A Locke Dictionary

GW00481169

B

THE
BLACKWELL PHILOSOPHER DICTIONARIES

A Locke Dictionary

John W. Yolton

BLACKWELL
Reference

The right of John W. Yolton to be identified as author of this work has been
asserted in accordance with the Copyright, Designs and Patents Act 1988.

First published 1993
Reprinted 1993

First published in USA 1993

Blackwell Publishers
108 Cowley Road
Oxford OX4 1JF
UK

238 Main Street
Cambridge
MA 02142
USA

ISBN 0–631–175–474 (hardback)
      0–631–175–482 (paperback)

British Library Cataloguing in Publication Data

A CIP catalogue record for this book is available from the British Library.

Library of Congress Cataloging-in-Publication Data

A catalog record for this book is available from the Library of Congress.

Typeset in Baskerville 10/12pt by Acorn bookwork, Salisbury, Wilts
Printed in Great Britain by T.J. Press (Padstow) Ltd, Padstow, Cornwall.

This book is printed on acid-free paper.

Epigraph

A good portrait of Locke would require an elaborate background. His is not a figure to stand statuesquely in a void: the pose might not seem grand enough for bronze or marble. Rather he should be painted in the manner of the Dutch masters, in a sunny interior, scrupulously furnished with all the implements of domestic comfort and philosophic enquiry: the Holy Bible open majestically before him, and beside it that other revelation – the terrestrial globe. His hand might be pointing to a microscope set for examining the internal constitution of a beetle: but for the moment his eye should be seen wandering through the open window, to admire the blessings of thrift and liberty manifest in the people so worthily busy in the market-place, wrong as many a monkish notion might be that still troubled their poor heads. From them his enlarged thoughts would easily pass to the stout carved ships in the river beyond, intrepidly setting sail for the Indies, or for savage America. Yes, he too had travelled, and not only in thought. He knew how many strange nations and false religions lodged in this round earth, itself but a speck in the universe. There were few ingenious authors that he had not perused, or philosophical instruments that he had not, as far as possible, examined and tested; and no man better than he could understand and prize the recent discoveries of 'the incomparable Mr. Newton'. Nevertheless, a certain uneasiness in that spare frame, a certain knitting of the brows in that aquiline countenance, would suggest that in the midst of their earnest eloquence the philosopher's thoughts might sometimes come to a stand. Indeed, the visible scene did not exhaust the complexity of his problem; for there was also what he called 'the scene of ideas', immaterial and private, but often more crowded and pressing than the public scene.

George Santayana,
Some Turns of Thought in Modern Philosophy

Contents

Introduction

An effective method to use in discovering and understanding what an author says and means is to trace his use of those words that seem to be important or central in his writings. Importance can sometimes be determined by frequency of use, by chapters and books devoted to a particular term, by words that were seized upon by opponents in criticizing that author. It is necessary to pay attention to an author's use of traditional terms and concepts: does he accept the usual doctrines associated with those terms, or does he attack or replace those concepts? The words used are of course the expression of doctrines, so a word-use dictionary is a useful tool for revealing the doctrines of a writer.

Such a dictionary is especially appropriate when reading an author such as John Locke, whose writings cover a variety of topics and contain some systematic presentation of views. To trace his use of a term over several books can be salutary in correcting those interpretations by a critic who limits his attention to one or two works. Developing a sensitivity to an author's use of words can also be instrumental in preventing us from assuming that those words have in his thought the same meaning as they have in our philosophy. Philosophers have not always been good listeners to the voices of their contemporaries and predecessors; they are often prone to find in the writings of previous philosophers doctrines and meanings that they work with and value, rather than undertaking a serious examination of those earlier writers in order to determine what they actually said. Locke was himself sensitive to these dangers of mis-reading; in both *An Essay concerning Human Understanding* and an essay on how to read St Paul's Epistles, he sketched some very specific and practical rules for understanding a text written so far in the past, and in a difficult foreign language. But the same rules for tracing the author's actual use of words, placing them in their verbal and historical context, apply to reading any text, even one, such as Locke's various books, written in our own language. A seventeenth- or eighteenth-century use of a word may have a quite different sense from our use of that same word.

This *Locke Dictionary* presents Locke's use of words from 'abstraction' to 'zealots', citing explicit passages where those words occur, allowing his use to inform us of the doctrines, theory, concepts and opinions those words entail. With only one exception ('empiricism'), all the entries are words used by Locke. Sometimes the presentation of word-use has been the occasion for discussing some general topic, e.g., religion, science, government. Where possible, some indication is given of previous writers' doctrines. In some cases, an indication is given of the influence or fate, in later writers, of some doctrine in Locke's works. References to secondary literature are sometimes given at the end of an entry; a more extended list of secondary sources can be found in the bibliography.

The reader of this dictionary will soon discover that many of the central issues in Locke's thought are clustered in a number of words and concepts. For example, his account of virtue is related to his discussion of morality, good and evil, happiness, sin; his account of essences is linked with those of substance, and of the corpuscular hypothesis; logic, inference, demonstration, deduction, proof comprise another group of terms revealing Locke's thought. The entries are based on most of his writings, some that he did not publish, and a few on his correspondence. So this dictionary is intended to help the person who is interested in almost any topic dealt with by Locke, whether it be those central doctrines so much discussed in his account of knowledge and reality, or his theory of government, his commitment to religious toleration, his larger religious views, his study on education, his pamphlets on money, his remarks about women. There are also brief entries on the books he published (and several he left unpublished), with an outline of their content, origins, different editions. A fuller description can be found in part A of the bibliography. The bibliography contains two other parts: one on the works of seventeenth-century and other pre-nineteenth-century authors, the other on some of the secondary literature on all of Locke's writings and life.

There is, then, a wealth of information in this *Locke Dictionary*, most of it direct from what Locke himself wrote, either paraphrased or in his own words. Where different interpretations have been offered on some particular topic, these are noted, but I have tried not to impose my reading on his texts. Locke speaks for himself through these entries. The dictionary is not a substitute for Locke's own writings, but it can be useful as a starting point. The reader interested in a specific topic can start by reading the relevant entries and then go to Locke's full text. A person with a general interest, or one who just has a curiosity about Locke, may find browsing in the dictionary valuable. There are about 130 entries. There may be others that some readers would think should have been included. I have had to be somewhat selective, balancing the goal of being comprehensive in covering the total Locke corpus against the obvious importance and centrality of some of the doctrines in such works as his *Essay concerning Human Understanding* or *Two Treatises of Government*. My hope is that those who consult this dictionary will come to appreciate both the depth and extent of Locke's interests and involvements in the intellectual, religious, and social issues of his time.

What can we learn about a man from his books? In most cases, we can discover an author's beliefs, theories, and attitudes about the subjects on which he writes. Some writers are not so easy to decipher as others are. David Hume tends to examine previous systems of philosophy, not always revealing his own views (e.g., as in Book I of his *Treatise*). With Locke, the writing is much more straightforward, although the doctrines he offers or attacks are often rather complex and obscure. We can discover Locke's own interests by surveying the books he published: interests in the education of children, in defending a simple, reasonable Christianity; interests in science and medicine. His other preoccupations are revealed in other sources: his journals and notebooks, his correspondence with a wide variety of people, his library. The older biographies of King and Fox Bourne and the more recent biography by Cranston (see the bibliography) contain many details about his life and thought. More recent specialized studies such as Richard Ashcraft's *Revolutionary Politics* (1986) have added new information – in Ashcraft's case, about Locke's stay in Holland. Other scholars are at work filling in details of his early years, of his youth. The eight volumes of correspondence are also a rich source of information on Locke's attitudes and his place in the intellectual scene of the seventeenth century.

The seventy-two years of Locke's life (1632–1704) were marked by much social unrest in England and by several dramatic political events: a civil war between parliament and King Charles I which ended in the trial and execution of that king; another king, James II, deposed and replaced by a foreign monarch. Locke's father was briefly a soldier in that civil war, Locke himself was implicated, through his association with the Earl of Shaftesbury, in plots against Charles II; and, when Locke returned from Holland after James II was deposed, he sailed in one of the ships in the fleet bringing William III's wife, Mary, to England. Locke held several governmental offices, he turned down others, and he was a confidant and perhaps an adviser to Shaftesbury while the latter was active in political affairs during the reign of Charles II.

Well-read in philosophy, religion and science, Locke collected a large library on these and other subjects. He studied medicine at Oxford, developed friendships with several prominent doctors (Thomas Sydenham is the best-known), and with the leading chemist of the day, Robert Boyle. He also knew Newton and other important men in the

Royal Society. Locke developed other friendships with scientists, theologians and men of letters during his several visits to France and his long stay in Holland. A traveller himself, he read and collected travel books, using some of their information in his own works. He was educated at two of England's most prestigious institutions, Westminster School and Christ Church at the University of Oxford. He held several appointments at Christ Church until his expulsion on the order of Charles II in 1684.

He was not always in residence at Christ Church, even during his years as a member. His meeting with Anthony Ashley Cooper, the future Earl of Shaftesbury, led to his joining the Shaftesbury household as secretary and assistant to Shaftesbury, as well as medical adviser. His association with Shaftesbury brought him into contact with political affairs of the country, since Shaftesbury played a prominent role in parliament, a role that eventually placed him (and by implication Locke) in jeopardy. Discussions with Shaftesbury undoubtedly sharpened Locke's interest in the nature and structure of government. Perhaps it also led him later to offer suggestions for alleviating a crisis over coinage.

Along with his involvement in practical affairs, Locke continued his interests in intellectual, more theoretical, matters. While at Christ Church, he gave lectures on moral philosophy and wrote several tracts on the legitimate role of government in the lives of citizens. He did not publish any of these early writings on morality, law and politics, but they served as a base from which he went on to his mature views, views which were not always identical to his earlier ones. His wide reading and extensive note-taking, as well as discussions with friends, added information, ideas and stimulation for his publications from 1689 on. He was in his late fifties before his first books appeared, but several of them had been developing over the years, even while he was in Holland trying to be inconspicuous. The result was a series of books published in a relatively short period, 1689–95. The years that remained until his death in 1704 were devoted to revising his books for new editions, replying to a few critics, and writing his last work, commentaries and notes on the Epistles of St Paul.

Locke's rich and varied life cannot of course be captured in such a brief survey, but it may give the reader some appreciation of Locke as a man of broad interests, great energy, and the source of some major intellectual contributions to philosophy, political theory and education. A brief listing of some of the more significant dates in his life may also help:

1632   Born, 29 August
1646   Admitted to Westminster School
1652   Elected to a studentship at Christ Church, Oxford

1656   Graduated BA
1658   Graduated MA
1664   Appointed Censor of Moral Philosophy at Christ Church
1667   Joined Shaftesbury's household in London
1668   Elected Fellow of the Royal Society
1671   Wrote first draft of the Essay
1673   Served as secretary to the Council of Trade until the end of 1674
1675   Awarded the degree of MB (Bachelor of Medicine)
1683   Arrived in Holland where he stayed until 1689
1696   Appointed a commissioner of the Commission for Trade and
       Plantations
1704   Died, 28 October

System of citations

Conduct = *The Conduct of the Understanding*, followed by section number; in *Works* (1823).

Corr. = *The Correspondence of John Locke*, ed. E.S. de Beer, Clarendon Press, 8 vols, 1976–89. Cited by letter number, followed by volume and page numbers.

Essay = *An Essay concerning Human Understanding*. Location of reference and quotations is given in arabic numbers; e.g., 4.3.6 = Book 4, chapter 3, section 6. Except for the first occurrence in an entry, only the numbers will be given; e.g., 2.8.8. References are to the 1975 edition by P.H. Nidditch. The 'Epistle to the Reader' is referred to by page numbers.

Essays = *Essays on the Law of Nature*. Page references are to this work as edited by W. von Leyden.

Paraphrases = *A Paraphrase and Notes upon the Epistles of St. Paul*, ed. A. Wainwright (1987), 2 vols. Paging is continuous through the two volumes, so only page numbers are given.

Reasonableness = *The Reasonableness of Christianity*. Page references are to the *Works* edition of 1823, volume vii.

ST, Some Thoughts = *Some Thoughts concerning Education*, ed. J. and J. Yolton (1989). References are to section numbers.

Two Tracts = *John Locke: Two Tracts on Government*, ed. Philip Abrams, 1967.

Two Treatises = *Two Treatises of Government*. Citations are given as *T*1 or *T*2 and a section number: e.g., *T*2, §10 means that section in the second treatise on civil government.

Works = *The Works of John Locke*, A New Edition Corrected, 10 vols, 1823.

A

abstraction One of the many activities (operations) of the mind whereby particular ideas are made to represent all objects of the same kind. Making ideas representative of a class requires the mind to consider its ideas as appearances separate from other existences and from 'the circumstances of real Existence, as Time, Place, or any other concomitant *Ideas*' (*Essay*, 2.11.9; cf. 3.3.6). Locke calls ideas considered in this abstractive manner 'naked appearances', a term indicating its separation from particular relations as well as ignoring questions of 'how, whence, or with what others' these appearances reach the mind (see also 2.12.1). In abstraction, the mind considers 'an *Idea* under no other Existence, but what it has in the Understanding' (4.9.1). Considering ideas in this way is, as Cartesians said, to treat them as modes of mind. Ideas so considered become 'the Standards to rank real Existences into sorts' (2.11.9). These standards are general ideas.

abstract or general ideas (and words) Ideas considered just as modes of mind are referred to by Locke as *abstract* and as *general* ideas. He also speaks of *abstract complex ideas* in his discussion of essences (*Essay*, 2.32.6). These ideas are abstract because they are the product of the mental operation of abstraction, ignoring the particularity of ideas. What is left after this process are *general* ideas (universals) whose function it is to help us in classification as to kinds (2.11.9). Abstracting to produce general ideas is not an ability animals have; it is this ability which 'puts a perfect distinction betwixt Man and Brutes' (2.11.10). Sorting or 'binding' things into bundles is one of the first acts of the mind after it has acquired some ideas (2.32.6, 7). Attaching a name to the general idea is also important: the idea is the standard, its name is the mark for a class. The idea is described by Locke as 'being something in the Mind between the thing that exists, and the Name that is given to it' (2.32.8). The generality of words is simply a function of their being signs of general ideas.

Locke accepted the ontology of particulars ('all things that exist are only particulars', 3.3.6), so it was important for him to find a way to deal with kinds which would not violate that ontology. Ideas too are particulars but they can be artificially viewed as general ideas and hence as ideas of kinds. The peculiarity of Locke's account is that, since all that exists is particular, there are no kinds in nature, just as there are no general ideas in the mind. Generality is a particular way of considering ideas and things (cf. 3.3.11).

Locke suggested how such a process from particularity to generality may operate in a child. A child's ideas of persons, as the persons themselves, are particular. At some time in his development, after the child has more experience of persons and things, he notices that 'there are a great many other Things in the World' than the persons and objects with which he is acquainted (3.3.7). These other persons and objects share some qualities: there are resemblances between them. The idea of 'man' and its name are thus formed; they catch the qualities and features shared by many persons. The process is the one described by Locke as abstracting, leaving out of the ideas of persons whom they know the particular features, considering or retaining only 'what is common to all' (3.3.7). Further delimiting the shared properties produces ideas of more generality, such as of animal or animality. Even the metaphysical categories of *being* or *substance* are accounted for in this way (3.3.9).

A shorter account of the psychology of the formation of general ideas can be found in 4.7.9, a passage that Berkeley later seized on in his rejection of what he took to be Locke's claim that there *are* abstract general ideas, existent ideas which are not particular. In that passage, Locke remarks that 'abstract *Ideas* are not so obvious or easie to Children, or the yet unexercised Mind, as particular ones.' He goes on to say that general ideas are 'Fictions and Contrivances of the Mind'. In order to remind the reader that he has not violated his particularist ontology by his account of abstraction and generality, Locke even says of the general idea of a triangle (the idea of a figure which is 'neither Oblique, nor Rectangle, neither Equilateral, Equicrural, nor Scalenon; but all and none of these at once') that such an idea or such a figure 'is something imperfect, that cannot exist'.

There is some ambiguity in this passage about whether what cannot exist is the idea or the triangle, but since Locke does say of abstract ideas that they are fictions, he seems to be denying the existence of both under the description he gives. Berkeley read the same passage as saying we can frame in our mind 'such an idea of a triangle as is here described' (*A Treatise concerning the Principles of Human Knowledge*, Intro., §13). Berkeley said he could not *conceive* such an abstract idea, although he did say he could 'consider some particular parts or qualities separated from others'; he could even *imagine* or *represent* 'to my self the ideas of those particular things I have perceived' in different combinations and even separated (*ibid.*, §10; cf. §16). 'Considering' is also accepted in section 11. Nor was Berkeley denying that there are *general* ideas. In fact, his account of these is the same as Locke's: 'an idea, which considered in itself is particular, becomes general, by being made to represent or stand for all other particular ideas of the same sort' (*ibid.*, §12). What Berkeley objected to was the claim that general ideas were acquired through abstraction, since the result of that process was, he thought, an abstract general idea: a particular idea, not a fiction, which had the contradictory features of being neither this nor that. Berkeley read Locke as saying his ontology of ideas included some definite ideas which were not particular but general and abstract in themselves, not just in their representative capacity (cf. §15).

Berkeley and Hume were committed to the same particularist ontology as was Locke: 'He that knows he has no other than particular ideas, will not puzzle himself in vain to find out and conceive the abstract idea, annexed to any name' (*Principles*, §24). Hume also accepted the generally received philosophy 'that every thing in nature is individual' (*Treatise*, I, I,VII, p. 19). Since it is absurd in reality for there to exist a triangle 'which has no precise proportion of sides and angles', it is also absurd in idea. Thus, abstract ideas are 'in themselves individual, however they may become general in their representation' (p. 20). Hume also agrees that words help us recall similar objects: the mind does not need the fiction of an abstract general idea since it has the capacity, aided by past experience, to think of any number of resembling objects. Hume's *Enquiry concerning Human Understanding* echoes Locke on this point: 'all general ideas are, in reality, particular ones, attached to a general term, which recalls, upon occasion, other particular ones, that resemble, in certain circumstances, the idea, present to the mind' (p. 158n.). Locke had said:

> *General and Universal*, belong not to the real existence of Things; but *are the Inventions and Creatures of the Understanding*, made by it for its own use, *and concern only Signs*, whether Words, or *Ideas*. Words are general, as has been said, when used, for Signs of general *Ideas*; and so are applicable indifferently to many particular Things; And *Ideas* are general, when they are set up, as the Representatives of many particular Things: but universality belongs not to things themselves, which are all of them particular in their Existence, even those Words, and *Ideas*, which in their signification, are general. (3.3.11)

He went on in this section to characterize the 'Generals' as 'nothing but the Capacity ... of signifying or representing many particulars' (cf. *Elements of Natural Philosophy*, in *Works*, iii. 229). These 'generals' (especially the ideas) become, in Locke's modification of the traditional doctrine of essence, general essences (3.8.1). The debate over abstraction and abstract ideas did not start with Locke and Berkeley. Berkeley refers to Aristotle and some scholastics who held versions of abstraction. Many of the logic books known to Locke devoted attention to these issues. (See *Abstraction, Relation and Induction*, by Julius R. Weinberg, 1965, pp. 3–60.)

analogy   There was a tradition prior to Locke of using analogy as a way of helping man understand things divine. After Locke, too, writers took up that theme. Interestingly, Locke refers to reasoning by analogy more in natural than in supernatural contexts. Analogy is not an important concept for him, but it receives a few references, even one relating to scientific experiments: 'Analogy is of great use to the mind in many cases, especially in natural philosophy; and that part of it chiefly which consists in happy and successful experiments. But here we must take care that we keep ourselves within that wherein the analogy consists' (*Conduct*, §40). He gives an example in this section of the use of 'the acid oil of vitriol' and 'the spirit of nitre or vinegar'. *Essay* 2.15.11 raises the question of whether angels or other spirits have any analogy with our experience. Analogy helps us form judgements or guesses where knowledge does not extend (4.8.9). What effects the qualities and powers of objects will have can only be determined by experience or 'by Analogy [we can] guess what Effects the like Bodies are, upon other tryals, like to produce' (4.3.29). An earlier passage had made more of this same point: the operations of nature are for the most part unknown to us. In particular, what the causes of observed effects are is beyond our knowledge: 'Analogy in these matters is the only help we have, and 'tis from that alone we draw all our grounds of Probability' (4.16.12). He goes on in this section to give a variety of examples where analogy helps, including our judgement about the chain of being extending upwards as well as downwards. He refers there to the 'rule of analogy' and to a 'wary reasoning by analogy'.

In his account of the nature of the mind and its operations, Locke employs a number of analogies. These are explanatory devices which aid him, in lieu of a psychological vocabulary, in articulating cognitive processes (*see* RESEMBLANCE; *see also* TABULA RASA).

After Locke, a writer who borrowed from Locke but who also found fault with some of his doctrines, Peter Browne, included some brief discussion of analogy in his *The Procedure, Extent, and Limits of Human Understanding* (1728), and then gave a more extended treatment of analogy in his *Things Divine and Supernatural Conceived by Analogy with Things Natural and Human* (1733). A more famous writer on this topic was Joseph Butler (*The Analogy of Religion Natural and Revealed*, 1736).

animals *see* BRUTES

animal spirits Locke announces at the beginning of the *Essay* that 'I shall not at present meddle with the Physical Consideration of the Mind' (1.1.2). What he rules out of consideration are such matters as the role played by the motion of animal spirits in sensation and the acquisition of ideas, or whether ideas do in fact depend upon matter. He characterizes these questions as 'speculative'. The reference is to the physiology of sense perception and awareness. There had been by Locke's time a fair amount of examination of muscles and sense organs. One of the dominant theories explaining bodily motion and awareness, even (early in the eighteenth century) voluntary muscular motion, involved animal spirits. That theory viewed the nerves as hollow tubes with a subtle fluid moving within; the fluid was called 'animal spirits'. Almost every tract or treatise dealing with sense perception, awareness or the passions referred to or assumed some physiological correlation. In their works on optics, both Descartes and Malebranche employed the animal spirit physiology extensively. Up until David Hartley in 1749, who invoked the theory of nerves as strings that vibrate when stimulated, animal spirits were the generally accepted theoretical concept. That theory also appears in Hume's *Treatise* in many passages, the journal *The Spectator* popularized the theory, and Locke, despite his disclaimer, refers to animal spirits in at least eight passages in the *Essay*, even offering an explanation of the phenomenon of cold and hot hands in water in terms of the movement of animal spirits (2.8.21; cf. 1.1.2; 2.1.15; 2.8.4,12; 2.10.5; 2.27.13; 2.33.6; and 4.10.19). There is also a passage in *Some Thoughts concerning Education* in which Locke raises the question of whether frightful and terrifying objects that disturb children and carry on into adult life may not be from 'an habitual Motion of the Animal Spirits, introduced by the first strong Impression' (§115).

The 2.33.6 passage is especially interesting since it seems to allow for the possibility of thinking and willing being 'but trains of Motion in the Animal Spirits, which once set a going continue on in the same steps they have been used to, which by often treading are worn into a smooth path, and the Motion in it becomes easy and as it were Natural'. The rest of this passage draws back from the possibility that thinking and willing are *nothing but* motions of animal spirits (i.e., brain events) by suggesting that the *cause* of thinking and willing may be the motion of animal spirits. That Locke was close to saying thought is a property of the brain was a charge many writers made later (*see* THINKING MATTER).

In the eighteenth century, especially in France, the power of physiological explanations of mental states and processes posed a threat to traditional mind-body dualism. The more complex physiological theories

became, the more they were associated with what was perceived to be a
growing materialism. Locke's name was linked to a number of French
materialists, e.g., Voltaire, Diderot.

appearance This is a word of more importance for its use in the
eighteenth century (especially with Kant) than with Locke (or Hobbes,
who also used the term). Nevertheless, Locke's use of 'appearance' and
'appear' has an interest of its own in relation to his way of talking about
ideas. There are two main uses of the word in Locke's *Essay*, one for the
way objects appear and the other for ideas. He speaks of 'the outward
Shape and Appearance of a Man' while discussing the question of whether
shape and figure are necessary for immortality (4.4.15). He talks there of
the visible parts and figure of a man. The more intriguing use is in
connection with physical objects. For example, he notes that he can
change the appearance of the paper in front of him by writing on it
(4.11.7). The fact that the characters he makes on the paper remain there
is part of his argument against scepticism. Under the supposition that our
senses might be altered 'and made much quicker and acuter', he concludes that 'the appearance and outward Scheme of things would have
quite another face to it' (2.23.12). While discussing duration, he refers to
a man observing 'the Revolution of Days and Nights', finding 'the length
of their Duration to be in Appearance regular and constant' (2.14.5).
While presenting the MOLYNEUX PROBLEM, he speaks of the experience we
have of 'what kind of appearance convex Bodies are wont to make in us',
and of judgements altering the appearances (2.9.8).

In his analysis of time, he speaks of the appearance of ideas 'one after
another in our Minds', the distance 'between any parts of that Succession,
or between the appearance of any two *Ideas* in our Minds' (2.14.3). The
appearance of ideas in succession is sometimes faster, sometimes slower,
but overall more or less constant (2.14.4). He raises the question of
whether ideas in the mind may be caused by motion, but whatever the
cause is, the ideas we have 'include no *Idea* of Motion in their Appearance'
(2.14.16). It is the successive appearance of ideas in the mind that gives
us the idea of duration. Locke suggests that 'any constant, periodical
Appearance, or Alteration of *Ideas* in seemingly equidistant Spaces of
Duration' could make as good a way of distinguishing TIME intervals as
the revolutions of the sun (2.14.19).

The talk of ideas as appearances is sprinkled throughout the *Essay*. The
'Epistle to the Reader' speaks of a simple idea as '*that simple appearance,
which the Mind has in its view, or perceives in it self, when that Idea is said to be
in it*' (p. 13; cf. 1.4.20). He also speaks of the ideas of coldness, hardness,
of smells, colours and tastes as being '*one uniform Appearance*, or Conception

in the mind' (2.2.1). The term 'conception' is a reminder that 'appear' and 'appearance' when applied to ideas do not carry a visual meaning. So much of Locke's description of ideas and the workings of the mind is done in the language of vision: it was a handy analogy, especially in the absence of any firm psychological vocabulary. He characterizes memory in one place as 'the appearance of those Dormant Pictures', depicting the mind searching with the 'Eye of the Soul' for a forgotten idea, or as old ideas being 'rouzed and tumbled out of their dark Cells, into open Daylight, by some turbulent and tempestuous Passion' (2.10.7). Particular ideas 'received from particular Objects' are made general 'by considering them as they are in the Mind such Appearances, separate from all other Existences, and the circumstances of real Existence, as Time, Place, or any other concomitant *Ideas*' (2.11.9). This same passage refers to such general ideas constructed by abstraction as 'precise naked Appearances in the Mind'. He gives an example of colour: 'Thus the same Colour being observed to day in Chalk or Snow, which the Mind yesterday received from Milk, it considers that Appearance alone, makes it a representative of all of that kind' (*ibid.*). Specific colours such as white and red can be placed under the heading of 'colour', but they themselves have nothing in common that can be left out 'to make them agree in one common appearance' (3.4.16). Simple ideas, e.g., of a particular colour, can be said to be true: 'their Truth consists in nothing else, but in such Appearances, as are produced in us and must be suitable to those Powers that God has placed in external objects' (2.32.14). It is, Locke suggests, the texture of a violet which 'by a regular and constant operation' produces the idea of blue. Whether that colour is 'in' the violet or only a mark by means of which we distinguish violets from other flowers, it is the appearance which we call 'blue' (*ibid.*).

archetype   Locke uses this old word to characterize the relation between ideas and their referents. In contrasting real with fantastical ideas, he says the real have a 'Foundation in Nature' or a 'Conformity with the real Being, and Existence of Things, or with their Archetype' (*Essay*, 2.20.1). Similarly, adequate in contrast with inadequate ideas are said to 'perfectly represent their Archetypes, which the Mind supposes them taken from' (2.31.1). Adequate ideas also stand for and refer to their archetypes. Ideas of substances are imperfect and inadequate as copies of their originals or archetypes because of Locke's scepticism about our knowledge of the real essence of substance (2.31.6; cf. 4.4.11). Complex ideas of modes and relations *are* themselves originals and archetypes of actions and relations, a use of this term which reflects in part Locke's technical concept of *mixed modes* (2.31.14). In fact, all complex ideas excepting those of substances are '*Archetypes* of the Mind's own making, not intended to be the Copies of any thing, nor referred to the existence of any thing, as to their Originals' (4.4.5). Mathematical and geometrical truths are another example of archetypes: the properties of geometrical figures apply to real, existing objects because those figures are the archetypes for objects. The things to which those properties apply must agree with those archetypes in the mind of the mathematician. Even though those figures have an '*Ideal Existence*' in the mind, he knows they will hold true of real objects because the ideal is the original for the real (4.4.6).

assent   The definition of 'assent' is 'the admitting or receiving any Proposition for true, upon Arguments or Proofs that are found to per-swade us to receive it as true, without certain knowledge that it is so' (*Essay*, 4.15.3). In stating the purpose of his *Essay*, Locke included, after the enquiry into the 'Original, Certainty, and Extent of humane Know-ledge', the 'Grounds and Degrees of Belief, Opinion, and Assent' (1.1.2). As well, the *Essay* was to 'examine by what Measure, in things whereof we have no certain Knowledge, we ought to regulate our assent' (1.1.3). The reference to measures is to his discussion, late in that work, of probability, including historical testimony and even revelation. The dif-ferent 'measures' justify or warrant different *degrees* of assent. In those late chapters, sometimes 'assenting' means 'receiving it for true', as when a mathematician affirms the three angles of a triangle to be equal to two right angles. In that case, the cause of assent is the 'Veracity of the Speaker' (4.15.1). Many propositions on which we reason and act are not known to be true (we do not have 'undoubted Knowledge of their Truth'), but we assent to them resolutely 'as if they were infallibly demonstrated' (4.15.2). But there are degrees of assent from such examples as these of 'full *Assurance* and Confidence, quite down to *Conjecture*, *Doubt*, and *Dis-trust*'. My past experience, what I have learned, is a factor in what persuades me of some report, e.g., of men walking on frozen water (4.16.5).

Locke recognizes that our assent does not always have in actual view the reasons that have once persuaded us: our memories do not retain or have readily available those reasons (4.16.1). We are often persuaded '*of several opinions, whereof the Proofs are not actually*' in our thoughts. We may not even be able to recall the proofs or reasons (4.16.2). In trying to convince someone of your opinions, you must give that person time to run over the grounds or reasons before expecting him to assent, particularly if it is a matter of dislodging a firmly held belief (4.16.4). Probable propositions which require our assent are of two sorts: those concerning matters of fact or observation open to human testimony and those which are beyond 'the discovery of our Senses [and] are not capable of any such Testimony' (4.16.5). Locke devotes several sections to the different kinds of testimony about matters of fact and the relevant degrees of assent warranted in his discussion of probability (4.16.6–11). The discussion of those matters which lie beyond our observation and testimony covers a variety of topics, including miracles and matters of faith (4.16.12–14).

Another area where assent (sometimes he writes 'consent') plays a role is in Locke's polemic against innate ideas and principles. He has an extended discussion of the argument for innate principles from an appeal to universal consent. That argument was used to support both logical or epistemic and moral principles. Locke rejects the claim and the argument on the grounds that there are no principles universally accepted or known by all people (children included), and those principles that do enjoy wide recognition are the result of learning. In some passages, assent generally is linked with the faculty of reason making us assent to certain truths (1.2.8). Locke's main claim about our assent to truths is that it is a function neither of reason (although that faculty plays an important role) nor of some supposed 'native inscription' (natural impression), but of the understanding itself and the faculties involved in experience and observation (1.2.11; cf. 1.2.5). In his *Conduct*, Locke urges us to regulate our assent to claims and doctrines 'by the evidence which things carry with them' (§33; cf. §34). In 1.2.16, a rather Cartesian-sounding passage, 'assenting to' is equated with 'perceive', as in perceive (i.e., understand) the truth: 'the Truth of it appears to him [the child], as soon as he has setled in his Mind the clear and distinct *Ideas*, that these Names stand for.' Examples of assent following upon clearly understanding the ideas comprising some proposition are '*That One and Two are equal to Three, that Two and Two are equal to Four*', or '*That two Bodies cannot be in the same place*', or '*That White is not Black*' (1.2.18). The assent to such propositions is said to be given by the understanding (1.2.20; 2.11.1).

Assent to moral propositions is more complex; it requires reasoning and discussion, not just clear and distinct ideas (1.3.1; 1.3.4). Locke also distinguishes between assenting to a truth and assenting to a command (1.3.12). He is careful to distinguish assenting to speculative and to practical propositions, whether truths or commands. The latter assent must be reflected in action. To the suggestion that 'those who live by Fraud and Rapine, have innate Principles of Trust and Justice which they allow and assent to' (1.3.2), he uses a concept of *tacit* assent which plays an important role in his *Two Treatises*. To this suggestion, 'That the *tacit assent of their Minds agrees to what their Practice contradicts*', Locke, perhaps anticipating a question later raised against the concept of tacit consent in *Two Treatises*, explains that the actions of men are 'the best Interpreters of their thoughts' (1.3.3; cf. 1.3.22). Practical principles do not end only in contemplation: they 'must produce Conformity of Action, not barely speculative assent to their Truth'. Whether a person could be said to assent to the law of contradiction and not reflect that assent (whether tacit or express) in action is doubtful, but it is more difficult to think of clashes between thought and action in this case of logical principles.

One of the more important aspects of Locke's discussion of assent is his analysis of wrong assent, why people so frequently 'give their Assent contrary to Probability' (4.20.1). This chapter of the *Essay* contains some fascinating examples; it also reveals a subtle understanding of human nature. Locke is often at his best when discussing defects and errors in the acquisition of knowledge or the formation of beliefs: the misuse of words, wrong and unnatural association of ideas, accepting propositions against the preponderance of evidence. Truth and happiness were two strong goals for him, error and misery evils to be avoided. In this chapter, he lists four reasons or explanations why people assent to propositions against their likelihood of being true, against their probability.

The first is the lack of opportunity to 'make Experiments and Observations' which would provide proofs or evidence for some propositions (4.20.2). The 'greatest part of Mankind, who are given up to labour, and enslaved to the Necessity of their mean Condition', are in this state (*ibid.*). The picture Locke paints of the state of working men is probably accurate: they spend all their time and pains 'to still the Croaking of their own Bellies, or the Cries of their Children'. Locke does not seem to be criticizing or defending the plight of the workers when he goes on to say: ''Tis not to be expected, that a Man, who drudges on, all his Life, in a laborious Trade, should be more knowing in the variety of Things done in the World, than a Pack-horse, who is driven constantly forwards and backwards, in a narrow Lane, and dirty Road, only to Market, should be skilled in the Geography of the Country' (*ibid.*). This condition is the result of 'the natural and unalterable State of Things in this World'. Nevertheless – and here is Locke's censorious voice – should the working man really desire to acquire some knowledge, especially about matters of religion, he could find time to give consideration to those concerns, instead of 'Things of lower Concernment' (4.20.3).

Locke is more censorious about those societies where men of large fortunes have the means to surround themselves with books and have the time to search for truth and well-grounded opinion, but are prevented from such free enquiry. He refers to societies 'where Care is taken to propagate Truth, without Knowledge; where Men are forced, at a venture, to be of the Religion of the Country; and must therefore swallow down Opinions, as silly People do Empiricks Pills, without knowing what they are made of, or how they will work, and have nothing to do, but believe they will do the Cure' (4.20.4).

Working conditions and social conditions militate against free enquiry, and lead to the forming of assent without evidence. A second cause of wrong assent is the lack of skill in using and assessing evidence. There are people 'who cannot carry a train of Consequences in their Heads, nor weigh exactly the preponderancy of contrary Proofs and Testimonies, making every Circumstance its due allowance' (4.20.5). Locke recognizes the different abilities we have; there is 'a difference in Men's Understandings, Apprehensions, and Reasonings'. In some cases, so great is the difference that Locke makes the bold assertion that 'one may, without doing injury to Mankind, affirm, that there is a greater distance between some Men, and others, in this respect, than between some Men and some Beasts' (*ibid.*).

A third reason for some people's assenting against the evidence or likelihood of some proposition is that they do not want proofs to support their beliefs (4.20.6). This sort of people have leisure and fortunes that enable them to seek proofs, but 'the hot pursuit of pleasure, or constant drudgery of business' engages their time and interest. As well, 'Laziness and Oscitancy [dullness] in general, or a particular aversion to Books, Study, and Meditation' keep them from having any serious thoughts. Locke shows some disdain of this sort of person: they 'think themselves miserable in coarse Cloaths, or a patched Coat, and yet contentedly suffer their Minds to appear abroad in a pie-bald Livery of coarse Patches, and borrowed Shreds, such as has pleased Chance, or their Country-Tailor, (I mean the common Opinion of those they have conversed with,) to cloath them in' (4.20.6).

The fourth and last reason for wrong assent, for embracing error, concerns the wrong measure of probability, even when presented clearly with the evidence (4.20.7). There are four causes for this kind of wrong assent: the assuming of uncertain and non-evident propositions as *principles* for thought and action; the blind acceptance of some received hypothesis; allowing a predominant passion or inclination to cloud our mind; or relying upon untested authority. Sections 7 to 10 mention such principles: those claimed to be innate, those that custom and education have instilled in children's minds, and claims of infallible doctrines such as transubstantiation (*see* PROBABILITY).

Section 11 illustrates the blind reception of some hypothesis, fixed view, entrenched opinion. Locke looks to the academic world for his example of unexamined assent. 'Would it not be an insufferable thing for a learned Professor, and that which his Scarlet would blush at, to have his Authority of forty years standing wrought out of hard Rock Greek and Latin, with no small expence of Time and Candle, and confirmed by general Tradition, and a reverend Beard, in an instant overturned by an upstart Novelist?' (4.20.11). Can such a man consider the possibility that 'what he taught his Scholars thirty years ago, was all Errour and Mistake; and that he sold them hard Words and Ignorance at a very dear rate'?

The rest of *Essay* 4.20 (§§13–18) contains some equally keen observations and illuminating examples of the influence of passion and authority on assent.

association of ideas   In his *Conduct of the Understanding*, Locke refers to the chapter added to the fourth edition of his *Essay* (1700) on the association of ideas. He says that in that chapter (2.33) he gave a description of the phenomenon (he says he treated it 'historically') but gave no remedies for it (*Conduct*, §41). He calls it a 'disease of the mind as hard to be cured as any; it being a very hard thing to convince any one that things are not so, and naturally so, as they constantly appear to him' (*ibid.*). He speaks of the 'unnatural connexions' which become by custom 'as natural to the mind as sun and light, fire and warmth go together, and so seem to carry with them as natural an evidence as self-evident truths themselves'.

The way to prevent this disease is to be careful that in the early years of childhood, 'ideas that have no natural cohesion come not to be united in their heads' (p. 277). Care should be taken that the child not join any ideas together 'in any other or stronger combination than what their own nature and correspondence give them' (*ibid.*). *Some Thoughts* urges parents not to allow 'any fearful Apprehensions [to] be talked into them, nor terrible Objects surprize them' (§115). The result of such an experience is that it 'often so shatters, and discomposes the Spirits; that they never recover it again; but during their whole Life, upon the first suggestion, or appearance of any terrifying Idea, are scatter'd and confounded; the Body is enervated and the Mind disturb'd, and the Man scarce himself, or capable of any composed or rational action.' The child should also be encouraged to make frequent examination of the ideas that are linked together in his mind in order to determine whether this association of ideas be 'from the visible agreement that is in the ideas themselves, or from the habitual and prevailing custom of the mind joining them thus together in thinking' (*Conduct*, §41). Habit and custom make it difficult for us to avoid such unnatural associations; the confusion of two different ideas linked in the mind by a customary connection tends to make those two ideas one. Our heads are accordingly filled with 'false views' and our reasoning marked by false consequences (*ibid.*).

Such association of ideas is often reflected in our actions and arguments, for example, the 'Obstinacy of a worthy Man, who yields not to the Evidence of Reason, though laid before him as clear as Day-light' (*Essay*, 2.33.2). Education can be one of the causes of this disease, but tracing it to this source does not give us a clear understanding of how it arises (2.33.3). He refers to this disease of the mind as a sort of madness, apologizing for using such a harsh term as 'madness', since the disease can appear in very rational minds. This is not a madness in opposition to reason; 'there is Scarce a Man so free from it' (2.33.4). Nor is it the result of 'the power of an unruly Passion'.

Before he added this chapter to the *Essay*, Locke had said that mad men 'do not appear to me to have lost the Faculty of Reasoning: but having joined together some *Ideas* wrongly, they mistake them for Truths' (2.11.13). The cause of the disease he describes under the heading of the 'association of ideas' is similar to that in more recognizably mad men. The mad men he has in mind are those who, e.g., think they are kings, or that they are made of glass (2.11.13). These men still use reason in drawing the correct conclusions from what they believe themselves to be; they expect to be treated as a king, or they take precautions so that their bodies will not break. These mad men have not forsaken reason; they put 'wrong *Ideas* together, and so make wrong Propositions, but argue and reason right from them' (*ibid.*). There are also degrees of madness: the disorder of ideas is more pronounced in some than in others. The cases of madness cited by Locke in this earlier chapter are more extreme than the madness he describes in the added chapter; the former affects only a few men, but the latter is 'a Taint which . . . universally infects Mankind' (2.33.4), hence the importance of presenting this kind of madness under its proper name so that prevention and cure may be found.

Some ideas have 'a natural Correspondence and Connexion one with another' (2.33.5). He does not give any examples here of natural connections, but in his suggestion for a demonstrative morality, and in his account of DEMONSTRATION generally, he presents some examples of conceptual connections of ideas – examples of one idea naturally, by its very nature, linking with others (*see* LOGIC). There is another kind of 'Connexion of *Ideas* wholly owing to Chance or Custom' (*ibid.*). These ideas become so firmly linked that it is difficult to separate them: 'the one no sooner at any time comes into the Understanding but its Associate appears with it; and if they are more than two which are thus united, the whole gang always inseparable shew themselves together' (2.33.5).

For anyone with a knowledge of Hume's *Treatise of Human Nature*, the next few sections in this chapter of Locke's *Essay* will sound very familiar. Custom, Locke writes, 'settles habits of Thinking in the Understanding, as well as of Determining in the Will, and of Motion in the Body' (2.33.6). The various 'Sympathies and Antipathies observable in Men, which work as strongly, and produce as regular Effects, as if they were Natural' are taken to be natural when in fact they are the result of a purely accidental connection of two ideas (2.33.7). Some antipathies (he does not name any) are natural and 'depend upon our original Constitution, and are born with us', but most of our likes and dislikes are the result of custom and chance association. A great many accidental associations begin in childhood, hence the importance that those who have children or are in charge of their education should be careful to 'prevent the undue Connexion of *Ideas* in the Minds of young People' (2.33.8). For example, 'The *Ideas of Goblins and Sprights* have really no more to do with Darkness than Light; yet let but a foolish Maid inculcate these often on the Mind of a Child, and raise them there together, possibly he shall never be able to separate them again so long as he live, but Darkness shall ever afterwards bring with it those frightful *Ideas*, and they shall be so joined that he can no more bear the one than the other' (2.33.10).

Various other examples are mentioned or discussed: hatred of a particular person caused by thinking often about the injury that person inflicted on you, the result being that you can hardly separate the pain from your idea of that person (2.33.11); or the association of pain and sickness with a particular room where a friend died, leading you to avoid entering that room again (2.33.12). Another example: a man cured of madness 'by a very harsh and offensive Operation'; even though the man was very grateful to be cured, he could not disassociate the pain of the cure from the person who performed the offensive operation. Seeing that man again, or even just his image, 'brought back with it the *Idea* of that Agony which he suffer'd from his Hands' (2.33.14). Still another example, perhaps of greater importance to Locke, is of the child who has an aversion to a particular book, or books in general, because of the association of that book with the pain he suffered at being harshly corrected so often by his teacher (2.33.15). Perhaps the most intriguing example is of the gentleman who learned to dance in a room that happened to have an old trunk in the corner. 'The *Idea* of this remarkable piece of Household-stuff, had so mixed it self with the turns and steps of all his Dances, that though in that Chamber he could dance excellently well, yet it was only whilst that Trunk was there, nor could he perform in any other place, unless that, or some other Trunk had its due position in the Room' (2.33.16).

An example of particular significance for Locke's philosophical doctrines and a controversy he found himself in shortly after the publication of the *Essay* in 1690, is that of the association of the idea of being and matter, that association established by either education or thought about such concepts (2.33.17). Such an association may prevent our forming the idea of the existence of 'separate Spirits', i.e., angels, or even, the implication seems to be, of mental as well as physical events. His examples of wrong, unnatural and dangerous associations of ideas also include one of the doctrines of the church: 'Let the *Idea* of Infallibility be inseparably join'd to any Person, and these two constantly together possess the Mind, and then one Body in two Places at once, shall unexamined be swallowed for a certain Truth, by an implicit Faith, when ever that imagin'd infallible Person dictates and demands assent without enquiry' (2.33.17). A more forthright rejection of this doctrine is found in an early journal entry in 1676. Transubstantiation should not be a matter of faith, but rather of philosophy: 'It is a thing we exercise our senses and knowledge on and not our faith, and so clear that there is not room to doubt. For the reality and essence of bread being in respect of us nothing but a collection of several simple ideas, which makes us know it, disting- uish it from flesh, and call it bread, it is as impossible for a man, where he finds that complex idea to know it to be flesh or receive it for such, as it is to believe himself a loaf' (*Essays*, p. 278; a slightly different version of this comment appears in *Essay*, 4.20.10). It is by 'custom and the terrible name of heresy' that men may be 'frightened from regarding their own ideas', that it is bread, not flesh (*Essays*, p. 278). Some philosophical differences are also traced to 'wrong and unnatural Combinations of *Ideas*' (2.33.18). 'Irreconcilable opposition between different Sects of Philosophy and Religion' arises because of the failure to be sufficiently critical of what doctrines are accepted.

A good summary of Locke's account of this disease of wrong association of ideas follows this last example: 'That which thus captivates their Reasons, and leads Men of Sincerity blindfold from common Sence, will, when examin'd, be found to be what we are speaking of: some indepen- dent *Ideas*, of no alliance to one another, are by Education, Custom, and the constant din of their Party, so coupled in their Minds, that they always appear there together, and they can no more separate them in their Thoughts, than if they were but one *Idea*' (2.33.18). It is these results of custom and association which are the basis for seeming to give sense to jargon or to make demonstrations of absurdities and nonsense (*ibid.*).

Implicit in Locke's warnings about bad association of ideas, especially his caution to parents and tutors about avoiding such links between certain experiences and specific ideas or beliefs, is a recognition of the positive, character-forming conditions for raising children. His *Some Thoughts concerning Education* is filled with advice on ways to stimulate a desire to learn, advice on the importance of reinforcement of good habits and good examples. But he does not develop, as Hume did later, a psychology which places association of ideas at the centre of the account of knowledge and belief. By examining the dark side of association, by characterizing it as a disease, a form of madness, Locke may have been responsible for the subsequent attention given to association. Locke believed he was the first to stress this aspect of the way the mind works. Writing to William Molyneux on 26 April 1695, he spoke of his plan to add a chapter to the *Essay* on this topic, referring to it as the 'Connexion of Ideas' and commenting that it 'has not, that I know, been hitherto consider'd and has, I guess, a greater influence upon our minds, than is usually taken notice of' (*Corr.* 1887; v. 353).

Most commentators dispute Locke's claim to be the first to notice this phenomenon, pointing out that earlier writers had recognized some of the ways in which thoughts are related to other thoughts. Hobbes, for example, talked of 'mental discourse' or the 'discourse of the mind', meaning the 'train of thoughts' moving through the mind (*Leviathan*, Pt I, ch. III). 'When a man thinketh on any thing whatsoever, His next Thought often, is not altogether so casual as it seems to be. Not every Thought to every Thought succeeds indifferently' (*ibid.*). Hobbes went on to show how one thought leads to another, and that thought in turn gives rise to a third or more thoughts. His account of the succession of connected thoughts is brief and it lacks the feature that caught Locke's attention: the fixation on two associated ideas which we are unable to separate. The train or connection of ideas for Locke was much more specific than it is for Hobbes's mental discourse. David Hartley, who wrote extensively about the association of ideas, is probably correct in saying that 'the Word *Association*, in the particular Sence here affixed to it, was first brought into Use by Mr. *Locke*' (*Observations on Man*, 1749, Pt II, §II, p. 65). The sense to which Hartley refers is 'The Influence of Association over our Ideas, Opinions, and Affections'. He says that that influence is so great and obvious 'as scarce to have escaped the Notice of any Writer who has treated of these' features. Hartley does not mention any of these writers in this passage, only saying that 'all that has been delivered by the Antients and Moderns, concerning the Power of Habit, Custom, Example, Education, Authority, Party prejudice, the manner of learning the manual and liberal Arts, &c. goes upon this doctrine as its Foundation' (*ibid.*). Hartley's discussion of this phenomenon is more concerned with the physiological correlates of mental associations than it is with the psychological phenomena. He couples his famous doctrine of vibration of nerves with the doctrine of the association of ideas (in some passages, he seems tempted to identify them).

At the beginning of his discussion of vibrations and associations, Hartley refers to 'what Mr. *Locke*, and other ingenious Persons since his Time, have delivered concerning the Influence of *Association* over our Opinions and Affections' (*ibid.*, p. 5). One of these ingenious persons was

John Gay who, in a 'Preliminary Dissertation concerning the Fundamental Principles of Virtue or Morality', wrote about the ways in which pleasure often gets associated with certain experiences, leading some men, for example, to identify money with happiness (in Edmund Law's translation of William King's *De Origine Mali*, 1731; King's book appeared in 1702). He gives other examples, some of which involve what he calls 'improper objects', but none of his examples quite has the obsessive quality of those cited by Locke. Nor are those kinds of examples found in Hume's elaborate analysis of association of ideas in his *Treatise* (1739–40). Locke's added chapter was accurately summarized by Chambers in his *Cyclopaedia* (1728). Later in the century, Joseph Priestley agreed with Hartley that Locke was the first to notice what Priestley calls 'the mechanical association of ideas', citing only the 2.33.6 passage from Locke's *Essay* about the physiology of association, not the psychology (*Hartley's Theory of the Human Mind*, 1775, Introductory Essay II, pp. xii–xiii).

atheism Locke's attitude towards atheism (the denial of the being of God) was stark and intolerant: atheists are not to be tolerated at all. A fundamental reason for such an attitude is that 'Promises, covenants, and oaths, which are the bonds of human society, can have no hold upon an atheist' (*A Letter concerning Toleration*, in *Works*, vi. 47). In responding to John Edwards's charge that he, Locke, gave in his writings occasion for atheism, Locke labelled atheism a crime, even suggesting that atheists were mad and should be 'shut out of all sober and civil society' (*A Vindication of the Reasonableness of Christianity*, in *Works*, vii. 161). Atheism, or lending support for atheism, was charged against Locke by other writers, charges based upon several doctrines of the *Essay*, the rejection of innate ideas being prominent among those doctrines. Thus, it is not surprising that in his reply to Edwards, Locke remarks, rather testily, that atheism 'should be very warily charged on any one, by deductions and consequences, which he himself does not own, or, at least, do not manifestly and unavoidably flow from what he asserts' (*ibid.*; a similar remark is in *Two Treatises*, 1, §154).

Locke did recognize that recent travel literature had disclosed whole nations that did not have an idea of God (*Essay*, 1.4.8). He also admitted that 'the Complaints of Atheism, made from the Pulpit, were not without Reason' (*ibid.*). He even suggests that there may be some atheists among the population of his own time, people who hide their atheism because of 'the fear of the Magistrate's Sword, or their Neighbour's Censure'. It would be interesting to learn who were the 'profligate Wretches' who 'shamefacedly' own to be atheists.

In the *Essay* chapter on our knowledge of the existence of God, Locke expresses the opinion that the question of whether having the idea of God does or does not prove his existence is not the best way to silence atheists (4.6.7). In an early entry in his journal, he offered a suggestion for silencing atheists or for convincing them they were wrong. Suppose, he wrote in 1676, the 'probability lay on the Atheist side'. If they were right in saying there is no God, what faces them is only annihilation or eternal insensibility; that is the best they can hope for. Those who believe that God does exist have the possibility of everlasting happiness. If these believers turn out to be wrong about there being a God, annihilation is the worst that can happen to them. But should the atheist be wrong, he faces with certainty infinite misery. Such a set of reflections might silence the atheist. (See R.I. Aaron and J. Gibb, *An Early Draft of Locke's Essay*, Oxford, Clarendon Press, 1936, where this and a few other journal entries are printed, p. 82; this journal entry is reproduced in *Essay*, 2.21.70.)

Locke knew that his contemporaries saw atheism as linked with Epicureanism because of what was perceived as their heavy reliance on atomism as the cause and explanation of all events. Ralph Cudworth had written extensively about the ancient atomists and Epicureans for just this reason, to show the link with atheism (*The True Intellectual System*, 1678). Another Cambridge Platonist, Henry More, also wrote against atheism in his *An Antidote Against Atheisme* (1653). Cudworth and More were serious authors, but there were other authors such as John Edwards or William Carroll, who threw around the charge of atheism against any doctrine or suggestion that to them seemed 'unorthodox'.

axioms   *see* MAXIMS

B

belief Belief, opinion, and faith are often interchangeable in the *Essay*, especially when Locke writes about improper grounds for belief. All three are closely related to assent, which in turn is discussed in the account of probability. Sometimes Locke gives a descriptive account of how beliefs or opinions arise or are cultivated. Children, for example, are often led to a belief in matters of religion or morality because of the 'Superstition of a Nurse, or the Authority of an old Woman' (*Essay*, 1.3.22). When children are grown up, the ill-grounded opinions continue to prevail, are even taken to be the '*impress of God and Nature*' (1.3.23). Most people have 'some reverenced Propositions' which serve as principles to judge truth and falsity or right and wrong (1.3.24). It is difficult to break free from or to challenge the 'received Opinions of their Country or Party' (1.3.25). The reasons some people believe in innate principles may be, Locke suggests, traceable to such unexamined, false, even absurd principles instilled in the minds of children before the use of reason, and prior to the recognition of the proper grounds for belief and assent.

Locke names three grounds for belief, only one of which is a proper normative base for justified belief, reason and evidence. A second, revelation, is accepted with some qualifications and only for specific types of claims. A third ground for belief (added in later editions of the *Essay*), enthusiasm, is rejected (4.19.3). This last so-called ground commanded Locke's attention because those who use it claimed it as revelation. Instead, these men take away from both reason and revelation, substituting for both 'the ungrounded Fancies of a Man's own Brain' (4.19.3). Distinguishing good from bad grounds for belief constitutes what has been called Locke's 'ethics of belief' (see H.H. Price, *Belief*, 1969, and J.A. Passmore, 'Locke and the Ethics of Belief', 1978), although he is not always clear about when he is speaking *normatively* (and hence, about justified belief) and when he is more concerned with *describing* how beliefs are formed and assent given. He does say that what 'makes me believe, is something extraneous to the thing I believe; something not evidently joined on both sides to, and so not manifestly shewing the Agreement, or Disagreement of those *Ideas*, that are under consideration' (4.15.3). Both the causes of and the reasons for belief are explained mainly under the headings of 'probability' and 'faith or reason'.

The nature and origin of belief continued to be a topic of discussion by philosophers after Locke. Hume relied heavily upon the natural foundations of belief in the nature of man, and Reid developed this theme even further; both writers found the source of practical beliefs for guidance in action in human nature. The doctrines and artificial beliefs and principles of philosophers were attacked by both Hume and Reid. In the nineteenth century, Cardinal Newman elaborated an account of belief and assent which took issue with Locke particularly. Belief in contrast to knowledge became a standard topic in twentieth-century philosophy.

Bible   Locke was an avid collector and a close student of the Bible. In his library, he had twenty-eight copies, printings of the sixteenth and seventeenth centuries, in Greek, Latin, Hebrew, English and one in Dutch. Of the New Testament, he had two dozen copies, again in a range of languages: Greek, Latin, Syriac, French, Italian, and Spanish. He also had several Concordances and a number of interpretations of the Bible. His own *Reasonableness of Christianity* had as a subtitle, 'As Delivered in the Scriptures'. His *Paraphrases of St. Paul's Epistles* gives his own analysis of those central Christian writings. He urged everyone to read and study the Scriptures: 'If the reading and study of the Scripture were more pressed than it is, and men were fairly sent to the Bible to find their religion; and not the Bible put into their hands only to find opinions of their peculiar sect or party; Christendom would have more Christians, and those that are would be more knowing and more in the right than they are now' (*A Second Vindication of the Reasonableness*, in *Works*, vii. 294). Not only are the Scriptures a source of religion, they also contain a morality: they are one of the best 'Discourses of Morality' (*ST*, §185). The study of morality has high priority on Locke's reading list for gentlemen: 'the Morality of the Gospel' far exceeds the ancient and modern books. To give a man a full 'knowledge of true Morality, I should send him to no other Book, but the New Testament' ('Mr. Locke's Extempore Advice', reprinted in *Some Thoughts*, ed. Yolton and Yolton, 1989, p. 321).

Locke was very particular about the way children should be exposed to the Bible. It was important for them to read it, but the usual practice, which Locke characterized as 'the promiscuous reading of it through, by Chapters, as they lie in order', is of no advantage at all 'either for the perfecting their *Reading*, or principling their Religion' (*ST*, §158; cf. §190). Many parts of the Bible are too difficult for a child to understand: e.g., 'the Law of *Moses*, the Song of *Solomon*, the Prophecies in the Old, and the Epistles and *Apocalypse* in the New Testament' (*ST*, §158). The principles of religion are to be drawn from the Bible 'and in the Words of the Scripture', but only those that are 'suited to a Child's Capacity'. Locke makes a distinction between those parts of the Bible that could be used to help children learn to read, and those that are suited for religious and moral instruction. For reading, 'the Story of *Joseph*, and his Brethren, of *David* and *Goliath*, of *David* and *Jonathan*' are suitable (*ST*, §159). For instruction, moral rules, such as the Golden Rule and others scattered up and down in the Bible, are recommended.

It was important for Locke that children learn their moral rules in the words of the Scriptures, not in those of some secondary version written by men 'prepossess'd of Systems and Analogies' (*ST*, §159). Children are to learn the catechism, giving their answers to the questions in the exact words of the Scripture. A possible secondary reading could be 'a good History of the Bible' for young people, but there were none such that Locke recommends (*ST*, §190). It would also be useful to have 'a short and plain Epitome made' of the Bible, 'containing the chief and most material Heads, for Children to be conversant in as soon as they can read' (§191).

Locke's stress on having children read parts of the Bible itself, not some second-hand account of what it says, reflects his antipathy towards the systems of divinity and the interpretations of the Bible which made doctrinal claims Locke could not find in his Bible. The first of his *Two Treatises of Government* was occupied mainly with showing Filmer that his claims for patriarchal government and for the sole authority of the father in families were nowhere to be found in or supported by the Bible. Locke's exchange with Bishop Stillingfleet over certain doctrines in the *Essay* was concerned with trying to convince the Bishop that what the Bishop claimed was in the Bible was not there: e.g., the doctrine of the Trinity or the resurrection of the same body. On the Trinity: 'My lord, my Bible is faulty again, I do not remember that I ever read in it either of these propositions, in these precise words, "there are three persons in one nature or, there are two natures and one person". When your lordship shall show me a Bible wherein they are set down, I shall think them a good instance of propositions offered me out of Scripture' (*Second Reply to the Bishop of Worcester*, in *Works*, iv. 343). On the resurrection of the same body: 'The resurrection of the dead I acknowledge to be an article of the Christian faith; but that the resurrection of the same body, in your lordship's sense of the same body, is an article of the Christian faith, is what, I confess, I do not yet know' (*ibid.*, p. 303). He goes on to say that he cannot find in the New Testament any reference to the same body. Locke insisted that nothing in his *Essay* was inconsistent with or rejected by the Bible. He ends his postscript to his first reply to the Bishop's attack with this eloquent statement:

> The holy scripture is to me, and always will be, the constant guide of my
> assent, and I shall always hearken to it, as containing infallible truth,
> relating to things of the highest concernment. And I wish I could say, there
> were no mysteries in it: I acknowledge there are to me, and I fear always
> will be, but where I want the evidence of things, there yet is ground enough
> for me to believe, because God has said it: and I shall presently condemn
> and quit any opinion of mine, as soon as I am shown that it is contrary to
> any revelation in the holy scripture. But I must confess to your lordship,
> that I do not perceive any such contrariety in any thing in my Essay of
> Human Understanding. (*A Letter to the Right Reverend Edward, Lord Bishop of
> Worcester*, in *Works*, iv. 96)

The Bishop found Locke's use of the term 'idea' disturbing, not really
understanding that he often used it as a synonym for 'thought'. Locke
held strong views about how to read and understand a text. He insisted
that the first step in reading any book, the Bible included, is to 'get to
myself, the best I can, the signification of the words' of that book (*Second
Reply*, iv. 341). When dealing with a text such as the Bible, it is even more
important to 'understand the words and phrases of the language I read
it in, i.e. to form ideas they stand for'. Moreover, 'If there be any word
or expression, which in that author, or in that place of that author, seems
to have a peculiar meaning, i.e. to stand for an idea, which is different
from that which the common use of that language has made it a sign of,
that idea also I endeavour to form in my mind, by comparing this author
with himself, and observing the design of his discourse, so that, as far as
I can, by a sincere endeavour, I may have the same ideas in every place
when I read the words, which the author had when he writ them' (*ibid.*,
pp. 341–2). Locke also comments on some of the difficulties in reading a
text, especially one in a foreign language, in the third book of his *Essay*,
which was devoted to the nature and use of language. Words, in whatever
language, depend to a large extent 'on the Thoughts, Notions, and *Ideas*
of him that uses them', so even men of the same language and country
may misunderstand one another (*Essay* 3.9.22). He cites Greek authors in
particular in this passage, suggesting that 'in almost every one of them'
we will find in effect 'a distinct Language, though the same Words'. When
trying to understand writers of a different age and language than our own,
we need to remind ourselves that those authors very probably had
'different Notions, Tempers, Customs, Ornaments, and Figures of
Speech, etc. every one of which, influenced the signification of their
Words' (*ibid.*). Some meanings of words may be lost and unknown, other
words require constant reference to the way the author uses them and we
should place them in the context of that usage.

Locke then applies these general remarks to the interpretation of the Old and New Testaments, complaining that 'the Volumes of Interpreters, and Commentators' of those books illustrate the difficulties he has just mentioned (3.9.23). He admits that 'Though every thing said in the Text [of the Scripture] be infallibly true, yet the Reader may be, nay cannot chuse but be very fallible in the understanding of it.' His most detailed and sustained discussion of these hermeneutical points is found in his *Paraphrases of St. Paul's Epistles*. The preface to that work, which carries the title, 'An Essay for the Understanding of St. Paul's Epistles, by Consulting St. Paul Himself', is an essay on the use and abuse of the Bible, with particular attention to St. Paul. It is an essay that can be read with profit today, with almost any text in mind. Some of the points and recommendations, even warnings, he makes are as follows:

(1) Paul's correspondents would have been familiar with what he wrote about; they would be able easily to know his meaning. Removed in time as we are, 'we have no Information of the Occasion of his writing, little or no Knowledge of the Temper and Circumstances those he writ to were in' (*Paraphrases*, p. 103).

(2) The language was Greek, a dead language now but one of 'a very witty volatile People, Seekers after Novelty, and abounding with Variety of Notions and Sects, to which they applied the Terms of their common tongue with great Liberty and Variety' (*ibid.*). Furthermore, while the terms were Greek, 'the idiom or Turn of the Phrases may be truly said to be Hebrew or Syriack' (p. 104).

(3) St Paul has a particular style of writing and many new thoughts and doctrines; his mind is filled with a 'Crowd of Thoughts, all striving for Utterance'. Hence the pace of his writing and its implicit ideas made for difficulty of understanding (*ibid.*).

(4) The fact that the Epistles were divided into verses and chapters can mislead us, as well as enable different sects to extract and remove from their context passages that support their own doctrines and interpretations (p. 105) Letters were continuous discourses, as was also much of the Bible, especially the New Testament (p. 106). One of Locke's favourite objects of attack – the different sects and interpreters of the Gospel, who look to the Bible for their beliefs, not for what is really there – comes in for criticism here (pp. 106–7).

(5) Many interpreters of the Bible do so through their own philosophical doctrines. It is wrong to 'go about to interpret' the words of the Scripture 'by Notions of our Philosophy, and the Doctrines of Men deliver'd in the Schools. This is to explain the Apostles meaning by what they never thought of whilst they were writing, which is not

the way to find their Sense in what they deliver'd, but our own' (p. 114).

Locke then proceeds in his commentary to practise what he lays down in this prefatory essay.

brutes With his suggestion that animals differ from men in not having a reasonable soul or a language, Descartes launched a debate which ran well into the eighteenth century. Descartes argued that the motion of animals is controlled entirely by the mechanism of their bodies. In fact, he even identified many of the movements of the human body as run by physiology. Besides the affront to the normal attitude towards God's creatures, Descartes's claim, which was viewed as saying animals were machines, raised theological questions for those who were inclined to say animals do have souls, albeit perhaps not rational ones. The question was, if animals do think and reason and have ideas (as some writers, including Locke, believed), do they also have souls which are immortal? The subject of animal souls generated a large number of tracts and pamphlets in the seventeenth and eighteenth centuries.

Locke does not devote a chapter to this topic, but there are a number of passages which reveal his response to the ongoing debate. In sketching his account of the *chain of being*, a chain where there are no chasms or gaps, Locke remarked that between some men and some animals there are great differences, but 'if we compare the Understanding and Abilities of some Men, and some Brutes, we shall find so little difference, that 'twill be hard to say, that that of the Man is either clearer or larger' (*Essay*, 4.16.12). At the same time, in criticizing some religious practices and ceremonies for not conforming to reason, Locke laments: 'So that, in effect Religion which should most distinguish us from Beasts, and ought most peculiarly to elevate us, as rational Creatures, above Brutes' makes 'Men often appear most irrational, and more senseless than Beasts themselves' (4.18.11). Without any clearly discernible boundaries between animals and men (3.6.27), it is not surprising that some of our mental functions are shared with some animals.

Brutes (Locke's usual way of referring to animals) 'probably have several *Ideas* distinct enough', but they are unable to compare ideas any 'farther than some sensible Circumstances annexed to the Objects them-selves' (2.11.5). Similarly with adding and enlarging ideas, '*Brutes* come far short of Men' (2.11.7). He reaffirms here that an animal does acquire ideas 'and retain together several Combinations of simple *Ideas*, as poss-ibly the Shape, Smell, and Voice of his Master, [which] make up the complex *Idea* a Dog has of him'. The dog is not able to put those ideas together himself and make a complex idea. Nevertheless, Locke speaks of the ideas that dogs have *directing* them 'in the knowledge of several things'. The most important difference between man and brutes is that 'the power of *Abstracting* is not at all in' brutes (2.11.10). The process of abstraction, which Berkeley later denied, is what for Locke 'puts a perfect distinction betwixt Man and Brutes' (*ibid.*). He does not want to deny reason to brutes, only wishing to assert that their reasoning is done with *particular*, not general, ideas (2.11.11). The memory that Locke ascribes to some animals involves particular ideas as well. One example of memory in animals involves birds who can learn tunes. The effort which he thinks is observable of the bird trying to 'hit the Notes right' puts it past doubt with Locke 'that they have Perception, and retain *Ideas* in their Memories, and use them for Patterns' (2.10.10).

Interestingly, in 2.11.11, Locke referred to those who say animals are 'bare machines', and here in 2.10.10 he admits the possibility that the motion of birds may be solely a function of mechanism.

> For though I should grant Sound may mechanically cause a certain motion of the animal Spirits, in the Brains of those Birds, whilst the Tune is actually playing; and that motion may be continued to the Muscles of the Wings, and so the Bird mechanically be driven away by certain noises, because this may tend to the Birds Preservation: yet that can never be supposed a Reason, why it should cause mechanically, either whilst the Tune was playing, much less after it ceased, such a motion in the Organs of the Bird's Voice, as should conform it to the Notes of a foreign Sound, which imitation can be of no use to the Bird's Preservation.

The machine of the body, even of humans', was often said to run itself, moving limbs, but few accepted mechanism as the only way in which body and limbs can be moved. Similarly for Locke's bird: it is both mechanical and reasoning, it both responds to physical stimuli and works with ideational content. In a later passage, the identity (sameness) of an animal is located in the organization of parts sustaining one common life, that life being compared to the working of a watch. The difference between the animal and the watch is that 'the fitness of the Organization, and the Motion wherein Life consists' with animals 'begin together, the Motion coming from within' (2.27.5). In a watch, the motion is imposed from without.

Animals appear in Locke's *Essay* to illustrate various points: e.g., about classification or about species characteristics. There is the strange, imported cassowary to be seen in St James's Park (2.25.8): Locke challenges those who believe in real essences to determine the boundaries of the species to which this animal belongs without using the observed qualities (3.6.9). It is by a listing of the observed qualities that we can come to attach a name to that type of animal (3.6.3; cf. 3.11.21). There is also the talking parrot, used by Locke to make the point that even if the conversation of that Brazilian parrot reported by Sir William Temple did occur, we would still say it was a parrot, not a man (2.27.8). Parrots are cited elsewhere to make the point that merely repeating words, as children do when first learning to speak, is not really speaking (3.1.1; 3.2.7).

Locke also had a non-theoretical interest in animals, perhaps even a moral interest. He chastises children who are cruel to animals. He tells us that he has 'frequently observed in Children, that when they have got possession of any poor Creature, they are apt to use it ill: They often *torment*, and treat very roughly young Birds, Butterflies, and such other poor Animals which fall into their Hands, and that with a seeming kind of Pleasure' (*Some Thoughts*, §116). He urges mothers who allow their daughters to have pets, e.g., dogs, squirrels, birds, to make sure the children 'keep them well and look diligently after them, that they wanted nothing, or were not ill used' (*ibid.*). Locke's main interest in these remarks about the care of animals is the effect cruel behaviour towards animals will have on the child's character, but there is a suggestion of a secondary concern for animals as well. In an earlier section in this same work, where Locke comments on the difficulty of extirpating bad habits acquired by children, he refers to dogs and horses 'or any other Creatures' who, once they have been taught some tricks, are difficult to retrain. His comment reveals his view of children as well as of animals: 'none of these Creatures are half so wilful and proud, or half so desirous to be Masters of themselves and others, as Man' (§35).There are other ways in which Locke finds animals better than men. One obvious way is in terms of their sense organs: 'the pig and the ape, and many of the quadrupeds, far surpass men in the sharpness of the senses' (*Essays*, p. 147). Relying on travel books and their reports of societies where children were exposed or old people killed, Locke is led to comment that men 'surpass brutes in savageness' (*ibid.*, p. 173). He refers in *Two Treatises* to societies that sell children, characterizing this practice as the 'the most unnatural Murder, humane Nature is capable of': the 'Dens of Lions and Nurseries of Wolves know no such Cruelty as this' (*T*1, §56). He believed that nature teaches all things a general rule of 'self Preservation, and the Preservation of their Young'. He is appalled that some men violate nature and behave in ways never found among animals. Animals, he assures us, 'will Hunt, Watch, Fight, and almost Starve for the Preservation of their Young, never part with them, never forsake them till they are able to shift for themselves' (*ibid.*). Reason places men 'almost equal to Angels', but when reason is

forsaken, men sink 'to a Brutality below the level of Beasts' (*T*1, §58).
Another natural rule which men do not always obey is steadfastly obeyed
by animals: 'in those viviparous Animals which feed on Grass, the
conjunction between Male and Female last no longer than the very Act of
Copulation: because the Teat of the Dam' is sufficient to take care of the
offspring without any help from the male. But in other animals, e.g.,
beasts of prey or birds, the male stays and helps raise the young (*T*2, §79).

Animals are used by Locke in a less praiseworthy way when he
describes the man who transgresses the law of nature by killing others.
The murderer has abandoned reason and declared war on all mankind.
Therefore, he 'may be destroyed as a *Lyon* or a *Tyger*, one of those wild
Savage Beasts, with whom Men can have no Society nor Security' (*T*2,
§11). An act of aggression, even that of a thief, may lead to designs on
the life of another, placing the aggressor and those he attacks in a state
of war: 'And one may destroy a Man who makes War upon him, or has
discovered an Enmity to his being, for the same Reason, that he may kill
a *Wolf* or a *Lyon*; because such Men are not under the ties of the Common
Law of Reason' (*T*2, §16). There are also a number of passages where
Locke compares people living under an unjust ruler to herds of animals
kept for man's use and pleasure (*T*2, §§163, 172, 181). His doubt (or
realism) about the altruism of human nature is expressed in another
passage where animals are used as an illustration. He remarks that even
in an absolute monarchy, 'Subjects have an Appeal to the Law, and
Judges to decide any Controversies, and restrain any Violence that may
happen betwixt the Subjects themselves' (*T*2, §93). But he questions
whether 'this be from a true Love of Mankind and Society', or from a
concern for 'Power, Profit, or Greatness' of those who rule. In the same
way, one who has animals 'that Labour and drudge only for his Pleasure
and Advantage' keeps them from hurting or destroying each other, but
not out of any real concern for the animals (*T*2, §93). There may be a
tone of censure here, though it may only be directed at the unjust ruler,
not to the keeper of animals.

That man has a right to use animals as need arises to ensure man's
preservation, was never in doubt by Locke. It was the teaching of the
Bible (Genesis 1: 29–30; see *T*1, §§25, 26, 39, 40). Along with the earth,
animals are given by God to all mankind (*T*2, §27).

C

cause   The term 'cause' is closely associated with the terms 'produce' and 'power' in Locke's *Essay*. He writes as if we actually observe a quality or a substance beginning to exist, receiving that existence 'from the due Application and Operation of some other Being' (2.26.1). Observing that heat constantly melts wax, or that fire turns wood to ashes, we acquire the idea of cause and effect. As so often in this work, Locke slides from talking of *ideas* being caused to a change of *qualities* in substances being caused. The meaning of 'cause' is simply that 'which makes any other thing, either simple *Idea*, Substance, or Mode begin to be' (2.26.2). Unlike the more cautious Hume in the next century, Locke ascribed real causes to ideas, substances and modes, not just constant, uniform sequences. He identified several different kinds of causal action: *creation* ('when a new Particle of Matter doth begin to exist, *in rerum natura*, which had before no Being'); *generation*, when existing particles are rearranged to form a new particular individual ('this Man, this Egg, Rose, or Cherry'); *making*, when some external process produces 'a sensible Separation, or *juxta* Position of discernible Parts'; or *alteration* of some of the qualities of some object (2.26.2).

Locke speaks of powers in objects producing or causing ideas or sensations in us; that is what makes the idea real and adequate (2.30.2, 2.31.2). He admits that we do not know the precise nature of the causes of our sensations or ideas (e.g., the number and degrees of particles), but he accepts the corpuscular hypothesis about the structure of matter as the best explanation of the cause of our ideas and the cause of changes in other bodies (4.2.11). He shows no hesitation in affirming that ideas do have physical causes, but, as with most writers, he professes ignorance as to the details of the causal relation between matter and mind, between particles and sensations (see 4.11.2). In some passages, he speaks of *appearances* being caused by objects (2.9.8). In his discussion of substances and their qualities, he is keen to emphasize the fact that the cause of the coexisting qualities (the cause of their union) is unknown (2.23.6–9), but he always works with the principle that the ideas, sensations, or appearances that we experience do have causes, powers, in the objects which account for them. His more cautious statements admit that we do see or experience various effects but do not know their causes; that is why he accepts the corpuscular theory as probable only. Strictly, causes do not come 'within the scrutiny of humane Senses' (4.16.12), they cannot be examined by our senses. Nevertheless, he offers some interesting examples, probably borrowed from writers such as Boyle or Hooke, giving the probable nature of the corpuscles of matter and how they may act to produce the phenomena we observe (4.16.12). The chapter on primary and secondary qualities has many more examples; even some physiological causes are identified (2.8).

While Hume also recognized an underlying physiological structure for our thoughts, feelings, sensations and passions, even offering a few physiological explanations for mental events, and while he has a number of references (especially in his *Enquiry concerning Human Understanding*) to the 'ultimate springs and principles' in nature, he argued that we cannot observe causal efficacy, necessary connection, or powers. Our idea of cause for Hume has its origins in feelings and beliefs about the future being like the past. These feelings and beliefs arise when we experience the uniformities of events. Locke was more confident and more outspoken about there being causal powers at work in the world, but he does admit that we cannot observe those powers.

chain of being   The notion of degrees of reality or of a scale of being dates back at least to Plato. It can be traced through the centuries, taking various forms in the course of its history. (See A.O. Lovejoy, *The Great Chain of Being*, Harvard University Press, 1936.) Contemporaries of Locke frequently referred to the chain, e.g., Thomas Browne, William Petty, Sir Matthew Hale, Bishop John Wilkins, Robert Boyle (all of whose works Locke had in his library). From the fact that 'in all the visible corporeal World, we see no Chasms, or Gaps', Locke feels confident in asserting that 'there should be more *Species* of intelligent Creatures above us than there are of sensible and material below us' (*Essay*, 3.6.12). In *The Reasonableness of Christianity*, Locke speaks of 'infinite numbers and degrees of Spirits' beyond us (in *Works*, vii. 134; cf. *Essay*, 4.3.27). The *Essay* is less expansive, saying only that there are at least *several* degrees of angels (2.10.9). The details of the descending scale are not fully filled in, but presumably it reaches to the insensible particles of matter (2.8.13; *see* SPIRITS).

The examples he offers as evidence of the lack of chasms or gaps in the visible universe are a combination of observation reports, mythology, and some rather wild, unsupported claims: fishes that have wings and fly, birds that live in the water, seals that live on land and in the water, porpoises that 'have the warm Blood and Entrails of a Hog', and 'what is confidently reported of Mermaids, or Sea-men' (3.6.12). He also refers to some brutes (not named) 'that seem to have as much Knowledge and Reason as some that are called Men'. Elsewhere, Locke claims to have seen the issue of a cat and a rat (3.6.23). Other references to monstrous human births (a subject which fascinated Locke) probably were seen as lending support to his acceptance of the chain of being (3.3.17; 3.6.22, 27). He even claimed that 'the Animal and Vegetable Kingdoms, are so nearly join'd, that if you will take the lowest of one, and the highest of the other, there will scarce be perceived any great difference between them' (3.6.12).

Commitment to the chain of being, especially to some of the reported examples of the absence of any fixed boundaries between biological species, runs counter to today's known biological facts. Locke has little to say about biology. The chain of being seems incompatible with the notion of natural kinds. Locke is firm in his assertion that the kinds or classes we use are man-made, as his particularist ontology implies. Depending upon how we interpret his discussion of real essences, that ontology may run into trouble there, unless the text can be shown to reject unequivocally the old doctrine of fixed kinds in nature.

changelings   There were several different meanings to this term. Sometimes it refers to the notion of a child supposedly left by fairies, perhaps as a substitute child. Other times – and this was the sense in which Locke used this term – it refers to a half-witted person, an idiot or imbecile, perhaps misshapen and lacking in reason. Locke uses this example of changelings to illustrate several metaphysical and moral points. For example, he casts doubt on the claims for fixed real essences: 'Monsters, in all the Species of Animals, and of Changelings, and other strange Issues of humane Birth' (*Essay*, 3.3.17). Another passage on substance raises questions about the criteria for classification: 'Shall the difference of Hair only on the Skin, be a mark of a different internal specific Constitution between a Changeling and a Drill, when they agree in Shape, and want of Reason?' (3.6.22). Later in Book Four, the question of essence and classification arises again. Writing as if he has had reports of some changelings 'who have lived forty years together, without any appearance of Reason', he suggests that to say those changelings 'are something between a Man and a Beast' assumes that 'man' and 'beast' 'stand for distinct species so set out by real Essences' (4.4.13). In the next section of that same chapter, he also raises the question of the fate of such creatures in the next world, saying he is not concerned with that topic; they are in God's hands.

With his novel distinction between *physical* and *moral* man, changelings come in for a different use: the question whether 'a Child or Changeling be a *Man* in a physical Sense' is irrelevant to questions of what makes a *moral* man (3.11.16). In the long chapter on liberty (the chapter title is 'Power'), he contrasts the importance of being guided by reason in our actions, raising the rhetorical question: 'Would any one be a Changeling, because he is less determined by wise Considerations, than a wise Man?' (2.21.50). He was there discussing the notion of freedom as a total lack of determination of the will, even by reason or law. His comment: it is not 'worth the Name of *Freedom* to be at liberty to play the Fool'.

children   There are frequent discussions of children in Locke's writings. Sometimes children are used to illustrate or support some claim, e.g., about the origin and development of ideas, or about the absence of innate truths. Other times, children's rights and obligations are the focus of Locke's attention, as they are in both parts of *Two Treatises*. That work also talks of the relation between parents and children, and the role of both in civil society. Filmer is taken to task in the first of these treatises for his attitudes towards children, especially Filmer's claim that 'the Power of Parents over their Children' is '*Supreme Power*, and like that of Absolute Monarchs over their Slaves, Absolute Power of Life and Death' (*T*1, §51; cf. §§52–5). The most concentrated attention given to children is of course in Locke's *Some Thoughts*, a 'how-to' book for parents on raising and educating their children, helping them towards rationality and virtue.

The amount of space given over to discussions of children in his written works was unusual. There were other tracts on education, but to include detailed discussions of children in a political treatise, or even in works of psychology and theories of knowledge, is at this time quite rare. Locke was himself keenly interested in children, he knew and observed many of his friends' young children, he spent long periods living in several households with children, and children seem to have liked the bachelor Locke. It was important for him to understand the minds and passions of children. His descriptive accounts of the human understanding required him to pay some attention to the genesis of awareness. His interest in the importance of moral education made it imperative for him to understand child psychology (*see* SOME THOUGHTS CONCERNING EDUCATION).

coexistence   When Locke defines knowledge in Book Four of the *Essay* as our perception of the relations of ideas, one of four such cognitive relations he distinguishes is coexistence. His listing reads '*Co-existence*, or *necessary connexion*' (*Essay*, 4.1.3), but what he says earlier and later makes it clear that these are different relations; at least, necessary connections are not available to us, are not revealed in experience. If they were discoverable, they would still be examples of coexistence, but unlike those we can discover, they would be *necessary* coexistences. He spends many sections on what the consequences would be for our knowledge of the world, were we able to discover necessary connections in nature, such connections at the corpuscular level, between real and nominal essences, or between primary and secondary qualities. In lieu of such knowledge, coexistence is the relation on which our science is built, out of which natural histories of phenomena are made. Experience and observation constitute our method for discovering the coexistence of qualities. Locke characterizes our knowledge of this relation as 'short', indicating its dependence upon experience which is limited, but he stresses that 'the greatest and most material part of our Knowledge' concerning the materials (the substances) that interest scientists consists in that relation (4.3.9). He tends to speak of 'ideas' being found coexisting when he sometimes means 'qualities'. It is coexisting *qualities* that are the bases for our scientific knowledge. For example, 'Our *Idea* of *Flame* is a Body, hot, luminous, and moving upward, of *Gold*, a Body heavy to a certain degree, yellow, malleable, and fusible.' The accuracy and reality of our knowledge of such substances as gold, lead, water, oil depend upon how careful our observations have been of the qualities that occur together and under what conditions (see 4.4.12; 3.3.15; 2.30.5).

In Book Two of the *Essay*, Locke applied the restriction of our knowledge to minds and immaterial spirits as well as to kinds (sorts) of physical substances. In the case of immaterial spirits, our idea is constructed from 'those Operations of our own Minds, which we experiment daily in our selves, as Thinking, Understanding, Willing, Knowing, and Power of beginning Motion' (2.23.15). With physical substances, Locke speaks of an unknown cause of the union of coexisting qualities (2.23.6), a cause which is beyond our knowledge but about which the corpuscular theory offers an hypothesis.

cohesion   The problem of accounting for the cohesion of particles of matter was recognized by Locke and most scientists then as important but difficult to solve. The 'glue' or 'cement' which holds individual particles together and preserves groups of them in a stable union was not understood until after Newton. There were several explanations offered, explanations discussed by Locke in the *Essay*: the pressure of ambient bodies, the pressure of the air or aether (2.23.23–27). Locke discusses and rejects these explanations. He appeals to cohesion in many passages. For example, hardness is described as 'a firm Cohesion of the parts of Matter, making up masses of a sensible bulk' (2.4.4), or the extension of body is described as 'nothing, but the cohesion or continuity of solid, separable, moveable Parts' (2.4.5; cf. 2.23.17). An oak tree differs from a mass of matter in being a *specific* group of particles organized in a particular way: the mass of matter is 'only the Cohesion of Particles . . . any how united' (2.27.4). Not only does Locke think we cannot discover the particular insensible constitution of any bit of matter, it was even more important for him to remark that we do not have an understanding of cohesion itself. Thus, our knowledge of nature is doubly limited.

commonwealth In drawing the lines between civil government and religious societies, Locke remarks that 'The Commonwealth seems to me to be a society of men constituted only for the preserving, and advancing their own civil interests' (*A Letter concerning Toleration*, in *Works*, vi. 9). His *Two Treatises* gives a more precise definition of this term, indicating that it is not identical to civil government: 'By *Common-wealth*, I must be understood all along to mean, not a Democracy, or any form of Government, but *any Independent Community* which the *Latines* signified by the word *Civitas*, to which the word which best answers in our Language, is *Common-wealth*, and most properly expresses such a Society of Men, which Community or City in *English* does not, for there may be Subordinate Communities in a Government' (*T*2, §133). Although the chapter in which this section occurs is entitled 'Of the Forms of Commonwealths', the 'forms' really refer to the government set up for the community by the majority of its members. Locke has earlier in this work argued that where men unite into a society, the majority has, as he says in this chapter, 'the whole power of the Community, naturally in them', so they 'may imploy all that power in making Laws by Officers of their own appointing' (*ibid.*, §132). The forms of the governmental structure may include democracy, oligarchy, monarchies of various forms (hereditary, elective), or some mixture of these.

In a very early tract, Locke outlined different views about the nature of civil government and the locus of civil power, but he declined to opt for any particular view. He simply says that 'God wished there to be order, society and government among men. And this we call the commonwealth' (*Two Tracts*, pp. 231–2). He does say that 'In every commonwealth there must be some supreme power without which it cannot truly be a commonwealth: and that supreme power is exactly the same in all government, namely, legislative' (*ibid.*, p. 132). In *Two Treatises*, he speculates on the possible origins or early forms of commonwealths, suggesting that 'if we look back as far as History will direct us, towards the *Original of Common-wealths*, we shall generally find them under the Government and Administration of one Man' (*T*2, §105). A father's

'Preheminency might in the first institution of some Common-wealths, give rise to, and place, in the beginning, the Power in one hand' (§106). He considers the possibility that '*a Family* by degrees *grew up into a Commonwealth*' with the fatherly authority passing to the son (§110). Nevertheless, a family is not a commonwealth or a political society (§86). The ruler of a commonwealth is different in function from the ruler of a family or the captain of a ship (§2). The beginning of a commonwealth or political society (the latter seems to be the former plus forms of government) occurs when people who were in a state of nature agree to 'unite into a *Community*' and give up some of the rights and powers they have in the state of nature. Consent is all the 'compact' that is required. A political society is 'nothing but the consent of any number of Freemen capable of a majority to unite and incorporate into such a society' (§99).

Political power is defined as the '*Right* of making Laws with Penalties of Death, and consequently all less Penalties, for the Regulating and Preserving of Property' (§3). The 'force of the Community' is employed in administering the laws, and the commonwealth is defended from foreign attack. The legitimate authority of the commonwealth applies only to the members, not to foreigners (§9). Punishment for transgressions of the laws of the society is in the jurisdiction and power of the commonwealth. The magistrate makes and applies the 'Judgments of the Commonwealth', but those judgements are in effect the judgements of the members or their representatives (§88). The main reason for uniting into a commonwealth 'and putting themselves under Government, *is the Preservation of Property*' (§124). Wherever the 'Legislative or Supreme Power of any Common-wealth' lies, whoever fulfils that function must do so 'by establish'd *standing Laws*, promulgated and known to the People, and not by Extemporary Decrees' (§131). Those laws must be for the good of the people. Taxes cannot be raised on property '*without the Consent of the People*' and the '*Legislative* neither must *nor can transfer the Power of making Laws* to any Body else, or place it any where but where the People have' (§142). All the power of the legislative is delegated from the people (§§137, 141).

Involved with Locke's concept of a commonwealth and its form of government are the notions of community, majority, and a unified, integrated whole. Even in the state of nature, everyone belongs to or forms one large community, the community of mankind (§128). When a person unites with others to form a commonwealth and then a political society, that move is one of incorporation: 'That which makes the Community, and brings Men out of the loose State of Nature, into *one Politick Society*, is the Agreement which every one has with the rest to incorporate, and act as one Body, and so be one distinct Commonwealth' (§211; cf. §§120,

95). The members of such a community, of a commonwealth, 'are united and combined together into one coherent living Body' (§212). Locke goes on in the next sentence to say, 'This *is the Soul that gives Form, Life, and Unity,* to the Common-wealth', seeming to add a soul to the analogy between the coherent unit that is a commonwealth and a living body. Perhaps the fact that the body is living qualifies it for being a soul as well. The contrast is with the situation when the commonwealth is dissolved through various possible causes: then we have a 'confused Multitude' (§219). Under that situation, 'the Bonds of Society' are broken, bonds which 'keep every part of the Body Politick in its due place and function' (*ibid.*). The order and connection of the parts is gone.

The analogy of the living body with functioning parts and a soul appears in several sections of this treatise. Joining together and consenting '*to make one Community* or Government', people are 'incorporated and make *one Body Politick*, wherein the *Majority* have a Right to act and conclude the rest' (§95). The community is made 'one Body, with a Power to Act as one Body, which is only the will and determination of the *majority*' (§96). The analogy of the body politic is elaborated even further in this last section by Locke's talking of the force necessary to move that body; the force is supplied by the majority. Everyone is bound to accept the majority decision, the act of the majority passes for the act of the whole (see §§97, 98). The only other way to move the body politic is by every individual consenting – not a very practical alternative. Illness alone would keep some members 'away from the publick Assembly' (§98). Locke's conviction that the majority must be the moving force is strong: 'For where the *majority* cannot conclude the rest, there they cannot act as one Body, and consequently will be immediately dissolved again' (§98; cf. §99).

Depending upon the specific form of government a commonwealth has, the working of the body politic, especially the way in which the majority could 'act the whole', would differ. Whatever form is followed – even the mixed form Locke uses at the end of *Two Treatises* of a hereditary ruler and two assemblies, one of hereditary nobility, the other of representatives appointed by the people – he seems to say that those filling official roles do so as public persons, within the confines of working for the good of the people (§151). Modern readers tend to read Locke's account of commonwealth and political society as a plan for democracy, but he does not say democracy is the only form of government that will fit his model. The dramatic denouement of *Two Treatises*, where he discusses what would happen when the trust of the people has been violated, talks of king and prince. The famous answer to the question, '*Who shall be Judge* whether Prince or Legislative act contrary to' the people's trust?, may have been intended as a bold challenge to the existing institutions in England: '*The People shall be Judge*' (§240). If the people's judgement is to be expressed by the will of the majority through the representatives chosen by the people, the assembly of representatives would seem in that situation at least to be the ultimate locus of power. Even in less severe situations, e.g., 'if a Controversie arise betwixt a Prince and some of the People, in a matter where the Law is silent, or doubtful, and the thing be of great Consequence, I should think the proper *Umpire*, in such a Case, should be the Body of the *People*' (§242). The body of the people is the community as a whole, not each member in particular: 'The *Power that every individual gave the Society*, when he entered into it, can never revert to the Individual again, as long as the Society lasts, but will always remain in the Community; because without this, there can be no Community, no Commonwealth' (§243; *see* REPRESENTATIVE).

compact or contract 'That Men should keep their Compacts, is certainly a great and undeniable Rule of Morality' (*Essay*, 1.3.5). The early *Essays on the Law of Nature* make keeping promises an obligation derived from nature, from the law of nature (p. 119). Without that natural obligation, 'it is not to be expected that a man would abide by a compact because he has promised it' (*ibid.*). In that essay, Locke identifies two 'factors on which human society appears to rest, i.e. firstly, a definite constitution of the state and form of government, and, secondly, the fulfilment of pacts'. He also writes of 'the faithful fulfilment of contracts'. The word 'compact' tends to be used more often than 'contract', but there are passages, such as this one, in which both terms occur. Peter Laslett has suggested that 'compact' in Locke's usage is more informal, carrying the sense of an agreement between people (a promise), while 'contract' may have a more formal, legal sense (see his edition of *Two Treatises*, p. 112). Elsewhere, Locke refers to a compact we 'enter into with God or with our fellow men' (*Two Tracts*, p. 225). The *Essays* distinguish *tacit* contracts 'prompted by the common interests and convenience of men, such as the free passage of envoys, free trade, and other things of that kind', from 'an expressly stated contract, such as the fixed boundary-lines between neighbouring peoples, the prohibition of the purchase and import of particular goods, and many other such things' (pp. 161–3). These examples of tacit or express contracts are not derived from the law of nature: they are examples of *positive*, not *natural*, consent. Is there a suggestion here that 'compact' goes with 'natural', while 'contract' is linked with positive law?

A few other specific examples of compacts can be found in *Two Treatises*. He refers to countries such as England where land is held in common by compact; hence 'no one can inclose or appropriate any part, without the consent of all his Fellow-Commoners' (*T2*, §35). Where land is scarce, '*Communities* settled the Bounds of their distinct Territories, and by Laws within themselves, regulated the Properties of the private Men of their Society, and so, *by Compact* and Agreement, *settled the Property* which Labour and Industry began' (*T2*, §45; cf. §28). He also mentions the temporary contract between a master and a servant: the servant sells some of his time and service (§85). In his account of property, Locke showed how in the pre-political society, where all is common, private property could be acquired without 'any express Compact' (§25). When value was placed on gold and silver, men found a way to have unequal and disproportionate possessions by a 'tacit and voluntary consent', but not by compact (§50; *see* PROPERTY).

There are also examples of what cannot be done by compact. A man '*cannot*, by compact, or his own Consent, *enslave himself* to any one, nor put himself under the Absolute, Arbitrary Power of another, to take away his Life, when he pleases' (§23). A father's compact with a government cannot bind his children (§73). This same point is made more strongly later in *Two Treatises*: "'Tis true, that whatever Engagements or Promises any one has made for himself, he is under the Obligation of them, but *cannot* by any Compact whatsoever, bind *his Children* or Posterity' (§116; cf. §118). In the first of *Two Treatises*, Locke's attack against Filmer included rejecting the notion that 'a Man can alien his Power over his children, and what may be transfer'd by compact, may be possessed by Inheritance' (*T1*, §100). A father's power over his children can be forfeited by carelessness or indifference (he cites the example of selling children); it cannot be transferred by compact.

Another example that receives more attention is the marriage compact or contract. The first of *Two Treatises* distinguished the power of a father through begetting from the power of a husband founded on contract (*T1*, §78). In that same passage, he speaks of 'the conjugal contract'. In the second of *Two Treatises*, he explains that '*Conjugal Society* is made by a voluntary Compact between Man and Woman' (§78). The rest of that section fills in some of the details of that compact. Although it consists 'chiefly in such a Communion and Right in one anothers Bodies, as is necessary to its chief End, Procreation; yet it draws with it mutual Support, and Assistance, and a Communion of Interest too'. Care and education of children is also part of the commitments under the marriage contract. The next few sections elaborate on the conjugal society formed by such a compact. That compact need not always be for life, unless some positive law 'ordains all such Contracts to be perpetual' (*T1*, §81). The wife has by contract some specific rights, including the 'Liberty to *separate* from' the husband (§82). Locke adds, however, 'where natural Right, or their Contract allows it', implying that the liberty of separation could be written into the contract. The reference to natural right as a possible exclusion of such liberty is unclear. More details are given in §83 (*see* WOMEN).

It is the formation of the political or civil society that is usually called to mind when the term 'contract' is mentioned. Men make various promises and compacts with others in the state of nature as well as within civil society. A compact whereby men agree 'together to enter into one Community, and make one Body Politick' moves them from the state of nature to civil society (*T*2, §14). Such a compact is described as the 'original' compact by means of which each man incorporates with others 'into *one Society*', with obligations to 'every one in that Society' (§97). This compact or agreement carries with it the understanding that each member gives up the powers each had in the state of nature, giving that power now to the majority (§99). It is this compact that 'did, or could give *beginning* to any *lawful Government* in the World' (§§97, 171). Subsequent to the beginning of civil society, a person who happens to be living in that country is subject to its benefits and protection, but such a person is not a member of that community. Membership can only come about 'by positive Engagement, and express Promise and Compact' (§172).

The concept of a social contract is found in writers before Locke, even as far back as the ancient Greeks (see entry, 'Social Contract', in Wiener, *Dictionary of the History of Ideas*, vol. IV, 1968). Hobbes just before Locke, and Rousseau in the eighteenth century, are the two figures most often cited in this tradition of social contract theory (Hobbes, *Leviathan*, 1651; Rousseau, *Du contrat social*, 1762).

conception   The way of ideas associated by Locke's contemporaries with some of his new doctrines (and challenges to old doctrines) was also a new language, a new way of talking about knowledge, belief, and mental operations. There was not available to Locke a developed psychological vocabulary. He recognized and alerted his readers to the fact that he made heavy use of the term 'idea'. He also explicated his use of the term 'perception', since he relied upon that term also fairly frequently, e.g., in the definition of knowledge and the different relations of ideas. The terms 'impression' and 'appearance' are also part of the emerging psychological vocabulary, his way of talking about mind. Another term in this language of mind is 'conception', a word sometimes used with 'notion', at other times used instead of 'idea'. Still additional uses of 'conception' refer to what we can understand or comprehend, two other words in this vocabulary.

The most frequent use of 'conception' (or its plural form) is to indicate where our comprehension is unclear, confused or inadequate. He notes in his discussion of innate principles that there are many different and contrary ideas and conceptions of God (*Essay*, 1.4.14). Some of those are linked with 'gross Conceptions of Corporeity', an unsuitable conception for God (1.4.15), or with 'absurd and unfit conceptions' (1.4.16). In Book Three of the *Essay* on language, he speaks of 'gross and confused Conceptions and unaccurate ways of Talking and Thinking' (3.6.30; cf. 3.10.22). He also says we sometimes give a wrong name to our conceptions (3.6.33). In another passage, he writes of the notion that other creatures may have a different sense modality from ours, this being far from 'our Notice, Imagination, and Conception' (2.2.3). He characterizes the notion of substantial forms as a confused conception (3.6.10), and he says some disputes are 'more about the signification of Words, than a real difference in the Conception of Things' (3.9.16). Other passages refer to 'our general or specifick conception of Matter' (4.10.10), of something that is 'above our conception' (4.10.15), and he does not think it is 'beyond our Conception' to think of the size, figure, and extension of one body causing changes in another body (4.3.13).

He comments in another passage that definitions do not always give us a clear conception of the meaning of a word (3.4.4). Writing about relations, he uses 'idea' and 'notion' as well as 'conception': having a 'clear conception' (2.25.8; cf. 2.16.7), or a clear conception of power (2.21.72). His usual way of describing words as signs is to say they refer to ideas, but 3.1.2 describes sounds as '*Signs of internal Conceptions*'. Words signify the ideas or conceptions of the speaker; if a person tries to apply words as marks immediately to the ideas other people have, he would 'make them Signs of his own Conceptions, and yet apply them to other *Ideas*', mixing the two vocabularies together (3.2.2). In the same chapter, he says conceptions are communicated by words (3.2.6). In 4.18.3, he speaks of 'Impressions delivered over to others in Words, and the ordinary ways of conveying our Conceptions one to another'. In his analysis of our idea of space, he remarks that 'Many Ideas require others as necessary to their Existence or Conception', apparently allowing for a conception of some ideas (2.13.11). A passage in the *Conduct* says conceptions are 'nothing but ideas, which are made up of simple ones'; such conceptions are complex ideas (§29; in *Works*, iii. 258).

Some specific conceptions are mentioned. Raising some doubts about the ideas of substances, he says that the idea of corporeal substance 'is as remote from our Conceptions, and Apprehensions, as that of Spiritual *Substance*' (2.23.5). Commenting on how the 'Workmanship of the All-wise, and Powerful God, ... exceeds the Capacity and Comprehension of the most Inquisitive and Intelligent Man', he compares that lack of comprehension to the lack of understanding by the 'most ignorant of rational Creatures' of the 'best contrivance of the most ingenious Man': their conceptions fall short of those artful contrivances (3.6.9; cf. 2.24.3). The complex idea of a genus is said to be but 'a partial Conception of what is in the *Species*' (3.6.32). The terms 'matter' and 'body' are said to 'stand for two different Conceptions' (3.10.15). The smell of a rose conveys '*one uniform Appearance*, or Conception in the mind' (2.2.1). He also uses the term 'conception' while analysing space and motion (2.15.1; 2.23.28).

Locke's use of this term ranges from a substitute for 'idea', to another way of characterizing the contents of thought, to acts of conceiving and understanding. Of the various faculties and operations of the mind distinguished by most standard logic manuals of that period, conception was often discussed. Hume later suggested that all those faculties are just variants of conception.

Conduct of the Understanding   On 10 April 1697, Locke wrote to his friend William Molyneux:

> I have lately got a little leisure to think of some additions to my book [*An Essay concerning Human Understanding*], against the next edition [the fourth, of 1700], and within these few days have fallen upon a subject that I know not how far it will lead me. I have written several pages on it, but the matter, the farther I go, opens the more upon me, and I cannot yet get sight of any end of it. The title of the chapter will be Of the Conduct of the Understanding, which, if I shall pursue, as far as I imagine it will reach, and as it deserves, will, I conclude, make the largest chapter of my Essay. (*Corr.* 2243; vi. 87)

The chapter was never incorporated into the *Essay* (it would probably have been longer than 2.21 on 'Power', which was 73 sections); it was first published in his *Posthumous Works*, in 1706, edited by Peter King. Shortly before his death, Locke spoke again about the *Conduct*, this time in a letter to Peter King of 4 October 1704: '*The Conduct of the understanding* I have allways thought ever since it first came into my mind to be a subject very well worth consideration, though I know not how, it seems to me for any thing I have met with to have been almost wholly neglected: what I have done in it is very far from a just treatise' (*Corr.* 3647; viii. 413). He goes on to explain to Peter King that, as he thought of 'miscarriages' of understanding, he put down some thoughts about remedies for those faults. It takes up 137 octavo pages as the lead piece in the *Posthumous Works*. In it, Locke ranges over a wide variety of topics, most of which receive treatment in his *Essay*. The *Conduct* is a treatise on method, written in less technical language than the *Essay*. He writes about reasoning, ideas, principles, practice and development of habits of reasoning, arguments, reading, words and much else. It is a useful work to consult for a more informal approach to these topics.

connexion (necessary)   Locke (and others at that time) often uses the term 'connexion' to mean 'necessary connexion'. He seems to have accepted the notion of such connections in nature, but the limitations of our faculties (our 'uncurable Ignorance' is how he characterizes it at one point, *Essay*, 4.3.25) prevent us from discovering them. Contingent, coexisting relations are for us the only grounds for science. His discussion of this necessary connection is linked with the concept of real essence and the corpuscular structure of matter. For example, were our complex ideas of substances the real essence (if the ideas captured or reflected the real essence of bodies), the properties we discover in bodies would be *deducible from* those ideas and their necessary connection with the real essence. However, we have no reason to think that the malleability of iron has a necessary connection with any other of the qualities we find coexisting with it, e.g., its colour, weight or hardness. He speaks of all the observed qualities 'flowing from' the real essence or from the internal constitution (i.e., 'the Figure, Size, and Connexion') of the solid parts of the matter of gold, iron, etc. He also speaks of that internal constitution as the *cause* of its observed qualities. The reason that science (Locke writes 'Humane Science') is narrow and limited is that our knowledge is limited to observed coexistences of qualities. Our ideas of the substances of scientific enquiry 'carry with them, in their own Nature, no visible necessary connexion' among the qualities (4.3.10). An example is given in 4.3.13: we can conceive the possibility of a causal relation between the size, figure and motion of two bodies, but we cannot discover any *connection* between impulse and motion. Nor can we discover any such connection among the various primary qualities, or between those qualities and our sensations. In this latter case, Locke says there is not even a 'conceivable *connexion* betwixt' the primary qualities and our sensations. Nor will any analysis of our ideas yield a knowledge of nature. Even were we able to discover the microstructure of bodies, we could never 'discover any necessary *connexion* between them, and any of the *secondary Qualities*' (4.3.14). There *are* a few conceptual connections among our ideas, e.g., 'Figure necessarily supposes Extension, receiving or communicating Motion by impulse' presupposes solidity; but in general, 'Our Knowledge ... reaches very little farther than our Experience' (4.3.14, 16, 28).

The limitation of our knowledge of bodies to observed coexisting

qualities, and our lack of knowledge of any necessary connection among
qualities or between primary and second qualities, or between primary
qualities and our sensations, means that we have very little *general* or
universal knowledge of nature, little that carries *'undoubted Certainty'*.
Locke instances the proposition, 'All gold is fixed', but what he says holds
for any general proposition about gold: that it is yellow, that it is
malleable, etc. Necessary connections are not discovered in experience,
no generalization can be affirmed with anything other than probability,
unless we just mean to call attention to our definition of gold (4.6.7–10).
In these sections, Locke is concerned to affirm the contingent nature of
our knowledge of physical bodies. The same limitation holds for our
knowledge of 'man'. We normally mean by that term 'a Body of the
ordinary shape, with Sense, voluntary Motion, and Reason join'd to it',
but we have no knowledge of 'the real Constitution on which Sensation,
power of Motion, and Reasoning, with that peculiar Shape, depend, and
whereby they are united together in the same Subject' (4.6.15). We lack
any knowledge of necessary connections among these qualities or between
them and the real constitution on which they depend. Similarly, in talking
of actions and intentions, Locke remarks that there is no discoverable
necessary connection (he writes here, 'natural connexion') between 'the
outward and visible Action' and the intention of the man who commits
murder or sacrilege (3.9.7). Thus, such generalizations as 'all men sleep
by intervals', 'no man can be nourished by wood or stones', 'all men will
be poisoned by hemlock' cannot be asserted with certainty, as true
generalizations. Similar remarks hold also for general claims about chemical substances.

Far from lamenting our lack of certainty in science, Locke views that
lack as a distinct advantage. Instead of trying to derive a science of nature
from our ideas, we are driven to the *things themselves*. Experience, he
asserts, *'must teach me,* what Reason cannot' (4.12.9). Some readers may
find a regret on Locke's part that human knowledge is so limited, limited
to experience and observation, but it was the announced programme of
the Royal Society to replace speculation, books of authority, and all claims
for demonstrative knowledge by careful experiments and detailed observations. When Locke refers to our 'State of *Mediocrity'*, saying that 'natural
Philosophy is not capable of being made a Science', he is simply pointing
out that our knowledge of nature should be based upon experience and
observation (4.12.10). It is a *deductive* science of nature derived from a
discovery of real essence or necessary connections that Locke rejects as
possible. An *experimental* science is within our power; it was being constructed by the scientists Locke knew – Boyle, Newton, Sydenham.

We might still ask, if Locke was not lamenting our inability to construct
a deductive science based upon the discovery of necessary connections,

why does he spend so much time telling us what it would be like? He characterizes a knowledge of the necessary connections of the qualities and powers of bodies as enabling us to know 'without trial' several of the operations of bodies upon other bodies (4.3.25). We would be able, for example, 'to tell before Hand, that *Rhubarb* will purge, *Hemlock* kill, and *Opium* make a Man sleep' (4.3.25). The comparisons are with the knowledge we have of the properties of a square or triangle, or the knowledge a watchmaker has about the workings of the clock without trial or observation; e.g., 'that a little piece of Paper laid on the Balance, will keep the Watch from going, till it be removed; or that some small part of it, being rubb'd with a File, the Machin would quite lose its Motion' (*ibid.*; cf. 4.6.11). If there is any longing expressed in these passages for a non-experimental deductive science of nature (what he refers to as a 'perfect science of nature'), it does not deter Locke from agreement with the Royal Society scientists on the importance of experimental science. These passages do, however, suggest that Locke accepted the notion of necessary connections in nature which other intelligences than human may have or could have access to.

conscience   This is not a term used very often by Locke, but it is important in reminding us of a concept frequently used by writers contemporary with and just earlier than Locke. The term appears in some of his earliest writings, some that he never published. After 1690, it fades out of his use. In the first of two early treatises (published recently as *Two Tracts on Government*, ed. Abrams, 1967), Locke defines conscience as 'nothing but an opinion of the truth of any practical position, which may concern any actions as well moral as religious, civil as ecclesiastical' (p. 138). In the second of these tracts, he narrows the definition to moral actions: 'The law of conscience we call that fundamental judgment of the practical intellect concerning any possible truth of a moral proposition about things to be done in life' (p. 225). He goes on to refer to the light of nature implanted in our hearts by God, describing that light as 'an inner legislator (in effect) constantly present in us whose edicts it should not be lawful for us to transgress even a nail's breadth' (*ibid.*). Divine law 'binds the consciences of men' (p. 226). He warns against false appeals to conscience, and those who appeal to conscience as a way of avoiding obeying some positive law of the civil magistrate. Locke was sceptical that 'private men's judgments' could function as the measure of 'the equity and obligation of all edicts' (p.137). He offers no criterion or test for distinguishing merely private opinion from that divine, inner legislator; he was mainly concerned in those tracts with the abuse of appeals to conscience.

In his *Essays on the Law of Nature*, written about the same time as these two tracts, he speaks of conscience as evidence that God exists (pp. 109, 155), but he prefers the argument from sense and reason as a way of showing there is a God. He discusses the argument that had been used about conscience as proof of 'the existence of a law of nature'. That argument said that 'the fact that "no one who commits a wicked action is acquitted in his own judgement"', shows there is such a law (pp. 117, 167). Locke was not favourably inclined towards this argument; but it is clear that he writes with many of his contemporaries in mind who did invoke such an argument, even some who said laws of nature are innate. Nevertheless, Locke gives some role to conscience in these essays: 'Indeed, all obligation binds conscience and lays a bond on the mind itself, so that not fear of punishment, but a rational apprehension of what is right, puts us under an obligation, and conscience passes judgement on morals, and, if we are guilty of a crime, declares that we deserve punishment' (p. 185). Making the point that 'the binding force of civil law is dependent on natural law', he closes the sixth essay by remarking that 'we should not obey a king just out of fear, because, being more powerful, he can constrain . . ., but for conscience' sake, because a king has command over us by right' (p. 189).

The *Essay* defines conscience as 'nothing else, but our own Opinion or Judgment of the Moral Rectitude or Pravity of our own Actions' (1.3.8). That opinion is not derived from God; it can arise from education, from other people, or just from the customs and practices of our society. In that passage, he was writing against those who argued for innate moral rules. Conscience was often invoked by those writers as evidence for innateness. The 'inner legislator' of *Two Tracts* tends in the *Essay* to be reason, not conscience. However, Locke does say that 'In the great Day, wherein the Secrets of all Hearts shall be laid open, it may be reasonable to think, no one shall be made to answer for what he knows nothing of; but shall receive his Doom, his Conscience accusing or excusing him' (2.27.22).

Two Treatises employs the notion of conscience in a few passages. For example, no one can be 'oblig'd in Conscience to submit to any Power, unless he can be satisfied who is the Person, who has a Right to Exercise that Power over him' (*T*1, §81). The same point is made later about 'the Duty of my Obedience, and the Obligation of Conscience I am under' to another person (*T*1, §120; cf. §122). The discussion in the second of *Two Treatises* of the power all men have in the state of nature to punish those who transgress the laws of nature urges men to listen to what 'calm reason and conscience dictates' (*T*2, §8). The question of whether someone has put himself in a state of war with me is one 'I my self can only be Judge [of] in my own Conscience, as I will answer it at the great Day, to the

Supream Judge of all Men' (*T*2, §21). A later passage says that foreigners, 'by living all their Lives under another Government, and enjoying the Priviledges and Protection of it, though they are bound, even in Conscience, to submit to its Administration' are not members of that commonwealth (*T*2, §122).

consciousness   In rejecting the Cartesian notion of thought being the essence of the soul, because it entails that the soul always thinks (which he took to be false), Locke is led to define 'consciousness'. It is 'the perception of what passes in a Man's own mind' (*Essay*, 2.1.19). No one, he insists, can tell me I was conscious (e.g., in sleep) if I was conscious of nothing. The notion that a man can think without being conscious that he is thinking was for Locke not just false, but an absurdity, just as absurd as to say a man is hungry but does not feel hunger. Hunger 'consists in that very sensation, as thinking consists in being conscious that one thinks' (*ibid.*; cf. 2.1.12). The claim of innate ideas and principles is rejected, *inter alia*, for the same reason: it requires us to have ideas but not be conscious of them. If it be said that innate ideas are in the memory, and hence not always 'actually in view', when called up they would have to come with a consciousness of having been known or perceived before (1.4.20). It is the 'consciousness of having been in the mind before' that distinguishes memory from other modes of thought.

The term 'consciousness' is not used only in connection with memory. Locke reports the case of a blind man who lost his sight when he was a child and then had it restored. The colours he experienced with his renewed sight were 'convey'd to his mind, and that without any consciousness of a former acquaintance' (1.4.20). In his discussion of different degrees of knowledge, Locke asks whether a man 'be not invincibly conscious to himself of a different Perception, when he looks on the Sun by day, and thinks on it by night' (4.2.14). In a few passages, phrases such as 'perceive it' or 'be sensible of it' play a role similar to 'is conscious of'. A better-known use of 'consciousness' is found in his discussions of *personal identity*. Consciousness is an ever-present phenomenon, whether it be linked with memory or just our present perceptions. Neither perceiving some present object or event nor recalling it is the same as consciousness: consciousness accompanies these and every mode of thought (see the phrase, 'if these Perceptions, with their consciousness', 4.27.10; *see* PERSON).

consent   In his discussion of the epistemic sense of 'assent', as in assenting to or believing a proposition, Locke was concerned to identify justifying or warranting grounds for assenting. That discussion also contains some descriptive accounts of how beliefs arise. In his polemic against innate ideas and principles, Locke attacked the argument from a supposed universal *consent* to certain speculative and moral propositions. There is another, performative, use of 'consent' in his political writings, e.g., *Two Treatises*, which is the legitimating act for political society. This political use of 'consent' carries rights and obligations with it. The concept of a social contract or compact was part of a tradition prior to Locke. That concept assumes free consent on the part of those who agree to join the society formed by their joint action. Locke brought the notion of political consent into greater prominence than had been the case with other writers.

Having rejected in the first of *Two Treatises* Robert Filmer's claim that men are born in subjection to their parents, especially to the father (*T*1, §6), Locke recognized that 'in the first Ages of the World, and in places still', fathers did become a kind of 'prince', a ruler over their children (*T*2, §74). The legitimacy of such a relation after 'the Minority of his Children' has passed arises only from 'the express or tacit Consent of the Children'. Consent, not paternal right, operates in such situations. This consent is described by Locke as *tacit* and *natural*. The government children have been under during their minority 'continued still to be more their Protection than restraint' (*ibid.*, §75). The rudiments for the later move into political society are present in this family example, although there are differences and greater complexity in political consent.

Locke believed that history had in fact shown, what reason affirms, that 'the *Governments* of the World, that were begun in Peace, had their beginning laid on that foundation, and were *made by the Consent of the People*' (§104). Thus his insistence that 'the *beginning of Politick Society* depends upon the consent of the Individuals, to joyn into and make one Society' (§106). One of the defects in the state of nature is the lack of a standard of right and wrong agreed to by 'common consent' (§124). Positive law in political societies must rest not only on natural law, but on the '*consent of the Society*': that consent is necessary for the laws of government (§134). The consent that is necessary for civil law and for civil society is not just an agreement to form a civil polity: it is a consent to make '*one Body Politick*, wherein the *Majority* have a Right to act and conclude the rest' (§95). In order to act as one body, the will of the majority must operate. Thus, *individual* consent constitutes the community, the consent of the majority runs the community: 'the *act of the Majority* passes for the act of the whole' (§96). Each member (Locke says 'every Man'), through the consent to join, 'puts himself under an Obligation to every one of that Society' (§97; §§98, 99). In later passages while discussing taxation, 'his own consent' is equated with 'the Consent of the Majority' (§140).

In his concept of a body politic and of the majority's will representing individual consents, Locke was echoing features to be found in Hobbes and was anticipating aspects of Rousseau's social contract. One of the more obscure features of Locke's account of consent, a feature still lively debated today, is his use of the distinction between *express* and *tacit* consent. What criterion do we use to determine *tacit* consent? In the epistemic uses of this notion in the *Essay*, Locke insisted on manifestations in behaviour of the belief in virtue (1.3.3). In the political context, the question he posed was: 'what ought to be look'd upon as a *tacit Consent*, and how far it binds, i.e. how far any one shall be looked on to have consented, and thereby submitted to any Government, where he has made no Expressions of it at all' (*T2*, §119). Does this last clause imply the possibility of a consent without *any* expression, verbal or behavioural? The details and implications of his answer to that question continue to occupy the attention of scholars and political scientists, but his immediate answer is that 'every Man, that hath any Possession, or Enjoyment, of any part of the Dominions of any Government, doth thereby give his *tacit Consent*, and is as far forth obliged to Obedience to the Laws of that Government, during such Enjoyment, as any one under it' (§119; *see* ASSENT).

corpuscular hypothesis In speaking of active and passive powers of bodies, Locke traces those powers to the 'Texture and Motion of Parts', even though he admits that 'we cannot by any means come to discover' that texture or motion (*Essay*, 4.3.16). We do not even have '*clear Ideas* of the smalness of Parts, much beyond the smallest, that occur to any of our Senses: and therefore when we talk of the divisibility of Matter *in infinitum*' we have only a very confused idea of 'Corpuscles, or minute Bodies' (2.29.16). We do have clear ideas of division and divisibility, but when we try, as the corpuscular hypothesis says, to reduce the size of particles to the insensible level, we end with obscurity. Nevertheless, he uses this hypothesis to account for the action of bodies upon other bodies, for the observable qualities of bodies, and for the causal theory of perception. He tells us in that passage that he accepted this hypothesis 'as that which is thought to go farthest in an intelligible Explication of the Qualities of Bodies'. *Some Thoughts* says that 'the Modern *Corpuscularians* talk, in most Things, more intelligibly than the *Peripateticks*' (§193). That hypothesis does not give us any insight into the nature of bodies; for that, we would need to discover 'what Qualities and Powers of Bodies have a *necessary Connexion or Repugnancy* one with another' (*Essay*, 4.3.16).

Locke offers this hypothesis as an account of why the same water feels hot to one hand, cold to the other. Warmth or heat on this hypothesis is '*nothing but a certain sort and degree of Motion in the minute Particles of our Nerves, or animal Spirits'* (2.8.21). Thus, if the motion of the particles or corpuscles in the nerves of one hand increases while that in the other hand decreases, the difference will be affected by the motion of the particles of water, resulting in different sensations. Simple ideas are sometimes referred to as 'appearances or sensations' produced by the 'Size, Figure, Number, and Motion of minute Corpuscles singly insensible' (4.2.11). Elsewhere, these insensible corpuscles are said to be the 'active parts of Matter, and the great Instruments of Nature, on which depend not only all their secondary Qualities, but also most of their natural Operations' (4.3.25).

Locke's friend the chemist, Robert Boyle (whose works Locke knew very well), had invoked the corpuscular hypothesis as an explanation for many of the phenomena he studied in his laboratory. Other scientists, e.g., Henry Power, Robert Hooke, and Isaac Newton, used this hypothesis. It has sometimes been called the 'mechanical philosophy'. It can also be traced back in various forms to the ancient Epicureans and atomists. It constituted the more or less standard view of matter and its causal powers before and after Locke. Locke agreed with Boyle and Newton on the importance of the concept of 'cohesion': what holds matter together, even keeping individual corpuscles from flying apart. The corpuscular hypothesis was gradually edged into the background as science came to find forces and powers in matter, e.g., gravitation, electricity, magnetism. In the eighteenth century, a number of scientists were even taking the view that the amount of hard, corpuscular matter in the universe was very small. Locke perhaps foreshadowed some of this evolution in the concept of matter by the stress he placed upon *powers*, but he *did* use the corpuscular theory and he did take it as the best hypothesis so far constructed (cf. §193 in *Some Thoughts*).

D

deduction The closest Locke gets to deduction in the logical sense is when he couples it with demonstration. But since his account of demonstration stresses the showing of the relations of ideas and perceiving the connections, and in the light of his negative evaluation of the syllogism as a method to knowledge, we can say that deduction for Locke does not carry the meaning we would give it in our logic books. A passage in *Essay* 2.31.6 comes close to a formal sense of that term: he says 'all the Properties of a Triangle depend on, and as far as they are discoverable, are deducible from the complex *Ideas* of three lines, including a Space.' *Essay* 4.2.7 speaks of 'long deductions' where a demonstration may require a number of intermediate ideas before we can perceive the connection between the extremes. A passage late in the same book refers to 'the evident deductions of Reason in demonstrations' (4.28.5). We use our reason when we follow a demonstration; some demonstrations have many steps in reasoning before knowledge is produced or shown. Each step in the reasoning has intuitive certainty. The faculty of reason that follows a demonstration is, it seems, the same as deduction; at least, it is very closely linked with it. The three terms – inference, deduction, and reasoning – are all very tightly related. It would be difficult to give separate definitions or characterizations of them. In some instances, we fail to find intermediate ideas, we cannot always find the 'medium' between ideas and hence we fail in our efforts to demonstrate some connection of ideas. In a long demonstration, a long deduction, we may fail to find connecting ideas in part of the demonstration. In such a case, 'we come short of Knowledge and Demonstration' (4.3.4; cf. 4.3.19, where he speaks of long deductions again). Another passage speaks of recalling a proof for some probable truth: we must recall it 'in the same order, and regular deduction of Consequences' as applied in the original proof.

There is a variety of other occurrences of 'deduction' in the *Essay*, most of them very close to the sense of 'infer' or 'conclude'. For example, referring to the mind's putting ideas into propositions, he says that sometimes the truths are obvious right away, while at other times 'deductions made with attention' are required (1.4.22). Or, he remarks, we are apt to make deductions from ideas, or parts of ideas (2.29.14). Another section suggests that were there a monkey that had the use of reason and could understand general signs, and deduce consequences, the monkey would be subject to laws, as any rational creature is (3.11.16). In 4.8.11, he speaks of the lack of 'plain and clear deductions of Words one from another'. One meaning of the term 'reason' is 'clear and fair deductions' from principles (4.17.1). The truth of moral rules depends upon certain principles from which they 'must be deduced', perhaps a reference to his notion of a demonstrative morality (1.3.4). Moral rules are also said to be 'the most obvious deductions of Humane Reason' (1.3.12).

definition   Locke was sceptical of the traditional notion of definition in terms of genus and species. To define man in this way as a rational animal is much less informative than to say that the word 'man' stands for 'a solid extended Substance, having Life, Sense, spontaneous Motion, and the Faculty of Reason' (*Essay*, 3.3.10). The meaning of 'man' is much better conveyed by the descriptive definition. What is important for any definition is to make another person 'understand by Words, the *Idea*, the term defined stands for' (*ibid.*); it is '*the shewing the meaning of one Word by several other not synonymous Terms*' (3.4.4). Definition is especially important for moral words: it is '*the only way, whereby the precise Meaning of moral Words can be known*' (3.11.17). The stress in Locke's discussion is on meaning and understanding, using words to convey the meaning of ideas and to help others understand our thoughts and words. Another way Locke characterizes definition is to say it *enumerates* the simple ideas contained in the complex idea. Only complex ideas can be defined.

Locke remarks that previous writers have not considered 'what Words are, and what are not capable of being defined', the result being 'great wrangling, and obscurity in Men's Discourses' (3.4.4). The Port Royal logic of Arnauld and Nicole had identified some words that do not need to be defined, words where a definition would be useless, but they did not say there are words that *cannot* be defined (*La Logique, ou L'Art de penser*, 1662). Since defining for Locke is enumerating the simple ideas in a complex idea, it follows that the simple ideas cannot be defined. Acquisition of simple ideas cannot be accomplished by words, by definitions; these ideas (e.g., of colour, sounds, tastes) are acquired through experience with the qualities of objects. Definitions can sometimes make us understand the names of things which 'never come within the reach of our Senses', so long as none of the terms in the definition stands 'for simple *Ideas*, which he to whom the Explication is made, has never yet had in his Thoughts' (3.4.12). In our own time, Bertrand Russell enunciated a very similar principle when he distinguished between knowledge by description and knowledge by acquaintance: '*Every proposition which we can understand must be composed wholly of constituents with which we are acquainted*' (*Problems of Philosophy*, 1912, p. 58). Locke even uses the word 'acquainted' when he goes on to remark that even when someone has been acquainted with an idea he may not know that a particular word stands for that idea (3.4.13).

Locke pokes fun at some of the past attempts to define simple ideas (3.4.8). Nor does he find modern philosophers any better, whether they attempt to explain the causes of simple ideas or, as the atomists do, define motion as the '*passage from one place to another*' (3.4.9). He also distinguishes translation from definition, the former being the replacement of words that have the same signification (3.4.9).

The topic of definition has received much attention from Plato and Aristotle down to our own time. Locke's discussion is most usefully situated in the context of writers such as Hobbes, Descartes, Pascal, all of whom had something to say about definition. The more immediate context for Locke is the Port Royal logic. There are a number of similarities between that logic and Locke's account of definition: the distinction between definition of names and things; the arbitrariness of definition of names; the fact that many name-definitions do not refer to properties of the world; warnings against confusing the two kinds of definitions; and the dangers of unclear definitions (see *La Logique, ou L'Art de penser*, Pt I, chs XII and XIII). After the seventeenth century, definitions continue to receive widespread treatment. The subject is still frequently discussed in logic books and in many works dealing with theory of knowledge (see *Definition* by Richard Robinson, Clarendon Press, 1950; the article on 'Definition' in *The Encyclopedia of Philosophy*, ed. Paul Edwards, 1967).

demonstration Locke defined knowledge in terms of the relation between ideas, specifically the '*perception of the connexion and agreement, or disagreement and repugnancy of any of our ideas*' (*Essay*, 4.1.1). Their connection or disconnection must be perceived by us before knowledge occurs. He followed Descartes in identifying an immediate perception (awareness) of these relations as 'intuition'. No reasoning is required for such immediate awareness. As with Descartes also, intuition often requires the help of demonstration, the use of intervening ideas to reveal to us the connections with other ideas. Such non-immediate awareness of the agreement or disagreement of two ideas by means of demonstration is necessary when we (Locke writes 'the mind') cannot bring together the ideas we wish to relate so as to 'shew' their connection or repugnancy (4.2.2). The use of intervening ideas as a way of showing the agreement of any two other ideas is called 'proof'. It becomes 'demonstration' when 'the Agreement or Disagreement by this means plainly and clearly [is] perceived' (4.2.3). The perception resulting from a demonstration may take time and effort, 'pains and attention': 'A steddy application and pursuit is required to the Discovery: And there must be a Progression by steps and degrees, before the Mind can in this way arrive at Certainty' (4.2.4; cf. 4.17.2). Prior to demonstration there is doubt. While certainty results when the demonstration is successful in showing us the connection of ideas, demonstrative certainty lacks some of the lustre and full assurance of intuition (4.2.6).

Demonstration involves intuition: I must perceive immediately the relation in each step of the demonstrative progression. As Descartes had also stressed, we must be able to hold in view all the steps in a demonstration so that we can perceive immediately at the end the relation between the first and last steps (4.2.7). The process of demonstration enables us to *juxtapose* the two ideas we enquired about and thus make 'an immediate comparison' of them (4.3.3). In that way, the agreement or disagreement of two ideas is *shown*, revealed to the mind, made evident. This combination of 'showing' or 'disclosing' and 'juxtaposition' is stressed again by Locke when he offers his account of inference and informal logic (4.17.4). He there argues that the syllogistic form fails to make the relations of ideas perspicuous. What is required is that the mind or perceptive faculty be able to view ideas together, 'taking a view of them laid together, in a *juxtaposition*' (4.17.4). That same sentence speaks of 'the Eye', as if he means literally laying out on paper the ideas in verbal dress side by side. In a demonstration, the steps in the progression would be laid out on paper so that the eye and the mind can view the connections.

Other passages in the *Essay* reinforce the basic notion of demonstration as 'showing'. Commenting upon our lack of knowledge of the numbers and motion of particles involved in the causation of different degrees of whiteness, Locke says we cannot demonstrate 'the certain Equality of any two degrees', but when the differences are apparent to our senses, we *are* able to demonstrate (i.e. show) the difference (4.2.13). In an earlier passage, he speaks of dogs and elephants giving 'all the demonstration of' (showing all the signs of) thinking that we can imagine, short of telling us they are thinking (2.1.19). The fact that there is no universal consent over a list of truths that are innate is said to be a 'demonstration' that there are none (1.2.4).

The syllogism was not a useful mode of demonstration, but Locke's attacks against the other standard notion, that demonstration starts with general principles (logical and metaphysical ones), was more radical. Attacks against Aristotle and syllogistic reasoning were becoming common, new logics based upon an understanding of how the mind works were emerging (e.g., the Port Royal logic, J. P. de Crousaz's logic).

Locke's rejection of basic principles on which demonstrations were to be built began with his polemic against the claim for innate speculative truths; that rejection was then extended to maxims and axioms as the foundations for demonstrating truths and the relation of ideas. John Sergeant's criticism of Locke in his *Solid Philosophy Asserted* (1697) was in large part motivated by Locke's new concept of demonstration as 'making evident', replacing the older notion of deducing from principles. The striking difference between the standard view and Locke's new account of demonstration can be seen by reading Sergeant's *The Method to Science* (1696). Locke referred to the principles of identity and contradiction ('Whatsoever is, is' and 'It is impossible for the same thing to be and not to be') as 'those magnified Principles of Demonstration' (1.2.4). In that passage, he was only concerned to argue that these principles did not have universal assent, one of the claimed criteria for innateness. Later in the *Essay*, these principles or maxims are charged with being useless or even leading to meaningless or absurd conclusions. At their best, these logical principles produce verbal truths, unrelated to the world (4.7.16). With the principles of identity and contradiction, we can demonstrate both that 'there may be a *Vacuum*, and that there cannot be a *Vacuum*' (4.7.14). Another 'truth' that can be demonstrated from these principles is that 'Infants, and Changelings are no Men' (4.7.17).

Locke speaks of Newton's discoveries and demonstrations of several propositions, new truths discovered not by the use of those logical principles or others such as 'the whole is bigger than a part', but by 'finding out intermediate *Ideas*, that shew'd the Agreement or Disagreement of the *Ideas*, expressed in the Propositions he demonstrated' (4.7.11). The reference is to Newton's 'Advances in Mathematical Knowledge', indicating that Locke extended to mathematics and geometry his concept of demonstration. If we understand the definition (or essence) of a particular figure, e.g., an *ellipsis*, we will be able to discover all the properties of that figure 'and demonstratively see how they flow, and are inseparable from it' (2.31.11). When we demonstrate that the three angles of a triangle are equal to two right angles, 'What do we more but perceive, that Equality to two right ones, does necessarily agree to, and is inseparable from the three angles of a Triangle' (4.1.2). Locke then makes a remark that looks as if he were distinguishing between the demonstration itself and our perception of what is demonstrated or shown. Mathematical demonstrations do not, he says, themselves depend upon our senses, but examining with our eye the diagram drawn on paper leads to the certainty we acquire. All his other remarks about demonstration find him denying such a distinction: a demonstration is not a demonstration unless it aids us in perceiving the connection between the different properties of a figure, between the idea of a triangle or an ellipsis and some other idea about those figures.

Given his concept of demonstration as showing, making evident, the relations between ideas, it should come as no surprise to find those passages in the *Essay* which speak of demonstration in morality (e.g., 3.11.16). Moral words and ideas were members of the class of what Locke called 'mixed modes', 'such Combinations of *Ideas*, as the Mind puts together of its own choice' (3.11.15). There may or may not be 'standing Patterns' in the world to which these modes or ideas refer. The meaning or signification of such names of actions 'cannot be made known, as those of simple *Ideas* [can], by any shewing' (*ibid.*), by pointing to examples, but there is another way of showing their signification: demonstration, presenting the conceptual relations between moral ideas. Just as the definition of geometrical and mathematical terms is man-made (even if God-made, the point holds), so are the definitions of moral words: 'the precise real Essence of the Things moral Words stand for, may be perfectly known; and so the Congruity, or Incongruity of the Things themselves, be certainly discovered, in which consists perfect Knowledge' (3.11.16). Locke chastises those who do not take care to be clear and precise in their moral discourses. With a definition, *'the precise Meaning of moral Words can be known'* (3.11.17). In Locke's language, there are no external archetypes for these words; the words are themselves the archetypes or standards to which actions either conform or not.

> It is far easier for Men to frame in their Minds an *Idea*, which shall be the Standard to which they will give the Name *Justice*, with which Pattern so made, all Actions that agree shall pass under that denomination, than, having seen *Aristides*, to frame an *Idea*, that shall in all things be exactly like him, who is as he is, let Men make what *Ideas* they please of him. For the one, they need but know the combination of *Ideas*, that are put together within in their own Minds; for the other, they must enquire into the whole Nature, and abstruse hidden Constitution, and various Qualities of a Thing existing without them. (3.11.17)

Just as 'The Mathematician considers the Truth and Properties belonging to a Rectangle, or Circle, only as they are in *Idea* in his own Mind' (4.4.6), so the moral philosopher does the same. If there are existing triangles in the world, they must have the properties defined by the mathematician's idea of a triangle. If there are any acts of justice, murder or ingratitude in the world, those actions must fit the descriptions specified by the moral terms of our language. The mathematician intends 'Things no farther than they agree with those his *Ideas*'. The moral philosopher intends actions only as they agree with his mixed-mode ideas and words. It is because of these features of mathematics and morality that Locke is able to say so confidently (he says 'it follows from' these features) that *'moral Knowledge* is as *capable of real Certainty*, as Mathematicks' (4.4.7). Where some properties of geometrical figures may not be immediately clear, demonstration can make them so. Where some of the connections between different moral ideas may be obscure, demonstration can show us those connections by using intermediate ideas which make those relations perspicuous. Moral demonstration, then, consists in tracing the various relations our ideas of actions have to one another (4.4.9; cf. 4.12.8).

Demonstration in mathematics and geometry has certain advantages over the demonstration of moral ideas: (1) there are sensible marks and diagrams we can use to represent numbers and figures and (2) moral ideas are more complex than those of number and figure (4.3.19). The juxtaposing of ideas in mathematics and geometry can thus be more easily and directly shown, literally drawn. Words are the representations of moral ideas, so there is a sort of substitute for diagrams when we write those words on paper and order the progression from one to another, but the difficulty Locke finds is that the ideas behind the words often vary in meaning from person to person. Thus, the importance of fixing our mixed-mode ideas precisely. The complexity of moral ideas also raises difficulties for memory: the mind cannot easily hold all the progressions of moral demonstrations in one view (4.3.19). This difficulty can be partially overcome by good definitions, 'setting down that Collection of simple *Ideas*, which every Term shall stand for; and then using the Terms steadily and constantly for that precise Collection' (4.3.20).

Locke provides us with a few examples of simple, short moral demonstrations. Should we not understand immediately the proposition *'Where there is no Property, there is no Injustice'*, the connection can be shown by explaining that the idea of property is that of a right to some thing, and that the idea of injustice is that of 'the Invasion or Violation of that right' (4.3.18). Similarly, by understanding that the idea of 'government' is that of 'the establishment of Society upon certain Rules or Laws, which require Conformity to them', and the idea of absolute liberty means doing whatever one pleases, the truth of *'No Government allows absolute Liberty'* is perceived to be as certain as any truth in mathematics (*ibid.*). There are more complex demonstrations in the chapter on 'Reason' (4.17).

The introduction of the short examples in 4.3.18 inserts a different notion into moral demonstration from that of just showing the conceptual connections between moral ideas. He makes the bold assertion that 'the measures of right and wrong might be made out' by demonstration; not just the relations between moral ideas, but the *measures* of right and wrong.

Demonstration is there described as proceeding from 'self-evident Propositions, by necessary Consequences, as incontestable as those in Mathematicks'. The fact that this version of moral demonstration is inserted after Locke has given another example of showing interconnections of ideas may shed light on what appears to be a quite new and much more rigorous and formal concept of demonstration. The example there is of the idea of 'a supreme Being, infinite in Power, Goodness, and Wisdom, whose Workmanship we are, and on whom we depend; and the *Idea* of our selves, as understanding, rational Beings' (*ibid.*). Had Locke used the law of nature in this context, we could relate this remark to what he had written many years previous to the *Essay*, in his lectures as Moral Censor at Oxford. There is a harmony between the law of nature and our rational nature. It follows that 'all those who are endowed with a rational Nature, i.e. all men in the world, are morally bound by this law' (*Essays*, p. 199). Locke makes it abundantly clear in the *Essay* as well, that the true measure of right and wrong is God's law (2.28.8). It was self-evident to Locke that there is a God (although he also produces a demonstration of his existence) and that we are his workmanship, but how he thought we could from these principles derive the law of nature (for that is the measure of right and wrong) is never explained.

It was clearly *this* demonstration of the measures of right and wrong, not just the showing of conceptual connections, that Locke's friend, William Molyneux, urged Locke to produce: 'One Thing I must needs insist on to you, which is, that you would think of Obleidging the World, with *a Treatise of Morals*, drawn up according to the Hints you frequently give in Your Essay, Of their Being Demonstrable according to the Mathematical Method' (*Corr.* 1530, 27 August 1692; iv. 508). In his response, Locke remarked that the task was difficult, but he promised to try his hand when he had some leisure (*ibid.*, 1538, 20 September 1692; iv. 524). By 1695, in his *Reasonableness of Christianity*, Locke's confidence that such a demonstration could be produced, or that many people could benefit from it, had not increased. There, he suggested that the task was too difficult for 'unassisted reason [i.e., reason without revelation] to establish morality in all its parts, upon its true foundation, with a clear and convincing light' (in *Works*, vii. 139). The 'long and sometimes intricate deductions of reason' are more than most men can absorb. That the deduction or demonstration (perhaps these are different for Locke?) he had in mind in that work would produce the measures of right and wrong seems confirmed by his remark that human reason had never, up to the time of Christ, had 'an entire body of the "law of nature," ' derived from 'unquestionable principles by clear deductions' (*ibid.*, p. 140). Such a body of ethics, he says again, 'proved to be the law of nature, from principles of reason, and teaching all the duties of life; I think nobody will say the world had before our Saviour's time' (p. 141). His early *Two Tracts* characterizes the New Testament as 'a perfect rule in so far as it provides general standards of conduct from which all other particular rules derive and can be deduced' (p. 234).

The notion of a demonstrable morality can be found in other writers contemporary with Locke and earlier, but no one seems to have paid as much attention as Locke to the first and the main part of his suggestion: the tracing of conceptual connections. What he says about the demonstration needs to be placed with his critical comments on the syllogism and his own positive remarks about an informal logic of use. It has been the other undeveloped notion of a demonstration of the laws of nature, of moral obligation and the measures of right and wrong, that has intrigued more recent writers on Locke. Attempts have been made to show that Locke's hope was to assimilate moral obligation to logical validity, or to construct a practical syllogism whose conclusion would tell us what we ought to do. Whether these suggestions reflect what he had in mind in that 4.3.18 passage is difficult to determine. In view of his explicit identification of demonstration in mathematics and geometry with the laying out of diagrams, the juxtaposition of figures and properties, I rather suspect that it was *this* concept of demonstration that he had in mind when he spoke of a demonstrative morality. Even the measures of right and wrong, the laws of nature, God's laws, might emerge from a juxtaposing of such ideas as a wise and good God and man as the workmanship of God. If these two ideas were for Locke self-evident, perceived intuitively, immediately, it just might be possible to discover some relations between these two ideas and other mixed modes. That the law (or laws) of nature could be discovered or made perspicuous in this way seems, however, very doubtful.

duration   *see* TIME

E

education   *see* SOME THOUGHTS CONCERNING EDUCATION

empiricism, empirical   These are not terms in Locke's lexicon. They have been applied to his account of the source of knowledge and the method of science. Locke is classed as an empiricist by commentators for various reasons, the most general being his stress upon experience and observation as the source of ideas and knowledge. The tendency has been to overlook or down-play the fact that 'experience and observation' for Locke cover both sensory and reflective experience. Empiricism is a label that many people associate with sensation and sense experience. Condillac in eighteenth-century France helped to foster this limited view of Locke's account (Condillac called his *Essai sur l'origine des connoissances humaines*, 1746, a 'supplement' to Locke's *Essay*), although Condillac too included reflection in his analysis. The label 'sensualist' became associated with Locke and Condillac by nineteenth-century French historians, e.g., Victor Cousin.

Other aspects of Locke's thought which have lent themselves to the empiricist label are his rejection of innate ideas, the metaphors of the mind as a blank tablet or dark closet, his stress on making natural histories of phenomena (in medicine, of diseases and symptoms), his reluctance to form hypotheses and general theories before sufficient data has been collected. Locke *was* concerned with the question of method, how to improve knowledge and understanding. In his *Conduct of the Understanding*, he suggests how to reach a balance between fact-gathering and organizing the facts with general theories and hypotheses (*see* HYPOTHESES). In that work, he contrasts those whose knowledge is 'very little improved by all that crowd of particulars, that either pass through or lodge themselves in their understandings', with those who 'draw general conclusions, and raise axioms from every particular they meet with' (§13). The proper balance is some combination of these two approaches, 'taking material and useful hints, sometimes from single matters of fact', carrying these in your mind 'to be judged of, by what' is subsequently discovered in experience and by observation as confirming or falsifying tentative general principles. The confirmation process should, he says, be done by 'a sufficient and wary induction of particulars'.

The reference to those who are content with a crowd of particulars or a 'heap of crudities', may be to the medical physicians cited by such ancient writers as Sextus Empiricus (e.g., in his *Against the Logicians*). Locke was part of the new attitudes in medicine, working with Dr Thomas Sydenham on cataloguing the symptoms of various diseases in order to understand their causes and discover remedies. The term 'empiric' or 'empirick' designated (to use the definition in Dr Johnson's *Dictionary of the English Language*, 1755) such 'Physicians as form'd themselves Rules, and Methods on their own Practice and Experience; and not on any Knowledge of Natural Causes'. Locke compared those who seek truth without knowledge to people who are forced to 'swallow down Opinions, as silly People do Empiricks Pills, without knowing what they are made of, or how they will work, and have nothing to do, but believe they will do the Cure' (*Essay*, 4.20.4). Johnson also indicates that the term 'empiricism' had the sense of 'dependency on experience without knowledge or art, quackery'. Chambers, in his *Cyclopaedia* (1728), gives the same information, including the reference to quacks and charlatans. As late as 1768–71, in the first edition of the *Encyclopaedia Britannica*, these definitions are repeated. In his *Monadology*, Leibniz refers to 'the *empirical physicians* who practise simply, without any theory', adding that all of us are 'empiricists in three-fourths of our actions', citing our expectation that 'there will be day-light to-morrow ... because it has always happened so up to the present time' (*Monadology*, §28).

Essay concerning Human Understanding   This is one of Locke's major books. Many years in composition, begun as a response to some questions raised in a small discussion group, written and expanded at different times while Locke was busy with other activities, this work went through three drafts before reaching publication. The first two drafts (called A and B) are dated 1671, the third (draft C) is of the mid-1680s. (The first two drafts have been edited by Peter H. Nidditch and G.A.J. Rogers. The third draft is in preparation, edited by Rogers.) An abridgement of the *Essay* appeared in a French-language journal, the *Bibliothèque universelle*, in January 1688. That abridgement did not contain Book 1 with its rejection of innate ideas and principles, but it received several negative reactions because of the notice that innate truths were attacked in that work. When the full version was published in 1690, it was not long before reactions, some warm with praise, many of an almost excited negative nature, appeared in print or were reported and passed on to its author. (The full story of the reactions to this work are chronicled in Yolton, *Locke* *and the Way of Ideas*, 1956.) It was seen as a dangerous book by some because many standard, long-held doctrines and beliefs were either attacked or ignored. Its aim was, as Locke explained in the introduction, 'to enquire into the Original, Certainty, and Extent of humane Knowledge; together, with the Grounds and Degrees of Belief, Opinion, and Assent' (1.1.2). The four books that comprised the *Essay* were devoted to innate notions, ideas, words, and knowledge and opinion. These simple headings hide a depth of analysis and breadth of issues on a wide variety of subjects, both traditional and new. It can be described as a work on theory of knowledge, philosophy of science, metaphysics, method, or psychology. Its influence on subsequent thought in these areas has been extensive. The *Essay* received wide attention in a variety of eighteenth-century French journals. It stirred controversy as well as praise and imitations in Britain and France. In fact, it was a very influential book in eighteenth-century Europe. It went through four editions in Locke's lifetime, with revisions in some of the editions. The fifth edition, which Locke did partly revise, did not appear until after his death; he died in the autumn of 1704, and the fifth edition was published in 1706. Several French translations appeared from 1700 to mid-century, a German translation in 1757, and a Latin in 1701. Numerous reprints were published in the eighteenth century of an abridgement made in 1696 by John Wynne, including French and Italian translations thereof.

Essays on the Law of Nature   These were probably lectures Locke gave at his college, Christ Church, Oxford, when he was Moral Censor, around 1664. For a time after that period, he considered revising and publishing these essays, even as late as the early 1690s. But his interest after that faded; his major writings absorbed his attention. These essays were not published until 1954 when Dr W. von Leyden edited and translated them from their original Latin, with Latin and English texts on opposite pages. He also included a long, informative introduction on the history of the essays and their context within other writings on the topic of the law of nature. (See *John Locke: Essays on the Law of Nature*, ed. W. von Leyden, Clarendon Press, 1954.)

Locke's essays are written in the form of examination topics typical of the university programme. Students were asked to debate specific questions; usually those debates had to be conducted in the form of logical syllogisms, thus testing supposed skill in logic as well as substantive knowledge. Locke's lectures may have been useful for students who were anticipating examinations. Some of the topics, in the form in which they are put by Locke, appear in the eighteenth century on lists of examination papers. Locke's first essay is: 'Is there a rule of morals, or law of nature, given to us?' His answer is 'yes'. He then proceeds to discuss the question and support his affirmative answer. The second essay asks: 'Can the law of nature be known by the light of nature?' Locke's answer is again 'yes'. Other essays raise different questions: 'Is the law of nature inscribed in the minds of men?': Locke says 'no'. 'Can reason attain to the knowledge of natural law through sense-experience?': the answer is 'yes'. Dr von Leyden prints eight essays in all, plus a speech Locke gave when he ceased being Moral Censor.

The topics of these essays are very close to the ones Locke attacks in his polemic against innate ideas and principles in the first book of his *Essay concerning Human Understanding*. The language of the innatists appears in these early *Essays*, but Locke's firm answer of 'no' to the question of inscription in the mind indicates his rejection of innate principles in the 1660s. A good understanding of the position he attacks in his *Essay* will be furthered by reading these *Essays*. They also give some information about Locke's views on the law of nature and what it sanctions.

essence   Locke explains that the original meaning of the term 'essence' is 'the very being of any thing, whereby it is, what it is' (*Essay*, 3.3.15). On the traditional metaphysics, what exists, what there is, is either a substance or a quality. Qualities cannot exist by themselves; they must be qualities *of* some thing, some substance. Two kinds of substance were recognized, material and immaterial, body and mind. Each kind of substance had a defining property, an essential quality which makes it a material or immaterial substance. Thus, bodies were considered material or corporeal substances whose essential quality was extension. That quality was what made body (or matter) what it is. Its being is to be extended. Similarly, mind, soul or spirit was considered an immaterial substance with the essential quality of thought, at least for finite minds or souls. Descartes is a good example of a philosopher who worked with this two-substance ontology: *res extensa* and *res cogitans*. Since the essence of a kind of substance is its very being, as Locke says, Descartes and others were committed to saying the soul always thinks, just as matter is always extended. A bit of matter that was not extended would not be matter. A soul which is not always manifesting thought would not be a soul. Unextended matter and non-thinking mind are, on this view, inconceivable and contradictory notions.

Locke challenged these traditional doctrines in a number of ways. He announces at the beginning of the *Essay* that he will not examine wherein the essence of mind consists (1.1.2), but he later takes issue with Descartes by arguing that it is probable that thinking is not the essence, although it is the action of mind (2.19.4). His reason for rejecting thought as the essence of mind or soul is that there are degrees of thinking, levels of awareness, fluctuations in thinking. The essence of a thing does not change; if it did, the very being of that thing would change. Locke also believed that we in fact do not always think, dreamless sleep being one example. Locke's rejection of thought as the essential property of mind or soul was a radical claim, a challenge to the generally accepted notions about mind and substance. Some of his readers saw this as opening the possibility for an alteration in the notion of mind, even perhaps giving support to a material soul. But Locke offered an even more radical and dangerous challenge to the doctrine of substance: he did not think we can discover the unchanging essences of either kind of substance. The phrase 'unknown essence' is used frequently (e.g., 2.23.3; 2.32.18). He even suggested that our idea of God is limited and perhaps incorrect: His essence may be different from our idea; God may be simple and uncompounded while our idea of God is complex, made up of existence, knowledge, power, wisdom, etc.

Locke may not have thought he was being radical in expressing these views since he begins 3.3.15 by saying that 'the *Essences* of Things are Thought, by some ... to be wholly unknown' (the 'some' are not identified), and he continues by saying, as if reporting on current usage, that the term 'essence' has almost lost its original meaning; it now has been 'applied to the artificial Constitution of *Genus* and *Species*' (3.3.15). The term 'artificial' contrasts with the characterization of the original meaning which identified the essence as the 'real, internal constitution of things', a phrase which is Locke's adaptation of the scientific, corpuscular account of matter. The change from *real* to *artificial* essence, from what he names the 'real essence' to the 'nominal essence', reflects a number of other doctrines in the *Essay* about abstract ideas, classes, the rejection of a knowledge of necessary connections in nature, and his overall stress upon experience and observation.

He further clarifies the notion of real essence of corporeal substances by describing two opinions about them. The one opinion holds that there is a fixed number of essences 'according to which, all natural things are made, and wherein they do exactly every one of them partake' (3.3.17). In this way, natural things belong to species, to kinds. Locke believed this opinion has impeded progress in science, in our knowledge of natural things. Moreover, it is incompatible with the 'frequent Productions of Monsters, in all the Species of Animals, and of Changelings, and other strange Issues of humane Birth' (*ibid.*). As well, he finds the notion of unknown essences quite unclear; knowledge will not be aided by such a concept. The other opinion, which Locke says is the more rational of the two, looks 'on all natural Things to have a real, but unknown Constitution of their insensible Parts, from which flow those sensible Qualities, which serve us to distinguish them one from another, according as we have Occasion to rank them into sorts, under common Denominations' (*ibid.*). The distinguishing of things does not refer to distinguishing one *particular* from another (your pen from mine), but to the distinguishing of *kinds* of natural things, e.g., gold, silver, or lead (3.3.18). Each particular has its own internal constitution which accounts for its set of qualities. That constitution, that real essence, perishes when the object ceases or undergoes radical change, e.g., a change from grass today, becoming flesh of sheep and part of the man who eats the sheep. The real essence of grass, as of all particulars, is generable and corruptible, unlike the fixed kinds of essences of the first opinion (3.3.19). It is the nominal essence which on Locke's account remains unchanged unless our names for things (e.g., 'man', 'horse') were to change.

One of his reasons for rejecting the first opinion about real essences was the claim that they are unknown. The second opinion also claims the real internal constitution is unknown, but Locke was reluctant to cast aside this notion of real essence, even though most of his attention was focused on the *nominal* essence, the essence which we construct out of observed coexisting qualities. He accepted the corpuscular hypothesis as the best explanation of observed phenomena. To that hypothesis he added the notion that the observed qualities 'flow from' the internal constitution of bodies. At one point in his exchange with Stillingfleet, the Bishop of Worcester, Locke thought the Bishop was saying that the real essence flows from the substance. 'Here I must acknowledge to your lordship, that my notion of these essences differs a little from your lordship's; for I do not take them to flow from the substance in any created being, but to be in every thing that internal constitution, or frame, or modification of the substance, which God in his wisdom and good pleasure thinks fit to give to every particular creature, when he gives it a being' (*Mr. Locke's Letter to the Bishop of Worcester*, in *Works*, iv. 82). That relation of 'flowing from' has a causal role, but it also would have a logical role to play were we able to know the real essences, in this sense of 'essence' (*see* CONNEXION (NECESSARY)).

This logical or conceptual relation between real essence and the qualities of an object is exemplified for Locke by geometrical figures. Our idea of an *ellipsis* contains 'the whole Essence of that Figure' and we can discover all of its properties demonstratively (2.31.11). The essence or formal constitution of a triangle is available to us through its definition (3.11.22). Were the internal constitution of the substance we call 'gold' similarly known, we would be able to discover all its properties from that internal structure. It is not clear from what he says about geometry whether he considered the concepts of figures to be man-made, or whether he thought of such figures as having some ontological status. But whichever view he accepted, the real essence of geometrical figures (their definitions) contains the information about all their properties.

There is another area in which the conceptual relation between concepts and consequences is fixed and knowable, the action concepts that Locke called 'mixed modes'. These concepts, e.g., of obligation, drunkenness, hypocrisy, are constructed or formed by the mind, either to describe some relations between people or to serve as standards or criteria for actions. These are *kinds* of actions: hence the concept or, as Locke sometimes calls them, 'notions', refer to species, but those species are determined by us, by our society; they constitute the customs and mores of a society. Since the essences of these mixed modes are determined by us, an understanding of the words or concepts gives us a knowledge of all the properties of those terms. The essences of these species or kinds of actions 'are nothing but the abstract *Ideas* in the Mind, to which the Name is annexed' (3.5.1). The understanding of mixed modes and the understanding of geometrical figures open for us further knowledge about those modes and figures. Their properties are contained in or flow from their concepts. In these examples of classes or kinds, the *nominal* essence (the name or idea) is the same as the *real* essence. The 'formal structure' is in effect a definition.

The relation between real and nominal essence in natural things would be similar were we able to know and understand the formal constitution (the microstructure) of gold, silver, or lead. Since that structure is not available to us, it is the nominal essence for natural things that becomes all-important. In each case, that of geometrical figures, of mixed modes, and of physical substances, the known, nominal essence is an idea or name, an abstract idea with names attached (3.6.2). With geometrical figures and action concepts, the nominal and real essences are the same. With physical substances such as gold or silver, we do not know whether the nominal essence reflects in any way the real internal structure, although Locke accepted the scientific hypothesis which preserves the 'flow from' relation in its causal form. Moreover, Locke's account of the different kinds of qualities of body (primary and secondary) employs the causal relation between the internal, insensible corpuscular structure and those qualities.

In the formation of those essences called 'mixed modes', we are not obliged to construct them by observing coexisting qualities, but nominal essences of physical substances must be carefully based upon existing qualities. What qualities we group under a class name or idea may be arbitrary, reflecting those combinations which are important and useful in science or medicine, but the arbitrary and artificial nature of these nominal essences must not ignore existing combinations. The progress of science depends upon our classifications being accurate reflections of what qualities exist and appear together in our experience. If gold proves useful for chemists, our nominal essence and class name for gold must catch those qualities that the chemist finds useful, 'a Body yellow, of a certain weight, malleable, fusible, and fixed' (3.6.2). In medicine, it is even more important to ensure that the names of diseases and illnesses (e.g., hysteria, dropsy, gout) refer to sets of observed qualities that are symptoms for those illnesses. Cures require a careful charting of the history of diseases, 'a work of time, accurateness, attention, and judgment' (Locke to Thomas Molyneux, 20 January 1693, *Corr.* 1593; iv. 629). Locke was more confident about the possibility of penetrating behind the external symptoms of diseases to the 'specific nature or peculiar ferment or fault' of each disease than he was about discovering the internal structure of physical substances (see quotation from Locke's journals for 22 July 1678 in Dewhurst, *John Locke – Physician and Philosopher*, 1963, p. 136). What is important in physic as well as in physics is to record the coexisting qualities, to construct natural histories of diseases and of physical phenomena. On those careful observations, we then build our classifications of kinds of substances and diseases.

Most of Locke's examples of essences are taken from chemistry, the subject of Robert Boyle's work, with which Locke was so familiar. Although he uses the term 'species' for sorts and kinds, little attention is paid to biological species. There is one interesting illustration of the difference between real and nominal essence which hints at an underlying biological or physiological structure as the real essence of man. The complex idea of man to which Locke refers is made up of voluntary motion, sense, reason, a body of a certain shape. This is 'the *nominal Essence* of the *Species*' (3.6.3). The foundation for these qualities is that 'Constitution of *Man*, from which his Faculties of Moving, Sensation, and Reasoning, and other Powers flow; and on which his so regular shape depends'. Angels and God have a knowledge of that constitution, but our knowledge fails to be that extensive. We are no closer to understanding the inner constitution of man than we are the inner structure of chemical substances. There is no suggestion that Locke thought of man's constitution as corpuscular, although he does use the analogy, in this passage, of the clock-maker's knowledge of the wheels, springs and pulleys of the Strasbourg clock. Men and animals nevertheless have real essences on which their faculties and qualities, their motions and perceivings, depend.

If the inner constitution of things, whether animate or inanimate, plays such a causal role in the manifest qualities and operations, did Locke believe the real essence determined classes, species? Did he, we might ask, believe there were *natural* classes, not the kind cited under the first opinion about real essence but under his own notion of internal constitution? We may find an answer to this question in other sections of 3.6. For example, 3.6.4 remarks that if we take 'away the abstract *Ideas*, by which we sort Individuals, and rank them under common Names', the notion of *essentiality* vanishes. As an individual, 'there is nothing I have' that is essential to me, although as this particular individual it is 'necessary for me to be as I am; GOD and Nature has made me so' (3.6.4). He began that section by remarking again on the ordinary use of the word 'essence': it relates to sorts of things. I become a member of a sort, only when my attributes or actions fit the abstract idea, the class term. The same requirement holds for physical substances. If some particular bit of matter has only some of the properties specified by our word 'iron' or 'gold', we would not say it lacked something essential as *that* piece of matter. 'It would be absurd to ask, Whether a thing really existing, wanted any thing *essential* to it' (3.6.5). Even more decisive against the notion of natural kinds is Locke's insistence that 'to talk of specifick Differences in Nature, without reference to general *Ideas* and Names, is to talk unintelligibly' (*ibid.*). Locke's real essence is not a 'sortal', it does not determine classes and species; it is, in effect, the particular constitution on which depend all the properties of the particulars that make up the world. Indirectly, we can say that his real essences play a role in classification, that they relate to a sort, in the sense that the qualities and properties which are used by us to divide particulars into kinds 'flow from' the real essence of each particular object or individual (*see* SORTS, SORTALS).

The more cautious conclusion would be to say Locke only claims that *our* classifications are based on the nominal essence, the qualities *we* collect under an idea or name. After all, he denies we can know real essence. However, Locke clearly accepted the principle that 'all that exists is particular' (a principle accepted later by Hume), so his general ontology seems to exclude species (3.3.1). He does not deny 'that Nature in the Production of Things, makes several of them alike', especially in 'the Races of Animals, and all Things propagated by Seed' (3.3.13). The similitude between particulars is not so steady or uniform as to form classes, as Locke's remark about the chain of being makes clear: fishes with wings, birds that live in water, animals that reason (3.6.12). We might want to say that when we add existence in time and place, Locke's real essence individuates particulars, while his nominal essence groups those particulars into classes for our use. 'Why do we say, This is a *Horse*, and that a *Mule*; this is an *Animal*, that an *Herb*? How comes any particular Thing to be of this or that *Sort*, but because it has that nominal Essence, Or, which is all one, agrees to that abstract *Idea*, that name is annexed to?' (3.6.7). Whatever final conclusion we draw on the question about Locke and natural kinds, *Essay 3.6* and *2.23* merit close and detailed study.

experience   At the end of his long discussion and rejection of the claims for innate ideas and propositions in the first book of the *Essay*, Locke announces that in the rest of that work he has tried 'to raise an Edifice uniform, and consistent with it self, as far as my own Experience and Observation will assist me' (*Essay*, 1.4.25). He says that he will support his principles by appeal 'to Mens own unprejudiced *Experience*, and Observation'. At the end of his account of the acquisition of some particular ideas, he repeats his remark about appealing to experience and observation for deciding whether he is right about the origin of ideas (2.11.15). In this programme, Locke was echoing the official method of the Royal Society whose members in turn took their inspiration from Francis Bacon. The historian of that society, Thomas Sprat, praised Bacon for his defence of 'Experimental Philosophy' (*The History of the Royal Society*, 1667, p. 35). Sprat characterized the goal of the Royal Society scientists as: 'to make faithful *Records* of all the Works of *Nature*, or *Art*, which can come within their reach' (*ibid.*, p. 61), what Locke and others called 'making natural histories of phenomena'. Voltaire later called Bacon the 'father of experimental philosophy' (*Letters concerning the English Nation*, 1733, Letter XII, preceding Letter XIII on Locke). Diderot and d'Alembert (the editors of the great Enlightenment *Encyclopédie*) also praised Bacon for his programme of experience-based investigations of nature. Locke cites Bacon on method in his *Conduct of the Understanding*.

Locke also follows Bacon in his opposition to trusting formal rules of reasoning and relying upon authorities. The injunction of the Royal Society was reinforced by Locke: look to the things themselves, do not be prejudiced by past authority or by current linguistic usage. The discovery of matters of fact by careful experience and experiments became the new methodology of science. A man's 'constant and never-failing Experience', Locke said, gives us the truth of matters of fact: 'all the stated Constitutions and Properties of Bodies, and regular proceedings of Causes and Effects in the ordinary course of Nature' (4.16.6). It is constant experiences which support the probabilities of general principles and predictions. Trained and practised observers can often anticipate 'what Experience has not yet discovered' (4.6.13). Since we lack a knowledge of real essence and necessary connections, our knowledge of nature must be based on experience: '*Experience here must teach me*, what Reason cannot' (4.12.9; cf. 4.12.10; 4.3.16, 17; see *Conduct*, §13). Writers who stress experiments and observations, as opposed to hypotheses and speculative systems, are recommended for the student (*Some Thoughts*, §193).

The investigation of natural events, the science of nature, for us is limited to what we can discover through experience, observation and experiments. The investigation of human understanding, the science of mind (which was Locke's area of interest in the *Essay*), must also proceed by experience and observation. Much of his analysis of the understanding is done in the language of ideas. He hoped that those who want to confirm his account of the origin of ideas will consult their own experience (2.1.1). His general claim of the origins of ideas is that they arise in the mind from experience and observation, observation of external objects and experience of the operations of the mind (2.1.2). Habits of perception result from repeated experiences, e.g., leading us to judge space, figure and motion of objects by the use of light and colours (2.9.8). Every man's experience shows him the force of habit in relation to pleasure and pain (2.21.69). More importantly for his account of the nature of ideas, experience shows us that we cannot make simple ideas; the mind is passive in receiving them (2.22.2). If we use observation and experience instead of relying upon pre-formed theories, we will discover few signs 'of a Soul accustomed to much thinking in a new born Child' (2.1.21). Here and later he had his eye on the Cartesian claim that the soul always thinks (see 2.19.4). Children only acquire those ideas which 'Experience and the Observation of things, that come in their way, furnish them with' (1.4.2).

Experience is appealed to in other passages to account for specific ideas. One way in which we can acquire certain complex ideas is through the experience of watching men wrestle or fence (2.22.9). He appeals to every man's experience to confirm his claim that ideas of physical substances are acquired from observing coexisting qualities (2.23.3). The ideas of body (the 'power of *communication of Motion by impulse*') and of souls (the 'power of *exciting of Motion by Thought*') are furnished every day by experience (2.23.28). Experience assures us of the existence of extended and thinking substances, of 'the Existence of such Beings' (2.23.29). Sometimes experience runs counter to what we find conceivable: we cannot conceive how 'any thing but impulse of Body can move Body', but we have in our selves a 'constant Experience' of voluntary motion produced 'in us only by the free Action or Thought of our own Minds' (4.10.19). By reflecting on what passes in our selves, 'we find by Experience, that barely by willing it, barely by a thought of the Mind, we can move the parts of our Bodies', thereby acquiring the idea of the beginning of motion (2.21.4).

From experience we also learn some of the limitations of language. For example, attempts to explain simple ideas by words will fail; they must be experienced in order for us to know what they are (2.4.6); we have few names for tastes and smells, and we must leave these to be discovered by the thought and experience of each individual (2.18.5). It is also by experience that we learn that not every word in a language has an exact and clear signification (3.3.10). Experience will 'easily convince any one' that a definition cannot make the meaning of the word 'light' understood by a blind man; simple ideas cannot be acquired by definitions (3.4.10).

General truths are limited to what can be discovered through observation and experience (4.3.28) and the grounds of probability are judged by the conformity of 'any thing with our own Knowledge, Observation and Experience' (4.15.4). Chemists learn by experience that some samples of a substance they take to be sulphur or antimony differ in some of their qualities as experienced before (3.6.8). Locke even credits experience with convincing us 'that *we have an intuitive Knowledge of our own Existence*' (4.9.3).

Appeals to experience thus run throughout the *Essay* on a number of different topics. Locke's general programme in that work was to substitute for the claims of innate ideas and truths an experience-generated alternative, an alternative which followed in the footsteps of the Royal Society and Bacon. Experience by itself does not produce all our ideas, their production is aided by activities of the mind. The details of Locke's appeals to experience in his account of the human mind can be found in the account of the acquisition of ideas, in his dual analysis of sense perception and reflection. Berkeley and Hume carried forward this stress on experience-based knowledge, as did Condillac in France. There was a tendency in writers after Locke to overlook his reflective experience as a source of ideas and knowledge; this was especially true with Condillac and later French historians of philosophy. The concept of experience for Locke was broad, general and diverse. Its full nature is revealed by tracking three other terms in his writings: TABULA RASA, INNATENESS, and TEMPERS.

F

faculties The ascription to the mind of various faculties (e.g., sense, reason, memory) goes back as far as Plato. Usually these faculties are task-oriented, each having a specific function in awareness and knowledge. Descartes's rule 12 in his *Rules for the Direction of the Mind* distinguishes four faculties: intellect, imagination, sense-perception, and memory. These four are also at work in his *Meditations on First Philosophy*. Hobbes in the *Leviathan* works with sense, imagination and reason. When in his *Treatise of Human Nature* Hume searches for the source of our belief in the existence of body, he examines in turn sense, reason and imagination. Many eighteenth-century logic books were organized around faculties; some such as William Duncan's *The Elements of Logick* (1748) follow Locke's *Essay* rather closely. In his *Cyclopaedia* (1728), Ephraim Chambers identifies two faculties of the soul, understanding and will. Chambers also points out that the term 'faculty' had an application to bodies as well, the general definition being 'a *Power*, or Ability of performing an Action'. With this general definition, Johnson cites as powers of the mind imagination, reason and memory (*A Dictionary of the English Language*, 1755).

Thus, on either side of Locke, the notion of faculties of the mind was commonplace. For Locke in particular, this notion enabled him to describe the actions of the mind, the mind being for him, despite his own talk of passivity and a *tabula rasa*, very active. He speaks of 'the rational Faculty' (*Essay* 1.2.4), of the faculty of thinking (2.1.15, 20; 4.3.6), of faculties of enlarging, compounding, abstracting and reasoning (2.1.22). These are all powers of the mind, as is also willing (2.6.2). Perception is the first faculty of the mind exercised about ideas, 'the first Operation of all our intellectual Faculties' (2.9.15). The next faculty is retention, a power to retain ideas for a while or to revive them later (2.10.1, 2). The mind also has the faculty or ability to discern and distinguish different ideas (2.11.1). We also have faculties of moving, sensing and reasoning (3.6.3). When he deals with understanding and will as faculties and powers of the mind, Locke pauses to deny that they are 'real beings' or 'distinct agents' (2.21.6). It is clear that all of the faculties and actions of the mind are abilities we have, not reified agents. The ability to will

actions or to refrain from acting is one of the more important of our
abilities for Locke (see 2.21.4, 17, 20, 29).

The various abilities of the mind are often characterized by Locke as
natural faculties (4.18.3, 9; 4.3.27; 1.3.13), faculties that we are endowed
with (4.11.14; see *Conduct*, §4). But we must learn to use our faculties
properly and to recognize their limitations. Progress in knowledge can be
made so long as 'we entertain all Objects in that Way and Proportion,
that they are suited to our Faculties' (1.1.5; cf. 4.11.2; 4.12.11). It was
his conviction in the existence of our faculties for acquiring ideas and
knowledge which was one reason for rejecting innate ideas (1.2.1). God
has fitted our senses, faculties and organs 'to the conveniences of Life'
(2.23.12; 4.10.1) and for our preservation (4.11.8).

faith   There are two different uses of this term in Locke's writings: one
is epistemic and secular, the other is epistemic and theological. The first
of these uses is found in the introduction to the *Essay* where he announces
that part of his method for determining the '*Bounds* between Opinion and
Knowledge' will be to 'make some Enquiry into the Nature and Grounds
of *Faith*, or *Opinion*: whereby I mean that Assent, which we give to any
Proposition as true, of whose Truth yet we have no certain Knowledge'
(1.1.3). The terms 'faith', 'opinion', and 'belief' tend to be used interchangeably in that work (e.g., 4.2.14; 4.15.3). In some passages, Locke
writes 'assent or faith' (e.g., 4.15.2). The first sense of this term is even
defined in one passage as 'a firm Assent of the Mind' (4.17.24). Assent
or faith should not be given uncritically, as Locke laments some people
do, 'lazily enslaving their Minds to the Dictates and Dominions of others'
by a blind or implicit faith (1.4.22).

The other use of the term 'faith' is in the religious context. Our assent
to revelation is a faith 'which as absolutely determines our Minds, and as
perfectly excludes all wavering as our Knowledge it self' (4.16.14). This
faith 'carries with it Assurance beyond Doubt, Evidence beyond Exception' (*ibid.*). In fact, Locke says 'we may as well doubt of our own Being,
as we can, whether any Revelation from GOD be true.' Faith is defined
in this context as 'a setled and sure Principle of Assent and Assurance'
which leaves no room for doubt. *However*, Locke insists, 'we must be sure,
that it be a divine Revelation, and that we understand it right.' Further
qualifications are placed on religious faith in the chapter on faith and
reason (4.18). There, he wants to determine the boundaries between faith
and reason as a way of deciding 'how far we are to be guided by Reason,
and how far by Faith' (4.18.1). It is too easy just to say of some particular
claim or doctrine that it is above reason. Faith is now defined as 'the
Assent to any Proposition, not thus made out by the Deductions of

Reason; but upon the Credit of the Proposer, as coming from GOD, in some extraordinary way of Communication' (4.18.2). When Locke goes on to say that '*Faith* can never convince us of any Thing, that contradicts our Knowledge', he means to say 'it ought not convince us' (4.18.5). Divine faith, his term for this kind of faith, should be limited to propositions which are supposed to be divinely revealed. Locke was not being facetious when he said that what God has revealed is certainly true, but the problem comes when we try to determine the criteria for REVELATION (*see* REASON). Nor did Locke want to draw the boundaries so firm between reason and faith that the former was excluded from religion. It was important for him to insist that Christianity was *reasonable*; otherwise the way is open for enthusiasts and 'those extravagant Opinions and Ceremonies, that are to be found in the several Religions of the World' (4.18.11).

Two other features of religious faith appear in other writings of Locke. In his *A Letter concerning Toleration*, he affirmed that 'All the life and power of true religion consists in the inward and full persuasion of the mind; and faith is not faith without believing' (in *Works*, vi. 10–11). A very early work expressed the same sentiment: 'the essence and soul of religion consists' in the 'inner worship of the heart which God demands' (*Two Tracts*, p. 214). In his extended account of Christian faith in his *The Reasonableness of Christianity* he identifies belief in Jesus as the Messiah as the defining trait of a Christian (*Works*, vii. 17–18, 113, 114). He insisted that he was not talking solely about an historical belief or faith; it is a justifying and saving faith as well (*ibid.*, pp. 101–2). Along with this saving faith there must go a good life, and that requires repentance (p. 105). Still a slightly different feature is added to religious faith in Locke's *A Paraphrase and Notes upon the Epistles of St. Paul*, a trust in or a personal allegiance to Christ. As Arthur W. Wainwright points out, this element of trust as part of the Christian faith placed Locke closer to the Calvinists, Armenians, and Socinians (see his two-volume edition of that work, Clarendon Press, 1987, pp. 41–2).

freedom (*see* LIBERTY)

G

God This is a term that occurs frequently throughout Locke's writings. The first of his *Two Treatises of Government* was an extended challenge to Sir Robert Filmer's argument that Adam was monarch of the world as soon as God created him, and all legitimate rulers thereafter inherit the right to rule from Adam. In various writings, Locke identifies the law of nature as God's law (e.g., *Essays*, VI, p. 187). His *Some Thoughts concerning Education* stresses the importance of giving the child ('imprinting' on the child's mind) a true notion of God (§136). In that same work and in *The Reasonableness of Christianity*, the Bible is taken as the word of God. In these writings and most prominently in the *Essay*, references to God indicate Locke's understanding of his nature, our knowledge of him, what God has given us (faculties and laws), and how we will be judged. There are also some interesting passages that offer scenarios involving God's actions as a way of illustrating some metaphysical doctrine defended by Locke.

God's nature is indicated in explicit passages but also in some of the descriptive names Locke employs. Besides the usual 'Supreme Being', 'the Almighty', or 'the Great God', there are a number of descriptions stressing God as 'Our Maker', 'the Author and Maker of all things', 'the bountiful Author of our being', 'the all wise Architect'. Related to these are those descriptions that depict God as the sustainer of the world: 'the eternal independent Author of them [all spirits] and us', 'the infinite Author and Preserver of all things', or 'the Sovereign disposer of all things'. Still other names reveal some of God's attributes: 'the Father of all Spirits', the 'first eternal thinking Being', the 'infinite wise Author of our being', 'all wise and powerful God', 'the all wise Agent' or 'the infinite wise Contriver of us and all things'. Several indicate Locke's acceptance of the limitations of our knowledge: 'the incomprehensible supreme Being' or 'the infinite incomprehensible God'. Some explications of these descriptions are found in the *Essay*. For example, God has no beginning, is eternal, unalterable and is everywhere (2.27.2). In an earlier passage, Locke explains that the term 'infinite' applies mainly to God's duration and ubiquity, but figuratively to his power, wisdom and goodness

(2.18.1). What we mean by speaking of God's attributes as infinite is that his acts and objects are infinite in number and extent. There is also a passage in the early *Essays* where Locke warns that 'God has created us out of nothing and, if he please, will reduce us again to nothing' (p. 187).

Some references to God in the *Essay* reflect doctrines Locke has argued for. In his attack on the Cartesian notion of the soul always thinking, he tells us that God always thinks, never slumbers or sleeps (2.1.10). Many writers around Locke and into the next century insisted on the passivity of matter, only minds or spirits can be active or initiate action. Locke's God is pure spirit and is only active, 'pure Matter is only passive' (2.23.28; but *see* POWERS). God as the author of matter 'is truly above all *passive Power*' (2.21.2). In *Some Thoughts*, Locke instructs the tutor to introduce the child to the Bible before the study of bodies, as a way of counteracting the easy impression from the study of bodies that explanations in science can ignore God (§191). There, Locke remarks that 'by mere Matter and Motion, none of the great Phaenomena of Nature can be resolved, to instance but in that common one of Gravity, which I think impossible to be explained by any natural Operation of Matter, or any other Law of Motion' (§192). He even offers as explanation of the deluge which faced Noah that God could have altered 'the Centre of gravity in the Earth for a time' (*ibid.*). God is also invoked to support Locke's suggestion about the possibility of thinking matter: because of God's power, because he is the creator and maker of all things, he could have superadded thought to a bit of organized matter (4.3.6). The replies to Stillingfleet's attack on this suggestion elaborate how this might have been done. Similarly, it is not impossible for God to make a creature with different sense organs from those we have (2.2.3). In his polemic against innate ideas, Locke appeals to the fact that God has given us sight and a power to receive light by our eyes from external objects as one reason for discarding the claim of innate ideas: this would be contrary to God's purpose (1.2.1). In the chapter on primary and secondary qualities, Locke refers to God as a way of illustrating the causal theory of perception which supposes no similarity between the motion of particles and our ideas: just as God has linked the idea of pain to the 'motion of a piece of Steel dividing our Flesh, with which that *Idea* hath no resemblance', so it is not impossible to conceive 'that God should annex such *Ideas* [as colours and smells] to such Motions [of corpuscles] with which they have no similitude' (2.8.13). In arguing for his concept of space as separate from body, Locke suggests the thought experiment of God placing 'a Man at the extremity of corporeal Beings', then supposing the man to 'stretch his Hand beyond his Body' into space (2.13.21). The next section argues for the same notion of space by having God stop all motion in the universe and then annihilate some particular body or bit of matter. It is obvious,

Locke says, 'that the Space, that was filled by the parts of the annihilated Body, will still remain, and be a Space without Body' (2.13.21 *bis*). God also enters Locke's attack against the syllogism: 'But God has not been so sparing to Men to make them barely two-legged Creatures, and left it to *Aristotle* to make them Rational' (4.17.4). God has given us a mind that can reason 'without being instructed in Methods of Syllogizing'.

Locke also identifies God as the source of several useful faculties and aids. In general, God has given man 'Whatsoever is necessary for the Conveniences of Life, and the Information of Vertue' (1.1.5; a claim found in the Bible, 2 Peter 1:3). God has also given us the ability to discover truth without the need for innate ideas (1.3.22; cf. 2.23.12). As well, God has 'given us the power over several parts of our Bodies, to move or keep them at rest, as we think fit' (2.7.3). He has annexed pain to the experience of certain objects in order to aid our preservation (2.7.4). He has put into us 'the *uneasiness* of hunger and thirst, and other natural desires' to motivate us for the preservation of our life (2.21.34).

The one remaining feature of Locke's references to God concerns our knowledge. While several of his descriptive labels of God affirm his incomprehensibility to man, Locke asserts firmly that the *existence* of God is known for certain (e.g., 4.11.13; 4.17.2). Our faculties 'plainly discover to us the Being of a GOD' (4.12.11). How is that discovery made? *Essay* 4.9.2 says we have that knowledge by demonstration. In the early *Essays*, the inference by reason to God is drawn after reflecting upon what we discover about the world (its order and beauty) by means of our senses, a kind of argument from design (pp. 153–7). God is said to show 'Himself to us as present everywhere', but Locke means 'show' in the sense that 'after reflecting' we conclude that God is there. The more systematic account of the 'demonstration' of God's existence is given in *Essay* 4.10. In that chapter, Locke proceeds from the knowledge of our own existence (an intuitive knowledge, he claims) to the conclusion that '*there is an eternal, most powerful, and most knowing Being*' (4.10.6). From 'something exists' to 'something cannot come from nothing', to 'something exists with perception and knowledge', to 'there has to be a first knowing being', Locke lays out the steps that lead us to his conclusion, 'God exists.' This is 'so fundamental a Truth, and of that Consequence, that all Religion and genuine Morality depend thereon' (4.10.7). He goes on to spend a number of sections establishing the immateriality of God and arguing for the impossibility of thought arising from matter, as some materialists were claiming (4.10.10–19).

good and evil   Locke's forthright statement in *Essay* 2.20.2 that 'Things then are Good or Evil, only in reference to Pleasure or Pain' lends some credence to the claim that he accepted some kind of hedonism, or that there is a hedonistic tendency to his concept of good and evil. He continues in this same passage by saying: 'That we call *Good*, which *is apt to cause or increase Pleasure, or diminish Pain in us; or else to procure, or preserve us the possession of any other Good, or absence of any Evil.*' He gives a correspondingly similar definition of evil in terms of pain. Even happiness is characterized as pleasure: 'in its full extent [happiness] is the utmost Pleasure we are capable of, and *Misery* the utmost Pain' (2.21.42). Good and evil come in degrees, so that a lesser evil may sometimes be preferred over a lesser good. The restatement in 2.28.5 confirms that he really does mean that good and evil are 'nothing but Pleasure and Pain, or that which occasions, or procures Pleasure or Pain to us'. But this same section goes on to describe *moral* good and evil, linking it to 'the Will and Power of the Law-maker', clearly meaning God. His early *Two Tracts* makes the same point: 'were there no law there would be no moral good or evil' (p.124), and 'moral actions imply a law as a standard of good and evil' (p.221). Both passages refer to divine law. Pleasure and pain become the rewards and punishments given us on the day of judgement (cf. 2.28.6; *see also* LAW).

In writing about the law of nature, Locke says 'the nature of good and evil is eternal and certain' (*Essays*, p. 121). Without natural law 'there would be neither virtue nor vice, neither reward of goodness nor the punishment of evil' (*ibid.*, p. 119). In *Some Thoughts*, Locke says that 'Good and Evil, *Reward* and *Punishment*, are the only Motives to a rational Creature' (§54). The important question for Locke is, will men be motivated by present or future good? He believes that we do not always judge good and evil in terms of pleasure and pain; sometimes things that '*draw after them Pleasure and Pain*' are also judged to be good or evil (*Essay*, 2.21.61). Are we far-sighted enough to govern our lives in this world with an eye for what draws pleasure or pain after it in the next world? In the first edition of the *Essay*, Locke said that the greater good does determine the will, but with the second edition he tells us that he changed his mind somewhat: the greater good will not determine the will unless our desire, raised proportionally to the greater good, makes us uneasy, causing us to want that good (2.21.35; *see* UNEASINESS). He gives various examples of people being content with lesser goods. He also throws in the biblical injunction, 'till he *hungers and thirsts after righteousness*'. Greater visible good does not always raise our desires in proportion. Absent good does not always make part of our present happiness. He is rather sceptical about our ability to fix our thoughts on the future eternal state. Most people 'cannot deny, but that it is possible, there may be a state of eternal durable Joys after this life, far surpassing all the good is to be found here' (2.21.44). He continues in this passage to extol the joys of heaven and our future state, but lamenting that many people will 'not be moved by this greater apparent good, nor their *wills* determin'd to any action, or endeavour for its attainment'. At the same time, Locke believes that men can be brought to prefer the joys of eternal life if they can be made to see 'that Virtue and Religion are necessary to [their] Happiness' (2.21.60). The way to bring a man to understand where his happiness lies, Locke tells us, is to 'let him look into the future State of Bliss or Misery, and see there God the righteous Judge, ready to *render to every Man according to his Deeds*' what they are entitled to on the basis of their life in this world (*ibid.*).

government   The generic sense of this term is the action of governing, or guiding or directing. Locke uses it in this way in *Some Thoughts* where the tutor is frequently referred to as the 'governour' (e.g., §§94, 195). The tutor's task, along with the parents', is to govern the child's activities and attitudes in such a way that in time the child will be able to act responsibly on his own; the government of the tutor will no longer be necessary. In *Two Treatises*, Locke fought a battle with Robert Filmer over the nature and legitimacy of political government. Locke recognized that history may give us examples of societies being formed 'under the Government and Administration of one man' (*T*2, §105). Families also may have left the governing to the father. Filmer had argued for the continuation of paternal rule as justified, hence his spirited defence of monarchy as descended from Adam. Even if it be said that 'every Man ... was born subject to his Father', the 'subjection due from a Child to a Father, took not away his freedom of uniting into what Political Society he thought fit' (§102). Locke conjectured that history will also reveal that many governments have been established by the consent of the people. Locke's case against Filmer rests on the strong claim that '*Politick Societies* all *began* from a voluntary Union, and the mutual Agreement of Men freely acting in the choice of their Governours, and forms of Government' (*ibid.*). Another definition of government is given later: 'a Society of Rational Creatures entered into a Community for their natural good' (§163).

H

happiness There are in Locke's writings different views about the nature of happiness. Happiness as a goal and motive for action, even as a social value, was an ancient notion. It has frequently been linked, sometimes identified, with pleasure (Epicureans) or utility (Hume, Mill). For the Christian, happiness refers to, and may only be possible in, a future life. All of these various strands and linkages with happiness are found in Locke's writings. His two earliest writings, *Essays on the Law of Nature* (written in 1664 but only published in 1954) and his Valedictory Speech as Censor of Moral Philosophy at Oxford (published in 1954 along with the *Essays*), present two sides of this complex idea. The Valedictory Speech is a stylized lament, in part humorous and satirical, about the difficulty of attaining happiness in this life. The question raised in that speech was 'Can Anyone be Happy in this Life?' Locke's answer was 'no'. But Essay VIII in the *Essays* gives a more hopeful account, assuming that we follow the law of nature, God's law. Following that law 'gives rise to peace, harmonious relations, friendship, freedom from punishment, security, possession of our property, and – to sum it all up in one word – happiness' (p. 215). The *Essay* identifies 'true' happiness as our greatest good and 'the highest perfection of intellectual nature' (2.21.51; cf. 2.21.53); but he does not give many details of what such happiness is or what leads to it. In 2.21.60 he indicates that virtue and religion are necessary to happiness, reminding the reader of 'the future State of Bliss or Misery' resulting from God's judgement. The *Essay* closes by linking virtue and happiness, characterizing ethics as 'the seeking out those Rules, and Measures of humane Actions, which lead to Happiness, and the means to practise them' (4.21.3). He also indicates that a knowledge of God relates to our happiness (4.10.1). Early in the same work, Locke claims that God has, 'by an inseparable connexion, joined *Virtue* and publick Happiness together' (1.3.6). The Christian has the happiness or misery of another life in mind (1.3.5); a rational being reflects seriously on that same 'infinite Happiness and Misery', the 'exquisite and endless Happiness', as the eternal rewards of a virtuous life here (2.21.70).

The link in Locke's opinion between virtue and happiness is thus evident. At the same time, this eudemonic strand in his account needs to be considered in conjunction with other passages which deal with pleasure. When he says that nature 'has put into Man a desire of Happiness, and an aversion to Misery' (1.3.3), does he consider the desire to be one for virtue, for virtue as a means of attaining happiness? His work on education says that virtue, along with power and riches, are valued 'only as Conducing to our Happiness' (*ST* §143). The forensic term 'person' belongs 'only to intelligent Agents capable of a Law, and Happiness or Misery', seeming again to link morality with happiness (2.27.26). But in explicating his concepts of delight or uneasiness, he says 'satisfaction', 'delight', 'pleasure', and 'happiness' are 'different degrees of the same thing' (2.7.2). The long chapter on 'power' comes even closer to defining happiness as pleasure: '*Happiness* then in its full extent is the utmost Pleasure we are capable of' (2.21.42). He goes on in that section to define 'good' as 'what has an aptness to produce Pleasure in us'. Pleasure and happiness appear together in other passages (e.g., 2.23.33). Self as a conscious thinking thing is conscious of pleasure and pain and capable of happiness or misery (2.27.17), a capability which is clearly within our control if we act properly (cf. §1 of *Some Thoughts*). Other passages stress the need to 'suspend the satisfaction of our desire in particular cases' for the sake of 'our real happiness' which is described as 'our greatest good' (2.21.51). *Some Thoughts* calls attention to the importance of children's acquiring the habit of mastering their desires and inclinations, of resisting 'the importunity of *present Pleasure or Pain*', since these are habits which are 'the true foundation of future Ability and Happiness' (§45).

hypotheses In harmony with many scientists of his day, Locke insisted that experience and observation must precede generalizations and hypotheses. Whatever hypothesis we form in physical science must be based upon matters of fact; we should conduct our observations and our collecting of facts (our natural histories) free of all hypotheses (*Essay*, 2.1.10). Our own hypotheses should not be 'the Rule of Nature' (2.1.21). He also criticized 'Men whose Understandings are cast into a Mold, and fashioned just to the size of a *received Hypothesis*' (4.20.11). Robert Hooke, the microscopist and active member of the Royal Society, spoke of the rule the Society had of avoiding '*Dogmatizing*, and the *espousal* of any *Hypothesis* not sufficiently grounded and confirm'd by *Experiments*' (*Micrographia*, 1665). Locke puts the point carefully late in the *Essay*. An hypothesis should not be accepted

> *too hastily* (which the Mind, that would always penetrate into the Causes of Things, and have Principles to rest on, is very apt to do,) till we have very

well examined Particulars, and made several Experiments, in that thing
which we would explain by our Hypothesis, and see whether it will agree
to them all; whether our Principles will carry us quite through, and not be
as inconsistent with one *Phenomenon* of Nature, as they seem to accommo-
date, and explain another. (4.12.13)

Similar sentiments can be found in Robert Boyle, William Molyneux, and
others. Locke made the same sort of cautious remarks about the use and
formation of theories and hypotheses in medicine. Writing to Dr Thomas
Molyneux on 20 January 1693, expressing views that Locke shared with
Molyneux and the famous Dr Sydenham, Locke's friend, he describes
general theories as 'for the most part but a sort of waking dreams' (*Corr.*
1593; iv. 8). He criticized those doctors who try to fit the phenomena of
diseases to some prior theory. Only upon the ground of careful observation and recording of the history of diseases can good hypotheses be built.
Even then, hypotheses 'serve as an art of memory to direct the physician
in particular cases, but not to be rely'd on as foundations of reasoning,
or verities to be contended for' (*ibid.*; cf. *Essay* 4.12.13, where Locke refers
to well-made hypotheses as 'at least great helps to the Memory'). Until
we can 'discover how the natural functions of the body are perform'd, and
by what alterations of the humors or defects in the parts they are hinder'd
or disorder'd', hypotheses will remain 'suppositions taken up gratis'(*Corr.*,
ibid.).

In his most cautious moments, Locke disparaged general maxims and
principles along with hypotheses (4.12.12). Some of the defects of the
reliance on hypotheses are that our belief in them may hide their weakness
(3.10.14) or their authors cover some weaknesses with new words to make
them sound attractive (3.10.2). He also uses the word 'hypothesis' to refer
to doctrines with which he disagreed or views he believed false. For
example, the hypothesis that the soul always thinks (2.1.17, 18); the
hypothesis of plenitude, no empty space (2.13.23); some of the explanations of the cohesion of particles of matter (2.23.23); the hypothesis of a
fixed number of real essences (3.3.17); the hypothesis about the eternity
of matter (4.10.13, 17). The only hypothesis which Locke finds useful is
the corpuscular hypothesis: this is, he says (not quite speaking in the first
person), 'thought to go farthest in an intelligible Explication of the
Qualities of Bodies' (4.3.16). He reiterates this remark about the corpuscular hypothesis in *Some Thoughts*, while recommending the reading of
Cudworth's *True Intellectual System* for the history of hypotheses among the
Greeks (§193).

There is one other hypothesis mentioned by Locke in a favourable way,
although this is not a scientific hypothesis. As other writers including
Newton did, Locke held that the phenomena of gravity cannot be

explained 'by any natural Operation of Matter, or any other Law of Motion' (*ST*, §192). It could only be explained by 'the positive Will of a Superiour Being, so ordering it'. Calling this an hypothesis, he then suggests how Noah's flood could have been caused by God's altering the centre of gravity. He even replies to some objections against this theological explanation.

I

idea This is one of the most important and heavily used terms in modern philosophy. From Descartes to Leibniz and Kant on the Continent, from Locke to Reid in Britain, accounts of perception and knowledge employed the term 'idea'. Its precise nature and role vary in the different writers. The interpretations given to it by subsequent writers on modern philosophy have generated debate right down to our own time.

Almost at the beginning of the *Essay*, Locke apologized for 'the frequent use of the Word *Idea*', a word which he believes serves 'best to stand for whatsoever is the Object of the Understanding when a Man thinks' (1.1.8). He goes on to link his use of that word with other older accounts of knowledge, accounts that used words such as 'phantasm', 'notion', and 'species'. Locke's term 'idea' expresses, he says, what these other terms mean. The generic meaning is 'whatever it is, which the Mind can be employ'd about in thinking' (*ibid.*). Scholastic writers talked of sensible and intelligible species and adapted Aristotle's talk of the form of objects that can exist in matter or in mind. A seventeenth-century follower of Aristotle, John Sergeant, used the term 'notions'; and 'phantasm' is found in Hobbes. Each of these earlier accounts struggled with a way to explain how mind can know body, each sought to account for the transition from physicality to mentality.

Locke indicates, in a remark added to later editions of the *Essay*, that he was aware of the Cartesian heritage of the language and problems of this term. He had originally employed the terms 'clear' and 'distinct', terms with a central role in Descartes's account of knowledge and certainty. Locke explains that 'our *simple Ideas* are *clear*, when they are such as the Objects themselves, from whence they were taken, did or might, in a well-ordered Sensation or Perception, present them' (2.29.2). Even memory can present clear ideas so long as those ideas do not lack the 'original Exactness' they had when first acquired. In this passage, he writes as if the object presents the idea, as if the mind receives ideas from an 'outward Object' (2.29.4). In a passage in the 'Epistle to the Reader' (added in the fourth edition), Locke suggests that the terms 'clear' and 'distinct' may not be as well understood as people believe. He suggests substituting for these two the terms 'determinate' and 'determined'. His explication of these substitute terms uses the language of 'objects' also. '*By those denominations, I mean some object in the Mind, and consequently* determined, *i.e. such as it is there seen and perceived to be*' (p. 13). An *idea* is said to be determinate or determined when '*it is at any time objectively in the Mind*'.

In this added clarification, Locke is searching for a vocabulary that will help him point up the need to avoid disputes about words, one of his primary concerns in this work. He believes that if we have precise, determinate ideas as the referents for words, verbal disputes can be minimized, doubts and controversies can be at an end. Thus, the terms 'determinate' and 'determined', better than 'clear' and 'distinct', signify (1) '*Some immediate object of the Mind, which it perceives and has before it distinct from the sound it uses as a sign of it*' and (2) '*That this Idea thus* determined, *i.e. which the Mind has in it self, and knows, and sees there be* determined *without any change to that name, and that name* determined *to that precise Idea*' (p. 14). The phrase 'immediate object of the mind', reappears in later writers (e.g., Berkeley), and it echoes the language of Malebranche. Malebranche was explicit about the indirectness of our knowledge of physical objects: we only know ideas immediately, ideas given us by God on appropriate occasions. It is not clear from Locke's language of ideas as objects, as the immediate object of the mind, that he followed Malebranche in making ideas special objects. In fact, he attacked Malebranche on just this point in his *An Examination of P. Malebranche's Opinion of Seeing All Things in God* (in *Works*, 1823, vol. ix). There is something else about the passage from his 'Epistle to the Reader' that should make us pause if we are tempted to interpret Locke as making ideas special objects: he uses the important phrase, 'objectively in the mind'. For Descartes, this was a phrase that referred to the existence of *objects* in the mind. Ideas for Descartes play two roles, as modes of mind (modes of immaterial substance) and as the objects known. The earlier theories to which Locke refers by those terms 'phantasm', 'notion', 'species' were other ways in which physical objects could be said to exist in the mind, the underlying assumption being that what is known must be 'present with the mind' (a phrase frequently used later by Hume). If we were to say the immediate objects of the mind are ideas on these theories, and on Descartes's adaptation of those theories with *his* objective reality, we would be saying in effect that the objects themselves are the immediate objects of the mind, are present with the mind. Physical objects are rendered immediate to the mind by means of the transfer of the form of objects from physical to cognitive reality, or by the translation of sensible into intelligible species, or, as with Descartes, by ideas capturing objectively the reality of objects. The echo of these theories may seem to have become distorted in Locke's account, since he speaks of *ideas* being objectively in the mind. However, Descartes's ideas *have* objective reality, they represent and capture cognitively the reality of objects, so Locke's use may not be all that different.

Locke is close enough to Descartes's use of 'objectively' to give us reason for looking elsewhere in the *Essay* for indications of a Cartesian reading. Are the two sides of Descartes's 'objective reality of ideas' visible in the *Essay*, the representative, epistemic side and the ontic reality of objects? It has been the representative feature of ideas on which commentators on Locke have focused, finding in that feature reasons for saying our knowledge of objects for Locke is indirect, that what we immediately know or are aware of are ideas, not things. Locke says as much in the opening section of Book Four: 'Since *the Mind*, in all its Thoughts and Reasonings, hath no other immediate Object but its own *Ideas*, which it alone does or can contemplate, it is evident, that our Knowledge is only conversant about them.' The *Essay* ends on the same note: 'For since the Things, the Mind contemplates, are none of them, besides it self, present to the Understanding, 'tis necessary that something else, as a Sign or Representation of the thing it considers, should be present to it: And these are *Ideas*' (4.21.4). Malebranche had insisted that everyone agrees that we do not perceive external objects by themselves, that 'our mind's immediate object when it sees the sun, for example, is not the sun, but something that is intimately joined to our soul, and this is what I call an idea' (*De la recherche de la verité* (1674), trans. Lennon and Olscamp, 1980, p. 217). In his critique of Malebranche (*Des vrayes et des fausses idées*, 1683; English translation by Stephen Gaukroger, 1990), Arnauld chided Malebranche for basing his conclusion about ideas being the immediate object of the mind on such an absurd alternative as objects, such as the sun or moon, being united with the mind. Malebranche, Arnauld suggested, had confused spatial with cognitive presence to the mind. From the fact that 'external Objects be not united to our Minds', Locke draws a different conclusion in *Essay* 2.8.12: that some physical causal process affects nerves and brain, producing ideas in the mind. Corpuscular action of matter, not God, is for Locke the cause of our sensory ideas.

The extended exchange between Arnauld and Malebranche occurred while Locke was completing and preparing his *Essay* for publication. Locke followed that debate closely. Arnauld found Malebranche's ideas as special objects existing in the mind of God a misreading of Descartes, for whom ideas were modes of mind as well as the bearers of the reality of objects, but not themselves objects. Opposed to ideas as objects, Arnauld insisted that to have an idea of some object is the same as perceiving that object (Def. 3, ch. 5, p. 65 in Gaukroger's translation). The two terms 'perception' and 'idea' have slightly different meanings, close to the twofold nature of ideas for Descartes: 'Thus the *perception* of a square has as its most direct meaning my soul perceiving the square, whereas the *idea* of a square has as its most direct meaning the square in so far as it is *objectively* in my mind' (Def. 6, ch. 5, p. 66 in *On True and False Ideas*, tr. Gaukroger). There are a number of places in Locke's *Essay* in which the same equation of ideas and perception is found, without the stress on objective reality. For example,

> Whatever *Idea* is in the mind, is either an actual perception, or else having been an actual perception, is so in the mind, that by the memory it can be made an actual perception again. (1.4.20)

> To ask, *at what time a Man has first any* Ideas, is to ask, when he begins to perceive; having *Ideas*, and Perception being the same thing. (2.1.9)

> For our *Ideas*, being nothing but bare Appearances or Perceptions in our Minds . . . (2.32.1)

> [In 2.32.3, he repeats this last remark:] And so I say, that the *Ideas* in our Minds, being only so many Perceptions, or Appearances there. (cf. 2.1.3; 2.10.2)

Similarly in his *Examination of Malebranche*, Locke identified himself with 'one who thinks ideas are nothing but perceptions of the mind' (§15, in *Works*, ix).

When Arnauld tried to disabuse Malebranche of the notion that the objective reality of ideas did not mean physical objects were literally in the mind, he explained (as Berkeley did later) that 'exist in the mind' just means 'is perceived by the mind'. For example, 'I maintain that an object is present to our mind when our mind perceives and knows it' (*On True and False Ideas*, tr. Gaukroger, p. 65). Or, 'I maintain that a thing is *objectively* in my mind when I conceive it' (*ibid.*, p. 66). There is a remark in Locke's *Essay* which comes close to both these definitions, although it appears in a different context, in his rejection of innate truths of which we are not conscious. We must be aware of whatever exists in our mind: 'For if these Words (*to be in the Understanding*) have any Propriety, they signify to be understood' (1.2.5).

There are, then, passages in Locke's writings which use the language of Arnauld, supporting the interpretation that 'idea' was a term selected by Locke to refer to the content of thought – as we might say, 'I have an idea of a tree', or 'I have a thought of (am thinking about) that tree.' Hume employs the same term in the eighteenth century, explicitly equating 'idea' with 'thought' in his *Enquiry concerning Human Understanding*. 'Thought' and 'idea' are also interchanged by other writers from Locke to Hume. One anonymous author of a pamphlet which surveyed various

views about ideas in the seventeenth century favoured the identification
of thought and idea, confirming Locke's agreement with Arnauld's definition of ideas as perceptions (*A Philosophick Essay concerning Ideas*, 1705).
This same writer distinguished two different concepts of idea, ideas as
distinct beings (the view of Malebranche) and ideas as the thoughts we
have about some object. The latter, this writer says, was the more
common view.

There are other passages where Locke follows the language of ideas as
objects, lending support to those who find in the *Essay* a representative
theory of perception, where ideas, not physical objects, are perceived.
Locke's definition of KNOWLEDGE is also given in terms of the perception
of relations of ideas (*see* REPRESENTATION). It is this second use of the term
'idea' which many commentators today seize upon for their ascription of
a special-object interpretation of ideas (ideas as proxies for objects), but
we need to recognize those other passages which follow Arnauld's reading
of Descartes. It may be there is no clearly consistent account of ideas in
the *Essay*, but the inescapable fact is that both concepts of that term
identified by the anonymous 1705 writer are present in the *Essay* and in
the *Examination of Malebranche*. The debate between Arnauld and Malebranche over the nature of ideas is reflected in Locke's use of that term.
Each reader will have to decide whether the evidence places Locke with
Arnauld or with Malebranche.

There are two other aspects of Locke's account of ideas in need of
attention: his classificatory schema and his description of the acquisition
of specific ideas. His classificatory schema uses the compositional categories of simple and complex, and the ontological categories of mode,
substance and relation. Commentators have differed over the importance
of the simple–complex division. It does not seem to be a division of great
significance for Locke. In the early chapters of Book Two of the *Essay*, it
enables him to introduce some specific ideas, allocating them to reaching
the mind through one sense, several senses, reflection, or a combination
of sense and reflection (2.2.1–7; 3.3). The ideas he cites and discusses
under these classifications range from light and colours, sounds, noises,
solidity, space, extension, motion, to perception or thinking, volition or
willing, pleasure, pain, uneasiness, power, existence. Some of these ideas
or qualities (it is not always clear which) receive separate extended
analyses in other chapters, reflecting their special status and importance
for Locke. Especially inside those detailed analyses, the simple-complex
distinction disappears. It is Locke's concepts of space, time, power,
solidity which are more important than whether our ideas of these
properties are simple or complex. The ontological classification *is* more
important, although again the text suggests that his interest focused on

the substances, relations, and modes rather than upon our ideas of these. Of course, ideas themselves *are* modes of mind, just as they were for Descartes. The issue here is rather complicated because Locke appears to have opinions about the ontological status of space and time, as well as claims about our ideas of them.

The second additional topic not to be ignored when examining Locke's use of the term 'idea' is his account of how we acquire some of our ideas. Simple ideas such as colour, sound, taste arise in our mind almost against our will; we are, he says, passive in receiving that sort of ideas (although we do need to pay attention to what is happening around us and to our sense organs). In the case of the ideas of existence and unity, once we have any ideas in our minds, once we are aware of them, the idea of existence arises as a result of our *considering* those ideas 'as being actually there, as well as' considering 'things to be actually without us' (2.7.7). The operation of 'considering' marks our active participation in the acquisition of the simple idea of existence. Locke is explicit about the action of the mind producing complex ideas (2.2.2; 2.12.1). Of these activities, he mentions a few: combining, comparing, separating (as in abstraction). In the course of his presentation of the origin of other ideas, e.g., of cause (2.26.1) or power (2.21.1), other mental operations are at work: observing, reflecting, contemplating, and even considering certain principles. The mind for Locke is largely active.

identity One of the actions of the mind is comparing, comparing one thing with another for similarities and differences, comparing a thing with itself at different times. This latter action yields the ideas of identity and diversity: 'when considering any thing as existing at any determin'd time and place, we compare it with it self existing at another time' (*Essay*, 2.27.1). The 'very Being of things' is their identity, their sameness over time. Existing at a particular time and place excludes other objects from that time and place. The notion of *sameness* is the notion of 'the same with it self'. It follows, Locke says, that 'one thing cannot have two beginnings of Existence, nor two things one beginning'. The *beginning* of existence in time and at a place individuates any object, including finite intelligences: 'Finite Spirits having had each its determinate time and place of beginning to exist, the relation to that time and place will always determine to each of them its Identity as long as it exists' (2.27.2). The comparing of an object with itself is not an act of identifying; Locke was not writing about *criteria* for determining sameness. His concern was with the conditions under which we can acquire the idea of identity, of sameness. Seeing an object at a particular time and place, 'we are sure, (be it what it will) that it is that very thing, and not another' (2.27.1). What the idea of identity means, what sameness of being is, is having a particular time and place for its beginning and continuing to exist wherever it does. A particular particle of matter, an atom (that is, 'a continued body under one immutable Superficies'), taken in any moment of its existence, is 'the same with itself' (2.27.3).

Identity or sameness applies to complex bodies also, but in those cases, continuity of existence over times and places is not sufficient for sameness. In addition, 'same mass of matter' requires that the same parts, the same atoms, continue to make up that mass. Their arrangement and structure can vary, but not the number and sameness of parts. If just one atom or particle is taken away, it is no longer the same mass or same body.

With living matter, plants and animals, the specific particles are not part of the identity, since they change as the plant or animal grows and lives. Unlike a mass of matter, it is the *organization* that constitutes the same oak, the same horse. The living oak tree differs from a mass of matter in that while it is 'the Cohesion of Particles of Matter any how united' that constitutes the identity of a mass of matter, for the oak tree it is the disposition and organization of the parts towards a particular end or function which constitutes the life of that tree or plant (2.27.4). It is the common life which all the parts participate in that makes the sameness of plant or animal. When new particles are formed, replacing old ones, they are 'vitally united to the living Plant, in a like continued Organization'. Organization of component parts working towards ends also characterizes machines, but they differ from living organisms in that the force that sets the parts of a watch or any machine in motion comes from outside the machine. In an animal, 'the fitness of the Organization, and the Motion wherein Life consists, begin together, the Motion coming from within' (2.27.5).

Locke also applies identity to ideas. The first act of the mind 'when it has any Sentiments or *Ideas* at all [is] to perceive its *Ideas*, and so far as it perceives them, to know each what it is, and thereby also to perceive their difference' (4.1.4; cf. 4.7.4). A later passage says that it is 'by an intuitive Knowledge' that the mind perceives each idea to be what it is and to be different from any other idea (4.3.8). The identity of ideas is not linked with their beginning of existence, but with the fact that each idea is what it is and not another. The mind, for example, knows certainly that 'the *Idea of White*, is the *Idea* of White, and not the *Idea* of Blue' (4.7.4). So for all the ideas in a man's mind, 'He knows each to be it self, and not to be another; and to be in his Mind, and not away when it is there' (*ibid.*).

impressions Chambers's *Cyclopaedia* (1728), always a handy place to look for an indication of the uses of terms in philosophy, science and religion, defines 'impression' as 'a term in Philosophy, apply'd to the Species of Objects, which are supposed to make some Mark or *Impression* on the Senses, the Mind, and the Memory'. Under the term 'Imagination', Chambers characterizes that as designating 'a Power or Faculty of the Soul, by which it conceives, and forms Ideas of Things, by means of certain Traces and impressions that had been before made in the Fibres of the Brain, by Sensation'. Locke's use of 'impression' applies to both mind and body. There is also one use of impressions on the brain.

The brain passage is found in *Essay* 2.1.15. He suggests that it might be said 'that in a waking Man, the materials of the Body are employ'd, and made use of, in thinking; and that the memory of Thoughts, is retained by the impressions that are made on the Brain'. The notion of brain traces is found in many writers, e.g., Malebranche, Hume, and in Chambers's entries for 'brain' and 'image'. The bulk of Locke's references to impressions made on the body are to the sense organs, or just generally to the body. He speaks of a child knowing 'the Objects, which being most familiar with it, have made lasting Impressions', the example being the persons the child sees and talks with (2.1.22). Sensation is defined as 'such an Impression or Motion, made in some part of the Body, as produces some Perception in the Understanding' (2.1.23). He had in 2.1.21 referred to some 'violent Impression on the Body, [which] forces the mind to perceive, and attend to it'. If the mind fails to 'take notice' of what 'impressions are made on the outward parts' of the body, perception will not result (2.9.3). The 'impressions of sounding Bodies, made upon the Organ of Hearing' are one example (2.9.4). Dull impressions are cited in 2.9.15. Space, extension, figure, rest and motion 'make perceivable impressions both on the Eyes and Touch' (2.5). By means of such impressions (how, Locke does not say) we acquire the ideas of space, extension, etc. If the impressions made on any of our senses are 'exceeding quick, the Sense of Succession is lost' (2.14.10). He has just suggested that the succession of ideas (not impressions) is a better source for the idea of duration (2.14.9). Fixing our attention exclusively on one object, examining the ideas carefully, we may take no 'notice of the ordinary Impressions made then on the Senses, which at another Season would produce very sensible Perceptions' (2.19.3). Elsewhere, he writes of impressions of sounds (2.28.16), and of 'transient Impressions made by the Object' (2.29.3), but he does not specify where these impressions are made, on organs or in the mind. This last passage does use the example of hard wax resisting the impress of the seal, comparing this to the 'Organs, or Faculties of Perception'. 'Organ' or 'faculties' can be either body or mind, or both. While discussing adequate and inadequate ideas, he remarks, 'were there no fit Organs to receive the impressions Fire makes on the

Sight and Touch; nor a Mind joined to those Organs to receive the *Ideas* of Light and Heat, by those impressions from the Fire, or the Sun, there would yet be no more Light, or Heat in the World, than there would be Pain if there were no sensible Creature to feel it' (2.31.2). In this passage, impressions are clearly distinguished from ideas, although the latter are somehow received by means of the former. The phrase 'sensations or Ideas in us' precedes this sentence, suggesting that they may be the same. Sensations come from bodies which are their 'exciting Causes' (*ibid.*).

Locke may have picked up the term 'impression' from the innatists. As he reports, they claimed there were impressions on the souls of men, received in their first being (1.2.2), natural and original impressions (1.2.31), natural impressions on the mind (1.3.17), impressions of truth (1.3.3), and of general maxims (1.2.27). Locke was not opposed to the language of impressions or of imprinting (another term used by innatists), only the claim that some impressions are imprinted on the mind prior to all experience. He admitted that 'The Knowledge of some Truths . . . is very early in the Mind; but in a way that shews them not to be innate. For, if we will observe, we shall find it still to be about *Ideas*, not innate, but acquired: It being about those first, which are imprinted by external Things, with which Infants have earliest to do, and which make the most frequent Impressions on their Senses' (1.2.15). Examples of such early ideas are smells and tastes; the child is even said to have some truths based on these impressions, e.g., 'that sweet is not bitter' (*ibid.*).

Ideas of the operations of their minds come, if at all, later for children, 'Because, though they pass there continually, yet like floating Visions, they make not deep Impressions enough, to leave in the Mind clear distinct lasting *Ideas*, till the Understanding turns inwards upon it self, *reflects* on its own *Operations*, and makes them the Object of its own Contemplation' (2.1.8). Were it the case that the soul of a child has ideas 'of its own, that it derived not from *Sensation* or *Reflection*', the child would have ideas 'before it received any impressions from the Body' (2.1.17). Thus, having impressions on and from the body is a necessary step in acquiring ideas in the mind. Sometimes, Locke uses causal language for the relation between impressions and ideas. Motion 'made in some part of the Body' produces 'some Perception in the Understanding' (2.1.23). Motion in the body produces a perception, an awareness, whose content is an idea, an idea 'coeval with *Sensation*' (i.e., with an impression). Ideas are acquired by sensation as a result of 'the *Impressions* that are made on our Senses by outward Objects' (2.1.24). The mind, he says, is 'fitted to receive the Impressions made on it'; the referent of 'it' seems to be the mind, not the body. 'As the Bodies that surround us, do diversly affect our Organs, the mind is forced to receive the Impressions; and cannot avoid the Perception of those *Ideas* that are annexed to them' (2.1.25). Later, he tells us that '*Simple Ideas . . . are only* to be *got by* those *impressions* Objects themselves made on our Minds, by the proper Inlets appointed to each sort' (3.4.11). In this section on the names of ideas, he wants to stress the fact that words alone cannot give rise to ideas such as those of tastes and colours: only exposure to objects can do that. But does he mean to say that objects directly make impressions on the mind or, as the earlier passages said, that the impressions are made on sense organs? The reference to the 'proper inlets' is to sense organs, so the general account of first impressions, then ideas and awareness, may still hold. In 3.4.16, he speaks of the ideas of colours being 'produced in the Mind only by the Sight, and have entrance only through the Eyes' – no mention of impressions. He ends this section by saying: 'Extension, Number, Motion, Pleasure, and Pain . . . make Impressions on the mind, and introduce their *Ideas* by more Senses than one.'

We can see from these various passages that Locke did not have a clearly developed account of how from the causal action of external objects on the bodies of perceivers, awareness and ideas of objects and their qualities arise. In truth, no one in Locke's or the next century had such an account. Some, such as Malebranche and Leibniz, denied the possibility of physical causation affecting the mind. Nevertheless, the sequence accepted by Locke was the same as for most writers, even Malebranche and Leibniz, as well as Hume: physical impressions on sense organs and brain caused by external objects, then ideas and perception.

infallible, infallibility   There are two uses of these terms in Locke's writings: one is clearly pejorative, the other signifies evidence, conclusions, or rules which Locke takes to be certain. The fact that there are societies where the people worship many deities is infallible evidence that they lack an idea of the true God (*Essay*, 1.4.15). From the fact that we discover by experience that we sometimes think, we can 'draw this infallible Consequence, That there is something in us, that has a Power to think' (2.1.10). A man 'infallibly perceives two different *Ideas* to be different *Ideas*' (4.7.10). Identity propositions, e.g., 'the *Idea* of Yellow is the *Idea* of Yellow', is infallibly true and the 'Mind cannot but assent to such a Proposition' (*ibid.*). It is 'an infallible Rule, that where-ever the distinct *Idea* any Word stands for, is not known and considered, and something not contained in the *Idea*, is not affirmed, or denied of it, there our Thoughts stick wholly in sounds, and are able to attain no real Truth or Falshood' (4.8.13). We are said to have '*an intuitive Knowledge of our own Existence*, and an internal infallible Perception that we are' (4.9.3).

The pejorative use of these terms begins to appear when he attacks the claims for innate ideas and knowledge. Paraphrasing the attempts to prove innateness by appeals to universal consent, Locke presents this argument:

> The Principles which all mankind allow for true, are innate; those that Men of right Reason admit, are the Principles allowed by all mankind; we and those of our mind, are Men of reason; therefore we agreeing, our Principles are innate: which is a very pretty way of arguing, and a short cut to Infallibility. (1.3.20).

There may be a veiled reference to religious doctrines in a passage in 1.4.24: a reference to 'blind Credulity' by some men for certain principles. In the *Conduct*, he refers to a man 'muffled up in the zeal and infallibility of his own sect, and will not touch a book or enter debate with a person that will question any of those things which to him are sacred' (§3). He describes these men as wanting to have power over others by claiming 'the Authority to be the Dictator of Principles, and Teacher of unquestionable Truths'; they want to 'make a Man swallow that for an innate Principle, which may serve to his purpose' (*Essay*, 1.4.24). The suspicion that Locke may have religious persons and doctrines in mind is reinforced by his use of the analogy of swallowing principles in another passage. 'Let the *Idea* of Infallibility be inseparably join'd to any Person, and these two constantly together possess the Mind, and then one Body in two Places at once, shall unexamined be swallowed for a certain Truth, by an implicit Faith, when ever that imagin'd infallible Person dictates and demands assent without enquiry' (2.33.17). In another passage, he refers to countries where men 'are forced, at a venture, to be of the Religion of the Country; and must therefore swallow down Opinions, as silly People do Empiricks Pills' (4.20.4). Later in this same chapter, the swallow analogy is used explicitly against Papists:

> Take an intelligent *Romanist*, that from the very first dawning of any Notions in his Understanding, hath had this Principle constantly inculcated, *viz.* That he must believe as the Church (i.e. those of his Communion) believes, or that the Pope is Infallible; and this he never so much as heard questioned, till at forty or fifty years old he met with one of other Principles; How is he prepared easily to swallow, not only against all Probability, but even the clear Evidence of his Senses, the Doctrine of *Transubstantiation*? (4.20.10)

Antipathy to Papists is found as early as 1662, in a manuscript on the subject of infallibility. There, he speaks of 'sharp-sighted priests' who seek 'control over the conduct and consciences of men', of priests who 'insist that the Roman pontiff is the sole and infallible interpreter of the Holy Bible' ('John Locke's Essay on Infallibility: Introduction, Text, and Translation', John C. Biddle, *Journal of Church and State*, 19 (1977), p. 317). In a more serious vein, Locke remarks that the disagreements among Christians show that there 'has been no infallible interpreter' of divine matters (*ibid.*). Making a point he was to raise later about revelation, Locke comments that anyone who claims to be infallible would have to present infallible evidence of his infallibility, a task Locke believes cannot be done (*ibid.*, p. 321).

inference   Another term for inference is 'illation', and this is defined as 'the Perception of the connexion there is between the *Ideas*, in each step of the deduction, whereby the Mind comes to see, either the certain Agreement or Disagreement of any two *Ideas*', or their probable connection (*Essay*, 4.17.2). In another passage, Locke says 'To infer is nothing but by virtue of one Proposition laid down as true, to draw in another as true, *i.e.*, to see or suppose such a connexion of the two *Ideas*, of the inferr'd Proposition' (4.17.4). He gives the example of a proposition 'laid down': '*Men shall be punished in another World.*' Suppose that from this proposition another one is inferred, e.g., '*Men can determine themselves*'. The question for Locke is, has the mind 'made this Inference right'? The answer will be 'yes', 'if it has made it by finding out the intermediate *Ideas*, and taking a view of the connexion of them, placed in a due order' (*ibid.*). If the inference or the inferring was made without such a view of the connection of ideas, the inference is not a good or 'right' one. He speaks of the 'force' and 'reasonableness' of an inference when it is made with a view of all the intermediate ideas. He also speaks of the force and strength of an inference (*ibid.*). He criticizes rhetorical discourses as being led astray by some 'lively metaphorical Representations', causing the person or listener to 'neglect to observe, or [they] do not easily perceive what are the true' intermediate ideas.

  There are dangers to avoid in inferring. Inference is 'the great Act of the Rational Faculty' so long as we infer properly, but the 'Mind, either very desirous to inlarge its Knowledge, or very apt to favour the Sentiments it has once imbibed, is very forward to make Inferences' and hence is in too much haste, making an inference when it has not really perceived the connection, and hence, no inference was made or only a faulty one has occurred (4.17.4). Sometimes we can perceive the connection immediately, by an immediate comparing of ideas. In such cases reasoning is not needed. Then, it is 'by Discourse and Inference' that we make discoveries (4.17.15). The reference to discourse may be an indication that one way of helping someone perceive immediately the connection of ideas is by talking with him, talking about the connection and so bringing him to become aware of how the ideas are related. Demonstration is a kind of discourse, a means whereby I show you successive connections of ideas. Those connections must be 'intuited'; that is what 'immediate' perceiving is. Another form of inference involves probability. There, instead of intuiting or seeing immediately, we judge the connection of ideas (*ibid.*).

Illation or inferring is perceiving the connection of ideas, often within a demonstration. But how do we go about discovering intermediate ideas to connect two or more ideas? Sagacity is the name Locke uses for 'finding intermediate *Ideas*, that may shew the *Relations* and *Habitudes* of *Ideas*' (4.3.18; cf. 4.17.2). Another characterization of sagacity is 'A quickness in the Mind to find out these intermediate *Ideas*' that discloses the agreement or disagreement of other ideas (4.2.3).

The emphasis in his account of inference is on the activity of the mind. It is the inferring, the perceiving, that is important. The same stress is found in his account of demonstration: it is the showing, the understanding, that makes a demonstration. Judging is another related *activity* of the mind. Similarly, knowledge is dependent upon the products of the mind's perceiving (4.2.7).

innateness   Locke informs his readers that 'It is an established Opinion amongst some Men, That there are in the Understanding certain *innate Principles*; some primary Notions, . . . Characters, as it were stamped upon the Mind of Man, which the Soul receives in its very first Being; and brings into the World with it' (*Essay*, 1.2.1; cf. 1.3.13). In other passages, the language is of principles or truths 'written on their Hearts' (1.3.8), 'Propositions stamped on their Minds' (1.3.14), or 'Characters, and Marks of Himself [God], engraven in their minds by his own finger' (1.4.14). Much earlier than these passages were written, Locke used similar language in describing this belief. In the *Essays on the Law of Nature*, the opinion opposed to the one Locke favoured, that reason can discover the law of nature, is presented as saying that that law is 'written as it were on tablets' which lie 'open in our hearts' (p. 123), or as saying that the law of nature is 'stamped on our minds by inscription' (p. 125), or 'written in the souls of men' (p. 137; cf. pp. 143, 145).

Locke was referring to a view that can be found in many tracts and pamphlets earlier in his century. The language he used to describe that view is borrowed from those pamphlets. The metaphor of the 'finger of God' can be found in Richard Carpenter's *The Conscionable Christian* (1623): conscience is spoken of as a book 'euen in thine owne bosome, written by the finger of God, in such plaine Characters, and so legible, that though thou knowest not a letter in any other booke, yet thou maist reade this' (pp. 43–4). William Sclater, in *A Key to the Key of Scripture* (1611), employed the language of the law of nature 'written in the hearts of all men'. Matthew Hale, in *The Primitive Origination of Mankind* (1677), speaks of 'connate Principles engraven in the humane Soul' (p. 60). Nathanael Culverwel, in *An Elegant and Learned Discourse of the Light of Nature* (1654), claimed that 'There are stamp't and printed upon the being of man, some clear, and undelible principles, some first and Alphabetical Notions; by putting together of which it can spell out the Law of Nature' (p. 47). Another more cautious Cambridge Platonist, Henry More, in *An Antidote against Atheisme* (1653), opted for the notion of *implicit* knowledge, carefully denying the more vivid language of '*Ideas* flaring and shining to the *Animadersive faculty* like so many *Torches* or *Starres* in the *Firmament* to our outward sight' and '*Red Letters* or *Astronomical Characters* in an *Almanack*' (p. 13). More wished to dissociate himself from this literal language while still defending innateness. In denying the innateness of the law of nature, Samuel Parker, in *A Demonstration of the Divine Authority of the Law of Nature* (1681), complained that 'the plain Account of it has been obscured by nothing more, then that it has alwaies been described and discoursed of in metaphorical and allusive Expressions, such as *Engravings*, and *Inscriptions*, and the *Tables of the Heart*' (p. 5).

These are only a few of the many examples of the language of innateness and the doctrine that Locke describes and attacks in three chapters of Book One of his *Essay*. It was a *very* pervasive doctrine. That Locke had these compatriots in mind in his rejection of innate principles has been strangely resisted by commentators who, perhaps working with a view of philosophy which believes philosophers were always writing with philosophical predecessors in mind, have tried to find in Locke's polemic signs of Descartes or other major figures. The textual evidence seems overwhelming that it was tracts and sermons of the sort cited above that were the object of his attack. The only writer named by Locke (and this, he tells us, was added after he had written most of his attack) is Herbert of Cherbury in his discussion of innateness in *De veritate* (1624). What may have led some commentators to shy away from recognizing there were writers who did use the language Locke describes was that language itself. To sophisticated philosophers, the view described by Locke hardly sounds worth defending or attacking. Locke himself may have contributed to this tendency to search for reputable figures with a more substantial doctrine of innateness, since some of Locke's arguments against innate principles and ideas can be seen as applying to other versions of innateness. Nevertheless, the specific arguments Locke refutes are the ones appealed to by the writers of the pamphlets cited above.

Another feature of Locke's attack is revealed in that opening statement of the common opinion: it is *principles* that were said to be imprinted on hearts, minds, and souls – principles, propositions or truths. Ideas as innate are not discussed by Locke until chapter 4 of Book One of the *Essay*; they enter because on Locke's view, ideas are the components of propositions. The principles claimed to be innate were of two kinds. The first and most important (for indicating the focus of those many writers whose pamphlets Locke had in mind) are practical, moral principles, principles that tell us what to do, how we ought to act. Writers did not always give lists of the practical, moral injunctions they thought were innate, but high on the list of principles that were cited is 'There is a God.' We also find 'Promises are to be kept', 'we must honour and obey our parents', and 'we must not injure or harm any person.'

The other sort of principles said to be innate is logical or what were usually called 'speculative' ones, what Locke referred to as 'those magnified Principles of Demonstration, *Whatsoever is, is*; and *'Tis impossible for the same thing to be, and not to be*' (1.2.4). These were principles that some writers claimed were implicit in all reasoning and the basis for all demonstration. Such principles were also said to be self-evident, self-evidence being taken as an indication of innateness. Locke had strong objections to such an appeal to self-evident principles in reasoning or as a way of explaining demonstration (*see* MAXIMS). His main objection in Book One to the claimed innateness of such principles was that the list of innate speculative principles would be very large, since many truths are self-evident once we acquire specific ideas and understand certain terms. As a criterion for innateness, self-evidence is very misleading. The defenders of innateness did not always use the vivid language of red letters engraved on the soul for these speculative principles; they tended to say that these principles were assented to upon first hearing or after we come to use our reason. Locke had little trouble showing the weakness of this mark of innateness (1.2.6–14). These principles, and some identical propositions appealed to in accounts of logic, were not only not innate, they are of no use in reasoning and most of us reason without them.

It was practical principles, moral rules and injunctions about which Locke's attack on innateness was primarily concerned. It was this aspect of his discussion that brought forth strong attacks against him, since the prevalent view was, as William Sherlock expressed this view, that the denial of innate ideas, of any 'Connate Natural Impressions and Ideas of a God, and of Good and Evil', undermines religion and opens the way for atheism ('Digression concerning Connate Ideas', in his *A Discourse concerning the Happiness of Good Men*, 1704, pp. 161–2). Of the two ideas mentioned by Sherlock, it was the first, the idea of God, that gave the most offence when Locke denied its status as innate. Locke said openly that the proposition, 'God is to be worshipped', is 'without doubt, as great a Truth as any can enter into the mind of Man, and deserves the first place amongst all practical Principles' (1.4.7), but it is *not* innate, since the ideas composing this proposition are not innate (1.4.7–14).

Besides the strong but uncritical conviction that God implanted in man an idea of Himself along with the idea of good and evil, the usual appeal by the defenders of innateness was the claimed universality of these ideas. Especially with the growth of travel books about exotic lands, Locke had little trouble showing that there were no universally agreed-on principles of morality recognized in all societies, or even any common attitudes and customs. Nor did the travel literature support the contention that all societies had an idea of God (1.4.8, 15). Even were it the case that an idea of God or a particular notion of good and evil was found in all societies and all people, that fact would no more support the claim of innateness than would the fact that all nations have ideas of sun, heat, or number prove those ideas innate (1.4.9). Observation of children shows that they are not born with these ideas, that in fact these ideas are late in coming to children's attention (1.4.7).

For these ideas and for both types of principles claimed to be innate, Locke mounts a sustained attack against the reasons given for their being innate. That they are not found in all societies or all individuals was a factual claim he was able to make. That the retreat to the innateness of these principles being revealed by the assent they command when we gain the use of reason or upon first hearing, was shown by Locke to be conceptually confused. There is still another reason given by him for rejecting innate principles and ideas, a reason which rests upon a basic doctrine of his about the mind: if they were in the mind, we would be aware of them, even 'all *Children* and *Ideots*', since it is 'near a Contradiction, to say, that there are Truths imprinted on the Soul, which it perceives or understands not' (1.2.5). The concept of imprinting something on the mind involves awareness of what is imprinted: 'For to imprint any thing on the Mind without the Mind's perceiving it, seems to me hardly intelligible' (*ibid.*). No proposition 'can be said to be in the Mind, which it never yet knew, which it was never yet conscious of' (*ibid.*).

Keeping in mind that what Locke rejected as innate were speculative and practical propositions, truths, as well as the ideas of God and good and evil, we need to note that Locke *did* identify other sorts of principles which could be said to be innate, unlearned. Nature, Locke announces, 'has put into Man a desire of Happiness, and an aversion to Misery: These indeed are innate practical Principles, which (as practical Principles ought) do continue constantly to operate and influence all our Actions' (1.3.3; cf. *T2*, §§63, 67). These principles, these tendencies, *can* be found in all persons in every society. He even uses the language of 'imprinting' for these natural tendencies, but these are not, he insists, principles of knowledge regulating our actions. Later in this chapter, he makes the same point: 'Principles of Actions indeed there are lodged in Men's Appetites, but these are so far from being innate Moral Principles, that if they were left to their full swing, they would carry Men to the over-turning of all Morality' (1.3.13). The faculties of the mind are also described as 'inborn' (*Essays*, p. 127); and *Some Thoughts* makes a point of identifying a variety of character traits children are born with (*see* TEMPERS). So it was not innateness as such that Locke attacked: it was specifically principles of knowledge and moral action, with their attendant ideas, which were rejected as innate.

intuition   In the language of ideas which Locke uses to characterize knowledge, we are said to have intuitive knowledge when the mind perceives the relations of two ideas *immediately*, without the help of other ideas (*Essay*, 4.2.1; cf. 4.3.2). Another formulation has the ideas themselves disclosing their agreement or disagreement (4.1.9). It is truths that we acquire in this way. Intuitive knowledge is certain; the mind has no doubts about the truths (4.2.5). In a later passage, intuition, immediate viewing, is linked with self-evidence (4.18.5). None of these terms is, it may be felt, clear or self-evident. Descartes had also identified intuition and demonstration as two sources of knowledge. He explained his use of intuition in this way: 'By "intuition" I do not mean the fluctuating testimony of the senses or the deceptive judgment of the imagination as it botches things together, but the conception of a clear and attentive mind, which is so easy and distinct that there can be no room for doubt about what we are understanding' (*Rules for the Direction of the Mind*, rule 3).

In his effort to explicate what he means by 'intuitive' knowledge, Locke employs a number of analogies. He also gives a variety of examples. He compares it to bright sunshine which 'forces it self immediately to be perceived' (4.2.1), unlike demonstrative knowledge which requires a series of steps and which Locke compares to reflections in a series of mirrors (4.2.6). The mind is compared with the eye. A properly working eye 'will at first glimpse, without Hesitation, perceive the Words printed on this Paper, different from the Colour of the Paper' (4.2.5). Similarly for the mind, 'it will perceive the Agreement or Disagreement of those *Ideas* that produce intuitive Knowledge.' Thus, the mind perceives that white is not black; that a circle is not a triangle (4.2.1); that 'the *Ideas* of an obtuse, and an acute angled Triangle, both drawn from equal bases', are different (4.3.3); that certain numbers are equal or proportional

(4.3.19); that the arc of a circle is less than the whole circle (4.17.14); that non-entity is incapable of producing anything (4.10.3). We also have an intuitive knowledge of our own existence (4.9.3). Another example is 'that the *Idea* we receive from an external Object is in our Minds' (4.2.14).

J

judgment This is one of the more valued faculties of the mind. Judgement is defined as 'the thinking or taking two *Ideas* to agree, or disagree, by the intervention of one or more *Ideas*, whose certain Agreement, or Disagreement with them it does not perceive, but hath observed to be frequent and usual' (*Essay*, 4.17.17). It is also characterized as 'the acquiescing of the Mind, that any *Ideas* do agree, by comparing them with such probable *Mediums*' (4.17.16). Reason should be the guide of our judgement when we as free agents decide to act in specific ways. Judgement is a discerning faculty, it separates ideas from each other in terms of their differences. Even the least difference is important if we are to avoid being misled 'by Similitude, and by affinity to take one thing for another' (2.11.2). In this section, Locke was contrasting judgement with wit; wit seeks to bring together ideas which have 'any resemblance or congruity, thereby to make up pleasant Pictures, and agreeable Visions in the Fancy'. Judgement, we might say, is an analytic faculty, but it does require training and careful use. Hasty or uncritical judgements can mislead us, even in perception. References to judgement appear throughout the *Essay*. *Some Thoughts* also praises good judgement as a trait to be cultivated in children (§§40, 67, 122).

There is one positive role judgement plays in perceptual awareness, although this role is in a curious way a distorting or altering role. Locke draws a distinction between the visual appearance of objects and our perception of them. Judgement fills out the visual appearance, an appearance which is flat and comprised of light and colours, and turns it into a three-dimensional perceptual object (*see* MOLYNEUX PROBLEM).

justice In the first of *Two Treatises*, Locke remarks that justice 'gives every Man a Title to the products of his honest Industry, and the fair acquisition of his Ancestors descended to him' (*T*1, §42). The early *Essays on the Law of Nature* declares justice to be the 'chief law of nature and bond of society' (p. 109). He speaks there of *natural* justice. Since one of the main ends of civil government is the protection of property (property in the large sense of persons, lives, possessions), we can understand the close ties between property, law and justice. The proposition, *'Where there is no Property, there is no Injustice'*, is as certain 'as any Demonstration in Euclid' (*Essay*, 4.3.18). The *Essays* made the same point: 'For what justice is there where there is no personal property or right of ownership?' (p. 213). The two concepts of justice and property are discussed in relation to educating children where Locke urges parents to get children to share their possessions. He remarks that 'great Care is to be taken, that Children transgress not the Rules of *Justice*' (*ST*, §110). In the *Essay* 4.3.18 passage, he goes on to explain the conceptual connection between the idea of property and the idea of injustice. Property, and possessions in general, need to be acquired by honest labour and in accord with laws, natural or positive laws, not by force (*Essays*, p. 207). He urges us to analyse the complex idea of justice, break it down into its parts, so that we can have a clear idea of it. Since the idea of law is one of those component parts, we must understand what law is also (*Essay*, 3.11.9). In the state of nature, natural law applies; in political society it is civil law that specifies the details of ownership and penalties to offenders. The legislative body or designated authority in government *'is bound to dispense Justice*, and decide the Rights of the Subject *by promulgating standing Laws, and known Authoris'd Judges* (*T2*, §136).

Locke spends some time in the *Essay* explaining that the fact that justice is a mixed mode does not mean any person or society can define that term as they please. With mixed MODES, ideas for human actions, Locke's doctrine is that those ideas do not take their content from actions; rather, the ideas prescribe what actions fit the mixed mode. His way of putting that point with respect to moral ideas is to say they have 'no external Beings for *Archetypes* which they are referr'd to, and must correspond with' (3.11.17). Does this location of archetypes in ideas not leave him open to the charge, as he puts it against himself, that 'if *moral Knowledge* be placed in the Contemplation of our own *moral Ideas*, and those, as other Modes, be of our own making, What strange Notions will there be of *Justice* and *Temperance*? What confusion of Vertues and Vices, if every one may make what *Ideas* of them he pleases?' (4.4.9). Before looking at Locke's answer, we should ask, if the law of nature identifies duties and virtues (including justice), is not the objection Locke raises defeated before it starts? If it is defeated, can Locke maintain his doctrine of mixed modes for those moral ideas contained in the law of nature? There does not seem to be an answer to *our* question; the doctrine of mixed modes sits precariously between relativism and objectivism, between saying 'yes' to the objection Locke raises and 'no' to the one we have raised. The negative answer seems to threaten the doctrine of laws of nature.

Locke's reply to the charge of relativism – many different ideas of justice

– is given by comparing moral ideas to geometrical ideas. Someone could call a triangle by a different name, e.g., a trapezium, but the demonstration of the properties of the figure now called a trapezium would be the same as the demonstration for what others call a triangle (4.4.9). The change in name does not alter the idea. It is the *idea*, not the name, that is the mixed mode, that is the archetype. In the same way, moral ideas are distinct from what names people give them. For example, 'let a Man have the *Idea* of taking from others, without their Consent, what their honest Industry has possessed them of, and call this *Justice*, if he please. He that takes the Name here without the *Idea* put to it, will be mistaken, by joining another *Idea* of his own to that Name' (4.4.9). It is as if some ideas, those of geometry and morality, have a status independent of particular persons. Of course, Euclid or the first geometers constructed the ideas of triangles, squares, etc. For Locke, God constructs moral ideas, expressing them in natural law, and gives us reason to discover the laws and their moral content, a content Locke wants to describe as mixed modes when humans think of them. In one passage, he even describes mixed modes as *moral beings* (3.5.12) Cf. 2.28.14. Such beings in the case of some moral ideas such as justice have God's sanction. Justice would then seem to be a natural, not an artificial, virtue. Can it be both natural and a mixed mode?

K

knowledge In his *Conduct*, Locke said 'knowledge consists only in perceiving the habitudes and relations of ideas one to another' (§31; cf. §15). A more formal definition is found in the *Essay*: '*the perception of the connexion and agreement, or disagreement and repugnancy of any of our Ideas*' (4.1.2). Each of the terms in this definition is important for understanding the concept of knowledge with which Locke worked. 'Perception' tells us that knowledge is dependent upon one's awareness. Knowledge does not exist apart from us, waiting to be discovered. We tend to say books contain knowledge, we may speak of the book of knowledge, but what books contain is information (or misinformation). Once we have understood that information, *we* have acquired some knowledge. Similarly for acquiring knowledge about the world from our observation and experience of objects and events: it is *our* acquisition of ideas about the world which leads to knowledge. Just having ideas is not sufficient for knowledge; we must perceive 'the connexion and agreement, or disagreement and repugnancy' of our ideas. It is the *relations* of and between ideas, when we are aware of those relations, that constitute our knowledge, our knowing this or that. In some cases, we need the help of demonstration before we can perceive the relations between ideas, e.g., the relation between (the ideas of) any three angles of a triangle, equality, and two right angles. In this example, Locke leaves out the phrase 'the ideas of', speaking directly of perceiving that the 'Equality to two right [angles] does necessarily agree to, and is inseparable from the three Angles of a Triangle'. We may wonder what it is that we perceive when we acquire knowledge: do we perceive ideas or figures? (cf. 4.2.2, 3). In other cases, demonstration is not necessary; we perceive immediately and intuitively without help that, e.g., white is not black (4.1.2; 4.2.1). Here, ideas *are* present in his example: we perceive that the ideas of white and black do not agree.

There are four (more or less) relations of agreement or disagreement between ideas which, when perceived, yield knowledge. The first is identity or diversity. These are strictly two relations, but they work in tandem. The first act of the mind once it has acquired some ideas 'is to know each what it is, and thereby also to perceive their difference, and that one is not another' (4.1.4). To know an idea in this use means to perceive 'each *Idea* to agree with it self'. Such knowing is said to be infallible: 'A Man infallibly knows, as soon as ever he has them in his Mind that the *Ideas* he calls *White* and *Round*, are the very *Ideas* they are, and that they are not other *Ideas* which he calls *Red* and *Square*' (4.1.4). In 4.17.14, it is not only ideas that we perceive: 'Thus the Mind perceives, that an Arch of a Circle is less than the whole Circle, as clearly as it does the *Idea* of a Circle'.

The second relation of ideas distinguished by Locke in 4.1.3 is relation, an odd listing since it does not seem to designate any specific kind of relation, as identity and diversity (or the next two relations) do. His explication of this relation simply remarks on the importance of our being able to perceive the relations of ideas (4.1.5). He does speak of the perception of the relations *between*, not *of*, ideas as he did in 4.1.2, and of the relation between '*any two Ideas*, of what kind soever, whether Substances, Modes, or any other'. Does he mean there to be a difference between the agreement or disagreement *of* and *between* ideas? Identity, of course, is not a relation between *two* ideas, so there may be a difference there at least. But the oddity of this section continues: 'all distinct *Ideas* must eternally be known not to be the same, and so be universally and constantly denied one of another' (*ibid.*). Eternal knowledge is not mentioned elsewhere. Perhaps God's knowledge is also based on the perception of the relations of or between ideas. The point of this remark is to stress the importance of the fact that knowledge rests upon our ability to perceive 'any Relation between our *Ideas*, and find out the Agreement or Disagreement, they have one with another' (cf. 4.3.18). The next (Locke numbers it the third) sort of agreement or disagreement found *in* our ideas, '*co-existence*, or necessary *connexion*' (4.1.3), seems to be two relations. In a listing in 4.3.7, necessary connection is omitted: 'Identity, Coexistence, Relation, and real Existence' (see also 4.3.9–12). His brief explication in 4.1.6 does not speak of necessary connection, only of '*Coexistence*, or *Non-co-existence*' in the same subject. He has in mind the substance gold, the fixedness of gold, its 'power to remain in the Fire unconsumed'. Far from this being a *necessary* feature of the substance gold, it is just one quality which, along with yellowness, fusibility, malleableness and solubility, makes up our complex idea (the nominal essence) of gold (4.1.6). Human knowledge is limited and cannot extend to the real essences of substances or discover real, necessary connections in nature (see, e.g., 4.3.13, 14).

The last-named relation, real existence, is stated briefly in 4.1.7 as if it does not involve two *ideas* but the '*actual real Existence* agreeing to any *Idea*'.

The only example given in this section is 'God is'. Later, he gives as examples of our knowledge of real existence, the intuitive knowledge of our own existence, a demonstrative knowledge of God's existence, and a sensitive knowledge of the existence of the objects 'present to our senses' (4.3.21). His account of the intuitive knowledge we have of our existence does not explicitly use ideas. It is evident to me, he says, that '*I think, I reason, I feel Pleasure and Pain*' (4.9.3). He does not seem to want to say he knows that he feels pain by means of an idea; the *feeling* of pain gives him a perception of his own existence: 'I have as certain a Perception of my own Existence, as of the Existence of the Pain I feel' (*ibid.*). What we are said to be conscious of is not an idea, but 'our own Being'. The rather elaborate demonstration of God's existence starts from this perception of our own being and progresses to an intuitive knowledge of several principles, to the knowledge of an intelligent being (4.10.2–10). Ideas and relations of or between ideas are not mentioned.

In his general discussion of this last knowledge relation, real existence or what he calls the 'reality of our knowledge', Locke goes back to the language of ideas: ''Tis evident, the Mind knows not Things immediately, but only by the intervention of the *Ideas* it has of them' (4.4.3). Knowledge is said to be real 'only so far as there is a conformity between our *Ideas* and the reality of Things'. What kind of conformity is required and what are the marks or criteria for that conformity? The problem is stated in the language of ideas: 'How shall the Mind, when it perceives nothing but its own *Ideas*, know that they agree with Things themselves?' We know that our simple ideas are real, that they conform to reality, not, it seems, by our consulting ideas, but by discovering that we do not produce such ideas ourselves. From that realization we conclude that ideas 'must necessarily be the product of Things operating on the Mind in a natural way, and producing therein those Perceptions which by the Wisdom and Will of our Maker they are ordained and adapted to' (4.4.4). From the fact that '*simple* Ideas *are not fictions* of our Fancies', we can apparently conclude or know that those ideas 'carry with them all the conformity which is intended'. The example of such a conformity Locke gives is between the idea of whiteness or bitterness and the power in objects which produces those ideas. The knowledge relation of real existence clearly does not hold *between* two ideas, certainly not as Locke discusses it in these passages. Under pressure from Stillingfleet, the Bishop of Worcester, Locke attempted to reformulate this relation as one between two ideas: 'Now the two ideas, that in this case are perceived to agree, and do thereby produce knowledge, are the idea of actual sensation (which is an action whereof I have a clear and distinct idea) and the idea of actual existence without me that causes that sensation' (*Mr. Locke's Second Reply,* in *Works*, iv. 360). His further account in the *Essay* shows, however, that the idea of actual sensation is not involved, nor is it adequate to the task. If knowledge of the actual existence of objects is not based on a relation *between* ideas, can it be a relation *of* ideas?

If that real relation is revealed in or by the idea of whiteness, it might still fit Locke's definition of knowledge, although there is a problem about how we discover that relation. His discussion of our knowledge of the existence of objects says that it is the *receiving* of the idea of white, not the *idea* itself (nor the idea of actual sensation), which 'makes us know, that something doth exist at that time without us, which causes that *Idea* in us' (4.11.2). He continues: 'whilst I write this, I have, by the Paper affecting my Eyes, that *Idea* produced in my Mind, which whatever Object causes, I call *White*' (*ibid.*). The next section even speaks of 'those Things which he sees and feels', although elsewhere he distinguishes the *appearances* from the *powers* in objects, as if seeing objects may be having certain appearances (and ideas may be appearances, a Hobbesian term Locke frequently employs). Nevertheless, it is not simple ideas of sense alone which reveal the relation of real existence; it is the actual receiving of such ideas, together with some beliefs or theories about the nature of matter (that bodies have powers) and our awareness of not being the cause of those ideas. The same chapter gives additional *reasons* for placing sensations as the source of knowledge, what he earlier called 'sensitive knowledge' (4.3.5); but such knowledge requires reflection on and considerations of experiences of sensing: it is not revealed by the ideas of sense alone. Locke was not overly concerned with combating scepticism about the external world, as later writers were, but he did recognize that 'If it be true, that all Knowledge lies only in the perception of the agreement or disagreement of our own *Ideas*, the Visions of an Enthusiast, and the Reasonings of a sober Man, will be equally certain' (4.4.1). His response to this concern introduces more than the perception of the agreement or disagreement of ideas, so his formal definition of knowledge requires some qualification, at least in the instance of the relation of real existence.

Besides sensitive and demonstrative knowledge, intuitive knowledge is the source of certainty, greater certainty than the other two kinds of knowledge; it is the strongest degree of knowledge (see 4.2.1). The notion of degrees of knowledge had a tradition prior to Locke. Sometimes it was accompanied by the notion of degrees of reality, as with Plato or Descartes. Intuition was also important for Descartes in his analysis: he defined it as 'the conception of a clear and attentive mind, which is so easy and distinct that there can be no room for doubt about what we are understanding' (*Rules for the Direction of the Mind*, trans. Cottingham *et al.*, I, p. 14). An alternative characterization of intuition for Descartes is 'the indubitable conception of a clear and attentive mind which proceeds from the light of reason' (*ibid.*). Locke uses the analogy of light also, but the light perceived visually, not the metaphorical light of reason: this kind of knowledge is 'irresistible, and like the bright Sun-shine, forces it self immediately to be perceived, as soon as ever the Mind turns its view that way' (4.2.1; cf. 4.2.5). Locke followed Descartes also in saying intuition operates in demonstrative knowledge; it is required for seeing the connection between each step (4.2.7; 4.15.1). Intuition is also the way we know our own existence, that each idea we have is what it is, and it is the means for knowing all self-evident propositions. Two examples of self-evident propositions known by intuition (and hence, having intuitive certainty) are: 'it is impossible, for the same body to be in two places at once' (4.18.5), and 'bare *nothing can no more produce any real Being, than it can be equal to two right Angles*' (4.10.3).

Sensitive knowledge is important for Locke in enabling us to discover truths about the world, truths derived from experience and observation. Such knowledge has limitations, it cannot extend to the essential nature of body, it is restricted to observed coexistences and uniformities. Sensitive knowledge is more than adequate for experimental science. Science can be improved, our knowledge of nature extended and refined, if we learn to make more careful and detailed observations and eliminate some of the impediments that have infected previous work, such as relying on principles and maxims, using words without precise meanings, accepting doubtful systems for science, seeking certainty where only probabilities are possible.

One area about which Locke makes little comment, an area not covered explicitly by his account of knowledge, is self-knowledge or (more strictly) knowledge of the workings of the mind. This is an area in which Locke's 'reflection' operates. His accounts of the origin of specific ideas describe various mental operations which help in the acquisition of ideas. He does sometimes appeal to each man's own experience, and the *Essay* contains a wealth of material about the mind and its actions. That work contains, in fact, the beginnings of what Hume called the 'science of man' (i.e., psychology), a science to which Hume also made important contributions. Histories of psychology recognize Locke's place in the development of that discipline. Hume was explicit about the need to adopt the method of experience and observation for the science of man, for the descriptions of our cognitive and affective processes. Locke employs accounts of these processes but he does not address the methodology, or find a place for those accounts in his discussion and definition of knowledge. He identified the source of all ideas as either sensation or reflection, the latter sometimes being treated as *internal* sensation (e.g., 2.1.2–4). He also identified reflection as 'that notice which the Mind takes of its own Operations, and the manner of them' (2.1.4), but this 'notice' is improperly described as falling under sensitive knowledge. To intuitive, demonstrative, and sensitive knowledge, Locke needs to add reflective knowledge, what later came to be called 'introspection'. The importance of the *Essay* and of *Some Thoughts* in their detailed description of cognitive and affective processes should not be undervalued.

L

language As early as the 'Epistle to the Reader' in his *Essay*, Locke alerts us to the importance he gives to language in his analysis of knowledge and understanding. After praising the masters of science – Boyle, Sydenham, Huygenius, and Newton – he suggests that even greater progress could have been achieved '*if the Endeavours of ingenious and industrious Men had not been much cumbered with the learned but frivolous use of uncouth, affected, or unintelligible Terms, introduced into the Sciences, and there made an Art of, to that Degree, that Philosophy . . . was thought unfit, or uncapable to be brought into well-bred Company, and polite Conversation*' (p. 10). He complains that '*Vague and insignificant Forms of Speech, and Abuse of Language, have so long passed for Mysteries of Science; And hard or misapply'd Words, with little or no meaning, have, by Prescription, such a Right to be mistaken for deep Learning, and heighth of Speculation, that it will be easie to persuade, either those who speak, or those who hear them, that they are but the Covers of Ignorance, and hindrance of true Knowledge*' (*ibid.*). It is, he remarks, no easy matter to bring people to recognize that they have been '*deceived in the Use of Words; or that the Language of the Sect they are of, has any Faults in it*'.

The third book of his *Essay* is designed to '*make it so plain, that neither the inveterateness of the Mischief, nor the prevalency of the Fashion, shall be any Excuse for those, who will not take Care about the meaning of their own Words, and will not suffer the Significancy of their Expressions to be enquired into*' (*ibid.*). The last three chapters of that third book are devoted to the 'Imperfections of Words', the 'Abuse of Words', and the 'Remedies of the Foregoing Imperfections and Abuses'. There are three chapters on NAMES (the central core of Book Three), and one chapter on general terms (*see* ABSTRACT OR GENERAL IDEAS (AND WORDS)). The first two chapters are of a more general introductory nature: one on the 'Signification of Words'; the other (the first), on 'Of Words and Language in General'. There are also two short chapters on 'Abstract and Concrete Terms' and another on 'Particles', words that connect thoughts, ideas and propositions to each other.

There was a wide interest in language throughout the seventeenth and eighteenth centuries, an interest in the origin and nature of language.

Some writers claimed that there was a universal, natural language given to Adam by God and then lost, some sought to decipher from the Hebrew language the universal language, and others said man can construct such a universal language on his own. Some of those who argued for natural language talked of a 'harmony' between words and things; words were seen as expressing the essential features of things (e.g., Comenius, *Vis Lucis*, 1668). Other writers supported this view in different ways (e.g., W. Simpson, *Hydrologia Chymica*, 1669; J. Wilkins, *An Essay Towards a Real Character and Philosophical Language*, 1668). Leibniz defended a somewhat similar view in his *Nouveaux Essais*, 1765. (For a good discussion of Leibniz in relation to Locke, see Hans Aarsleff, 'Leibniz on Locke on Language', *American Philosophical Quarterly*, 1964. An extended account of the universal language view is given by James Knowlson, *Universal Language Schemes in England and France, 1600–1800*, 1975.)

Locke represents an opposing view: language and the signification of words are conventional, not natural, although his opening remark in chapter 1 of Book Three of the *Essay* speaks of God designing man as a sociable creature, making 'him not only with an inclination, and under a necessity to have fellowship' with others, but furnishing him also 'with Language, which was to be the great instrument and common Tye of Society' (3.1.1). In 3.11.1, speech is described as 'the great Bond that holds Society together'. He even speaks of *nature* suggesting unawares to the 'first Beginners of Languages ... the Originals and Principles of all their Knowledge', perhaps suggesting a link between language and knowledge (3.1.5). God or nature so furnished our organs 'as to be *fit to frame articulate Sounds*, which we call Words' (3.1.1), but sounds alone do not make a language. Two conditions are necessary in order to turn sounds into words. Sounds must be used as '*Signs of internal Conceptions*', made to 'stand as marks for the *Ideas*' in our minds (3.1.2). Sounds must also be able to stand for '*several particular Things*', for kinds or classes (3.1.3). Are these two conditions part of what God has furnished us, or what nature suggested to the first language-users? Nature fashioned our organs so that we can form articulate sounds, and the sounds we can make 'were by Nature so well adapted to that purpose', the purpose of making them *signs* of our ideas (3.2.1).

In this last passage, Locke writes 'words', not 'sounds', but that he did not mean to say nature (or God) gave us sounds with the two conditions that turn them into words is clear from the rest of that sentence: 'not by any natural connexion, that there is between particular articulate Sounds and certain *Ideas*, for then there would be one Language amongst all Men; but by a voluntary Imposition, whereby such a Word is made arbitrarily the Mark of such an *Idea*' (3.2.1; cf. 3.9.4). He then spends six sections on the signification of words. The main points of what has been considered a theory of meaning are the following:

(1) The ideas words stand for are their 'proper and immediate Signification' (3.2.2).
(2) Words are used to make known the ideas (thoughts) of the speaker.
(3) Words are voluntary signs.
(4) They cannot be signs of the qualities of objects, nor of the 'Conceptions in the Mind' of others.
(5) They may more or less correspond with the conceptions of others, but each of us, especially children, tends to use words for slightly different ideas. For example, the word 'gold' may for a child stand for the idea of a metal but also for the idea of the colour of a peacock's tail (3.2.3). That same word for some adults may refer to the idea of yellow colour and fusibility, others may add malleableness to the idea.
(6) Besides the proper and immediate signification of words being the ideas in the speaker's mind, men often 'in their Thoughts give them a secret reference to two other things' (3.2.4): (a) words are supposed to be the marks of ideas in the minds of other language-users; this is a necessary supposition for understanding; (b) men also 'often suppose their Words to stand also for the reality of Things' (3.2.5). The first supposition applies to what Locke calls 'modes', the second to 'substances'.
(7) The constant use of specific words to stand for or express particular ideas sets up a connection such that the words (names) 'almost as readily excite certain Ideas, as if the Objects themselves ... actually affect the Senses' (3.2.6).
(8) A danger in this association of word and idea is that we may focus our attention more on the words than on things (3.2.7). One of the slogans of the Royal Society, which Locke reinforced, was 'look to the things themselves, not words.' The point of this injunction was to stress the need for observation and the collecting of information on the behaviour of objects, rather than relying on textbooks and received opinions.

Locke ends this chapter by reaffirming the conventionalism of his view of language: '*Words* by long and familiar use, as has been said, come to excite in Men certain *Ideas*, so constantly and readily, that they are apt to suppose a natural connexion between them. But that they *signify* only Men's peculiar *Ideas*, and that *by a perfectly arbitrary Imposition*, is evident, in that they often fail to excite in others (even that use the same Language) the same *Ideas*, we take them to be the Signs of' (3.2.8).

Most of the imperfections of words are in fact improper uses of words. The objective of the three chapters on names is to make explicit precisely what the names of simple ideas, mixed modes, and substances can and cannot do, what it is that they identify. If we assume that our names for substances refer to and reveal the real essences of things, we will be led astray by words. Or if we fail to be very explicit about the referents of mixed-mode names (the archetypes or standards for actions), confusion and misunderstanding will result. He is more specific about the misuse and imperfections of words in chapter 9, distinguishing an ordinary or 'civil' use of language from a technical or 'philosophical' use. The latter is more demanding and requires greater clarity than the former. In this chapter, he expands on the difficulties in naming mixed modes and substances.

His list of abuses of words includes using them without clear and distinct ideas (3.10.2–4); '*Inconstancy* in the use of them' (3.10.5); '*affected Obscurity*' by using old words in new ways or 'introducing new and ambiguous Terms, without defining either' (3.10.6–13); or taking words for things, believing our words correspond with the real existence of things (3.10.14–16). There are other abuses identified in the rest of this long chapter (§§17–34). The remedies he recommends are addressed to ways of guarding against or correcting the abuses (3.11.1–27).

It is evident from the list of imperfections, abuses, and remedies, and from the practical orientation towards the acquisition and communication of ideas and knowledge, that Book Three is not a treatise on language, as many books at that time were. At the end of Book Two, Locke explains how he was led into discussing language. He had originally thought he could go from his analysis of ideas as the 'Instruments, or Materials of our Knowledge' to an account of 'what use the Understanding makes of them, and what Knowledge we have by them' (2.33.19). However, he came to appreciate that 'there is so close a connexion between *Ideas* and Words; and our abstract *Ideas*, and general Words, have so constant a relation one to another, that it is impossible to speak clearly and distinctly of our Knowledge, which all consists in Propositions, without considering, first, the Nature, Use, and Signification of Language' (*ibid.*). While discussing the imperfections of words, he again indicates that it was late in his thinking and writing about knowledge and understanding that he realized the necessity of giving some attention to language: 'I must confess then, that when I first began this Discourse of the Understanding, and a good while after, I had not the least Thought, that any Consideration of Words was at all necessary to it. But when having passed over the Original and Composition of our *Ideas*, I began to examine the Extent and Certainty of our Knowledge, I found it had so near a connexion with

Words, that unless their force and manner of Signification were first well observed, there would be very little said clearly and pertinently concerning Knowledge: which being conversant about Truth, had constantly to do with Propositions' (3.9.21). He was particularly concerned with how we can avoid mistakes in thinking and speaking which are due to our using imprecise, confused and unclear words. Men use words 'either to record their own Thoughts for the Assistance of their own Memory; or as it were, to bring out their *Ideas*, and lay them before the view of others' (3.2.2). When a man speaks to another, he does so 'that he may be understood; and the end of Speech is, that those Sounds, as Marks, may make known his *Ideas* to the Hearer' (3.2.8). Thus the importance of identifying the imperfection of words and the abuses of word-users, as well as sketching some of the remedies of both.

The role of language in society, even the notion of language as one of the bonds of society, appears in several of Locke's books. *Two Treatises* speaks of God 'having made Man such a Creature, that, in his own judgment, it was not good for him to be alone, [putting] him under strong Obligations of Necessity, Convenience, and Inclination to drive him into Society' (*T2*, §77). As an aid to this move into society, God also 'fitted him with Understanding and Language' (*ibid.*). The *Essays on the Law of Nature* speaks of 'a certain propensity of nature' urging man to join society and 'to be prepared for the maintenance of society by the gift of speech and through the intercourse of language' (p. 157). *Some Thoughts concerning Education*, which devotes a number of sections to the learning of foreign languages, notes that 'Men learn Languages for the ordinary intercourse of Society and Communication of thoughts in common Life' (§168). Speaking and writing are the ways in which men 'may let their Thoughts into other Mens minds' (*ibid.*).

The notion that language plays an important role in society was not uncommon. It is, for example, given prominence by Hobbes in a chapter on speech. Speech consists, Hobbes writes, 'of *Names* or *Appellations*, and their Connexion; whereby men register their Thoughts; recall them when they are past; and also declare them one to another for mutuall utility and conversation; without which, there had been amongst men, neither Common-wealth, nor Society, nor Contract, nor Peace' (*Leviathan*, Pt I, ch. IV, p. 100). In another passage, Hobbes expresses other views similar to those of Locke. 'The general use of Speech, is to transferre our Mental Discourse, into Verbal; or the Trayne of our Thoughts, into a Trayne of Words; and that for two commodities; whereof one is, the registring of the Consequences of our Thoughts; which being apt to slip out of our memory, and put us to a new labour, may again be recalled, by such words as they were marked by' (*ibid.*, p. 101). He goes on to use the terms 'mark' and 'sign' as Locke does: 'So that the first use of names, is to serve for *Markes*, or *Notes* of remembrance. Another is, when many use the same words, to signifie (by their connexion and order), one to another, what they conceive, or think of each matter.' These marks are called 'signs'. Hobbes also directs attention briefly to various abuses of speech, and he devotes a few paragraphs to names.

From the latter half of the seventeenth century until the end of the eighteenth, there is a plethora of books and treatises on language and what was later called 'linguistics'. Locke's discussion of language is often mentioned in later discussions. (For a comprehensive treatment of the writings on this topic, with some discussion of Locke, see Murray Cohen's *Sensible Words: Linguistic Practice in England, 1640–1785*, 1977.)

law   This is a term that plays an important role in Locke's account of morality and political society. It has a positive, not restrictive, sense: 'For *Law* in its true Notion, is not so much the Limitation as *the direction of a free and intelligent Agent* to his proper Interest, and prescribes no farther than is for the general Good of those under the Law' (*T2*, §57). The end of law is 'not to abolish or restrain, but *to preserve and enlarge Freedom*' (*ibid.*). He explains that the concept of a law is linked with and presupposes a law-maker and rewards and punishments (*Essay*, 1.3.12). The concept of law also carries the notion of obligation and duty (1.4.8). All the features of the concept of a law are found in the law of nature: 'For, in the first place, it is the decree of a superior will, wherein the formal cause of a law appears to consist; in what manner, however, this may become known to mankind is a question perhaps to be discussed later on. Secondly, it lays down what is and what is not to be done, which is the proper function of a law. Thirdly, it binds men, for it contains in itself all that is requisite to create an obligation' (*Essays*, pp. 111–13). The law-maker he has in mind in these passages is God (cf. *Essay*, 1.3.13); he was discussing the claims for innate ideas of morality and of God, but Locke would recognize the general truth of these conceptual connections. Before anyone can understand that he is bound by a law, there are several other bits of knowledge required: (1) 'he must know . . . that there is a law-maker, i.e. some superior power to which he is rightly subject'; (2) he must also know that 'there is some will on the part of that superior power with respect to things to be done by us, that is to say, that the law-maker, whoever he may prove to be, wishes that we do this but leave off that, and demands of us that the conduct of our life should be in accordance with his will' (*Essays*, p. 151). Another conceptual connection Locke identifies is the idea of government with the 'establishment of Society upon certain Rules or Laws, which require Conformity to them' (*Essay*, 4.3.18). It is the laws governing human actions in society, in the state of nature (the pre-civil society), between God and man, and between parents and children, that are discussed by Locke. The threefold distinction made in *Essay* 2.28.7 does not quite cover the variety of laws found in his writings, but it is a general indication of the scope: divine law, civil law and 'The Law of *Opinion* or *Reputation*'.

This last class of laws has worried some readers who have taken it as clashing with Locke's insistence upon God's law or the law of nature as the true measure of right and wrong, of virtue and vice. Some commentators have interpreted this identification of a class of laws based on opinion or reputation as Locke's own view of the basis for morality, despite his clear and unequivocal remark that only when the actions named as virtue or vice 'are co-incident with the *divine Law*' are they really examples of virtue or vice (2.28.10; cf. *Two Tracts*, p. 222, where he says divine law 'is that great rule of right and justice and the eternal foundation of all moral good and evil'). Locke's interest in these various kinds of laws was with describing and recommending rules and laws that do or ought to govern our actions.

Considerable attention is given by Locke to the parent-child relation. In *Some Thoughts*, where he is especially concerned with raising children to become rational, moral persons, he warns parents not to 'so heap *Rules* on their Children' that it becomes 'impossible for the poor little ones to remember a Tenth part of them' (§65). Use as few rules as possible was his advice, 'Make but few *Laws*, but see they be well observed' (*ibid.*). In the chapter on 'Parental Power' in *Two Treatises*, Locke is careful to draw the line between arbitrary, wilful and improper rules and laws imposed upon children (*T*2, §§65–74). The rules or laws relating to children do not seem to fit any of the three kinds of laws distinguished by Locke, although in the background of the parent-child relation are the divine laws, the laws of reason or nature. They may belong with the third class of laws, the laws of opinion, but only when those are consistent with God's laws.

There is another type of law, or another label, mentioned in several places: human laws (2.27.22), laws of mankind (*T*1, §47), laws of the community (*T*2, §§66, 82, 122, 197, 198), or laws of the land (*T*1, §88). These are labels for the laws which are established within a society to cover specific actions, obligations or transactions. Locke had great respect for law, especially for the laws of England. In *Essay* 4.16.10, he cites the specific law about the 'attested Copy of a Record' being good proof, but 'the Copy of a Copy never so well attested, and by never so credible Witnesses, will not be admitted as a proof in Judicature.' In *Some Thoughts*, he recommends young gentlemen to study law by first taking a look at 'our *English* Constitution and Government, in the ancient Books of the *Common Law*' (§187). The history of English law is important for giving us 'the reason of our *Statutes*' (*ibid.*). In specifying young gentlemen to read Cicero, Pufendorf, and Grotius (all of whom wrote on the law) Locke speaks of 'The *general Part of Civil Law* and History', urging the student to 'constantly dwell upon, and never have done with' them (*ibid.*, §186).

Two Treatises stresses the importance of civil law and of government founded on known laws. In entering into society, men have excluded force 'and introduced laws for the preservation of Property, Peace and Unity' (*T2*, §226). Men in the state of nature 'take Sanctuary under the established Laws of Government' (*ibid.*, §122; cf. §131). Civil laws, the laws established by civil government, embody the general customs and historic precedence embedded in the laws and practices of mankind, but civil laws for Locke must also conform to the laws of nature which are God's laws.

laws of nature In his attack against innate practical truths, Locke spoke of justice and the keeping of contracts. He identifies rules of justice with the very nature of humanity (*Essay*, 1.3.2). He goes on to contrast those people who follow these rules for convenience, with those who recognize them as laws of nature. To recognize a rule as a law of nature was to find that law binding on us as humans. The natural law tradition was well accepted by most writers (e.g., those authors Locke recommended young gentlemen to read, Grotius and Pufendorf), although there were some differences about its status and nature. Hobbes had his own peculiar twist to the concept, but in most writers the link is made with reason, morality and God. Locke's early unpublished *Essays on the Law of Nature* opens by asking the question, 'Is There a Rule of Morality, or Law of Nature Given to Us?' (p. 109). His answer is 'yes'. In that essay, he tells his students that the rule or law was known under several names or descriptions.

It was equated with 'that moral good or virtue which the philosophers of former times' searched for (e.g., the Stoics). The law of nature has also been identified as 'right reason, to which everyone who considers himself a human being lays claim' (p. 111). Reason in this context is not the faculty of reasoning, but rather a 'certain definite principle of action from which sprang all virtue and whatever is necessary for the proper moulding of morals'. Locke then gives a summary definition of that law of nature: 'the decree of the divine will discernible by the light of nature and indicating what is and what is not in conformity with rational nature, and for this very reason commanding or prohibiting' (p. 111).

Whatever the motive was for not publishing these lectures (one explanation might lie in the language he used which was very close to, sometimes identical with, that of the defenders of innate truths), it was not any change of mind about there being a law of nature which fits this description. The 1690 *Essay concerning Human Understanding* identified one of the kinds of laws men use to assess moral rectitude as the Divine Law: 'that Law which God has set to the actions of Men, whether promulgated to them by the light of Nature, or the voice of Revelation' (2.28.8). All men, he there says, recognize such a law. Similarly, his critique of Robert Filmer refers to the law of nature as 'the Law of Reason' (*T*1, §101). The second of *Two Treatises* says that 'it is certain there is such a Law, and that too, as intelligible and plain to a rational Creature, and a Studier of that Law, as the positive Laws of Common-wealths' (*T*2, §12). Civil laws are right only to the extent that they are founded on the law of nature. The rules made by the legislative branch of government must 'be conformable to the Law of Nature, i.e. to the Will of God' (*ibid.*, §135).

That Locke firmly believed there to be a law (or laws) of nature, and that it (or they) fits the general description he gives to it, is beyond dispute. What are less easy to determine are the specific information or injunctions prescribed by that law. Unlike positive, civil law, the law of nature is 'unwritten, and so no where to be found but in the minds of Men' (*T*2, §136). This feature of that law would seem to give Locke licence to use it to support whatever claims he wishes to make. He does not give a systematic list of laws that fall under this unwritten law of nature; but with the possible exception of some appeals to what the law says when writing about property, the few citations of natural law found in his works reflect the generally accepted moral rules of his day, even those defended by some of the innatists. Injunctions such as love God, tell the truth, be friendly, feed the hungry are found in the early *Essays*. *Two Treatises* speaks of 'the great Law of Nature, *Who so sheddeth Mans Blood, by Man shall his Blood be shed*' (*T*2, §11). The *Essays on the Law of Nature* lists as precepts of that law: 'sentiments of respect and love for the deity, obedience to superiors, fidelity of character, a friendly disposition, and all the other virtues' (*Essays*, p. 129). The chapter on property in *Two Treatises* refers to the 'original Law of Nature', which governs the beginning of property: what any man's labour has 'taken out of the hands of Nature' becomes that man's property (*T*2, §29). The law of nature also tells us what the limits are to property-acquisition: what I can take advantage of before it spoils (§31). There may be some special pleading in these property-acquisition examples of what the law of nature sanctions and commands, but the central feature of that law for Locke is its clear link with God, reason and morality.

Letters on toleration Toleration was a topic that interested Locke throughout his life, toleration by governments of religious practices and beliefs, toleration between religious sects for differences of beliefs and differing interpretations of Scripture. Locke had in fact little tolerance for intolerance, especially for those Christian prelates and church officials who tried to impose doctrines and dogmas which were not found in the Bible. He was strongly opposed to the use of force as a means of bringing people to the 'true religion'. True religion, he insists at the beginning of the first of four tracts he wrote on toleration, 'is not instituted in order to the erecting an external pomp, nor to the obtaining of ecclesiastical dominion, nor to the exercising of compulsive force; but to the regulating of men's lives according to the rules of virtue and piety' (*A Letter concerning Toleration*, 1689, in *Works*, vi. 6; translation of the Latin original, *Epistola de tolerantia*).

The subject of religious toleration was much discussed and debated in the 1680s and 1690s, especially in Holland. Locke lived for five years there between 1683 and 1688, most of that time in disguise and in hiding from what was believed by the English king to be subversive activity while Locke was secretary to Shaftesbury. He may even have been suspected of aiding dissident groups in Holland, prior to William and Mary's taking the English throne. Political, not religious, persecution was what Locke feared for himself. Holland had been the scene much earlier of religious clashes and persecution. Anyone writing on religious toleration in that country in the latter part of the seventeenth century would do so against that historical background. By the 1680s, Holland was in fact a refuge for many who fled religious intolerance in other countries. Holland was also the home of a group of theologians who stressed, as Locke was to do, simple, undogmatic beliefs: the religion and church of Christ was how they sometimes characterized their interpretation. They were known as the Remonstrants. (For a clear, brief account of this background, see E.S. de Beer's note, *Corr.* ii. 648–51.)

While living in Holland, Locke made a number of close friends; one in particular, the famous theologian Philip Limborch, was intimately involved with Locke's first publication on the topic of toleration. Probably written in 1685–6, Locke's *Epistola de tolerantia* was published at Gouda in 1689, with the help of Limborch. No author's name appeared anywhere, but the title page carried a long series of letters which were code for 'Limborch' the dedicatee, and 'Locke' the author. Only Locke and Limborch knew what those letters stood for. It was several years before Locke's authorship was discovered; even then, he refused to admit he was the author until a few months before his death in 1704. Strangely, he and Limborch even in their correspondence after Locke returned to England kept up the pretence that neither knew who the author was. There are at least ten letters between them in 1689 in which Limborch reports on the appearance of the *Epistola*, Locke expresses interest in having a copy,

Limborch sends him several copies (bound and unbound), reports on French and Dutch translations under way or planned, and details the keen interest in and speculation in Holland about the author and possible candidates (see *Corr.*, 1131, 1134, 1146, 1158, 1172, 1178, 1182, 1184, 1187; iii. passim; for a detailed account of this phenomenon and the various editions of the *Epistola*, see Raymond Klibansky's edition and J.W. Gough's translation, *Epistola de tolerantia*, Oxford, 1968).

Gough's 'translation' is a fairly close following of the original translation made by William Popple. The interest in toleration is evidenced by the fact that the first edition of Popple's translation in 1689 was followed by a second in 1690. The eighteenth century saw several translations into French and Dutch, and a second edition of the Latin in 1705. Jonas Proast attacked the *Epistola* in 1690, in his *The Argument of the 'Letter concerning Toleration' Briefly Consider'd and Answer'd*. Locke replied to Proast in the same year, his *Second Letter concerning Toleration*, to which Proast responded in 1691. Locke's *Third Letter for Toleration* (1692) was yet another response. Locke even wrote a fourth reply which was only published after his death in *Posthumous Works* (1706). The persistence with which Locke went over Proast's arguments for using force, the force of government, to bring people to the 'true religion', testifies to the strong feelings he had about the subject. The *Third Letter* is much the longest of the four; both it and the *Second Letter* are signed at the end 'Philanthropus', a further protection for his identity. These replies are written as if by a third party to the author of the *Letters* and to Proast.

In some of his private letters to Limborch (e.g., no. 1120), Locke reports on bills before the English parliament on toleration. After the Toleration Act was passed in May 1689, Locke wrote to Limborch: 'No doubt you will have heard before this that Toleration has now at last been established by law in our country. Not perhaps so wide in scope as might be wished for by you and those like you who are true Christians and free from ambition or envy. Still, it is something to have progressed so far' (*Corr.* 1147; iii. 633, de Beer's translation of Latin original). Locke's anonymous exchange with Proast reflects his concerns that the Toleration Act had not gone far enough. His four *Letters* give the details and the rationale for a stronger protection to toleration, and for wider toleration. The second and third of his letters are methodically written, somewhat repetitious (as such exchanges are), and not very stimulating. It is the first *Letter*, the *Epistola*, which is most interesting, the most valuable for a ringing statement of the need for toleration and the evils of intolerance.

The *Epistola* opens with an 'appeal to the consciences of those that persecute, torment, destroy, and kill other men upon pretence of religion, whether they do it out of friendship and kindness towards them, or no' (in *Works*, vi. 6). Locke might believe they acted in these ways out of kindness and concern, were these same 'fiery zealots' to correct in the same way 'their friends and familiar acquaintances, for the manifest sins they commit against the precepts of the Gospel' (*ibid.*). But he finds it difficult to believe they act as they do 'out of a principle of charity, as they pretend, and love to men's souls, that they deprive them of their estates, maim them with corporal punishments, starve and torment them in noisome prisons, and in the end even take away their lives' (*ibid.*, pp. 6–7). To compel men by 'fire and sword to profess certain doctrines, and conform to this or that exterior worship without any regard had unto their morals' is just a cover for trying to get people to join their particular party or assembly (p. 8). A danger is that under pretence of concern for the public good and the observation of laws, persecution and 'unchristian cruelty' will be used. Pretence of religion is no better justification for such actions; both may hide 'libertinism and licentiousness'. It is important to be clear about the boundaries between religion and civil government; the separation of church and state must be observed. The state has nothing to do with the salvation of souls, nor do religious sects have the right to force others to conform to their beliefs and practices. Any spontaneous society (which a church or sect is) has a 'fundamental and immutable right' to remove 'any of its members who transgress the rules of its institution; but it cannot, by the accession of any new members, acquire any right of jurisdiction over those that are not joined with it' (*ibid.*, p. 18).

The province of civil government, of the magistrate, is outward things such as property and possessions, not inward beliefs. The civil magistrate does not have the power to 'enforce by law, either in his own church, or much less in another, the use of any rites or ceremonies whatsoever in the worship of God' (p. 29). For Locke, there is a double reason for this proscription. One reason is that a church is a free society; the other and more fundamental reason is that 'whatsoever is practised in the worship of God is only so far justifiable as it is believed by those that practise it to be acceptable unto him.' Religion is a matter of 'the inward persuasion of the mind' (p. 11). A better-known statement of this principle occurs in a later passage: 'I may grow rich by an art that I take not delight in; I may be cured of some disease by remedies that I have not faith in; but I cannot be saved by a religion that I distrust, and by a worship that I abhor' (p. 28). He goes on to distinguish the outward form and rules of worship from the doctrines and articles of faith, taking up arguments defending the right of the civil magistrate to dictate or control either of these. Among the doctrines and articles of faith, some are practical, others speculative (p. 39). 'The magistrate ought not to forbid the preaching or professing of any speculative opinions in any church, because they have no manner of relation to the civil rights of subjects' (p. 40). For example, 'If a Roman Catholic believe that to be really the body of Christ, which another man calls bread, he does no injury thereby to his neighbour.' Or, 'If a heathen doubt of both Testaments, he is not therefore to be punished as a pernicious citizen.' The government's role is the protection of each person's property from encroachment of others; that is the reason people join a civil society.

Broad as Locke's tolerance was, it did not extend to those who deny the being of God. He seems to have practical moral reasons for withholding toleration from atheists: 'Promises, covenants, and oaths, which are the bonds of human society, can have no hold upon an atheist. The taking away of God, though but even in thought, dissolves all. Besides, also, those that by their atheism undermine and destroy all religion, can have no pretence of religion whereupon to challenge the privilege of a toleration' (p. 47).

letters to Stillingfleet   Locke wrote three replies to Edward Stillingfleet, the Bishop of Worcester, only the first of which carries the word 'letter' in its title. All three are written in the fashion of the time, as open public letters. Stillingfleet included a chapter in his *A Discourse in Vindication of the Doctrine of the Trinity* (1697) attacking a book by John Toland, *Christianity Not Mysterious* (1696). Toland's book used many Lockean terms and doctrines; it was considered heretical in relation to the standard theological doctrines accepted by most divines. Stillingfleet associated Locke's *Essay* with Toland's views and lumped Locke and Toland together under the heading, 'the new men of ideas'. Locke could not ignore an attack by a major figure of the church. His first response was *A Letter to the Right Reverend Edward Ld. Bishop of Worcester, concerning Some Passages Relating to Mr. Locke's Essay of Humane Understanding: In a Late Discourse of his Lordship's, in Vindication of the Trinity* (1697). Locke complained that he had been unfairly and inappropriately brought into a controversy over the Trinity, when his *Essay* says nothing about that theological doctrine. But Stillingfleet saw in several of the doctrines of the *Essay* threats to, if not rejections of, metaphysical notions that he took to be fundamental for a number of theological doctrines. What Locke said about our idea of substance and essence seemed to the Bishop to cast doubt on the reality of substance. Locke protested that he wrote only about the *idea* that we have of substance. The Bishop thought Locke made all knowledge dependent upon clear and distinct ideas, that on Locke's account knowledge was restricted to ideas, that we could not know whether there is an external world; and Locke's special concept of the person remained a mystery to the Bishop. In his *Letter*, Locke tried to answer and clarify all

the charges and problems Stillingfleet found in his *Essay*, all the while
insisting that he wrote that work 'without any thought of the controversy
between Trinitarians and Unitarians' (in *Works*, iv. 68).

The Bishop answered Locke's *Letter* in the same year, going over much
the same ground again. Locke responded with *Mr. Locke's Reply to the Right
Reverend the Lord Bishop of Worcester's Answer to His Letter* (1697), to which
the Bishop wrote another reply, *The Bishop of Worcester's Answer to Mr.
Locke's Second Letter* (1698). In that reply, the Bishop complained that
Locke went on too long, wrote too much in debating the issues. Perhaps
intentionally, Locke then wrote doubly long, *Mr. Locke's Reply to the Right
Reverend the Lord Bishop of Worcester's Answer to His Second Letter* (1699). The
long subtitle to this third reply gives an indication of the topics covered
in the whole exchange: 'Wherein, besides Other Incident Matters, What
His Lordship Has Said concerning Certainty by Reason, Certainty by
Ideas, and Certainty by Faith; the Resurrection of the same Body; the
Immateriality of the Soul; the Inconsistency of Mr. Locke's Notions with
the Articles of the Christian Faith, and their Tendency to Scepticism, Is
Examined'. Locke did not mention here the doctrine of the Trinity, about
which Stillingfleet kept trying to force Locke to say whether he accepted
it or not. By the time of his third reply, Locke was getting irritated and
impatient; his language is more sarcastic and biting. Towards the end of
this long response, after trying through the previous replies as well to
show the Bishop that what he claimed to find in Locke's *Essay* was not
there, Locke remarks: 'My lord, the words you bring out of my book are
so often different from those I read in the places which you refer to, that
I am sometimes ready to think you have got some strange copy of it,
whereof I know nothing, since it so seldom agrees with mine' (in *Works*,
iv. 406–7). The very last page of this third reply, and Locke's final
comment, is even more satirical: 'Before I conclude, it is fit I take notice
of the obligation I have to you for the pains you have been at about my
Essay, which I conclude could not have been any way so effectually
recommended to the world as by your manner of writing against it. And
since your lordship's sharp sight, so carefully employed for its corrections,
has, as I humbly conceive, found no faults in it, which your lordship's
great endeavours this way have made out to be really there; I hope I may
presume it will pass the better in the world' (*ibid.*, p. 498).

liberty The issue of freedom or necessity, the question: 'is man free or
are his actions determined (even predetermined)?', had been hotly
debated prior to Locke's turning his attention to that topic. The issue had
metaphysical, moral and theological implications. The wide scope of that
debate is indicated by the subtitle of Hobbes's tract, *Of Liberty and Necessity*

(1654): 'A Treatise, Wherein All Controversy concerning Predestination, Election, Free Will, Grace, Merit, Reprobation, etc., is Fully Decided and Cleared'. Locke's discussion of this topic is a good example of conceptual analysis. He placed that discussion in a chapter on power (*Essay*, 2.21), indicating the metaphysical (ontological) roots of the question: where does causal power lie, in finite agents or in God only? Power was an even broader concept in Locke's account of reality, MATTER itself having for him specific POWERS.

In that chapter (2.21), Locke was not primarily concerned with defending a position, but it is clear from numerous passages that he firmly believes that we as moral agents are free, that we do control many of our actions. His primary goal may be seen as a clarification of such concepts as freedom, will, power, necessity, power, and agency. He announces early in that chapter that it is evident 'That we find in our selves a *Power* to begin or forbear, continue or end several actions of our minds, and motions of our Bodies, barely by a thought or preference of the mind ordering, or as it were commanding the doing or not doing such or such a particular action' (*Essay*, 2.21.5). Liberty just is that power to act or not to act 'according to the preference of the Mind'; necessity is the lack of such a power (2.21.12). Such power belongs to agents, the power of acting or not acting (2.21.23–25). When we have that power, we are free. The locus of that power in persons is said to be the will, the will being nothing but a power to prefer or choose. That power or ability is really the ability of the actor, the agent. Sometimes Locke identifies the will as a power 'in the Mind to direct that operative Faculty of a Man' (2.21.29), but it is improper to ask, as many writers were doing, is the will free? The will just is a power men have. The debate should not be cast in the language of the freedom of the will; the proper question is, are we free? Locke was critical of faculty talk in general because, in debates of this sort, it tended to turn the faculty (e.g., the will) into an agent. Nevertheless, he does frequently describe aspects of man, rather than man himself, as being the agent. Some passages speak of the *mind* acting rather than the man or person. It is, he says at one point, 'the Mind that operates and exerts these Powers; it is the Man that does that Action; it is the Agent that has this power' (2.21.19).

This distinction between man and agent reflects Locke's special concept of the person and his distinction between the physical and moral man, between man and PERSON. As a man, I have various powers, e.g., of thinking, choosing, dancing, singing (2.21.18), or the power of moving parts of my body (2.21.48). Of particular relevance to moral man, to the person, is our ability to control our desires. One form of necessity sometimes cited is being under the sway of passions and desires. In his work on education, Locke goes to some lengths to urge the tutor and parents to train the child to ignore or control by reason his desires. Some desires, of course, are useful guides: the desire for pleasure (and happiness) and the avoidance of pain. These desires are part of the nature of man, but we must be selective in what we count as pleasure and happiness. Reason and deliberation must be able to decide what actions we ought to perform. One of the powers we have is the power to suspend 'any particular desire, and keep it from determining the *will*, and engaging us in action' (2.21.50). He goes on to explain that 'the determination of the *will* upon enquiry is *following the direction of that Guide*', the guide being some rule or law discerned by reason. A 'free agent' is defined as one who has 'a power to act, or not to act according as such determination directs'. He hastens to remark that this determination of the will by some guide (a set of rules) does not curtail the power that is liberty.

It was just this point on which much of the debate centred: does the determination of the will by rules or laws make the will or agent less free, or not free at all? What is the nature of that determination? Is it a form of causation, does it result from habituation, are reasons for acting also causes? Hobbes tangled with Bishop Bramhall over this question, Hobbes insisting that there is no escape from causation, even for agents. Subsequent debates over freedom and necessity in the eighteenth century (e.g., by Hume, Leibniz) continued to puzzle over this question. Kant also struggled to find some way to fit human agency into a world of universal causality. Locke did stress the importance of habituating the child to virtuous behaviour, but he also believed that habit was just a prelude to rational control and understanding. When reason takes charge, it is the person who acts; the agency belongs to the person or man. Self-determination is possible, Locke believed: it is the goal of education. These issues continue to be discussed today.

Liberty for Locke also had a central role to play in his political writings. In *Two Treatises*, discussions of freedom or liberty are often linked to the concept of person. The state of nature, the pre-civil society, is described as a state of liberty but not as a state of licence. The law of nature is the rule and guide for action in that state. Locke even characterized liberty in the state of nature as 'an uncontroleable Liberty, to dispose of his Person or Possessions', excluding suicide (*T*2, §6). Liberty becomes part of man's possessions, along with life and property: the function of civil government is the protection of all of these possessions (*T*2, §§87, 123). Every man is born to 'A *Right of Freedom to his Person*' (§§190, 194); natural liberty is 'to be free from any Superior Power on Earth', not free from God or from the constraints or guides of the law of nature or, in civil society, the positive laws. He insists that being free from the restraints and violence of others requires laws. Liberty is freedom 'to dispose, and order, as he lists, his Person, Actions, Possessions, and his whole Property, within the Allowance of those Laws under which he is' (§57; see also §§59, 63).

Locke also devotes some sections of *Two Treatises* to the freedom of children. They are born free as they are born rational, but both freedom and rationality have to be developed. Parents and tutor are the guides for the determination of his will until the child acquires the reason necessary 'to instruct him in that Law he is to govern himself by, and make him know how far he is left to the freedom of his own will' (*T*2, §63). Unrestrained liberty without the guidance of reason would reduce the child to the level of a brute.

logic Logic in the seventeenth and eighteenth centuries was in a transition period. Traditional school logic, the logic studied and used by students at universities, was Aristotelian. The many logic books written towards the end of the sixteenth and first half of the seventeenth centuries were designed more as manuals for instruction and use than as new contributions to the theory of logic or dialectic. The forms and divisions of logic became fixed, standard topics were rehearsed, the syllogism was always given prominence. At the instructional level, the significance of logic, especially of the syllogistic form, had become reduced to use in debate. In fact, examinations at Oxford and Cambridge universities, even well into the eighteenth century, required students to defend propositions *pro* and *con*, employing the mood and figure of syllogisms in oral debates. Questions of the truth or falsity of the propositions they were asked to defend were ignored. Cleverness, skill in scoring against one's debating opponent, turned logic into a game; its reputation as a serious study was greatly diminished.

As Descartes before him, so Locke rejected formal syllogistic logic as artificial, useless and irrelevant to knowledge. Francis Bacon's plea for a logic of discovery had little effect on the university curriculum. Nor did the more radical changes in the concept and content of logic embodied in the Port Royal logic of Arnauld and Nicole (which was influenced by Descartes) affect the practice in the schools. The very title of that Port Royal logic indicates its direction: *Logic, or The Art of Thinking*. The syllogism was not ignored in that logic but it takes its place in part three, after the two preceding parts on ideas and judgements. The art of *thinking*, not the art of *debating*: that shift in emphasis opened the way for others to begin the examination and study of the operations of the mind. Locke's *Essay* was a British application of that shift in the concept of logic.

The *Essay* also contains Locke's criticism of the older logics, especially their use in instruction (see esp. 4.17.4). The ability to think, reason, make judgements does not require a knowledge of the formal rules of logic. All of us get along quite well without the help of Aristotle. Not that we do not make mis-judgements, get confused by ambiguous and imprecise use of words, accept false principles uncritically. What Locke tried to do in that chapter, and also in Book Three on language, was to sketch a logic of use that would be based upon the natural association of ideas and conceptual connections. He recognized that he gave his readers only a sketch, a few suggestions, for such a natural logic unencumbered by artificial rules. He cites Richard Hooker's call for someone to provide 'the right helps to art and learning' (4.17.7). He does not claim to have answered that call but he does hope that his criticisms of the syllogism and his few brief examples of natural reasoning around conceptual connections will inspire others.

> It is sufficient for me, if by a Discourse, perhaps, something out of the way, I am sure as to me wholly new, and unborrowed, I shall have given Occasion to others, to cast about for new Discoveries, and to seek in their own Thoughts, for those *right Helps of Art*, which will scarce be found, I fear, by those who servilely confine themselves to the Rules and Dictates of others. (4.17.7)

Locke did go further towards developing a new logic in his *Conduct*, a work which starts with Bacon's call and then offers many informal remarks on method and ways of seeking knowledge. That work is a very important source for understanding Locke's notion of logic or the art of thinking. His critical attitude towards traditional logic in relation to teaching is present in his *Some Thoughts*, where he writes against having children debate in logical mood and figure. He also disparages the use of rules for thinking and reasoning, and he reminds parents that there are more important subjects than Latin and logic (see §§75, 94, 147, 166, 188, 189, 194). There were also a few eighteenth-century British logics that followed Locke's general format of including analyses of idea-acquisition and the various mental operations used in thinking.

M

matter The word 'matter' stands for an idea distinct from the idea of body, but matter and body are not in reality distinct: where there is matter, there is body, and where body, matter (*Essay*, 3.10.15). In this section, Locke is illustrating the ambiguity of words, especially as used by many writers. His clarification of the difference of meaning in these two words defines 'body' as 'a solid extended figured Substance', and 'matter' as 'a partial and more confused Conception, it seeming to me to be used for the Substance and Solidity of Body, without taking in its Extension and Figure' (*ibid.*). The latter two properties are necessary for particular bodies. A more formal definition of 'matter' is 'a solid Substance, which is every where the same, every where uniform.' There are many bodies but only one kind of matter composing them. The matter of bodies was, on the existing theory Locke accepted, corpuscular.

That generally accepted theory of matter usually included saying matter was passive and inert, incapable of self-motion. Corpuscularians insisted that God is the only active cause. Matter has the *passive* power of resisting change, but no *active* power. Without explicitly announcing he is doing so, Locke alters or modifies this standard view of passive matter. It was an alteration that went more or less unnoticed. He says that the insensible corpuscles are the active POWERS of matter (4.3.25). We can almost say that matter for Locke was essentially power.

One power Locke's matter does not have is thought. Matter is, he says, 'bare and incogitative' and incapable of producing thought (4.10.10). Warning against the uncritical use of general principles, Locke refers to 'that Principle of some of the old Philosophers, That all is Matter, and that there is nothing else' (4.12.4). What consequences such a principle, when taken as certain and indubitable, leads to can be seen in 'the Writings of some that have revived it again in our days'. Hobbes may have been one of the writers Locke had in mind. Cudworth had recently given a detailed and exhaustive historical account of the old philosophers who followed that principle (see his *True Intellectual System*, 1678). This claim that all is matter was important for Locke and Cudworth because it had not only metaphysical but theological consequences with which they disagreed. The metaphysical consequence was that there would be no room for thought or immaterial minds in a world of only matter. The theological consequence was either that there is no God or that God is material. Even if room could be found for God in such a world, the eternity of matter would detract from God's power, if not render Him useless.

Essay 4.10 on the knowledge and existence of God is Locke's concentrated refutation of what he refers to as 'this *corporeal System*' (4.10.17). It is in that chapter that Locke conclusively shows that he did not accept the notion that matter can think, a notion which he had briefly entertained earlier in that work (*see* THINKING MATTER). Sometimes Locke writes about *bare* matter, matter without motion: e.g., a pebble is 'a dead, inactive lump' (4.10.10). Such matter lacks the ability to add motion to its qualities. What qualities does 'bare' matter have? It is described as 'purely Matter', as if matter with motion added would be more than matter. What he means is that motion is not necessary for matter. With matter that is in motion, either 'the Motion it has, must also be from Eternity, or else be produced, and added to matter by some other Being more powerful than Matter' (*ibid.*). Does bare matter have *any* power?

Corpuscular matter, the matter of bodies that affects our senses and that brings about changes in other bodies, has primary qualities, among them being motion and rest. Even a simple grain of wheat and its parts each have solidity, extension, figure and mobility. At the insensible level, the parts of matter have these same primary qualities. Mobility is the power or ability to move. Is this power of mobility part of the nature of each corpuscle? If so, presumably it must have been added to bare matter by God. The same may be true for extension and figure, since Locke distinguishes between matter and body, the former referring only to solidity, to a solid substance. There is not of course such a substance really existing, since matter and body go together and are inseparable. Bare matter is a stage in creation, a stage at which God had to decide what other qualities besides solidity to add to that substance. In creating this substance, God creates a solid substance, solidity being for Locke the defining property of matter, not extension (*contra* Descartes). Extension, figure and motion are added properties, properties which God adds to what he has already at that stage created. The active powers of matter would seem then to be powers added to, not part of the nature of, matter. But an added (or, as he sometimes writes, 'superadded') power is still a power. Thus, the corpuscular matter of bodies possesses powers.

maxims *Essay* 4.7.1 remarks that 'There are a sort of Propositions, which under the name of *Maxims* and *Axioms*, have passed for Principles of Science.' The 'science' referred to is any organized body of knowledge and, for those who defended maxims, knowledge that is certain. Such maxims, it was claimed, are self-evident, a property which led many to say they were innate (innate speculative truths). In this chapter, Locke does not want to reopen the debate on innate truths (he gave his thorough critique of them in Book One). His objective here is to explore the claim that these self-evident principles influence and guide all knowledge. The claim that knowledge is derived from basic principles such as identity ('what is, is') or contradiction ('no thing can both be and not be') was prominent in Locke's century. One of his early critics, John Sergeant, defended this claim in a long book, *The Method to Science* (1696). Another critic, Henry Lee (*Anti-Scepticism*, 1702), argued a similar though more sophisticated case. The best-known critic of Locke, Leibniz, dealt at great length with Locke's rejection of maxims, and his rejection of formal logic (*Nouveaux Essais*, completed in 1704 but only published after Leibniz's death).

Locke understood the appeal to logical maxims for a source of knowledge as saying we start with principles and then derive from them in some way a bit of knowledge. Some writers, such as Sergeant and the defenders of innate principles, did write as if such was their claim. But the more sophisticated appeals to basic, primitive truths (Leibniz called them 'identical propositions') as having a role in knowledge referred to what is presupposed by certain specific claims or, as with Leibniz, about the formal order or formal structure of knowledge. These writers were not describing how in fact we acquire knowledge or make discoveries; the natural order of knowledge is not the logical order.

Such logical matters were of no concern to Locke; they were just another aspect of the old logics which he rejected also as not aiding the acquisition of knowledge. Locke's interest was with a description of the actual processes of the mind in perception, reasoning, memory, forming judgements. We reason and draw conclusions without the help of the syllogism, we acquire information about the world and ourselves through experience and careful observation. Moreover, logical maxims do not have a corner on the market for self-evidence; many propositions and truths are self-evident.

Locke does not just dismiss maxims: he goes into great detail about what they may be good for and where they have not been responsible for knowledge (4.7.11). His final remark is that where we have clear and determined ideas, maxims are irrelevant, and where we substitute maxims for unclear ideas, they are dangerous and lead us astray (4.7.20).

medicine Of the many subjects that interested Locke and occupied his time and attention – religion, morality, education, economics, politics, toleration, science – medicine is probably the most pervasive and long-lasting. Of course, religion and morality were dominant interests, too, but had he not been led into the political arena, albeit behind the scenes, by his association with Shaftesbury, Locke would probably have been a full-time practising physician. He attended the lectures of physiologists, anatomists, and chemists at Oxford, he read extensively in related areas, took copious notes that filled journals and notebooks, recorded recipes for cures and pharmaceutical recommendations, and built up associations with several doctors in Oxford and, later, elsewhere. He tried to bypass the normal curriculum requirements for a Doctor of Medicine degree (the MD), but that failed, or he decided not to pursue that possibility.

His first medical notebooks date from 1657 and 1659. He eventually filled numerous notebooks and made many entries in his journals relating to medical matters. Chambers, in the entry for 'medicine' in his *Cyclopaedia* (1728), remarks that after Harvey, medicine was 'free from the Tyranny of any sect, and is improved by the sure Discoveries in Anatomy, Chemistry, Physics, Botany, Mechanics, etc.'. Locke's interests were in all these areas. His friendship with Robert Boyle extended his knowledge of chemistry, especially as it related to medicine. Other doctors and scientists with whom Locke worked, corresponded or consulted include Willis, Lower, David Thomas, the famous Dr Sydenham. This last-named was a practising doctor with whom Locke worked and whose advice he sought frequently as he came across problems with his own patients. There are some writings in his hand which are probably Sydenham's ideas mainly, but these may well reflect Locke's own thoughts. Even late in life, while living with the Mashams, Locke apparently had a small medical practice in the local village. Throughout his life, friends sought his medical advice, he attended others, and prescribed for many. His most famous patient was Shaftesbury: Locke was involved in an operation that Shaftesbury said saved his life.

So while we cannot quite use the title 'Doctor Locke' in the absence of a formal MD degree, we can say that he was recognized as a medical man with good knowledge and an effective practice, although on a small scale. The details of this fascinating side of Locke can be found in Kenneth Dewhurst, *John Locke: Physician and Philosopher* (1963); in the standard biography of Locke by Maurice Cranston (1957); and in chapters I and II of François Duchesneau's, *L'Empirisme de Locke* (1973).

mind   None of Locke's books has the word 'mind' in the title. His *Essay* is about the understanding. The contemplated added chapter to that book was an essay on the conduct of the understanding, on how to use it properly in the service of truth and knowledge. His work on education, *Some Thoughts concerning Education*, is an extended set of instructions and advice on forming the mind of the child. The understanding *is* mentioned occasionally in that work, but it is the mind which the tutor and parents are concerned to form and develop. The traits or tempers of the child's mind must be accepted, controlled, turned to proper use. Locke's detailed account of these natural traits constitutes what he calls the '*Physiognomy of the Mind*' (*ST*, §101). The children's minds should be made 'supple and pliant, to what their Parents Reason advises them' (*ST*, §112; cf. §34). The child's mind is said to have thoughts and ideas, and frightful images sometimes occur there (e.g., *ST*, §§136, 138). For educational purposes, a sound body is as important as a sound mind, so attention is given in *Some Thoughts* to the health of both.

References to the mind in the *Essay* are about equal in number to those to the understanding. Both mind and the understanding have ideas and thoughts; both are active in performing certain operations, although the mind may be assigned more functions than the understanding. It would be difficult to extract from the *Essay* any clear distinction between the mind and the understanding. Sometimes, but by no means always, the understanding is a faculty of the mind. More often it is used interchangeably with mind. Ideas usually are located in the mind; it is the mind that enlarges, abstracts, considers, infers, concludes, but the understanding also, in certain passages, is assigned these same tasks. The mind is a source of many powers, as well as being the subject in the white paper or blank tablet analogy. The mind knows, perceives and is aware. Sometimes Locke (and other writers at this time) writes as if the mind, not the person, does these things. The tendency was to assign specific tasks to particular faculties of the mind, overlooking the fact that the person is the agent of thinking and acting.

There is not in Locke's writings what we would recognize as a 'philosophy' or 'theory' of mind, although the ingredients for some of our concerns in that area can be found, primarily in the *Essay*. Care must be taken, however, not to force some concepts or issues of later philosophers on to Locke's text. Locke was not much concerned with the mind-body problem, unlike Descartes, Malebranche or Leibniz. He accepted a causal theory of perception while admitting that he did not know how ideas or thoughts can be caused by physical and physiological processes. His interest was in describing the workings of the mind in sensing, perceiving, thinking and willing. A fixed vocabulary for such psychological description was lacking, so Locke had to use metaphor and analogy as well as new words in his account of the mind. In constructing that vocabulary, mind gets mixed in with other features of the general cognitive processes he described (*see also* UNDERSTANDING; FACULTIES).

miracles In a short *Discourse of Miracles*, written in the last years of his
life, Locke defines a miracle as 'a sensible operation, which, being above
the comprehension of the spectator, and in his opinion contrary to the
established course of nature, is taken by him to be divine' (in *Works*, ix.
256). Being contrary to the established course of nature is also rendered
as 'surpasses the force of nature in the established, steady laws of causes
and effects' (*ibid.*). He distinguishes between the *spectator*, 'He that is
present at the fact', and the *believer*, 'he that believes the history of the
fact'. The believer, Locke suggests, 'puts himself in the place of the
spectator'. Locke admits that what is in fact a miracle is rather uncertain
because it depends on the opinion of the spectator. What may be taken
to be a miracle by one person, may not seem to be so to another. A
consequence of the spectator-dependent definition is that some reports of
miracles may be of events that have 'nothing extraordinary or supernatural in them' (*ibid.*, p. 257). In the definition, Locke includes the
phrase, 'is taken to be divine', but he seems to allow for the possibility of
some non-divine miracles. His discussion focuses on those miracles that
are revealed by God.

How does a spectator determine whether some event he takes to be
contrary to the established course of nature is the work of God? Locke's
answer is tied to his account of REVELATION. The quick answer is that the
messenger bringing the word of God must have some 'credentials given
him by God himself' (*ibid.*). Miracles of the sort that interest Locke *are*
the credentials, but those miracles presuppose 'one only true God' (*ibid.*,
p. 258). The various miracles of Jesus reported in the Bible (calming the
waters, walking on water, curing a man with palsy, giving sight to a man
born blind) are signs of his being a messenger from God (p. 259). It may
take some spectators of such events several experiences before they are
convinced of the divinity of the messenger. In other instances, divine signs
may compete with other events that seem to surpass the laws of nature,
e.g., the deceptions of magicians. The spectator may be hard-pressed to
differentiate between magical and divine powers. The signs of greater
power convince.

> The producing of serpents, blood, and frogs, by the Egyptian sorcerers and
> by Moses, could not to the spectators but appear equally miraculous: which
> of the pretenders then had their mission from God, and the truth on their
> side, could not have been determined, if the matter rested there. But when
> Moses's serpent eat up theirs, when he produced lice, which they could not,
> the decision was easy. (*ibid.*, p. 269)

As well, the number and variety of Jesus's miracles confirm their 'extraordinary divine Power' (*ibid.*). Locke expresses confidence that God has taken care that 'no pretended revelation should stand in competition with what is truly divine.'

In his *Paraphrases of St. Paul's Epistles*, Locke glosses the text about miracles as 'what the spirit has revealed and demonstrated of it in the old testament and by the power of god accompanying it with miraculous operations' (*Paraphrases*, p. 172; cf. p. 237). In his *Reasonableness of Christianity*, Locke refers to Jesus's miracles as the way of convincing men that he was the Messiah (in *Works*, vii. 18–19). The early *Essays on the Law of Nature* opens by referring to God showing himself in the 'fixed course of nature now' and 'by the frequent evidence of miracles in time past' (p. 109). There is also some extended discussion of miracles in his *A Third Letter for Toleration*.

Locke's *Discourse of Miracles* was written after reading William Fleetwood's *An Essay on Miracles* (1701), and Benjamin Hoadly's response to Fleetwood in a *Letter to Mr. Fleetwood* (1702). Writing to his cousin, Peter King, shortly before his death, Locke refers to that *Discourse* and the occasion of his writing it: 'A learned friend or two as well as your self that have seen it were mightily for publishing of it. If upon serious consideration you and some other of my judicious friends think it may be of use to the Christian Religion, and not unseasonable at this time, and fit for the publique, For it being writ for my own satisfaction I never went beyond the first draught, you may doe with it as you think good' (*Corr.* 3647; viii. 413). The topic of miracles continued to be discussed throughout the eighteenth century, even though reason tended to overtake reliance on miracles in the writings of many of the leading figures. In the seventeenth century, Cudworth's *True Intellectual System* (1678) gave much attention to the topic. The miraculous for Cudworth is some event that is above nature, but some miracles are of a higher order than others. Those performed by Moses and Jesus fit the latter sort. In general, for Cudworth there are two main kinds of miracles. (1) Those events that 'could not be done by any *Ordinary* and *Natural Causes*' (p. 706). These events are supernatural but God could permit them to be done naturally. 'Naturally' turns out to mean 'the *Ordinary and Natural Powers of other Invisible Created Spirits, Angels* or *Daemons*'. (2) The second kind of miracle is those that are 'above the *Powers* of all Second *Causes*, or any *Natural Created Being*' (p. 707). This second kind can only be done by God. Cudworth also mentions Egyptian sorcerers and magicians.

A few years earlier than Cudworth, Edward Stillingfleet, who was to become Locke's main protagonist after 1690, devoted several chapters of his *Origines Sacrae* (1662) to miracles. The course of nature may be altered and things caused which are beyond the power of inferior causes (8th edn, 1709, p. 160). The term 'miracles' does not refer to 'mere Jugglers and impostures, whereby the Eyes of Men are deceiv'd'. In themselves, miracles are contrary to or above the course of nature. A true miracle is a production of something out of nothing (p. 161). He also contrasts the greater power of Christ's miracles with those of others and he stresses the importance of credentials indicating a divine origin (p. 164). He considers miracles to be matters of fact, in the sense that they are seen by many people, just as we see other events (pp.180–9). Chapter X is devoted to the differences between true and false miracles. The example of rod and serpent cited by Locke appears here: Moses's rod that turned into a serpent 'swallowed up' the rod-serpent of Pharaoh's magicians. He also refers to Moses turning dust into lice. His conclusion from these examples: 'Thus we see in the case of *Moses* how evident it was that there was a power above all power of *Magic* which did appear in Moses' (p. 225).

John Toland also devotes some attention to miracles in his *Christianity Not Mysterious* (1696), following the usual definition: '*A Miracle then is some Action exceeding all humane Power, and which the Laws of Nature cannot perform by their ordinary Operations*' (p. 150). But Toland, who like Locke was defending the reasonableness of Christianity, insists that the miraculous action 'must be something in it self intelligible and possible, tho the manner of doing it be extraordinary'.

In the eighteenth century, the most famous discussion of miracles is probably Hume's in his *Enquiry concerning Human Understanding*, a very critical discussion and a rejection of the possibility of miracles, or at least their intelligibility. Chambers's *Cyclopaedia* carried a brief account of miracles, drawing on earlier discussions, echoing some of Locke's remarks. Hume was attacked by several writers (e.g., George Campbell in 1762, Anthony Ellys in 1752). Voltaire added his thoughts to the topic, but the best-known of the writers on miracles were Thomas Woolston and William Paley.

modes   Modes are 'complex *Ideas*, which however compounded, contain not in them the supposition of subsisting by themselves, but are considered as Dependencies on, or Affections of Substances' (*Essay*, 2.12.4). Locke gives as examples the ideas 'signified by the words *Triangle, Gratitude, Murther, etc.*' Complex ideas are either combinations of simple ideas, or the result of mental operations on simple ideas, operations such as comparing, abstracting, compounding. In defining this term as a type of idea, Locke is aware that he is using that word 'in somewhat a different sence from its ordinary signification' (*ibid.*). Descartes used 'mode' when he was referring to a substance 'as being affected or modified' (*Principles* *of Philosophy*, Pt I, §56). There are modes of extension, thought and knowledge. To understand a mode, Descartes says, 'the concept of the thing of which it is a mode must be implied in' the concept of the mode (*Comments on a Certain Broadsheet*, in *The Philosophical Writings* trans. Cottingham *et al.*, vol. 1, p. 301). A mode for Spinoza is defined as 'the affections of substance, or that which is in another thing through which also it is conceived' (*Ethics*, Pt I, Def. V).

Both Descartes and Spinoza operate with the metaphysic of substance and attribute, both accept the two-substance doctrine: corporeal and incorporeal substances. This substance metaphysic is subdued in Locke's writings, perhaps even ignored. His defining of modes as ideas is another break with tradition. His modes come in two varieties, those that are different combinations of the same simple ideas, and those 'others compounded of simple *Ideas* of several kinds, put together to make one complex one' (2.12.5). As examples he cites beauty which is a combination of colour and figure causing delight in the beholder; or theft which is 'the concealed change of the possession of any thing, without the consent of the Proprietor' (2.12.5). Of simple modes, Locke has extended discussions of space, duration and expansion (2.13; 2.14; 2.15), and of number (2.16). Chapter 18 lists other types of modes, for example, of motion: slide, roll, tumble, walk, creep, run, dance, leap and skip (2.18.2). There are also modes of colour, tastes, smells. Reasoning, judging, volition are modes of thought (2.19.2). Pleasure and pain are two other modes that play important roles in his account of good and bad, as well as in human motivation (2.20). The idea of power is the mode whose discussion occupies more space in the *Essay* than almost any other, a total of seventy-two sections.

Another very important type of modes is what Locke calls 'mixed modes' (2.22). These are modes which combine different kinds of simple ideas, mixed kinds. They are not 'looked upon to be the characteristical Marks of any real Beings that have a steady existence, but scattered and independent *Ideas*, put together by the Mind' (2.22.1). Mixed modes are not real beings independent of the mind, but in one passage he calls them 'moral Beings', saying they have their 'original patterns' in the mind. The mind is active in framing these ideas; it does not have to determine whether they designate what exists in nature. Most of the mixed modes do describe actions, but they also prescribe, give the criteria for what counts as, e.g., hypocrisy, drunkenness (2.22.2). An understanding of actions can be given by explaining the words which signify the mixed-mode ideas. 'Thus a Man may come to have the *Idea* of *Sacrilege*, or *Murther*, by enumerating to him the simple *Ideas* which these words stand for, without ever seeing either of them committed' (2.22.3). Mixed-mode words are names of actions; they are sometimes an indication of what a society considers important: 'Thus, though the killing of an old Man be as fit in Nature to be united into one complex *Idea*, as the killing a Man's Father; yet, there being no name standing precisely for the one, as there is the name of *Parricide* to mark the other, it is not taken for a particular complex *Idea*, nor a distinct Species of Actions, from that of killing a young Man, or any other Man' (2.22.4).

There are three ways for acquiring mixed-mode ideas: experience and observation (e.g., watching men wrestle or fence), invention, and by explaining the names of actions. Explaining the names, explicating the simple ideas contained in the complex ideas of wrestling or fencing, is needed before we can understand what we are seeing. The particular simple ideas that comprise a mixed mode are often society-specific and always related to what is deemed important and worthy of particular names. For example, if men 'join to the *Idea* of Killing, the *Idea* of Father, or Mother, and so make a distinct Species from killing a Man's Son, or Neighbour, it is because of the different heinousness of the Crime, and the distinct punishment is due to the murthering a Man's Father or Mother', different from killing a son or neighbour (3.5.7). There are other particular examples of crimes or immoral acts which are given prominence because of the views of a society (cf. 3.5.6). In general, mixed-mode ideas and names pick out specific qualities and actions that are important for the life of a society, especially for the moral judgements of that society. The formation of such ideas and names is arbitrary, in the sense that the specific features included are not a function of what occurs; they are 'a voluntary Collection of *Ideas* put together in the Mind, independent from any original Patterns in Nature' (3.5.5).

There may be a problem for Locke with those moral ideas which are contained in the law of nature. Does he want to say that their status as mixed modes is different from that of other action words and ideas? If not, it may be difficult for him to say that an idea such as JUSTICE which is found in the law of nature is independent of any original patterns.

Since action is the great business of mankind, 'and the whole matter about which all Laws are conversant', mixed modes, especially those of thinking and motion, are a fundamental part of the fabric of society (2.22.10). The ideas of actions, with their names, help in the making of laws, enabling us to repress vice and disorder.

> Nor could any Communication be well had amongst Men, without such complex *Ideas*, with Names to them: and therefore Men have setled Names, and supposed setled *Ideas* in their Minds, of modes of Actions distinguished by their Causes, Means, Objects, Ends, Instruments, Time, Place, and other circumstances; and also of their Powers fitted for those Actions . . . (*ibid.*)

After Locke, the term 'mixed mode' does not appear very often. A good summary account of Locke's use of that phrase is found in Chambers's *Cyclopaedia* (1728), the entry for 'modes'. John Gay, in 'Preliminary Dissertation concerning the Fundamental Principles of Virtue and Morality', added to Edmund Law's English translation of William King's *De origine mali* in 1731, uses the term and some of Locke's examples (pp. xii, xv–xvii).

Molyneux problem   Locke notes that '*the Ideas we receive by sensation are often* in grown people *alter'd by the Judgment*' (*Essay*, 2.9.8). His example is of a shape and colour, a round globe of gold, alabaster or jet, where the colour is uniform over the surface. He says that the idea that is 'imprinted in our Mind, is of a flat Circle variously shadow'd, with several degrees of Light and Brightness coming to our Eyes' (*ibid.*). The term 'imprinted' is applied to the mind, not to the brain, so Locke must be saying that what we see under these conditions is a flat coloured circle. We do not strictly see a round object. Such strict seeing would seem to be limited to our earlier years, or perhaps to certain new experiences in adult life. What we do in fact see, what we are aware of, is a round golden object (if it is made of gold). This second kind of seeing is the result of learning: we have to learn to see three dimensions. What we experience, what we normally see, is the *appearance* of the round globe of a uniform colour. 'But we having by use been accustomed to perceive, what kind of appearance convex Bodies are wont to make in us; what alterations are made in the reflections of Light, by the difference of the sensible Figures of Bodies, the Judgment presently, by an habitual custom, alters the Appearances into their Causes' (*ibid.*).

It is the faculty of judgement which makes the alteration, returning to the causes of the experience. The causes to which Locke refers are not the light rays or the physiological processes in optic nerve and brain, but the existing round globe. What appears to me is what I strictly am said to see: 'a Plain variously colour'd'. What appears to me is in fact, as in a painting, 'variety of shade or colour, collecting the Figure'. Judgement makes that flat, coloured, shaded shape 'pass for a mark of Figure', a mark of a figure off the canvas. Judgement frames to itself the perception of a convex figure and a uniform colour.

What is not explained by Locke is what leads our judgement to alter the appearances. It cannot just be, as he claims, past experience (custom), since we never do perceive the globe as a flat circle; at least, we are never aware of a flat surface. We are unable to recall what it was like as an infant to learn to see objects. There may be a special situation in which a person would actually experience seeing a flat circle and then discover that its cause was a round globe. A person having such an experience would then understand that his original seeing was altered from the flat appearance to the full-bodied object. The situation for testing this possibility was of a man born blind who, as a result of an operation, came to have for the first time visual experiences. The case of the man born blind and then in later years made to see intrigued scientists and philosophers in the eighteenth century. Berkeley wrote about it; Leibniz, Condillac, Diderot, and Voltaire debated the results.

The problem was set for Locke by his friend William Molyneux, author of a work on optics, *Dioptrica Nova* (1692). Locke's account of the altering nature of judgement in visual perception was meant as an introduction to a question raised by Molyneux in a letter to Locke of 2 March 1693 (*Corr.* 1609; iv. 651). The answer that Locke gives to this question depends upon the assumption he makes of a difference between the visual appearance of an object and our perceptual awareness of that object. The perception reveals the way the object is, not just how it appears. The visual appearance works in the way in which a painting does: flat shapes of light and dark lead to our seeing objects. Locke's judgement learns, as it were, from experience what the painter has learned about lines, shade, and shapes on a flat surface making viewers see trees, people, tables, etc. Painters and our eyes begin with flat shapes but end with ordinary objects. The Molyneux problem, as it has been named, was a test for Locke's claim about visual appearances and the role of experience in altering what we are aware of, in changing the appearance into its cause.

Locke puts the problem in the words Molyneux used in his letter:

> *Suppose a Man born blind, and now adult, and taught by his touch to distinguish between a Cube, and a Sphere of the same metal* [Molyneux wrote 'suppose of Ivory'], *and nighly of the same bigness, so as to tell, where he felt one and t'other, which is the Cube, which the Sphere. Suppose then the Cube and Sphere placed on a Table, and the Blind Man to be made to see. Quære, Whether by his sight, before he touch'd them, he could now distinguish, and tell, which is the Globe, which the Cube.* (2.9.8)

Molyneux's answer was 'no', and Locke agreed. The problem as thus stated introduces another sense modality, touch, which Locke did not mention in his preliminary account of seeing. Perhaps in those preliminary remarks he did mean to say that the alteration of the visual experience was based upon tactile experiences, through touching, feeling and running one's hands over a globe of gold or alabaster. If so, then we have some useful information about the experience of seeing objects *as* objects: such seeing depends, as Berkeley was to say, upon touch. Where Berkeley speaks of visual experience *suggesting* the objects we touch and are aware of, Locke speaks of judgement *altering* our perceptions, but the processes are fairly similar. Berkeley speaks of two 'objects' of sight. 'In a strict sense,' Berkeley writes, 'I see nothing but light and colours, with their several shades and variations' (*New Theory of Vision*, §130). By custom and experiences of moving and touching, we learn to 'see' objects at a distance, not just light and colours. Berkeley remarks that the usual opinion is that 'something more is perceived by sight than barely light and colours', citing Locke's comment in 2.9.9 that sight also conveys to the mind space, figure and motion. Berkeley misses the 2.9.8 passage where Locke distinguishes two kinds of sight-objects.

Molyneux's answer of 'no' to his question was premised on the belief that the newly sighted person would have to learn that objects that affect his touch in a particular way also affect his sight in a particular manner: '*that a protuberant angle in the Cube, that pressed his hand unequally, shall appear to his eye, as it does in the Cube*' (2.9.8). The moral that Locke draws from this thought experiment is simply that our perceptual awareness is dependent upon experience and 'acquired notions'. He goes on to make a comment which sounds very much like Berkeley: light and colours *are* peculiar to sight, but these 'proper objects' of sight 'change the appearances' as a result of experience (2.9.9). Thus, what we take to be the product of sensation alone is often the product of sensation, experience and judgement working together. The proper object of sight 'serves only to excite the other, and is scarce taken notice of it self'. He instances the experience of reading a book or listening to someone speak: we take 'little notice of the Characters or Sounds, but of the *Ideas*, that are excited in him by them' (*ibid.*; cf. Berkeley's *New Theory of Vision*, §51).

The history of this problem between Locke and Molyneux dates back to 7 July 1688, before Molyneux knew Locke. On that date, Molyneux sent a letter to the editors of the *Bibliothèque universelle* after he had read the abridgement of the *Essay* which appeared that year *ibid.*, 8 (1688): 49–142). The problem was posed in that letter in very much the same terms as in the March 1693 letter. The latter led Locke to include the statement of the problem and his discussion of it in the second edition of the *Essay* (1694). In September 1695, Molyneux sent Locke a letter he had received from Edward Synge who offered an affirmative answer to Molyneux's question. Neither Locke nor Molyneux changed his opinion after reading Synge's analysis, an answer which drew on a distinction between ideas or notions and images. (For more details on this curious debate, including experiments to test the answers, see K.T. Hoppen, *The Common Scientist in the Seventeenth Century*, 1970, and Nicholas Pastore, *Selective History of Theories of Visual Perception, 1650–1950*, 1971.)

money Locke was a wise investor of his money and a shrewd manager of his property. The inheritance from his father appreciated considerably during his life as a result of his business acumen. He urged parents and tutors to help young adults learn how to keep accounts so that their estates later could be preserved (*Some Thoughts*, §210). The child should develop the habit of keeping a record of what he buys and pays for: 'This at least every body must allow, that nothing is likelier to keep a Man within compass, than the having constantly before his Eyes, that state of his Affairs in a regular course of *Accounts*' (§211). In that work, Locke also stressed the importance of having a good tutor; money spent on educating a child is money well spent, even if the tutor is expensive. A good tutor who can develop in the child a 'good Mind, well principled, temper'd to Vertue and Usefulness, and adorned with Civility and good Breeding, makes a better purchase for him [the father], than if he had laid out the Money for an Addition of more Earth to his former Acres' (*ST*, §90; cf. §92).

Aside from these few passages in *Some Thoughts concerning Education*, Locke did not have much to say about money in his published writings. There are two notable exceptions, one well-known and much discussed (in the chapter on property in *Two Treatises*), the other a series of pamphlets designed to influence a debate in parliament over interest rates and recoinage. Most commentators have, when examining his remarks about money, turned to *Two Treatises*. The second source for Locke's thoughts on money has only very recently received close attention from economic historians or from some commentators on Locke. Those pamphlets have now been edited with a long, detailed introduction by Patrick Hyde Kelly (*Locke on Money*, 1991). These writings reveal Locke's practical concerns and his considerable understanding of the value and role of money for the economy and trade of the nation.

Does the concept of money have a place in Locke's general philosophy? Kelly makes the interesting suggestion that money belongs to Locke's category of mixed modes. The term 'notion' may be the clue. Locke says in one passage that that term is the proper word to use when talking about mixed modes because that term indicates that the ideas making up those complex ideas have their 'Original, and constant Existence, more in the Thoughts of Men, than in the reality of things' (*Essay*, 2.22.2). The term 'notion' does occur in a few passages in Locke's tracts on money. In a section on 'Raising our Coin', he expresses the wish that 'those that use the Phrase of *Raising our Money*, had some clear Notion annexed to it' (*Locke on Money*, p. 304). He explains that that phrase can signify 'either *raising the value* of our Money, or *raising the Denomination* of our Coin' (*ibid*.). That same tract (it was in the form of a letter to a member of parliament, Sir John Somers) opens with the phrase, 'THESE *Notions*', and goes on to say modestly that '*If my Notions are wrong, my Intention, I am sure, is right*' (*ibid.*, pp. 209, 210). In another of these tracts on money, *Some Further Considerations*, Locke expresses the hope that what he has written may 'clear some Difficulties and rectifie some wrong Notions that are taken up about Money' (*ibid.*, p. 402).

Support for Kelly's suggestion that money is a mixed mode is found in the way Locke talks about money in the second of *Two Treatises*. For example, he says that 'Gold, Silver, and Diamonds are things, that Fancy or Agreement hath put the Value on', contrasting that value with the *real use* of gold, silver and diamonds (*T*2, §46). In section 48, he tells us what is required for the *invention* of money. Section 36 speaks of 'the *Invention* of *Money* and the tacit Agreement of Men'. Section 50 explains that gold or silver 'has its *value* only from the consent of Men'. The word 'notion' is not used in these passages but the terms 'agreement', 'invention', and 'consent' fit the language Locke employs when characterizing mixed MODES.

The discussion of money in the fifth chapter in *Two Treatises* is part of Locke's conceptual analysis of the origin of private property. It is one's labour and the possession of only what each can use before spoilage, with enough left for others, that comprise that analysis. With the invention of money, these conditions for ownership of property and possessions were changed: men could then have larger estates and greater quantity of possessions, since money became by invention and consent a surrogate for property (*T*2, §36). A piece of yellow metal keeps without decay or wasting and can be exchanged for meat or corn at any time (§37). Money is 'some lasting thing that Men might keep without spoiling', something that 'by mutual consent Men would take in exchange for the truly useful, but perishable Supports of Life' (§47).

monsters Locke refers several times to the 'frequent Productions of Monsters' in animals and humans (*Essay*, 3.3.17; 3.6.16; 3.6.22, 23). He reports that 'it has been more than once debated, whether several humane *Foetus* should be preserved, or received to Baptism' because they were so misshapen (3.6.26). He cites a case in France where the bishop was consulted in order to decide whether killing such a foetus would be murder (3.6.27). It is in that context that he mentions the story of the Abbot of St Martin who, though badly misshapen at birth, was luckily baptized and turned out to be rational and hence human. The question whether it would be murder to kill such strange issue, Locke insists, could only be answered by discovering if they had rational souls (3.11.20).

Most of these references rely upon reports of others, but Locke does claim to have seen 'the Issue of a Cat and a Rat' (3.6.23). All of these references are used to illustrate his claims that there are no fixed real classes in nature; but they also raise other issues about the CHAIN OF BEING or even moral issues such as when killing would be murder.

morality   Late in the *Essay*, in a section on the improvement of knowledge, Locke declares that '*Morality* is *the proper Science, and Business of Mankind in general*' (4.12.11). In a section intended for inclusion in the *Essay*, 'Of Ethics in General', morality is said to be 'the great business and Concernment of Mankind' (§3, p. 306, in *The Life of John Locke*, by Peter King, 1829). That planned addition to the *Essay* goes on to say that morality 'hath been generally in the world rated as a science distinct from theology, religion and law; and that it hath been the proper province of philosophers, a sort of men different from divines, priests, and lawyers, whose profession it has been to explain and teach this knowledge to the world'. What Locke criticizes in these writers on morality (he does not name any) is their failure to derive the rules they cite from 'their original, nor arguing them as the commands of the great God of heaven and earth, and such as according to which he would retribute to men after this life, the utmost enforcements they could add to them were reputation and disgrace by those names of virtue and vice' (*ibid.*, §4, p. 307). The most that such secular philosophers could appeal to was reputation and disgrace.

The ultimate source of morality is God, a point Locke makes in several passages in the *Essay*. For example, 1.3.6 says that 'the true ground of Morality . . . can only be the Will and Law of a God, who sees Men in the dark, has in his Hand Rewards and Punishments, and Power enough to call to account the Proudest Offender.' *Essay* 1.3.7 cites as 'the great Principle of Morality, *To do as one would be done to*'. He recognizes that there were other foundations claimed for morality. Some (he names Archelaus) say that 'Right and Wrong, Honest and Dishonest, are defined only by Laws, and not by Nature', while others say 'we are under Obligations antecedent to all humane Constitutions' (4.12.4). A Christian, a Hobbist and a heathen philosopher offer different reasons for saying 'Men should keep their Compacts' (1.3.5). Morality requires laws and rewards and punishments. Three kinds of laws are appealed to: divine law, civil law, and the law of opinion or reputation (2.28.6–7). That God has given to man a law 'whereby Men should govern themselves' (the law of nature), is a truth Locke firmly accepted. That law is the fundamental law of morality.

The philosophical analysis of the concepts of morality, law, and rule is important, as Locke's own account of these concepts indicates, but he has some important reservations about the analyses of those philosophers who have been seen as the men in charge of moral concepts. The danger of such secular conceptual analysis is that while we may acquire a clear idea of the terms justice, temperance, fortitude, theft and the actions they describe,

> all the knowledge of virtues and vices which a man attained to, this way, would amount to no more, than taking the definitions or the significations of the words of any language, either from the men skilled in that language, or the common usage of the country, to know how to apply them, and call particular actions in that country by their right names; and so in effect would be no more but the skill how to speak properly, or at most to know what actions in the country he lives in are thought laudable or disgraceful ... ('Of Ethics in General', §4, p. 307)

In the absence of any superior law besides that of society, moral teachers would degenerate into 'language masters', teaching us 'only to talk and dispute, and call actions by the names they prescribe' (*ibid.*, p. 308). Similarly, the ethics of the schools, built on the authority of Aristotle, teach us 'nothing of morality, but only to understand their names, or call actions as they or Aristotle does; which is in effect but to speak their language properly'. If morality is just about a set of definitions, we can acquire an understanding of what actions are considered virtues or vices, but if the talk of virtue does not refer to a 'law of a superior' who prescribes virtues for us, with the power of rewards and punishments, 'the force of morality is lost, and evaporates only into words, disputes, and niceties' (*ibid.*, §9, p. 310).

Action words are on Locke's account mixed modes; they contain criteria for an action being one of justice, murder or theft. He recognized that an action can be described in various ways. An action of holding a gun and pulling the trigger, e.g., 'may be either Rebellion Parricide. Murther. Homicide. Duty. Justice, Valor or recreation. & be thus variously diversified when all the circumstances put togeather are compard to a rule, though the simple action of holding the gun & pulling the triger may be exactly the same' (Draft A in *Drafts*, ed. Nidditch and Rogers, §23, p. 37). The multiplicity of descriptions of actions, and of the nature of human action, was revived in the 1950s, with a flurry of books and articles. One of the first and most interesting was Elizabeth Anscombe's *Intention* (1957). Once we determine what description fits a given action, we then need to know whether that action is morally good or bad (*Essay*, 2.28.4). Moral goodness is not the same as goodness; good and evil 'are nothing but Pleasure or Pain', but morally good and evil are 'the Conformity or Disagreement of our voluntary Actions to some Law, whereby Good or Evil is drawn on us, from the Will and Power of the Law-maker' (2.28.5). The law-maker is clearly God. The law of God secures and advances the general good of mankind, and that law is the law of nature 'which ought to be the Rule of Vertue and Vice' (2.28.11). Other sections in this chapter on relations and moral relations stress the same point (e.g., §§12, 15, 16).

Despite Locke's criticism of the conceptual analyses of secular philosophers, that same analysis was part of his account of the relation of ideas. Conceptual analysis of moral relations plays a role in his suggested demonstrative morality. Showing the conceptual connections between ideas is one way to demonstrate moral relations, but the more important and more debatable part of his suggestion of a demonstrative morality was the claim to derive from certain concepts and principles specific moral duties (*see* DEMONSTRATION). Despite the importuning of friends, Locke never did produce this part of a demonstrative morality. He may have changed his mind about its possibility, or he may just have turned his attention to other topics. Whatever the explanation of his failure to go further towards this intriguing suggestion, he had another, perhaps less rational, source for moral knowledge: the Bible. He instructs the tutor in *Some Thoughts* to have the child read no other 'Discourses of Morality, but what he finds in the Bible', and later perhaps when the youth becomes interested in systems of ethics, he might consult Tully's 'Offices' (§185). The study of morality 'becomes a Gentleman, not barely as a Man, but in order to his business as a Gentleman', what we today call 'business ethics'. For this study, there are many books of 'Ancient and Modern Philosophers. But the Morality of the Gospel doth so exceed them all, that to give a man a ful knowledge of true Morality, I should send him to no other Book, but the New Testament' ('Some Thoughts concerning Reading and Study for a Gentleman', reprinted in *Some Thoughts*, edited by Yolton and Yolton, p. 321). In that short piece of advice, Locke also suggests Tully's *De Officiis* as the best work by a secular philosopher.

The New Testament records Jesus's moral teaching: he cleared the moral law 'from the corrupt glosses of the Scribes and Pharisees' (*Reasonableness*, in *Works*, vii. 122). All the duties of morality were illustrated and inculcated in his disciples. Jesus's example and the New Testament are surer sources for moral knowledge than reason alone (*ibid.*, p. 139). Philosophers, those men who were not divines, priests or lawyers about whom Locke writes in 'Of Ethics in General', are again criticized in the *Reasonableness*:

> He, that any one will pretend to set up in this kind, and have his rules pass for authentic directions, must show, that either he builds his doctrine upon principles of reason, self-evident in themselves, and that he deduces all the parts of it from thence, by clear and evident demonstration: or must show

his commission from heaven, that he comes with authority from God, to deliver his will and commands to the world. (*Reasonableness*, p. 142)

Whether it is possible now, after Jesus has revealed the moral law, to reproduce or reinforce by demonstration the true morality, Locke does not say in that work. Perhaps it was such a possibility that he had in mind with his suggestion in the *Essay*. The *Reasonableness* still has reason agreeing with revelation. In Jesus's testimony, 'morality has a sure standard, that revelation vouches, and reason cannot gainsay, nor question; both together witness to come from God, the great law-maker' (p. 143).

motion   While discussing space, and pointing out that the parts of space are inseparable, Locke remarks that being inseparable entails those parts also being immovable. He then gives a short definition of motion: 'nothing but change of distance between any two things' (*Essay*, 2.13.14). Arguing against those who denied a vacuum (or empty space), he insisted that the idea of space is dependent upon the idea of solidity or filled space (2.4.3). As an illustration of this point, he suggests that we can have an idea of a single body moving while all others are at rest, thereby leaving behind a space without body. He is not saying that bodies can move in this way, alone, but the conception of a single body moving helps make the point about space: it is not, as some Cartesians said, the same as body (2.13.11). Our concept of motion requires the concept of space: 'Motion is not Space, nor Space Motion' (*ibid.*). God could 'put an end to all motion that is in Matter, and fix all the Bodies of the Universe in a perfect quiet and rest' (2.13.21 *bis*).

Motion appears in many lists of primary qualities of bodies: extension, figure, number, motion (2.8.12); texture and motion of the parts of objects, perhaps a reference to corpuscles (2.6.14); solidity, extension, figure, number and motion (2.8.22); bulk, figure, number, situation and motion (again, of the parts of bodies, but here it is bodies that we sense, 2.23.9); size, figure and motion (4.3.13); bulk, figure and motion (4.3.24). Other passages attribute motion, along with most of these same primary qualities, to the insensible corpuscles of bodies: figure and motion of the minute parts (2.23.13); bulk, figure, motion of the particles of water (2.23.26); size, figure, number and motion (4.2.11); figure, size, texture, motion (4.3.24); bulk, figure, motion (4.6.14).

One interesting feature of these lists is the occurrence of solidity on only one. Solidity is the only primary quality given a separate chapter for discussion (2.4). When Locke is responding to the Bishop of Worcester's attack on the suggestion that God could give the power of thinking to some systems of matter, Locke outlines a creation-scenario which has God creating a solid extended substance and then deliberating whether to add motion, a power of acting, to it (*see* THINKING MATTER). The *Essay* also talks of *bare* matter, matter without motion (4.10.10). In this passage, he is concerned to assert that it is impossible for 'bare incogitative Matter' to produce a thinking, intelligent being. He speaks of bare matter as 'a dead inactive Lump', and he says we cannot conceive that it 'can add Motion to it self, being purely Matter'. Both motion and thought are added in the initial stage of creating substances, motion being added to solid, extended substance, thought added to immaterial substance. But thought could have been added by God to the solid, extended substance, along with motion.

There is a difference between matter and body. The former can be 'bare', consisting only of solidity and extension. The latter has motion or the power of motion added to it. The '*primary* Ideas *we have peculiar to Body*, as contradistinguished to Spirit, *are the cohesion of solid*, and consequently separable *parts, and a power of communicating Motion by impulse*' (2.23.17). Precisely how bodies communicate motion by impulse is unclear to us, although we do know that 'as much Motion is lost to one Body, as is got to the other' (2.23.28). He speaks of 'the passing of Motion out of one Body into another', as if motion, not just the power of moving, is resident in bodies. He also makes a reference to a phenomenon 'observed or believed sometimes to happen', namely, the 'increase of Motion by impulse' (*ibid.*). Spirits, finite minds, also have a power to move bodies by thought, moving the limbs of their own bodies (2.23.17, 28). He characterizes such motion as 'spontaneous', a motion which animals also have. He even asserts that finite spirits themselves move (2.23.19). 'No Body can imagine, that his Soul can think, or move a Body at *Oxford*, whilst he is at London; and cannot but know, that being united to his Body, it constantly changes place all the whole Journey, between *Oxford* and *London*, as the Coach, or Horse does, that carries him' (2.23.20).

Motion comes into Locke's account elsewhere when talking about the motion of animal spirits, those physiological bodies that activate nerves and muscles and produce sensations in us (2.8.21; 2.9.3; 2.33.6; 4.10.19). He also makes a passing reference to the atomists' definition of motion, which he thinks is uninformative, and to the Cartesian definition, which he does not find any better (3.4.9).

Motion as a property (sometimes only as an accident) of matter was part of accounts of the physical world from Aristotle to Locke's time and beyond. It played a fundamental role in Hobbes's *Elements of Philosophy*, in Descartes's *Principles*, and in seventeenth-century science. It was important for Newton; Berkeley has an extended critique of Newton's account (along with space and time). Hume does not discuss it, but it comes in for some analysis by Kant. (For some historical accounts, see *Motion and Time, Space and Matter*, ed. Peter K. Machamer and Robert G. Turnbull (1976).)

N

names Both for Locke's ontology and for his account of language, names are an important class of words. In his particularist ontology, there are no general things, everything is particular. The only particular names are those proper names of persons, countries, cities, rivers, mountains. Sometimes animals (Locke mentions horses, in *Essay* 3.3.5) are given names. Any object could be given a proper name, but proper names have a limited use. The use of names is for communicating and understanding ideas and thoughts. Even were it possible, it would be pointless to 'heap up Names of particular Things'; that would not serve to communicate our thoughts to others (3.3.3). Communication occurs when 'by Use or Consent, the Sound I make by the Organs of Speech, excites in another Man's Mind, who hears it, the *Idea* I apply it to in mine, when I speak it' (*ibid.*). If I employ names of which only I know their meaning, communication will fail. Small groups of people might agree on a particular name for some object (e.g., their car, their horse or dog, even objects in a house), but the particularity of the names would preclude a wider, public understanding.

The question of how general words get formed was answered by Locke while discussing abstraction. In the account of names in 3.3, he uses some genetic examples, tracing the formation of general ideas from infancy and childhood. Words such as 'nurse' or 'mama' are first particular words, confined to specific individuals. Later, discovering similarities between his father or mother and other men and women, the child forms the idea of men and women (Locke only cites men), along with words for that class of individuals. The name 'animal' is formed by further abstracting operations (3.3.8; cf. 3.3.9). General names thus acquired are used in sorting things into classes.

Locke distinguishes three different kinds of referents for names: simple ideas, mixed modes and relations, and natural substances (3.4.1). The names for the first and third of these items *signify* ideas immediately but *intimate* '*some real Existence*, from which was derived their original pattern' (3.4.2). The names of mixed modes lack that external reference, they '*terminate in the* Idea that is in the Mind, and lead not the Thought any farther' (*ibid.*). In Locke's language of essence, the names of the first and second items signify the real as well as the nominal essence, but the names of natural substances signify rarely, if ever, 'any thing but *barely the nominal Essences* of those Species' (3.4.3). The names of simple ideas are less doubtful and uncertain than others. In their case, 'There is neither a multiplicity of simple *Ideas* to be put together, which makes the doubtfulness in the Names of mixed Modes; nor a supposed, but an unknown real Essence, with properties depending thereon, the precise number whereof are also unknown, which makes the difficulty in the Names of Substances' (3.4.15; cf. §16).

The names of mixed modes stand for kinds, mainly kinds of actions. Locke retains the language of essence in talking about mixed modes, saying that those names reveal the essence of what they name (3.5.1). But these essences are made by the understanding, 'made *very arbitrarily*, made without Patterns, or reference to any real Existence' (3.5.2). The names of mixed modes 'tie' the ideas together that have been selected to designate a kind of action (3.5.4; cf. §10). The names used in moral discourses may lose some of their meaning when translated into other languages (3.5.8). The names of mixed modes are also useful for indicating what species of actions are taken notice of in a particular society. For example, 'killing a Man with a Sword, or a Hatchet, are looked on as no distinct species of Action: But if the Point of the Sword first enter the Body, it passes for a distinct *Species*, where it has a distinct *Name*, as in *England*, in whose Language it is called *Stabbing*: But in another Country, where it has not happened to be specified under a peculiar *Name*, it passes not for a distinct *Species*' (3.5.11). The names of mixed modes, e.g., justice or gratitude, '*lead our thoughts to the Mind, and no farther*'; our thoughts 'terminate in the abstract *Ideas* of those Vertues' (3.5.12). This fact about the names of mixed modes leads Locke to say that the word 'notion' is a more accurate word for those names (*see* NOTIONS).

Mixed modes, and hence their names, often bring together a variety of ideas with no particular relation or connection to each other except as constituting and serving as the archetype for some actions. 'Thus the Name of *Procession*, what a great mixture of independant *Ideas* of Persons, Habits, Tapers, Orders, Motions, Sounds, does it contain in that complex one, which the Mind of Man has arbitrarily put together, to express by that one Name?' (3.5.13). We frequently learn the names of mixed modes before we acquire the ideas that constitute that mode. In the beginning of languages, this order was reversed. Children also learn names before they acquire and understand the ideas (3.5.15).

With the names of natural substances, the ideas of their qualities usually precede the names given to them. The formation of ideas of substances is not arbitrary; those ideas must be carefully taken from the objects we observe and experiment with. But the names for substances, as those for mixed modes, stand for kinds, what Locke calls 'sorts'. Locke was emphatic in his stress that the kinds of substances that we distinguish do not refer to any real essence, as older doctrines said. Our ranking of collections of coexisting qualities into classes is limited to those qualities, hence these ideas reveal the nominal ESSENCE only (3.6.1, 2). The names of natural substances enable us to distinguish kinds of things (3.6.20). In fact, without general names and the ideas they stand for, there would strictly be no species, no kinds of things for us (3.6.29). If I have only the name 'watch', the differences between silent and striking watches would not make different kinds of watches for me. To a person who has different names for silent and striking watches, those watches belong to different species of watch. The inward differences of mechanism, however, do not make different sorts of watch unless I have different names based upon my knowledge of the inward mechanisms of watches (*ibid.*). Locke wants to say the same about natural substances: kinds, classes, or species in nature are also a result of the work of the understanding in carefully collecting and naming coexisting qualities. The example of Adam naming new objects, objects he had not experienced before, illustrates this doctrine (3.6.46). It was a rather radical doctrine at that time but it is consistent with Locke's general account of the limits of human knowledge.

notions This is one of the more curious terms to be found in seventeenth- and eighteenth-century English writings. It is used by writers before and after Locke. In introducing his term 'idea', Locke explains that he uses that term to cover whatever has been meant by the terms phantasm, notion or species. All four words were understood by Locke to refer to 'whatever it is, which the Mind can be employ'd about in thinking' (*Essay*, 1.1.8). A writer who stressed, as did Locke, experiment and observation as the method to science, criticized 'the *notional Theorems* in philosophy', meaning theories not based on observation (Maynwaring, *Praxis medicorum antiqua et nova*, 1671). Culverwel characterized innate principles as 'Alphabetical Notions' (*An Antidote Against Atheisme*, 1655). Bishop Wilkins remarks that the construction of what he called a 'real character' for language should be made '*from the Natural notions of things*' (*An Essay Towards a Real Character and Philosophical Language*, 1668). A contemporary of Locke, John Sergeant, tried to adapt the Cartesian objective reality of ideas for his own purposes, making notions the objects as they exist in the mind (*Solid Philosophy Asserted*, 1697). Sergeant's notions were cognitive contents, meanings, as he termed them.

Sergeant's use of the term is a technical one; some of the uses in other writers were just ways of talking about thoughts or opinions.

The appearance of 'notion' in Locke's *Essay* covers more uses than these. In one or two places, he tries to offer a definition of the term for a very specific purpose, but there are many passages which employ the term 'notion' differently. Sometimes 'idea' and 'notion' are used interchangeably (e.g., 1.1.3; 2.14.5; 2.22.11). There are other references to 'vulgar' or ordinary notions (2.31.2, 12; 4.10.18). We also find many references to claims Locke believed to be false or worse: he calls them odd notions in 2.1.18 (that the soul always thinks); wrong notions influenced by custom (2.11.2; 2.21.69); people using their words for unsteady and confused notions (2.33.9; 3.10.4); and the imperfect notions children have (3.11.24). Locke mentions a number of specific notions. He remarks that blind persons cannot have any notions of colours or deaf men of sounds (2.2.2), and his account of memory reminds us that after some years 'there is no more Notion, nor Memory of Colours' (2.10.5). Substance is deemed an important notion (2.13.18): we are told what is required to have 'true distinct Notions of the several sorts of Substances' (2.23.7); he refers to 'this Notion of immaterial Spirit' (2.23.31); he speaks of the notions of gratitude and polygamy (2.28.9), of our notions of matter and thought (4.3.6), and even of a notion of God (4.8.6). When he discusses the claims for innate principles that involve God (e.g., that God is to be worshipped), he employs the term 'notion' more frequently than the term 'idea'. Phrases such as 'a notion of God', 'the notion of a law-maker', 'the notion of his maker', occur frequently in 1.4.8–15. When he deals with Herbert of Cherbury's account of common notions, principles or truths, the term 'notion' replaces 'idea' again (1.3.15; cf. 1.3.16, 17).

There are also places where Locke speaks of the origin and acquisition of notions. The innatist claimed that there are in the understanding 'certain *innate Principles*; some primary Notions' (1.2.1). Locke of course rejected that claim, insisting that all ideas are acquired from sensation or reflection. Some acquired notions (he uses the Cartesian phrase, 'adventitious Notions' in 1.2.25) can influence our perceptual judgements (2.9.8). The brief summary of his account of idea-acquisition speaks of 'the Originals of our Notions', seeming to suggest that those originals are ideas, that notions are derived from ideas (2.12.8), a suggestion that is explicitly applied to his analysis of causation: 'the Notion of *Cause* and *Effect*, has its rise from *Ideas*, received by Sensation or Reflection' (2.26.2). The chapter on faith and reason asserts that simple ideas 'are the Foundation, and sole Matter of all our Notions, and Knowledge' (4.18.3). The first chapter of Book Three on language notes the link between ideas and words, but uses the term 'notion' rather than 'idea':

> It may also lead us a little towards the Original of all our Notions and
> Knowledge, if we remark, how great a dependance our *Words* have on
> common sensible *Ideas*; and how those, which are made use of to stand for
> Actions and Notions quite removed from sense, *how their rise from thence, and*
> *from obvious sensible* Ideas *are transferred to more abstruse significations*, and made
> to stand for *Ideas* that come not under the cognizance of our senses; ...
> (3.1.5)

He wonders in this same passage 'what kind of Notions they were, and
whence derived, which filled their Minds, who were the first Beginners of
Languages'.

The linkage in 3.1.5 between actions and notions brings Locke close to
the one definition of 'notion' in the *Essay*. He contrasts the way our action
concepts are the standards for actions (actions are the referents of those
concepts) with the way our ideas of natural objects must be faithful to
the objects themselves. The essences of what he calls 'mixed modes' are,
he says, 'by a more particular Name called *Notions*; as by a peculiar Right,
appertaining to the Understanding' (3.5.12). He repeats this remark in
one of his replies to the Bishop of Worcester: 'the term "notion" is more
peculiarly appropriated to a certain sort of those objects, which I call
mixed modes' (in *Works*, iv. 133). There is, however, no systematic use of
this term when talking of mixed modes or human actions, so one is
puzzled about the point of these two passages.

Perhaps the important phrase in the 3.5.12 passage is the remark
that notions belong to the understanding, rather than to the senses or
reflection (cf. 'intelligible notions', 4.12.12). If so, the point may be that
notions are general terms. Mixed-mode words are type-words, designating actions such as murder, gratitude, justice. There are a few passages
where the generality of notions is noted. For example, the chapter on
general terms speaks of 'general Natures or Notions' as being 'abstract
and partial *Ideas* of more complex ones' (3.3.9), and 3.3.10 says that the
terms 'genus' and 'differentia' 'most properly suit those Notions they are
applied to'. Most disputes are said to be about '*general Propositions*, and
Notions in which Existence is not at all concerned' (4.4.8). The mind is
said to 'lay up those general Notions' which aid memory (4.12.3).

Had Locke given more attention to the term 'notion', had he found a
place for it in the way of ideas, he might have avoided some of the
criticism levelled against him. In the absence of any systematic treatment
of that term, the reader is left wondering about the frequency and
diversity of its uses in the *Essay*. The history of the term takes it into the
eighteenth century. Bishop Berkeley is the best-known user of it, a term
he found the need for in order to account for the fact that we do have

thoughts about minds. He could not say 'ideas' of minds since he restricted ideas to sensory experiences. The details of his use of notions have only recently been analysed. It is clear that for Berkeley, notions fill a non-sensory role. Another Irishman, Peter Browne (*The Procedure, Extent, and Limits of Human Understanding*, 1728), also appealed to this term. A major attack on Locke's ideas in favour of notions appeared in 1728, *Two Dissertations concerning Sense and the Imagination* (attributed, without substantiation, to a Zachary Mayne). Another tract in this tradition is *An Essay concerning Rational Notions*, 1733, by Charles Mayne.

P

Paraphrases   During the last few years of his life, Locke was busy writing paraphrases of St Paul's Epistles. He wrote on Galatians, 1 and 2 Corinthians, Romans and Ephesians, which were published after his death. The paraphrase on Galatians appeared in 1705, with subsequent editions in 1706, 1708, and 1718. The commentary on first Corinthians was published in 1706, a second edition in 1708. Second Corinthians appeared in 1706, Romans and Ephesians in 1707. An important essay on how to read the Epistles was published separately in 1707. In the same year, all the paraphrases and this essay were collected together into one volume. There were a number of other editions of the collection throughout the eighteenth century. There was a Dutch translation of Romans in 1768, and a German translation of the collection also in 1768. We now have a modern edition with a long introduction and notes by Arthur W. Wainwright (2 vols, Clarendon Press, 1987).

Writing paraphrases was a popular activity in the two centuries in which Locke lived. Some of the paraphrases that followed Locke's mention his or borrowed from them. His interest in St Paul (an interest which he shared with Newton) was part of a longstanding and deep commitment to biblical studies. His perceptive essay on how to read and understand an ancient text such as St Paul's letters reveals his sensitive efforts to present the meaning of what St Paul said in a language that Locke's readers could follow. His notes to the text and on specific doctrines explicate difficult passages.

passions   Locke does not have much to say about the passions. He recognizes that children and adults alike have passions and emotions, that we often act under the influence of some passion or other. Even the operations of the mind about its ideas sometimes have passions accompanying them (*Essay*, 2.1.4). Various passions are linked with pleasure and pain or good and evil. Uneasiness and desire are two other mental states closely related to Locke's brief account of the passions. His descriptions of passions are sometimes graphic: e.g., a boisterous passion 'hurries our Thoughts, as a Hurricane does our Bodies' (2.21.12). Elsewhere he refers to the power of an overwhelming passion (2.33.4). Restraining and moderating our passions free the understanding and enable it to examine problems and form judgements without bias (2.21.52). Passions can lead us to mistake the meaning of what someone says (4.16.11). He gives a short list of passions in his discussion of power (aversion, fear, anger, envy, shame), remarking that they can influence the will (2.21.39). He gives another list in the chapter on pleasure and pain: joy, sorrow, hope, fear, despair, anger, envy (2.20.7–13). In that chapter, he also gives some short definitions of each of those passions. Passions such as these are usually not found without desire and uneasiness.

In his writings on the raising and educating of children, Locke gives advice to parents and tutors on how to deal with the passions of children. We should, he tells us, remember that the child when grown up will have the same passions and desires we have (*Some Thoughts*, §41). Children have a variety of traits of character which the tutor and parents must learn to work with; some but not all of those traits can be suppressed; others need to be controlled and used, especially what Locke calls the 'predominate Passions' (§102). In general, passions in children should be subdued, certainly not encouraged (§112). Some passions can be useful: fear can quicken the child's industry. Fear is defined as 'an Uneasiness under the Apprehension of that coming upon us which we dislike' (§115). But Locke urges caution in the use of fear, especially in correction by punishment. The child should not be commanded out of passion (§81); and if corporal punishment is necessary, we should allow our passion to cool before punishing the child (§83). Beatings can become a passionate tyranny if we are not careful (§112). The tutor is also urged not to show emotions or passions in his dealings with the child (§84).

A 'prevailing passion' in adults can so pin down 'our thoughts to the object and concern of it, that a man passionately in love cannot bring himself to think of his ordinary affairs, or a kind mother, drooping under the loss of a child, is not able to bear a part as she was wont in the discourse of the company or conversation of her friends' (*Conduct*, §45).

The attention given to the passions by Locke was relatively minor, although what he says about pleasure and pain and uneasiness is closely related. He may have had the intention to say more about the passions. The chapter in the *Essay* on pleasure and pain ends with the comment that 'I would not be mistaken here, as if I meant this as a Discourse of the *Passions*' (2.20.18). He comments here that there are many more passions than he has mentioned, and those he has mentioned would merit a longer analysis and 'more accurate Discourse'. There is a rather extended journal entry for 16 July 1676 on pleasure and pain, the passions and emotions (printed in *Essays*, pp. 263–72). There were treatises on the passions both before and after Locke: Edward Reynolds, *A Discourse of the Passions* (1650); Descartes, *Les Passions de l'âme*(1649); Francis Hutcheson, *An Essay on the Nature and conduct of the Passions and Affections* (1728); Book II of Hume's *Treatise* (1740). Two well-known eighteenth-century encyclopaedias also carried long entries on the passions: Chambers, *Cyclopaedia; or, An Universal Dictionary of Arts and Sciences* (1728) and the Diderot-a'Alembert *Encyclopédie, ou Dictionnaire raisonné des sciences, des arts et des métiers* (1750).

perception   Locke tells us that the best way to understand what perception is is to reflect on what we do when we see, hear, feel, or think (*Essay*, 2.9.2). We reflect on 'what passes in our minds', one of the locutions Locke employs to refer to acts of perceiving, of being aware of some sensation or thought. He also identifies perception as the first faculty of the mind 'exercised' about our ideas (2.9.1). Perception is, he says, sometimes called 'thinking'; it is an *active* operation of the mind, a voluntary act of attending (cf. 2.6.2, where it is described as the power of thinking). There is a level of perception, 'naked' perception, where 'the Mind is, for the most part, only passive; and what it perceives, it cannot avoid perceiving' (2.9.1). This qualification, 'for the most part', refers to the fact that the stimuli on sense organs must *reach* the mind, *must be taken notice of* within the mind (2.9.3). The sensation of heat or the idea of pain must be produced in the mind, but that production cannot occur if we do not pay attention. Just what 'taking notice' is may not be clear; at least something more than physical causation must occur if we are to be aware of or perceive the sensation of heat or feel the pain. Perception, then, is clearly distinguished from physiology.

Locke reminds us of some experiences that illustrate the role of attention in perception. For example, we are concentrating upon some object or thought and fail to be aware of a bell ringing nearby: the sound fails to catch our attention, the mind 'takes no notice of impressions of sounding Bodies, made upon the Organ of Hearing' (2.9.4). The physical impulse must reach the 'observation of the Mind'. In the absence of attending to what goes on in the mind, no ideas will be 'imprinted' on the mind, no sensation will occur. Ideas are 'present in' the understanding (he frequently interchanges 'understanding' for 'mind') when perception occurs (cf. 2.19.3).

Locke then devotes three sections to children's perceptions in early years or even in the pre-natal state (2.9.5–7). In adults, sometimes the ideas we receive by sensation are altered by judgement, even without our being aware of the alteration (2.9.8; cf. 2.9.9). The Molyneux problem is inserted in this section, the question of whether a man born blind but newly sighted could identify by sight shapes he has been identifying by touch. The reason for this problem appearing in this section seems to be because Locke is stressing the role of experience in idea-acquisition. The innatists, he says, claim some ideas have no external cause, our perception of those ideas does not require any physical causal stimuli (*see* MOLYNEUX PROBLEM). It is the faculty of perception which distinguishes animals from '*the inferior parts of Nature*', e.g., plants. The motion of some plants (perhaps he means towards the light or because of a drop of water) is caused entirely by physical mechanisms within the plant (2.9.11). Animals of all sorts have some degree of perception (2.9.12). Even oysters or a cockle have some small degrees of perception: they have 'not so many, nor so quick Senses' as we do or as animals higher on the scale of being have (2.9.13). Old people have a loss of degrees of perception, even in some cases virtually no perception, no awareness (2.9.14). The degrees of perception might be said to parallel the degrees of being.

In a later chapter of the *Essay*, Locke distinguishes three kinds of perception, using the term 'understanding' rather than 'mind': (1) perception of ideas in our minds; (2) perception of the signification of signs; and (3) perception of the 'connexion or repugnancy' between ideas. Only the second and third are properly attributed to the understanding. The third kind of perception is the one that yields knowledge, since knowledge is defined by Locke as the perception of the relations of ideas (4.1.2; 4.3.1–3; 4.4.1; 4.7.2). This use of the term 'perception' is also found in many passages of his *Conduct* (e.g., §§6, 9, 13, 31).

person This term, Locke concludes in his discussion of identity and diversity, 'is a Forensick Term appropriating Actions and their Merit; and so belongs only to intelligent Agents capable of a Law, and Happiness and Misery' (*Essay*, 2.27.26). Any intelligent, rational being who is aware of the value of happiness and the evils of misery 'must grant, that there is something that is *himself*, that he is concerned for, and would have happy' (2.27.25). It is the awareness or consciousness that any intelligent being has of 'that something that is *himself*' which also makes that being aware that that self 'has existed in a continued Duration more than one instant' and that it may exist in the future. It is also this complex consciousness that enables that being to find 'himself to be the *same* self which did such or such an Action some Years since, by which he comes to be happy or miserable now' (*ibid.*).

The various terms used in these characterizations of the term 'person' reveal the domain of a person: it is a lawful, rational domain in which agents are motivated by a concern for happiness and virtue. Being a person is an active state in which actions are appropriated and recognized as actions for which the agent is responsible. We are clearly being directed by Locke to the moral, if not in the long run, the eschatological, domain. The odd locution, 'intelligent being', is used because Locke is identifying by the term 'person' an aspect of man. Earlier in this same chapter, he distinguished man from person. Man is a biological organism; each individual man is characterized by 'a participation of the same continued Life, by constantly fleeting Particles of Matter, in succession vitally united to the same organized Body' (2.27.6). We begin life as men (or, not to pre-empt gender, as humans); we can become persons. A person is not of course distinct from the man or human being, *moral man* is the successful combination of man and person, but my personhood is importantly distinguished from my manhood. Here is another definition of the term 'person': 'a thinking intelligent Being, that has reason and reflection, and can consider it self as it self, the same thinking thing in different times and places; which it does only by that consciousness, which is inseparable from thinking, and as it seems to me essential to it' (2.27.9).

Locke believed that humans have to work to keep above animals on the chain of being, an activity that requires us to become morally responsible persons living in accordance with the law of nature, God's law. Our very humanity is defined in this way, a humanity that is preserved in the family and in civic virtue, virtue which parents must cultivate in their children and which government officials must respect and protect. The process of education for Locke can be viewed as a development from man to person, from human to intelligent, rational, moral agents. *Two Treatises* might be said to be written with persons, not men, in mind, although this way of speaking is too artificial and presumes more conceptual continuity from the *Essay* and *Some Thoughts* to *Two Treatises* than may exist. But both the first and second of *Two Treatises* have frequent use of the term 'person', and many of those uses assume a man-person distinction. For example: 'the Persons of Men' (*T*1, §41); 'the Person of a private Father' (*ibid.*, §66); 'a Man's Person' (*T*2, §182). Other passages speak of a man disposing of his person or possessions (*T*2, §6), of uniting one's person to a commonwealth (§120), and of every man having a right of 'freedom to his Person' (§190), of men's persons being free by natural right (§194), or of the property men have in their persons (§173).

The notion of owning my person, of my personhood being part of my property, may strike our ears as strange, but it catches a central feature of Locke's concept of the person: it is something we have to acquire. The acquisition of actions talked about in one of his definitions is the process of accumulating actions that I accept as mine, that I take responsibility for, that have moral value, and that affect my happiness and moral worth. The definition of property in *Two Treatises* says that 'every Man has a

Property in his own *Person*' (*T*2, §27). The various lists of the kinds of items included in property most often mention life, liberty and estates or possessions (T2, §§87, 135, 171), but other listings include persons (e.g., §§57, 137). Besides life, which God gives men, the other items of property have to be acquired. Person or personhood is no different, even though the method of acquisition is different from that for land and goods (*see* PROPERTY).

There are other more standard uses of the term 'person' in Locke's writings, the application to the one who has authority being one of those; e.g., the person of the ruler where laws, the people, or custom determine who that person is. In his dispute with Robert Filmer, there are frequent uses of the term 'person' in this sense; e.g., we need to know 'the Person to whom this *Regal Power* of Right belongs' (*T*1, §§81, 107, 127, 162). That person is authorized to rule, or to do what mayors or lawyers or kings do. This is the public or civic person (*T*2, §§151, 205, 220). Such a person speaks for or represents the people. Hobbes had earlier distinguished the *natural* person, whose words and actions are considered as his own, from the *artificial* person, whose words and actions represent the words and actions of another man or group of men. An artificial person for Hobbes is similar to an actor on stage: his words and actions are owned by someone else (see Hobbes's *Leviathan*, Pt I, ch. XVI). Owning one's words (e.g., by copyright) or owning one's actions (owning up to them) are not such strange notions, but owning one's person is odd.

There was not much discussion in Locke's day of this feature of his concept of person, except indirectly: people found the distinction between man and person difficult to understand. In the next century, Bishop Butler and Thomas Reid vigorously attacked that distinction. There is also a discussion of this topic in Isaac Watts's *Philosophical Essays* (1733, Essay XII, pp. 287–306). One important but overlooked defence of Locke's concept of person was made by Vincent Perronet, in two tracts published in 1736 and 1738 (see his *A Vindication of Mr. Locke* and *A Second Vindication*, the latter now available in a reprint). Reverberations of Locke's stress on consciousness as constituting personal identity can be heard in France in such eighteenth-century writers as Condillac, Boulain-villiers, Buffon, Maupertuis and, in Switzerland, Charles Bonnet. The French translation of Locke's term 'consciousness' created difficulties for Locke's French translator, Pierre Coste and others (see Catherine Glyn Davies, *'Conscience' as Consciousness: The Idea of Self-Awareness in French Philosophical Writing from Descartes to Diderot*, 1990). In Locke's time, there was a theological notion which had some similarities to that distinction, the doctrine of the Trinity, three persons in one substance. One divine, William Sherlock, even employed something like

Locke's consciousness as a way of distinguishing the three persons of the Trinity (see his *A Vindication of the Doctrine of the Holy and Ever Blessed Trinity*, 1690; also, South's attack on Sherlock, *Animadversions upon Dr. Sherlock's Book*, 1693). Locke may have had this doctrine of the Trinity in mind (although more probably it was only the metaphysical doctrine of soul-substance) when he playfully explored the possibility of different soul-substances having the same person or of different persons residing in the same substance (2.27.12–24; cf. 1.4.4, 5). In our own time, philosophers have become fascinated with these puzzle cases, even adding to those discussed by Locke. The construction of complex puzzle cases has almost become an art form (see, e.g., Derek Parfit, *Reasons and Persons* (Oxford: Clarendon Press, 1984); Peter Unger, *Identify, Consciousness and Value* (New York: Oxford University Press, 1990)).

The more serious and disturbing part of Locke's account of person and personal identity (disturbing for Locke's contemporaries) was his dismissal of sameness of substance, of immaterial substance, as having no bearing upon sameness of person. If person *is* linked with an immaterial substance (our knowledge for Locke falls short of that), the substance does not make the person. Locke's readers accepted the standard two-substance ontology: bodies are material substances, souls or minds are immaterial substances. Locke's analysis of body was not made in terms of material *substance* but by reference to qualities such as solidity, extension, figure, and motion. His analysis of person was similarly made in terms of such qualities as awareness, concern, responsibility.

play *see* RECREATION

pleasure and pain   The simple ideas of pain and pleasure are received from the sources of ideas, sensation and reflection. They are also simple modes and hence cannot be defined; they can only be acquired from experience (*Essay*, 2.20.1). Locke explains that by pleasure and pain he means to refer to both body and mind, but he hastens to remark that all pleasures and pains are 'only different Constitutions of the Mind, sometimes occasioned by disorder in the Body, sometimes by Thoughts of the Mind' (2.20.2). Delight and uneasiness are the names he frequently uses for pleasure and pain (2.7.2). Various synonyms are satisfaction and happiness for the one, pain, torment, anguish and misery for the other. In a journal entry for 16 July 1676, there is another list of pains of the mind: weariness, sorrow, grief, melancholy, anguish, misery. Pleasures of the mind are there listed as mirth, delight, joy, comfort, happiness (*Essays*, p. 258). Good and evil are the causes of pleasure and pain – our passions are closely linked with them (2.20.3). Reflecting upon some past delight causes the idea of love; e.g., the love of some fruit or the love of one's children or friends. The thought of some object may cause us pain and give rise to hatred (2.20.4, 5).

God is said to have joined to some thoughts and sensations 'a *perception* of *Delight*', and God has annexed 'to several Objects, and to the *Ideas* which we received from them ... a concomitant pleasure' (2.7.3). God has similarly annexed pain to other objects as a way of warning us of possible harm (2.7.4). God's joining pleasure and pain to certain objects and thoughts is related to the innate principle Locke identified as part of human nature, the desire for happiness and aversion to misery (1.3.3). Elsewhere, 'nature' is substituted for 'God': 'it is wisely ordered by Nature ... that Pain should accompany the Reception of several *Ideas*' (2.10.3). Pain can also be a substitute for consideration and reason in children; it even acts more quickly than consideration in grown men, making 'both the Young and Old avoid painful Objects, with that haste, which is necessary for their Preservation' (*ibid.*).

Fear is one of the passions which plays a role in such guidance, but it is also sometimes necessary to overcome one's fears. Locke has some interesting comments about helping children deal with 'vain Terrors', such as the fear of frogs (*Some Thoughts*, §115). He talks also of the training of soldiers for warfare, by gradually getting them to distinguish between those things that are really dangerous and those that are not so (*ibid.*). With children, it is good to get them used to some pain, pain being the source of fear in children. He even recommends putting children in pain as a way of developing some of the Spartan virtues (*ibid.*). He condemns 'vicious Pleasures and Commendation' (§76), he notes that children find pleasure in being esteemed and valued (§57), and he criticizes parents who resort to the rod as a way of training children since 'This kind of Punishment, contributes not at all to the mastery of our Natural Propensity to indulge Corporal and present Pleasure, and to avoid Pain at any rate; but rather encourages it' (§48). Locke wants the child to gain 'Mastery over his Inclinations ... to *resist* the importunity of *present Pleasure or Pain*, for the sake of what Reason tells him is fit to be done' (§45).

Posthumous Works   In a letter to his cousin, Peter King, dated 4 and 25 October 1704 (Locke died on the 28th), Locke describes some papers of his on 'several subjects proposed to my thoughts, which are very little more than extempory views, layd down in suddain and imperfect draughts, which though intended to be revised and farther looked into afterwards, yet by the intervention of business, or preferable enquiries happend to be thrust aside and so lay neglected and sometimes quite

forgotten' (*Corr.* 3648; viii. 412). He left it to King's judgement whether
any of these should be published. Locke comments briefly on each item,
explaining the occasion for writing them and what state they were in. He
lists 'Of the Conduct of the Understanding', 'An Examination of P.
Malebranche's Opinion of Seeing All Things in God', 'A Discourse of
Miracles', and some 'Memoirs' of the first Earl of Shaftesbury. These all
are printed in the *Posthumous Works* (1706), with two pages of a preface,
'Advertisement to the Reader', which borrows sentences and phrases from
Locke's letter, thereby confirming that King was the person responsible
for putting these pieces together, although his name nowhere appears as
editor. Also included in the volume are two items not mentioned by
Locke, 'Part of a Fourth Letter for Toleration' and Locke's 'New Method
of a Common-Place-Book'.

powers The world as Locke understood and depicted it in various
passages in his *Essay concerning Human Understanding* is an active universe
filled with causal processes of different kinds: substances are *generated* by
internal principles activated by external, insensible causes; artefacts are
made by the juxtaposition of parts not previously connected; qualities of
objects are *altered* by the addition of new ones. These common types of
causal production exemplify powers at work in Locke's world, both the
physical and human worlds; but these powers pale before God's power of
creating, perhaps the archetype of active power. Making applies to God as
well as to man, but we only make artefacts such as machines or pictures
while God is *our* maker. The example of creation given by Locke in the
chapter on cause and effect is much lower on the scale of being: a new
particle of matter added to nature (2.26.2). God's creating power is even
such that he could have done what many of Locke's contemporaries
viewed with alarm and took to be a contradiction: give to certain complex,
organized systems of matter (perhaps a human brain) the active property
of thought.

When Locke discusses the *idea* of God and how we form for ourselves
the idea of an infinite being, he links God's power with his wisdom and
goodness. God's attributes are 'beyond the reach of our various Capacities', but we approach an understanding by extending the number or
extent 'of the Acts or Objects of God's Power, Wisdom, and Goodness'
(2.17.1). Our complex idea of 'the incomprehensible, supreme Being' is
made up of the simple ideas from reflecting and enlarging them: having
from 'what we experiment in our selves, got the *Ideas* of Existence and
Duration; of Knowledge and Power', etc., we then keep extending them
(2.23.33). One of the powers of the mind is this ability to enlarge some
of the ideas received from sensation and reflection. God has also given us

another power, 'the power over several parts of our Bodies, to move or keep them at rest, as we think fit' (2.7.3). Experience clearly reveals that we can excite motion by thought, but we no more understand how that works than we understand motion in bodies by impulse, although he thinks that the 'active power of Moving' (motivity) is 'much clearer in Spirit than Body' (2.23.28). Every moment of our waking life we discover this active power thought has for moving bodies. In this passage, Locke even raises the question, 'whether active power be not the proper attribute of Spirits, and passive power of Matter' (*ibid.*). By moving our arms or legs we can 'move our selves, and other contiguous Bodies'; in such motions are contained 'all the Actions of our Body' (2.7.3). The previous chapter identified the 'two great and principal Actions of the Mind' as 'the Power of Thinking' and 'the Power of Volition' (2.6.2). The latter is said to be a power given to our minds by God ('the Wise Author of our being'), the power 'to chuse, amongst its *Ideas*, which it will think on, and to pursue the enquiry of this or that Subject with consideration and attention' (2.7.3). Later, in 2.23.30, he describes thinking as 'a power of Action; i.e. a power of beginning, or stopping several Thoughts or Motions'.

In one passage, Locke says that the idea of power comes both from discovering that we move the parts of our bodies and 'from the effects also, natural Bodies are able to produce in one another' (2.7.8), but in the long chapter on 'power', he says the clearest idea of active power comes from 'reflection on the Operations of our Minds' (2.21.4). In that section, he is concentrating upon the power we have of beginning motion 'barely by a thought of the Mind', but the mind has other powers. Early in the *Essay*, he announces one of his goals, to try to discover the powers of the understanding (1.1.4). Section 7 of this same chapter says we can survey 'our own Understandings, examine our own Powers, and see to what Things they were adapted'. Besides the powers of the mind already mentioned, there is the power of retention, i.e., 'the Power to revive again in our Minds those *Ideas*' which have disappeared from our awareness (2.10.2). He recognizes that sometimes old ideas 'start up in our Minds, of their own accord'; and very often are 'rouzed and tumbled out of their dark Cells, into open Day-light, by some turbulent and tempestuous Passion' (2.10.7). Other times, the 'Mind . . . sets it self on work in search of some hidden *Idea*, and turns, as it were, the Eye of the Soul upon it' (*ibid.*). The mind also has the powers of comparing ideas (2.11.5), of repeating ideas (2.13.3; 2.17.3), of enlarging ideas (2.11.5), of abstracting (2.11.9). Specific examples are given of the formation of particular ideas by reference to some of the powers of the mind. For example, the idea of immensity is acquired from 'the power we find in our selves of repeating, as often as we will, any *Idea* of Space', and the idea of infinity is 'got from the Power, we observe in our selves, of repeating without end our own *Ideas*' (2.17.5,6). Other mental operations cited and used by Locke are said to proceed 'from Powers intrinsical and proper' to the mind (2.1.24). In a curious passage, Locke comments on 'how very *quick* the *actions of the Mind* are performed' (2.9.10). The mind takes up no space, is not extended and 'its actions seem to require no time'; many of its actions are 'crouded into an Instant' (*ibid.*).

More generally, the faculties and powers of moving, sensing and reasoning 'flow from' the constitution of man (3.6.3.). Locke found a similarity in the powers of man in the intellectual and material worlds. In both worlds, the materials are given to us (simple ideas in the former, objects and qualities in the latter); in neither can we create new items, but we can make new combinations. In such acts of making in the world of ideas, we have the active powers of combining, comparing, and separating (2.12.1). The mind is described as having a 'great power in varying and multiplying the Objects of its Thoughts' (2.12.2). Similarly with mixed modes, the mind 'often *exercises an active Power in the making*' of the several combinations of ideas that are the archetype for actions (2.22.2). The most frequent ideas out of which the mind makes mixed modes are those of thinking, motion and power (2.22.10). The first two of these are the ideas 'which comprehend in them all Action'. The idea of power designates that 'from whence these Actions are conceived to flow'. The 'flow from' locution is also used for material substances: qualities flow from the insensible constitution of a substance. Our names and ideas of actions distinguish one action from another by reference to their causes, means, objects, ends, instruments, time, place 'and other circumstances; and also . . . their Power fitted for those Actions'. He gives boldness as the power 'to speak or do what we intend, before others, without fear or disorder'. Powers or abilities of this sort sometimes turn into habits or dispositions. Testiness is 'a disposition or aptness to be angry' (*ibid.*). Material substances have dispositions also which Locke treats as powers. The parallels between the powers of the two kinds of substances often appear in the *Essay*. Power in both kinds of substance is said to be 'the Source from whence all Action proceeds, the Substances wherein these Powers are, when they exert this Power into Act, are called *Causes*; and the Substances which thereupon are produced, or the simple *Ideas* which are introduced into any subject by the exerting of that Power, are called *Effects*' (2.22.11). The power in 'intellectual Agents' is thinking and willing, in corporeal substances it is modifications of motion.

Following tradition, Locke distinguishes between active and passive power, the latter being the power or ability to receive change from some active power. His extended account of the origin of our idea of power in 2.21.1 reveals the activity of the mind in that acquisition.

> The Mind, being every day informed, by the Senses, of the alteration of those simple *Ideas*, it observes in things without; and taking notice how one comes to an end, and ceases to be, and another begins to exist, which was not before; reflecting also on what passes within it self, and observing a constant change of its *Ideas*, sometimes by the impression of outward Objects on the Senses, and sometimes by the Determination of its own choice; and concluding from what it has so constantly observed to have been, that the like Changes will for the future be made, in the same things, by like Agents, and by the like ways, considers in one thing the possibility of having any of its simple *Ideas* changed, and in another the possibility of making that change; and so comes by that *Idea* which we call *Power*.

Locke believed that our idea of active power, of the beginning of motion, comes only or most easily from reflecting on what 'passes in our selves, where we find by Experience, that barely by willing it, barely by a thought of the Mind, we can move the parts of our Bodies, which were before at rest' (2.21.4). We (Locke writes, 'the Mind') also have the power 'to order the consideration of any *Idea*, or the forbearing to consider it' (2.21.5). Both the power to move our body and the power over our thoughts and ideas are called 'the will'. Liberty is identified as the power we as agents have to 'do or forbear any particular Action, according to the determination or thought of the mind' (2.21.8). The issue of liberty or necessity is formulated in that long chapter around the idea of power. He concludes that chapter by returning to the distinction between active and passive powers. Active power for any substance is the putting itself in motion. This active power is strictly 'in no substance which cannot begin motion in it self, or in another substance at rest' (2.21.72). The same caution holds for thinking substances: a power to receive thoughts is passive power.

Do corporeal substances meet this criterion of *active* power? Locke raised the question in 2.23.28 of whether passive power is not the only kind of power matter has. He raises the same question in 2.21.2: 'whether Matter be not wholly destitute of *active Power*'. Several passages say that only *agents* have active power. Is there any kind of body, any particular corporeal substance, that is or could be an agent, or is it only humans (and God) who qualify as agents and hence are the only possessors of active power? His analysis of secondary qualities leads to the conclusion that they are powers of bodies in relation to our perception (2.21.3). He even says in this passage that the idea of power is 'a principal Ingredient in our complex *Ideas* of Substances'. This assertion is reaffirmed in 2.23.8:

'*Powers make a great part of our complex* Ideas *of Substances*' (cf. 2.23.10). The power a magnet has to operate on the minute particles of iron is cited in 2.23.9. The powers of gold (both active and passive) and of the sun are mentioned in 2.23.10. The power of '*communication of Motion by impulse*' is cited in 2.23.28, although he professes ignorance of how this power works. The ideas of whiteness and coldness and pain are said to be the 'Effects of Powers in Things without us, ordained by our Maker, to produce in us such Sensations' (2.30.2). Simple ideas are adequate because they are intended 'to express nothing but the power in Things to produce in the Mind such a Sensation' (2.31.12). We do not have adequate ideas of substances because we do not know all the active and passive powers any substance has (2.31.13). In 2.32.14, he repeats the earlier remark about our simple ideas: they are the perceptions 'God has fitted us to receive, and given Power to external objects to produce in us'. Simple ideas 'answer' the powers of objects. For example, the idea of the blue of a violet is in the flower 'only the Power of producing it by the Texture of its Parts, reflecting the Particles of Light' (§14; see also §15).

In Book Four, Locke talks again of the active and passive powers of bodies; they operate by means of the texture and motion of their parts (4.3.16). In that passage, he even talks of the 'necessary Connexion, and *Co-existence*, of the Powers' of bodies. Locke of course does not think our knowledge can discern these powers: 'we are ignorant of the several Powers, Efficacies, and Ways of Operation' of bodies (§24).

Of the three kinds of qualities discussed in 2.8, the secondary qualities and that third kind unnamed by Locke (those that cause changes in other bodies) are described as '*Powers barely*, and nothing but Powers' (2.8.24). No one, Locke remarks, thinks the whiteness and softness of wax when placed in sunlight are qualities of the sun. The powers of the sun are responsible for those changes. Similarly, we should not think the sensible qualities such as colour, smell, taste, that we are aware of when observing wax or any other objects, are real qualities of the object. In the object, these are only powers to bring about the appearances we experience. The status of primary qualities in objects is not quite as clear-cut, but it is the case that those qualities, or the particles that compose any bit of matter, exert the powers which result in the other two kinds of changes, changes in appearance to perceivers and changes in the constitution (and hence indirectly in the appearances) of other bodies (see 2.8.13). Even such a quality as 'fixedness' in gold is described as 'a power to remain in the Fire unconsumed' (4.1.6). In that intriguing passage in 4.6.11 in which Locke talks of the interrelatedness of all things ('Things, however absolute and entire they seem in themselves, are but Retainers to other parts of Nature'), he refers to the 'observable Qualities, Actions, and Powers' of objects which 'are owing to something without them'. In this passage he makes rather sweeping claims about the qualities 'by which we know, and distinguish' objects. Presumably he means sensible qualities. Since the ideas of primary qualities are produced in the same way as the ideas of secondary qualities (by the structure and motion of particles), Locke may intend this passage to apply to them as well. The *appearances* of things include both primary and secondary qualities, extended shape as well as colour and sound. What is lacking in our knowledge is, e.g., 'the Constitution within the Body of a Fly, or an Elephant, upon which depend those Qualities and Powers we Observe in them' (*ibid.*).

Corpuscles or particles are hard, have shape, are extended, in motion or at rest, and they are insensible. It is the configuration in particular masses of matter that enables them to manifest another property, the power to cause ideas in perceivers and the power to make changes in the properties of other bodies. Power is, in effect, another, perhaps the prime, primary quality of matter. The usual corpuscularian account, or the usual description of corpuscular matter given by those who wanted to protect God as the only *active* power, talked of matter as dumb, passive, inert and incapable of initiating motion: it was not self-active. The big battle in the eighteenth century over Locke's suggestion of thinking matter was waged over the claim that thought added to matter would make matter active. Of course, for traditionalists that possibility also violated a fundamental principle: each of the two kinds of substance had its essential property which could not be interchanged or added to the other. But most defenders of immaterialism (the view that there are two substances and that matter cannot think) also saw that Locke's suggestion would give to matter an active power and hence would go against their notion of inert, passive matter (*see* THINKING MATTER).

There was not the same apprehension over the powers of Locke's matter, the powers bodies have to initiate new ideas and new changes of bodily properties. 'Creative' would be too strong, but Locke's matter is far removed from the dumb, inactive matter defended by those who attacked the thinking-matter suggestion. Locke should have been attacked over his concept of matter, quite independently of the thinking-matter controversy. His active matter is obviously linked with the changes in the concept of substance which were taking place under Locke's hands. We lack a knowledge of the essence of material or of immaterial substance. Thus he was able to displace Descartes's extended and thinking substances with an active matter and a thinking, conscious, concerned person.

It is difficult to say which of these changes was the more radical. With the insertion into the concept of matter of the notion of powers (our principal idea of it), it must have seemed an innocent conceptual point to Locke to remark on the possibility of another power – thought – being added to matter. Whether he saw the connection between the *material* powers of matter and the power of thought, is not clear from his text. Nevertheless, at just about the same time that Newton elaborated his concept of gravity, of attraction and repulsion, Locke's *Essay* presented a power concept of matter. Newton was cautious about *his* powers, insisting that they were not part of the nature of matter. Locke may have been protected from the same attack Newton feared, since Locke wrote mainly about our *idea* of matter, not matter itself. After all, he disclaimed any knowledge of the essential nature of matter.

prerogative   Locke favoured written law so that people could know what they and their rulers could and could not do. The law of nature was, however, unwritten but he thought its dictates were clear. There is another area where unwritten laws (it might be better to call them 'judgements') operate in government. Locke recognized, as many other writers did, that written law could not cover all contingencies, could not be specific enough to enable rulers or the executive body to decide every issue. The executive branch of government accordingly has a power 'to act according to discretion, for the publick good, without the prescription of the Law, and sometimes even against it'. This power is called 'prerogative' (*T*2, §160). Such power and discretion operate within the general proviso, in the public good. The end of government is, Locke repeats often, 'the *preservation of all*' (*ibid.*, §159). Prerogative has another side to it: it is 'Peoples permitting their Rulers, to do several things of their own free choice, where the Law was silent, and sometimes too against the direct Letter of the Law, for the publick good' (*ibid.*, §164). The people can even take back some of the prerogative by instituting laws to cover some acts formerly done through the ruler's prerogative, but there will always be a need for discretionary action.

How is the judgement to be made that some action done by prerogative was for the public good? Locke openly recognized that there may be times when disagreements break out, but there is no criterion the people can appeal to against prerogative, at least not on earth. The very nature of acts done through prerogative is that there are no laws or criteria that can be used to test their propriety for furthering the good of the society. An appeal to heaven is, Locke suggests, the only recourse in such disputes (§168). At the very end of *Two Treatises*, when addressing the topic of tyranny and the dissolution of government, Locke mutes that stark conclusion about the only appeal being to heaven by saying '*The People shall be Judge'* (§240), the 'body' (the majority?) of the people should be the umpire (§241), but there he seems to assume a case where there would be little dispute among the people that the actions of the ruler or executive branch were against the public good. The issues here are delicate and complex, and have been the source of much debate.

probability   'The very notation [i.e., the central meaning] of the Word' *probability* is, Locke says, 'likeliness to be true' (*Essay*, 4.15.3). A probable proposition has arguments and proofs which 'make it pass or be received for true' (*ibid.*). This last clause indicates the close connection there is for him between probability and belief or assent. The arguments and proofs supporting some claim 'are found to perswade us to receive it as true', without our having certain knowledge of the truth. Lacking certainty, the arguments and proofs provide 'inducements' to take those claims as true (4.15.3, 4). Some ideas have 'an usual or likely' agreement; here, the judgement 'is properly exercised' in making probable propositions. Sometimes, probability can be so strong that the assent 'as necessarily follows it, as Knowledge does Demonstration' (4.17.16). In conversation, there is merit in 'the opposite Arguings of Men of Parts, shewing the different Sides of things, and their various Aspects, and Probabilities' (*ST*, §145). Since the extent of human knowledge is limited, well-grounded beliefs become the basis for most of our actions, probability becomes our guide (*Essay*, 1.1.5; 4.3.6). Locke compares the knowledge that we *do* have to seeing in 'broad day-light'; probability is the twilight 'suitable, I presume, to that State of Mediocrity and Probationship, he [God] has been pleased to place us in here' (4.14.2).

Locke's concept of probability is not a quantitative one: the arguments and proofs are not formal arguments (there is no logic of probability in his account), although he does talk of degrees of probability and of the preponderance of evidence. His account might be described as a psychology of probability, an account that recognizes the various factors that lead to belief and assent, and a recommendation for what should be the experiences and reports that merit our assent. There are rules and criteria for assessing the weight of the evidence or the degree of likeliness that some claim is true, but the basis for probable propositions and for our assent to them is conformity of claims 'with our own Knowledge, Observation and Experience' (4.15.4). The testimony of others, under specific conditions, can add to our inducements to believe certain claims. What experience and observation deal with are matters of fact (4.16.5). 'Where any particular thing, consonant to the constant Observation of our selves and others, in the like case, comes attested by the concurrent Reports of all that mention it, we receive it as easily, and build as firmly upon it, as if it were certain Knowledge; and we reason and act thereupon with as little doubt, as if it were perfect demonstration' (4.16.6). This is the highest degree of probability: 'when the general consent of all Men, in all Ages, as far as it can be known, concurs with a Man's constant and never-failing Experience in like cases, to confirm the Truth of any particular matter of fact attested by fair Witnesses' (*ibid.*). Examples of such highly probable propositions are: 'it froze in England last winter', 'there were swallows in the summer', 'fire warms and melts lead'. These propositions are near-certainties; assent to them is assurance.

The testimony of historians about certain features of human nature, e.g. that 'most Men preferr their private Advantage, to the publick', fits our experience; if all historians say that this was true of Tiberius, that report is extremely probable and gives rise to confidence (4.16.7). Particular matters of fact reported by historians have the next degree of probability, e.g., that there is such a city as Rome, that there was a man called Julius Caesar who was a general (4.16.8). Such reported persons and events have nothing in themselves that gives probability to the report: it is because those reports are 'by Historians of credit, and contradicted by' no writer that we cannot avoid believing them. Such reports 'carry' evidence, so much evidence that it 'naturally determines the Judgment' and leaves us little liberty to disbelieve it (4.16.9).

What happens when testimony or historical reports clash or contradict ordinary experience or even the normal course of nature? We must pay particular attention, weigh arguments and proofs for or against the testimony or report. Locke then calls attention to the various factors at work in testimony: a 'great variety of contrary Observations, Circumstances, Reports, different Qualifications, Tempers, Designs, Over-sights, *etc.* of the Reporters' (*ibid.*). He suggests a list of considerations that may guide us in deciding the probable accuracy of some report: the number of persons supporting a report, their integrity, their skill as witnesses. Second-hand reports, reports of what others reported, raise other problems: 'Passion, Interest, Inadvertency, Mistake of his Meaning, and a thousand odd Reasons, or Caprichio's' may lead to misleading or false reports (4.16.11).

So much for the possibility of matters of fact that can be observed and experienced. There is another class of probable propositions, of 'Propositions we receive upon Inducements of *Probability*', namely, those 'concerning Things, which being beyond the discovery of our Senses, are not capable of such Testimony' (4.16.5). This class of probable propositions ranges from assertions about the 'Existence, Nature, and Operations of finite immaterial Beings without us; as Spirits, Angels, Devils, *etc.*', to queries about the possible existence of 'material Beings; which either for their smallness in themselves, or remoteness from us, our Senses cannot take notice of, as whether there be any Plants, Animals, and intelligent Inhabitants in the Planets, and other Mansions of the vast Universe' (4.16.12), to suggestions about the imagined causes of the events and objects we do observe. For this last kind of claim, analogy is the basis on which we should construct our hypotheses. Locke gives us several examples where 'a wary Reasoning from Analogy' leads us to make probable conjectures about the corpuscular structure of matter and about the range of the chain of being.

Probability and probable reasoning were discussed briefly prior to Locke. The Port Royal logic of Arnauld and Nicole anticipates some of Locke's analysis (*La logique, ou L'Art de penser*, 1668, Pt I, ch. IV; Pt. IV, ch. XV; see also *John Locke e Port-Royal: il problema della probabilità*, by Luca Obertello, 1964). Bishop John Wilkins, *Of the Principles and Duties of Natural Religion* (1675), distinguishes knowledge from opinion or probability. For more on the early history of the concept of probability, see Ian Hacking's *The Emergence of Probability* (1975).

proof Demonstrative knowledge for Locke involves an intuition of the agreement or disagreement of ideas. That intuition frequently needs to be mediated by other ideas that link the ideas between which we are trying to discern the connection. Locke calls these mediating ideas, the ideas that intervene between two other ideas, 'proof' (*Essay*, 4.2.3, 7). The 'proof' of the connection between one idea and another lies in some other idea that is immediately related to each of the ideas under examination. In complex demonstrations, there is required a 'long train of Proofs', a series of ideas intervening between two other ideas, until the relation between the first and last can be 'seen' or perceived (4.2.6). Knowledge by intervening proofs is not as clear as intuitive knowledge, and complex demonstrations can lead to mistakes, but both intuition and demonstration yield certainty (4.2.3, 4, 5).

Just as a demonstration 'is the shewing the Agreement, or Disagreement of two *Ideas*, by the intervention of one or more Proofs', so probability is the appearance of agreement or disagreement 'by the intervention of Proofs' (4.15.1). A proof, then, seems to be *part of* or a *component of* a demonstration. Since he sometimes uses geometrical examples in talking about demonstration (e.g., the relation between equality, the three angles of a triangle, and two right angles), we might think that proofs are formal arguments such as Euclid's demonstrations. We might be tempted to say Locke had a mathematical or geometrical concept of proof. But his use of the term 'proof' to refer to intervening ideas in a demonstration should make us pause before drawing that conclusion. Moreover, when we examine what he has to say about DEMONSTRATION, we discover that his concept of it is rather more informal. A demonstration *shows* us the connection of ideas, it enables us to 'see' or perceive that connection. That perception results from intuition and proofs, the latter enabling us to extend our intuitions to other related ideas. Locke did allow that syllogisms do 'shew the connexion of the Proofs', but he believed the mind could discover that connection without the formality of syllogism and its rules (4.17.4). The stress in his discussion of demonstration, probability, and proof is on the way we are brought to perceive and assent to some proposition or claim as true or probable. There are arguments, both demonstrative and probable, which include evidence from experience and observation, the testimony of expert witnesses, and a more formal presentation of conceptual connections.

The term 'proof' is also used throughout the *Essay* and in the first of *Two Treatises* in a more ordinary, less technical way: e.g., the fact that not all nations have an idea of God proves that idea is not innate; or the inability to say what a particular word means is proof that you lack an idea for that word; or proofs drawn from Scripture.

properties Locke's use of this term is rather curious, unsystematic, but of some importance. It does not occur in the *Essay* until 2.23, the chapter on substances and his discussion of kinds of substances. He uses 'sorts' and sometimes 'species' instead of 'kinds'. Between that chapter and 3.6.6, the term 'properties' appears frequently, often in association with, or even as having the same meaning as, 'qualities'. In 3.6.6, he announces that properties belong to '*Species*, and not to Individuals'. The distinction between instances of particulars (i.e., individuals, this bit of gold, that man) and kinds or species runs throughout these many chapters and sections. The remark that properties relate to sorts, not to individuals, raises several questions: (1) 'do properties differ from qualities?', (2) 'what terms should we use to describe individuals?', and (3) 'are descriptions of individuals given in the language of kinds, the language that characterizes the species that an individual, a particular, represents?' These questions are confounded by several difficulties, one being the late appearance of 'property' in the *Essay*, another being Locke's very firm claim that kinds or sorts are made by man, not by nature, and a third being the unsystematic way in which 'properties', 'qualities', and even on occasion 'ideas' are used. It is worthwhile to trace the use of these words from 2.23.6 to the end of the *Essay* in 4.21.2. The appearance of the word 'idea' in many of these passages illustrates Locke's confession made in 2.8.8 (the discussion of different kinds of qualities of bodies) that he had often written 'idea' when he should have used 'quality', especially in places where he speaks of ideas 'as in the things themselves'. He there asked his reader to understand that he means 'the Qualities in the Objects which produce' the ideas we have.

In *Essay* 2.23.6, he is talking of the ideas we have or form of '*particular distinct sorts of Substances*'. He thinks the combination of ideas (!) coexisting and adhering in a substratum which is the cause of the union of those ideas is unclear because of the concept of a substance. The examples he uses throughout these passages are greatly varied; in this passage they are man, horse, sun, water, iron, gold, vitriol, bread. He talks of observing simple ideas in combination, of sensible qualities supposed to inhere in a substance; the section ends by using all three terms, speaking of 'observing those sensible Qualities, *Ideas*, or Properties, which are in that thing, which he calls the *Sun*'. It is clear that the topic in this section is particular *sorts* of substances. Section 14 of this same chapter talks again of ideas '*considered as united in one thing*'. The example here is a swan. He switches to 'properties' after giving a list of colours, long neck, red beak, power of swimming and 'some other Properties, which all terminate in sensible simple *Ideas*, all united in one common subject'. In 2.23.30, he again refers to 'primary Qualities, or Properties of Body'.

In another section, ideas of modes are 'voluntary Collections of simple *Ideas*, which the Mind puts together, without reference to any real Archetypes, or standing Patterns' (2.31.3). These ideas are themselves archetypes 'made by the Mind, to rank and denominate Things by'. The example is of a figure such as a triangle. He contrasts this kind of idea with the ideas of substances, remarking that we would like to 'represent to our selves that Constitution, on which all their Properties depend', a feat that is beyond our knowledge. He goes on to describe those men who think the names of substances do stand for certain real essences: they 'suppose certain specifick Essences of Substances, which each Individual in its several kind is made conformable to' (2.31.6). It is clear that these men, as depicted by Locke, suppose the essence to belong to a kind, not to an individual. They believe that they rank things by reference to those supposed real essences. Locke talks of observing collections of simple ideas 'constantly to exist together', remarking that 'such a complex *Idea* cannot be the real Essence of any Substance; for then the Properties we discover in that Body, would depend on that complex *Idea*, and be deducible from it, and their necessary connexion with it be known; as all Properties of a Triangle' are (*ibid.*). He then changes back to 'qualities'. The example is of iron: 'a Body of a certain Colour, Weight, and Hardness; and a Property that they look on as belonging to it, is malleableness.' Is the term 'property' applied only to malleableness? He says 'this Property has no necessary connexion with that complex *Idea*, or any part of it' (the idea

of gold). He understands these men to be referring to the *sorts* of things
and to their supposed real essences. The example is gold again with a few
additional qualities: 'shining yellowness; a greater weight than any thing
I know of the same bulk; and a fitness to have its Colour changed by the
touch of Quicksilver'. These features are then spoken of as 'properties':
'the internal Constitution, on which these Properties depend' (2.31.6).
But a few lines further on, it's back to 'qualities'.

   In this last passage, he has introduced a particular bit of gold, the ring
on his finger. He writes against the notion of a substantial form being the
real essence, rather than the corpuscular structure. Section 8 of this same
chapter speaks of qualities and powers of substances which make up our
complex ideas, pointing out that these ideas do not contain all the
qualities and powers of substances. He uses the language of simple ideas
united in the things. He is discussing inadequate ideas. He even ends by
saying 'it is impossible we should have adequate *Ideas* of any Substance,
made up of a Collection of all its Properties.' He also makes a passing
reference to his point about all the simple ideas of our complex ideas of
substances being powers, except 'only the Figure and Bulk of some sorts',
indicating that he is still talking about sorts, kinds, rather than the
particular ring. Nevertheless, he moves between talking about ideas,
qualities, and sometimes properties. This wavering about which term to
use is found in 2.31.10 where he comments: 'But no one, who hath
considered the Properties of Bodies in general, or this sort in particular'
can doubt that gold has many other properties. He speaks of 'this species',
and continues to use the term 'properties', saying all of them are inseparable from its internal constitution. He refers to the properties of a triangle
also. He never seems to refer to the 'qualities' of geometric figures. His
point in this section is that there are probably thousands, even an infinite
number, of properties in a sort of substance such as gold. Even our ideas
of mathematical figures would be inadequate if we had to collect all their
properties; luckily we do have the whole essence via the definition of such
figures: we can 'discover those Properties, and demonstratively see how
they flow from' their essences, their definitions (2.31.11).

   When he discusses true and false ideas, the term 'properties' appears
again: 'When the Mind *refers* any of its *Ideas* to that *real* Constitution, and
Essence of any thing, whereon all its Properties depend' (2.32.5). Later, he
says that our complex idea of gold does not contain the real essence since
'it contains but some few of those Properties, which flow from its real
Essence and Constitution' (2.32.24). These properties consist 'mostly in
the active and passive Powers' that objects have in relation to other things
(*ibid.*). He goes on to speak of 'the complex *Idea* of that kind of Things',
reminding us that he is not talking about individuals, but kinds of

individuals. The example here is a triangle, whose properties flow from its essence. He ends this section by remarking: 'So I imagine it is in Substances, their real Essences lie in a little compass; though the Properties flowing from that internal Constitution, are endless' (2.32.5). When he deals with general names, the term 'properties' is used again. A new idea of man can be made 'by leaving out the shape, and some other Properties signified by the name *Man*' (3.3.8). When, in this section, he contrasts his notion of real essence with the traditional one, he argues that the latter is falsified by the existence of monsters, since as he writes further on, 'it is as impossible, that two Things, partaking exactly of the same real *Essence*, should have different Properties, as that two Figures partaking in the same real *Essence* of a Circle, should have different Properties' (3.3.17). The triangle is also used as an example whose properties are founded on its essence. The situation is quite different with bits of matter, for example, the parcel of gold that makes the ring on his finger. There, it is not a definition, but the insensible parts 'on which depend all those Properties of Colour, Weight, Fusibility, Fixedness, *etc.* which are to be found in it' (3.3.18). The difference between mathematical figures and natural substances is not that the properties of the latter do not flow from the essence, from the internal constitution of particles, but that, unlike the triangle, we do not have a knowledge of that constitution. The term 'qualities' is used in this passage, but in 3.3.19, where the examples are grass, sheep, and man, it is the term 'properties' that is used. He also remarks in this last passage that 'the *Essence* of a *Species* [its nominal essence] rests safe and entire, without the existence of so much as one Individual of that kind', seeming to give to these essences something like the status of the essences of mixed modes.

The similarities between the ideas of mixed modes are extended in 3.5.16. The ideas of mixed modes and their names signify a real essence (since there is no difference in their case between real and nominal essence), and they are 'the Workmanship of the Mind'. This is the same language he uses when talking about the kinds of substances (3.5.14). All the properties of the species of actions (mixed modes) flow from and depend upon the complex ideas of those actions. In both cases, of mixed modes and substances, the boundaries of each sort or species are determined by the abstract idea. In contrasting the ideas of mixed modes with those of natural substances, Locke uses both 'qualities' and 'properties' (3.6.2). The real essence or internal constitution of substances is 'the foundation of all those Properties that are combined, and are constantly found to co-exist with the *nominal Essence*' (3.6.6). He continues in this section to refer to properties in relation to sorts of substances, although the term 'qualities' also appears in the example of gold. This is the section where he says that the term 'properties' belongs to sorts, not to individuals. He insists that the concept of 'essential' (he does not say 'essence') belongs to an object 'as a Condition, whereby it is of this or that Sort'. But again, the shift to quality talk occurs, he gives examples of sulphur, antimony, vitriol. He remarks that if these were distinguished into species 'according to their real Essences, it would be as impossible to find different Properties in any two individual Substances of the same *Species*, as it is to find different Properties in two Circles, or two equilateral Triangles' (3.6.8). In the next section he reverts to the language of 'ideas', speaking of the collection of sensible ideas that we observe which form the nominal essence, but he quickly falls back into quality language when he uses examples of plants, animals, iron, lead (3.6.9). A later section uses the language of properties when talking of species of spirits (3.6.17), and another section uses the language of properties flowing from different real essences (3.6.19). The mixture of qualities and properties is found in still later sections of this chapter (e.g., 3.6.47, 49; cf. 3.9.12). In 3.9.13, simple ideas are said to be found to coexist and to be 'united in the several Sorts of Things'; they become the standards that the names refer to (3.9.13). The rest of this section uses 'qualities' and 'properties' in a similar way, as standards for ranking kinds of things.

This partial survey of the use of the term 'properties', along with 'qualities' and sometimes 'ideas', is representative of many subsequent passages in Books Three and Four of the *Essay*. Some of those passages do discuss sorts of things, but there is no pattern of using 'properties' only when talking of sorting and kinds. In a few places in his exchange with Stillingfleet, the language is 'modes and properties' (*Mr. Locke's Letter to the Bishop of Worcester*, in *Works*, iv. 25, 27). That exchange does not help us resolve the question about properties and qualities: do they both relate to sorts, or do particular things *as particulars* have qualities, not properties? This question is not resolved on the basis of the texts. His use of 'properties' may just be a survival from scholastic and Aristotelian writers, but if, as these texts of Locke seem to suggest, he drew no significant distinction between qualities and properties, could he have just as easily said in 3.6.6 that qualities pertain to sorts, not to individuals? Such language would be odd, would leave the description of particulars without a vocabulary; it would at least require rephrasing: the notion of *essential* qualities relates to sorts. This seems to be the point Locke wants to make, when he discusses our abstract ideas of kinds of things, or when we talk of qualities or properties that are essential. Since we cannot discover the real essence (for Locke, the internal constitution of any bit of matter, organic or inorganic), we cannot say that any set of qualities or properties is essential for any bit of matter. 'Essential' for us can only refer to the nominal essence which we form, that collection of qualities or properties which we identify as types of things, as the standards for any particular's being an instance of what we call gold, lead, silver, water, horse, man, plant. Qualities or properties define sorts, our abstract general ideas and their names are sortals, and sortals are the workmanship of man, not of nature (*see* SORTS, SORTALS).

property   Locke's chapter on property in the second of *Two Treatises* has been the subject of much discussion by those writing about his political philosophy. Property is a central concept in his account of civil government. Political power is defined as 'a *Right* of making Laws with Penalties of Death, and consequently all less Penalties, for the Regulating and Preserving of Property' (*T*2, §3). Much of the first of *Two Treatises* was written against Robert Filmer's claims about property in his *Patriarcha, or The Natural Power of Kings* (1680). Filmer defended the thesis that God gave to Adam and his heirs dominion over the earth and its inhabitants. As Locke interpreted Filmer, this claim was startling: Adam had 'a Divine unalterable Right of Sovereignty, whereby a Father or a Prince hath an Absolute, Arbitrary, Unlimited, and Unlimitable Power, over the Lives, Liberties, and Estates of his Children and Subjects' (*T*1, §9). Filmer, Locke claims, said that Adam was monarch of the world: God gave him property and dominion over animals and children (*T*1, §23). Locke disputes Filmer's claim that the Bible anywhere gave Adam or any of his descendants exclusive dominion of property. One of the disputed passages, Genesis 1: 28, sets mankind above the other creatures and does give them a dominion over those creatures, but Locke insists that the passage also confirms 'the Original Community of all things amongst the Sons of Men' (*T*1, §40).

The difference of interpretation lies there: exclusive right to property or a right to use some of what is common. There is a difference between *having dominion* 'which a Shepherd may have', and *having full* property as an owner (*T*1, §39). On Filmer's interpretation, God gave Adam and *his* posterity ownership, not just dominion, over land and animals. Locke is not saying that ownership is improper. '*Justice* gives every Man a Title to the product of his honest Industry' (*T*1, §42). A qualification, which becomes important for Locke's second treatise analysis, says that another virtue, charity, 'gives every Man a Title to so much out of another's Plenty, as will keep him from extream want, where he has no means to subsist otherwise' (*ibid.*). Locke assures us that God would not give to anyone a property which would deny 'his needy Brother a Right to the Surplusage of his Goods'. What a man acquires through his industry descends to his children, so ownership is inherited; if there are no children, that property returns in a society to the community, or to the 'common stock of Mankind' (*T*1, §§88–90). The question of how anyone *could* acquire property is one that Locke says will be dealt with later, although the reference to a man's industry in §42 would seem to give at least a partial answer. Section 92 appears to give an additional explanation: the origin of property is 'from the Right a Man has to use any of the Inferior Creatures, for the Subsistence and Comfort of his Life'.

Locke opens the chapter on property in the second of *Two Treatises* (chapter 5) by reiterating his conviction that, as Psalm CXV. xvi says, God '*has given the Earth to the Children of Men*, given it to Mankind in Common' (*T*2, §25). The question is 'how any one should ever come to have a *Property* in any thing'. This question is put as a conceptual problem. He remarks that 'it seems to some a very great difficulty.' He points out that if Filmer's interpretation is correct, the result would be that only 'one universal Monarch, should have any property', since Filmer supposes that 'God gave the World to *Adam*, and his Heirs in Succession, exclusive of all the rest of his Posterity.' Locke then informs us that what he will do in this chapter is to show 'how Men might come to have a *property* in several parts of that which God gave to Mankind in common, and that without any express Compact of all the Commoners'. The word 'might' reflects the conceptual nature, even perhaps the tentative nature, of the analysis that follows.

The steps in Locke's account of how men *might* come to own property are as follows:

(1)   God gave the world to men in common, along with the faculty of reason, 'to make use of it to the best advantage of Life, and convenience' (*T*2, §26).

(2)   The fruits that 'the spontaneous hand of Nature' has produced, and the animals that feed on the earth, were given to mankind in common.

(3)   No one has 'a private dominion, exclusive of the rest of Mankind', in any of the productions of nature in their *natural* state.

(4)   Since the products of the hand of nature were given us for our use, 'there must of necessity be a means *to appropriate* them some way or other before they can be of any use, or at all beneficial to any particular Man.'

(5)   Appropriation in the case of food requires, if they are to do a man (Locke speaks of a wild Indian) any good, that it becomes 'a part of him'.

There is nothing exceptional so far in these steps, except perhaps step 5. The notion that edible property becomes a part of the person who consumes it is correct, but the suggestion seems to be that these sorts of items become my property by my eating them. When they are, in the biological sense, 'part of' me, they are mine. By making them disappear, by consuming them, I have also, Locke adds, prevented anyone else having a right to that food. So far, then, Locke has not mentioned the industry of the Indian as giving him a right to the food he picks.

Locke's next step adds an even more novel notion.

(6)   Even though 'the Earth, and all inferior Creatures be common to all Men', there is, even before any appropriation, some private property: 'every Man has a *Property* in his own *Person*' (§27). The notion of right is also present in this step: no one else has a right to my person.

Locke was sometimes obsessively concerned with someone having dominion over others. He chastised Filmer strongly for his claim for absolute dominion over others. The notion of part of *my* property being my PERSON may sound strange to our ears, but it is linked with Locke's special meaning of 'person', the moral agent who appropriates his actions and thus constitutes his personhood.

(7)   The next step in Locke's explanation of how men might come to have property in what is common (of course, the person is not part of the common), something else I as a person own, it is my labour, the labour of my body and the work of my hands. This too is not part of what is common (§27).

(8)   The reverse of the Indian making the products of nature part of himself now becomes the next step. By using the body and hands that I own (or the labour that I own through the use of body and hands), I mix my labour with nature's products, I join my labour to what the hand of nature produces. Just as the Indian made food his property by making that food part of his body, so now, by making my labour part of what nature provides, I make some portion of what is common mine, my property. Consuming the food nature provides is one way in which a part of what is common is removed from the common. Mixing labour with products of nature is another way to remove part of what is common. In both ways, no one has a right to what I have made my own, so long as (and here is an important qualification already anticipated by §29 of the first treatise) 'there is enough and as good left in common for others' (*T2*, §27).

(9)   Locke now combines the two modes of appropriation, eating and labouring. He now says that it is the gathering of acorns, not the

eating, which makes the acorns mine. It is not the *taking away* that makes them mine, although of course the nourishment I received from nature is mine (§28). It is the *adding to* nature that makes the food I cultivate and eat mine, giving me a 'private right' to the food. There is a significant difference between *taking from* and *adding to* nature more than was there.

Locke does not always stress the adding to nature in his examples, but it is clear that all taking involves some adding of labour. The next step in Locke's suggested account of privatization (of how it is possible to turn what God gave all mankind into private property) follows quickly.

(10)   Appropriating from what is common does not require the 'consent of all Mankind' (§28). He even claims a law of nature sanctions such appropriation (§30).

(11)   The same law of nature which permits appropriation in the way Locke has indicated (adding and taking) has a proviso: I can appropriate and enjoy so long as it does not spoil. Unlimited acquisition of property is forbidden by the law of nature. This principle gets modified later when Locke deals with the invention of money.

(12)   Section 32 applies the above account to land. Property in land is acquired in the same way as the products of nature. Here, the *adding to* of labour is more prominent. '*As much Land* as a Man Tills, Plants, Improves, Cultivates, and can use the Product of, so much is his *Property*.'

The significance for Locke of adding to nature is stressed by what he goes on to say in this and the following sections. In giving the earth to all mankind, God 'commanded Man also to labour'; God commanded that man 'subdue the Earth', i.e., 'improve it for the benefit of Life, and therein lay out something upon it that was his own, his labour' (§32). Farming the land annexes to that land something that is already the farmer's property, his labour. He also has property in his person, so person and labour go together to acquire additional property.

The account of how what was originally given to all is consistent with individual appropriation of part of what is common takes place within the two parameters specified in steps 8 and 11: that there is always enough goods and land left for others to privatize, and that what is taken does not spoil. So long as these two conditions are honoured, the 'taking' is negated: 'For he that leaves as much as another can make use of, does as good as take nothing' (§33). What God gave was not intended to remain common and uncultivated. Perhaps God did not really give the earth and its creatures to *all* mankind after all: 'He gave it to the use of the Industrious and Rational': labour was to be each man's title to land (§34). In commanding us to subdue nature, God 'gave Authority so far to *appropriate*. And the Condition of Humane Life, which requires Labour and Materials to work on, necessarily introduces *private Possessions*' (§35). The ground rules for acquisition, what Locke calls the 'measures of Property' (steps 8 and 11), work well in 'the first Ages of the World'; they even perhaps work in the world of Locke's time, although he recognizes that much of the world by then was populated (§36). Locke was convinced that 'the same *Rule of Propriety*, (viz.) that every Man should have as much as he could make use of, would hold still in the World, without straitning any body, since there is Land enough in the World to suffice double the Inhabitants' (*ibid.*).

The next clause in this section tells us why the rules of property-acquisition were upset: 'had not the *Invention of Money*, and the tacit Agreement of Men to put a value on it, introduced (by Consent) larger Possessions, and a Right to them'. But it was not just the invention of money, that upset the modest rules for adding to and taking away from what was common, which brought about rather drastic changes in the concepts of justice and charity described in *T*1, §42. These changes were also due to the appearance of a specific desire which was apparently not present in man in the first ages of the world, 'the desire of having more than Men needed' (*T*2, §37). This desire led to the invention of money; it also 'altered the intrinsick value of things, which depends only on their usefulness to the Life of Man' (§37). The importance of industriousness, of adding use-value to the land by cultivating it, is reinforced by several sections in which he talks about value. Uncultivated land is less valuable than cultivated land. Appropriating land by industry and labour increases 'the common stock of mankind' (*ibid.*). It is labour that '*puts the difference of value* on every thing' (§40; cf. §§41–43).

In section 39, Locke concludes that he has now shown how he can account for property without Filmer's exclusory supposition of Adam's private dominion over all the world. He summarizes his alternative in section 44:

> From all which it is evident, that though the things of Nature are given in common, yet Man (by being Master of himself, and *Proprietor of his own Person*, and the Actions or *Labour* of it) had still in himself *the great Foundation of Property*; and that which made up the great part of what he applyed to the Support or Comfort of his being, when Invention and Arts had improved the conveniencies of Life, was perfectly his own, and did not belong in common to others.

The two modifications to this account are the introduction of money and the regulation of property by consent in civil society. Civil laws regulate 'the Properties of the private Men of their Society, and so, *by Compact* and Agreement, *settled the Property* which Labour and Industry began' (§45). The introduction of money is the more serious challenge to Locke's account, since it leads to a greater quantity of possessions than would normally be possible. With money, the value of 'Fancy or Agreement' replaces real use-value 'and the necessary Support of Life' (§46). The introduction of money is preceded by trade and barter. If one man, being more industrious or clever than another, acquires more fruits than he can use, he may give some away or trade for other goods he has not laboured to acquire. The items in circulation are still the product of human labour, but now what a man owns may not be the direct product of his labour. Such a man has not wasted any of the common stock, nor has he damaged any possessions of others. The next step on the road to money is for someone to 'give his Nuts for a piece of Metal, pleased with its colour; or exchange his Sheep for Shells, or Wool for a sparkling Pebble or a Diamond'. Even if he keeps the nuts or shells or diamonds all his life, he has not invaded 'the Right of others' and he might 'heap up as much of these durable things as he pleased'. The 'just' bounds of his property have not been exceeded because at least one of the measures of property has not been violated: the metal or diamond does not spoil (§46). Different quantities of property follow upon the invention and use of durable goods such as metals or diamonds. Just as 'different degrees of Industry were apt to give Men Possessions in different Proportions, so this *Invention of Money* gave them the opportunity to continue and enlarge them' (§48). Since money has 'its *value* only from the consent of Men', they have in effect 'agreed to disproportionate and unequal Possession of the Earth' (§50).

Locke's analysis of the concept of property was written against a rich background of earlier discussions. Most of his predecessors, and some of his contemporaries, are standard figures in the history of political theory: Suarez, Grotius, Selden, Pufendorf. Locke wrote with Filmer most directly in mind but probably also, as Professor Tully suggests, James Tyrrell. Tully's book, *A Discourse on Property* (1980), can be usefully consulted for the historical material, as well as for a detailed presentation of Locke's account of property, an account which, together with Locke's other views on civil government, has been a staple in twentieth-century political theory, and sometimes the centre of rather fierce debate.

propositions The joining or separating of signs makes a proposition. Since there are for Locke two kinds of signs, ideas and words, there are correspondingly two kinds of proposition: mental and verbal. The first sort of proposition is 'nothing but a bare consideration of the *Ideas*, as they are in our Minds, stripp'd of Names' (*Essay*, 4.5.3). Mental propositions are made 'in our Understandings' without using words: the ideas that are the components of mental propositions are *'put together, or separated by the Mind, perceiving, or judging of their Agreement or Disagreement'* (4.5.5). It is difficult to work with mental propositions alone, since we use words to talk or think about them. It is difficult not to put words to our ideas. We *are* able to frame some ideas without words, for example, simple ideas such as white, black, sweet or bitter, triangle or circle; but in making propositions about complex ideas, 'we usually put the Name for the *Idea*' (4.5.4). Despite these difficulties, Locke does not want to give up the notion that there are mental propositions. To do so would come close to denying that there are ideas, at least complex ideas.

Locke recognizes that most men 'make use of Words instead of *Ideas*' in their thinking and reasoning (4.5.4). Verbal propositions are composed of words which are put together or separated *'in affirmative or negative Sentences'* (4.5.5). Whenever we perceive the agreement or disagreement of ideas, or even where we suppose there is agreement or disagreement, the mind 'does tacitly within it self put them into a kind of Proposition affirmative or negative' (4.5.6). The notion of a tacit proposition (cf. tacit consent in his political thought) is used when he explains that when ideas are sometimes said to be true or false, there is 'some secret or tacit Proposition' which we have in mind (2.32.1). Ideas are 'bare appearances' in our mind and cannot strictly have a truth-value. When Locke refers to 'metaphysical truth' (i.e., 'the real Existence of Things, conformable to the *Ideas* to which we have annexed their names'), he invokes the notion of tacit propositions again, a proposition 'whereby the Mind joins that particular Thing, to the *Idea* it had before settled with a name to it' (4.5.11).

Propositions, whether mental or verbal, have parts: ideas or words connected together to form sentences (3.7.1). Had those who defend innate principles paid attention to the component parts of those claimed innate propositions, they might have seen the impossibility of their claims (1.4.1). The logical principle, 'it is impossible for the same thing to be and not to be at the same time', contains ideas that are acquired late in a child's life: the ideas of impossibility and identity. Who could believe that children have such complex ideas prior to experience and some learning (1.4.3)? Similarly, the claim for innateness of the principle 'God is to be worshipped' requires the ideas of God and worship to be innate, ideas which again are acquired after childhood (1.4.7). In a later section, he speaks of the mind putting ideas into propositions (1.4.22); we know a proposition when we perceive the relations between the ideas of which that proposition consists (4.1.8), and propositions are said to contain ideas (4.1.9). We also make propositions with ideas or words (2.32.19).

Various kinds of propositions are referred to in the *Essay*: self-evident ones (1.1.19; 2.1.9), general propositions (2.10.2; 3.9.3), mathematical and logical ones, and others that are about reality (1.1.4; 4.4.6), and particular propositions (4.11.13). This last kind enters Locke's discussion of our knowledge of the existence of an external world, of things other than God and ourselves. We have a knowledge of our own existence by intuition; reason 'clearly makes known to us' the existence of God (4.11.1). The source of the knowledge of anything else can only be found, or can arise, from sensation: 'no particular Man can know the *Existence* of any other Being, but only when by actual operating upon him, it makes it self perceived by him' (*ibid.*). Just having an idea of some object 'no more proves the Existence of that Thing, than the picture of a Man evidences his being in the World, or the Visions of a Dream make thereby a true History'. It is the actual receiving of ideas in sensation that gives us the near-certainty, sense-certainty, that some particular object or event exists at that time: particular knowledge of a particular object at a specific time (4.11.2).

Locke is anxious to block the move from idea to existence; it is not the *having* of an idea, but the *receiving* it in sensation that warrants such a move. With his heavy reliance upon ideas, he wants to make it clear that just having an idea is no guarantee that there is an object in the world that corresponds to that idea. There is, however, one class of non-sensory ideas whose corresponding objects we can accept on the basis of revelation: other finite spirits (4.11.12). We cannot claim knowledge of such SPIRITS, but the proposition asserting their existence can be accepted as highly probable.

Locke concludes this chapter with a twofold division of propositions. (1) 'There is one sort of Propositions *concerning* the *Existence* of any thing answerable to such an *Idea*: as having the *Idea* of an *Elephant, Phoenix, Motion*, or an *Angel*, in my Mind, the first and natural enquiry is, Whether such a thing does any where exist?' (4.11.13). If we can have a knowledge of such objects, it is a knowledge only of particulars. (2) 'There is another sort of *Propositions*, wherein is expressed the Agreement, or Disagreement of our abstract *Ideas*, and their dependence one on another.' These propositions can be universal and certain. For example, 'having the *Idea* of GOD and my self, of Fear and Obedience, I cannot but be sure that GOD is to be feared and obeyed by me' (4.11.13). We cannot conclude that there are any men in the world from the certainty of this proposition, but we can say in whatever world men do exist, this proposition will apply and be certain. Propositions of this second sort have been called 'eternal truths', not, Locke hastens to add, for him 'because they are Eternal Propositions actually formed, and antecedent to the Understanding' (4.11.14). Nor are they eternal truths because, as the innatists claimed, 'they are imprinted on the mind' from patterns in God's mind. These propositions are eternal truths 'because being once made, about abstract *Ideas*, so as to be true, they will, whenever they can be supposed to be made again at any time past or to come, by a Mind having those *Ideas*, always actually be true.'

These universal propositions can be said to add to our knowledge, but not to our knowledge of existence, not even possible existence. Such propositions express conceptual truths, they deal with the relation of ideas. The ideas of God, man, fear, and obedience are the ingredients of a universal proposition that will be true in any world where there are men, and men who have those ideas. This proposition might be labelled 'instructive', to use a term Locke employs in *Essay* 4.8. In that chapter, and in 4.7 on maxims, he attacks other sorts of universal propositions that he believes can play no role in knowledge: trifling propositions.

While trifling propositions are certain, they 'add no Light to our Understanding, bring no increase to our Knowledge' (4.8.1). Some of these trifling propositions are purely identity ones: they simply assert the same terms of themselves. These may be merely verbal or some may even contain 'a clear and real *Idea*' (4.8.2). The proposition, 'What is, is', may help to show some absurdity in someone's argument, but by itself it teaches us nothing. There can be an unlimited number of such propositions of whose truth we can be infallibly certain, but none of them would give us any knowledge of anything in the world. These propositions are self-evident; some people 'think they do great service to Philosophy' (4.8.3). Locke grants that 'the foundation of all knowledge lies in the Faculty we have of perceiving the same *Idea* to be the same' and discerning its difference from all other ideas. This act of the mind does not work from any identical proposition, but it perceives and discerns identity and difference. It is trifling to claim that identity propositions can be used 'as Principles of Instruction' or as 'helps to Understanding' (*ibid.*). Locke is careful to be precise about what he means by an 'identical' or 'identity' proposition: a proposition 'wherein the same Term importing the same *Idea*, is affirmed of it self'. If there are other notions of identical propositions, they are not the object of Locke's attack.

Another kind of trifling proposition is '*when a part of the complex* Idea *is predicated of the Name of the whole*: a part of the Definition of the Word defined' (4.8.4). Such a proposition is found in the examples of definition rejected by Locke, where the genus is predicated of the species, or 'more comprehensive of less comprehensive Terms'. For example, 'Lead is a metal.' To a man who understands the complex idea of lead, he will already know it is a metal. Either a man has and understands the idea of lead or he needs to learn its meaning. In accord with Locke's concept of nominal essence, all the simple ideas that comprise the complex idea of lead or metal are acquired when we learn the idea. Locke does recognize that if we want to teach someone the meaning of the idea of lead, we might tell him it is a metal, assuming that he has and understands the signification of the term 'metal'. Thus this sort of trifling proposition can play an instructive role in the acquisition of specific ideas. It becomes trifling, it seems, when used with someone who already understands its meaning; understanding its meaning is to know all the simple ideas that constitute its nominal essence, e.g., that it is a body, very heavy, fusible and malleable (4.8.4). That the triflingness of this kind of proposition is a charge based on the assumption that people to whom we might utter one of these propositions already have and understand the definition is clearly indicated by Locke. 'Before a Man makes any Proposition, he is supposed to understand the terms he uses in it, or else he talks like a Parrot, only making a noise by imitation, and framing certain Sounds, which he has learnt of others; but not, as a rational Creature, using them for signs of *Ideas*, which he has in his Mind' (4.8.7). The same assumption holds for the hearer.

Another example of this sort of trifling proposition is 'All gold is fusible' (4.8.5). Again, it would seem useful for someone learning about gold, perhaps a child, who has learned that it is yellow and malleable, to be told that it is also fusible. Of course, if I am talking to someone who already has the idea of gold and who knows what it stands for, to tell him that gold is fusible or yellow is to tell him what he already knows. Hence, such a proposition is not instructive to that person. To attempt to use it in that situation is to trifle. Once we know the definition of gold, lead, man, or horse, it is non-instructive to affirm part of that definition of that term (cf. 4.8.6). Definitions themselves have a use, but the danger is that we may simply shuffle words. Locke was particularly concerned about moral discourse in this way; we could master the language of morals but only know what words describe what actions, without any understanding of the measures of right and wrong. His rejection of what he calls 'trifling' propositions is motivated by a similar concern.

If being told that man is an animal or a live body is not instructive, what would be an example of an instructive proposition? If I am told that 'in whatever thing *Sense, Motion, Reason,* and *Laughter,* were united, that Thing had actually a notion of GOD, or would be cast into a sleep by *Opium*', that would be an instructive proposition. It is instructive not only because it might give a person some new information; it is instructive because 'neither *having the notion of GOD, nor being cast into sleep by Opium*' is contained in the idea signified by the word 'man' (4.8.6).

In attacking identity propositions, as in his rejection of maxims and axioms, Locke was reinforcing his approach to knowledge and belief. He was concerned with how we in fact acquire knowledge, and he was insistent on placing that acquisition in the acts of perceiving, understanding, and judging. The acquisition of ideas is prior to the acquisition of knowledge or belief. Knowledge can arise for someone only after he has the relevant ideas, after those ideas have been placed into mental or verbal propositions. Knowledge is propositional. Having ideas involves understanding their meaning. Knowing takes place in this environment, against the background of idea-acquisition. Locke perhaps does not pay sufficient attention to learning the meanings of ideas when he discusses propositions and the acts of judging and knowledge, but he was convinced that neither in learning the meaning of an idea nor in acquiring new knowledge are identity propositions of any use. When, to a child, we say lead is a metal, that may be instructive to the child, giving him information about another quality of lead. In that situation, that proposition is not a trifling proposition; it is not for that person an identity proposition.

There was a tradition prior to and contemporary with Locke that found a use for axioms and identity propositions. That tradition was part of what Locke took to be the over-formalization of knowledge: it went along with stress on the syllogism as a method to knowledge. That same tradition contained the notion that there is a small set of propositions or principles which are the bases for knowledge. The distinction between knowledge and knowing on which Locke's analysis depends was not always recognized within that tradition. Leibniz was sympathetic to these notions but he did distinguish between the order of knowing and the natural or logical order of truth (see his *Nouveaux Essais*, his detailed analysis of Locke's *Essay*, the sections on Locke's 4.7 and 4.8). The most basic logical or epistemic principle for Leibniz was the identity proposition. His defence of those propositions in his *Nouveaux Essais* is not extensive, but his discussion of Locke's chapter on maxims (4.7) is more detailed. Leibniz's views are of course sophisticated and respectable, although they miss the main point of Locke's psychological account of knowledge. There were less sophisticated writers who made use of identity propositions in a way that illustrates what worried Locke about them. John Sergeant's *The Method to Science* (1696) has a long discussion of judgement and propositions which employs the kind of trifling propositions against which Locke wrote (Book II, Lectures I–IV, pp. 113–63). Sergeant's attack on Locke, *Solid Philosophy Asserted* (1697), also appeals to identity propositions, to which Locke reacted with many marginal comments, some on trifling propositions (see the Garland reprint, 1984, which is a reprint of Locke's copy with his marginalia). Later developments of this tradition used the label 'analytic' for propositions whose predicates were contained in their subject terms, contrasting these with 'synthetic' propositions; the most famous user of this distinction was Kant.

Discussion of the nature and status of propositions has a long history prior to Locke and subsequently in the late nineteenth and early twentieth centuries. Bertrand Russell, G.E. Moore and the early Wittgenstein gave propositions an ontological status somewhat similar to Locke's mental propositions. For an account of the treatment of propositions and judgements in the seventeenth and eighteenth centuries, with some account of earlier writers, see Gabriel Nuchelmans, *Judgment and Proposition from Descartes to Kant* (1983).

punishment   A succinct definition of punishment is one man lawfully doing harm to another (*T*2, §8). Locke is there writing about those who in the state of nature transgress the law of nature. The word 'transgress', and another used close by, 'trespass', would have religious overtones for Locke and his readers. That tone is reinforced by his descriptions of a man who violates the dictates of the law of nature:

(1)   The 'Offender declares himself to live by another Rule, than that of *reason* and common Equity, which is that measure God has set to the actions of Men' (*ibid.*).
(2)   He becomes 'dangerous to Mankind'.
(3)   His action is a 'trespass against the whole Species'.
(4)   By his action, he 'becomes degenerate, and declares himself to quit the Principles of Human Nature' (§10).
(5)   He is a 'noxious Creature' (§10).
(6)   He has 'declared War against all Mankind' (§11).

In this last passage, it is apparently acts of murder that Locke has in mind; he speaks of 'the unjust Violence and Slaughter he hath committed'. For such acts, the offender 'may be destroyed as a *Lyon* or a *Tiger*, one of those wild Savage Beasts' (§11; cf. §16). Locke mentions Cain's murder of his brother. In the section on the state of war, even theft seems to place one outside humanity. One man can be in a state of war with another if he has 'a sedate setled Design, upon another Mans Life' (§16). The use of force or violence against another man is an attempt to get that man into one's absolute power. From this characterization, Locke draws the startling conclusion that it is 'Lawful for a Man to *kill a Thief* because, even though the thief has not harmed the person he robs nor has any designs on that man's life, 'using force, where he has no Right, to get me into his Power', there is no reason to suppose that he 'who would *take away my Liberty*, would not when he had me in his Power, take away every thing else' (§18). Therefore, Locke concludes, it is lawful to 'kill him if I can'.

All of these comments on punishment are made with respect to the state of nature, prior to the formation of civil society and its laws. A civil society can presumably decide to deal differently with its criminals. It is important to realize that Locke is talking about the violation of the law (or laws) of nature, God's laws for man. Those laws deal with basic human values such as life and property; they define what it is to be human, what it is to be a moral agent, a person in Locke's technical sense of that term. These considerations ameliorate somewhat the stark, punitive tone of Locke's injunctions about those who transgress these laws. His tone, even in these passages of *Two Treatises*, is not always so harsh. He urges calm reason when punishing offenders, not 'passionate heats, or boundless extravagancy' of will (§8). The punishment should fit the crime, although he gives few details on how that could be decided. He also includes the notion of 'reparation': 'he who hath received any damage, has ... a particular Right to seek *Reparation*' (§10).

Restraint of the offender and example for others are two of the motives for punishing offenders against the law of nature. The concept of punishment in these passages is retributive, perhaps modelled on Locke's belief about how God will deal with us on judgement day. God 'sees Men in the dark, has in his Hand Rewards and Punishments, and Power enough to call to account the Proudest Offender' (*Essay*, 1.3.6). One of Locke's arguments against innate practical principles is that men do violate the laws of nature. Had they innate moral principles, they would know what those principles say; if they had an innate knowledge of them, they would not break them, certainly not without shame or fear (1.3.11). There is both a conceptual and a very practical point Locke wants to make. The conceptual point is that we cannot understand 'what Duty is ... without a Law; nor a Law be known, or supposed without a Law-maker, or without Rewards and Punishment' (1.3.12). Thus, the ideas of 'God, of Law, of Obligation, of Punishment, of a Life after this' are all linked together. The practical point Locke wants to make is that 'Ignorance or Doubt of the Law; hopes to escape the Knowledge or Power of the Law-maker, or the like, may make Men give way to a present Appetite' (1.3.13). If, as the innatists claim, all men know what their duty is, acting against such a known law would be acting in the full knowledge that 'the

Hand of the Almighty [is] visibly held up, and prepared to take Vengeance' (*ibid.*). Infinite happiness or infinite misery is the reward and punishment waiting for men; these are the enforcements of his law (2.21.70).

So the backdrop for Locke's discussion of punishment in the state of nature is this eschatological doctrine. Within a political society, the power of punishing, which each person in the state of nature has, is handed over to the community and its representatives. Whether the community metes out punishment of the same sort as Locke recommends for violations of the law of nature, whether civil punishment includes violations of the law of nature, are details Locke leaves unexamined. In general, civil law must not conflict with the law of nature, but laws of civil society may prescribe different punishments for some crimes. Could or would civil law prohibit the killing of a thief, for example? Would or should the civil polity consider a murderer as a wild, savage beast? The answers to these questions are not found in Locke's writings, but we should not overlook the fact that his harsh remarks about violators of the law of nature were directed to the situation in the pre-civil society.

When we turn to what Locke says about punishment in *Some Thoughts concerning Education*, we find a quite different attitude and tone. We should not be surprised at this difference of attitude, because Locke is concerned in that work with the raising and educating of children, with helping children become responsible moral persons. *Two Treatises* directed attention to adults who had ceased to be persons; *Some Thoughts* deals with children's development into persons. Locke shows a practical understanding of what will be effective with children: '*great Severity* of Punishment does but very little Good; nay, great Harm in Education' (*ST*, §43). He even offers a general claim: 'those Children, who have been most *chastised*, seldom make the best Men.' Corporal punishment, the use of the rod, is not much needed, is generally ineffective in helping the child learn, and can be very harmful for the child's character (§72). The one exception Locke allows for beating is for obstinacy or 'rebellion', but even there, it is 'the shame of the Whipping, and not the Pain [that] should be the greatest part of the Punishment' (§78; cf. §§79, 80). Psychological punishment is more effective with children than physical punishment. Whatever form the punishment takes, it should be consistent, applied with understanding and have the goal of correcting mistakes and faults; it should never be simply punitive.

There is one other area where the concept of punishment enters Locke's discussion, namely, in his various *Letters* on toleration. His antagonist there, Jonas Proast (e.g., *The Argument of the 'Letter concerning Toleration'*, 1690), argued for the use of force and penalties for dissenters from the 'true' religion. Punishment for those who have different religious views was just what Locke wrote against. As well, Proast's recommendations would mix church and state, a condition Locke also wanted to avoid. He responded at length to Proast in his second and third *Letters for Toleration* (in *Works*, vi).

Q

qualities In traditional metaphysics, the term 'quality' accompanies the term 'substance'. Substance was defined as something capable of existing by itself. Qualities require a substance for their existence. Qualities were divided into those that are essential to a kind of substance (in fact, they define the nature of a substance; e.g., material defined by extension) or accidental, qualities that are not essential for that kind of substance. Problems arose about essential qualities: if they define the kind of substance, how do they differ from the substance, can the substance exist without the essential quality? Locke avoids these problems since substance is downgraded in his ontology; at least our knowledge of substance is limited to the qualities we can discover, real essences cannot be known. We could almost say that Locke's ontology is one of qualities only, so long as we add the rider about our knowledge being limited to observed and experienced qualities. A further qualification needs to be made in order to indicate that Locke was not turning things into qualities, only saying that our *knowledge* of nature, of bodies, consists in the discovery of coexisting sensible qualities. Things, objects, both ordinary and metaphysical, inhabit Locke's world, but our knowledge of their nature is restricted to experience and observation, aided perhaps by a few hypotheses such as the corpuscular theory of matter.

He talks easily and frequently in the language of that theory, speaking, for example, of the insensible parts (particles) of some object on which the qualities depend (*Essay*, 3.6.2, 8). Those insensible particles are themselves described in terms of certain qualities: hard, round, extended, in motion or at rest. They also have specific powers. Scientists such as Robert Boyle (whose writings Locke knew well) and Isaac Newton used this corpuscular theory, Boyle rather extensively; but the general announced programme of the Royal Society was to extend and refine the observations and descriptions of phenomena. At the ordinary level, Locke talks of trees, water, houses, metals, food. There are frequently references in his *Essay* to such objects, to the qualities by means of which we identify and describe those kinds of objects (e.g., 2.23.4, 7). There are also references to familiar and ordinary qualities, to words as the names of qualities, of coexisting qualities, of leading or characteristical qualities (3.11.20, 21).

The contrast for the traditional metaphysics was between substance and quality. For Locke, the contrast is between ideas and qualities. The second book of the *Essay* traces the origin of many of our ideas, including our ideas of qualities. In 2.8.8, 'quality' is defined as 'the Power to produce any *Ideas* in our mind'. He employs the language of objects that have those powers, the power of a snowball 'to produce in us the *Ideas* of White, Cold*, and *Round*'. He speaks of ideas (sensations, perceptions) being *in* the understanding; qualities (powers) are said to be *in* the snowball, *in* bodies. A body, a bit of matter, on the corpuscularian theory is a certain grouping of insensible corpuscles. Those corpuscles are mainly powers on Locke's analysis; his concept of matter may conflict with the corpuscularian concept which made matter passive and inert. However, force and power were soon to replace, in the scientific theory of MATTER, the passive corpuscular concept (*see* POWERS). If bodies are essentially powers, what is the snowball in which the qualities are said to be located?

There may not be a clear answer to this question. In his explication of 'quality', Locke continues to talk as if there is a referent for object words. He distinguishes two main kinds of qualities. The first are called 'primary'; they receive various descriptions.

(1) They are 'utterly inseparable from the Body, in what estate soever it be';
(2) they stay the same through all changes, even changes made by force (pounding, crushing);
(3) our senses constantly find these kinds of qualities in 'every particle of Matter, which has bulk enough to be perceived'; and
(4) the mind finds these qualities inseparable from 'every particle of Matter, though less than to make it self singly be perceived by our Senses. *v.g.* Take a grain of Wheat, divide it into two parts, each part has still *Solidity, Extension, Figure*, and *Mobility*; divide it again, and it retains still the same qualities' (2.8.9). Even when we extend in our thoughts this division beyond the sensible level, the mind still assigns these qualities to the parts divided. Conceptually, any part of matter, whether sensible or insensible, has the primary qualities.

Locke gives different lists of primary qualities of matter, but they include at least the following: solidity, extension, figure, motion, rest (2.8.9), bulk, texture (2.8.10). Another term for these qualities is 'original', probably meaning the qualities which matter has prior to human perceivers, although Locke's creation-scenario talks of 'bare' matter, matter without some of these primary qualities (*see* THINKING MATTER). He also calls this first kind of quality 'real', to indicate that 'The particular *Bulk, Number, Figure, and Motion of the parts of Fire, or Snow, are really in them*, whether any ones Senses perceive them or no' (2.8.17).

The second main kind of body-qualities is called 'secondary'; these are said to be 'nothing in the Objects themselves, but Powers to produce various Sensations in us by their *primary Qualities*' (2.8.10, 14). The list of these qualities includes colours, sounds, tastes, smells. They are also called 'sensible' qualities, a somewhat misleading label if it is taken to mean that primary qualities are not also sensible when bodies are large enough to be perceived.

There is a third type of body-qualities; in a sense they are a subclass of the secondary ones. These qualities are also nothing but powers in bodies. The difference is that those called 'secondary' produce sensations in perceivers, while this third type produces changes in other objects which may or may not be perceived. The third type is a result of object-to-object causation, the second is object-to-perceiver causation. Both the second and third kinds are powers in objects. The light and warmth of the sun, its melting of wax, are all 'equally Powers in the Sun, depending on its primary Qualities; whereby it is able in the one case, so to alter the Bulk, Figure, Texture or Motion of some of the insensible parts of my Eyes, or Hands, as thereby to produce in me the *Idea* of Light or Heat; and in the other, it is able so to alter the Bulk, Figure, Texture, or Motion of the insensible Parts of the Wax, as to make them fit to produce in me the distinct *Ideas* of White and Fluid' (2.8.24).

In calling the second and third sorts of quality powers Locke speaks of them as 'mere' or 'barely' powers, but these powers are said to be *in* the object. Setting aside the question of what the object is that has these qualities (which may reduce to the question of what the corpuscles are), we should recognize that powers are a type of quality resident in the object. Bodies, whether sensible or insensible, have primary, secondary, and this third type of qualities. The second and third types are powers, but they are powers *of* and *in* the object. It may be important to notice that Locke assigns these powers to the 'insensible *primary Qualities*', or to 'the particular Constitution of' a body's primary qualities, not to its corpuscular structure (2.8.23). Bodies *have* the primary qualities independent of perceivers, and they or their primary qualities have the two sorts of powers whether they are manifest or not. The chemist, Robert Boyle, recognized such dispositional qualities (his word was 'dispositive'). Locke's account parallels that of Boyle closely as found in Boyle's *The Origine of Forms and Qualities* (1666).

The notion of dispositional qualities or powers, deciding on their reality-status, has posed difficulties for philosophers, but Locke's text seems clear that the powers he refers to are *in* bodies or are, as it were, qualities of the primary qualities of bodies. Thinking of qualities or powers as perceiver-independent poses no further difficulty. Whether the primary qualities and powers of a body or group of corpuscles are independent of other bodies is not entirely clear in Locke's text. There is one long, dramatic passage where he suggests a close interdependency among objects. After outlining the ways in which living plants and animals are dependent upon light, air, and water, and after claiming that if we place 'a piece of *Gold* any where by it self, separate from the reach and influence of all other bodies, it will immediately lose all its Colour and Weight, and perhaps Malleableness too; which, for ought I know, would be changed into a perfect Friability', and offering other similar examples, he concludes:

> This is certain, Things, however absolute and entire they seem in them-
> selves, are but Retainers to other parts of Nature, for that which they are
> most taken notice of by us. The observable Qualities, Actions, and Powers,
> are owing to something without them; and there is not so complete or
> perfect a part, that we know, of Nature, which does not owe the Being it has,
> and the Excellencies of it, to its Neighbours; and we must not confine our
> thoughts within the surface of any body, but look a great deal farther, to
> comprehend perfectly those Qualities that are in it. (4.6.11)

This passage and the examples he cites may conflict with his assertion earlier in the *Essay* that 'the particular constitution [its corpuscular structure], which every Thing has within it self' is had by that thing 'without any relation to any thing without it' (3.6.6). Possibly adding to potential conflict is Locke's talk of the qualities and powers of things 'flowing from' their internal constitutions (e.g., 2.23.3; 2.31.13; 3.6.19). That constitution is also what Locke calls the 'real ESSENCE' of things, his scientific (i.e., corpuscularian) substitution for the older concept of real essences as fixed natural kinds. The 'flow from' concept has causal connotations, but it is also linked with Locke's notion of a deductive knowledge of nature, were we able to know the real internal but insensible corpuscular structure of things. One passage illustrates the 'flow from' relation by reference to geometry: the properties of a triangle flow from its definition, 'three Lines including a Space' (2.32.24). Definitions in geometry play a role in relation to what can be derived from them similar to the role of Locke's real essences in relation to the qualities and powers of objects, at least of *kinds* of objects. Would those possible deductions from the corpuscular structure of bodies be made without reference to other objects?

R

reason Locke opens the chapter on reason in his *Essay* by distinguishing three different meanings (significations) in the English language for this term: (1) true and clear principles, (2) 'clear, and fair deductions from those Principles' and (3) the cause, especially the final cause (4.17.1). Instead of any one of these meanings, Locke uses the term 'for a Faculty in Man, That Faculty, whereby Man is supposed to be distinguished from Beasts, and wherein it is evident he much surpasses them' (*ibid.*). He recognizes that his account of knowledge as based on 'outward Sense and Inward Perception' raises the question how much is there a need for another faculty such as reason? He gives a firm answer: 'Very much; both for the enlargement of our Knowledge, and regulating our Assent' (4.17.2). Reason works with knowledge and opinion and assists all the other faculties, including those two operations of sagacity and illation so important in demonstrations. Between these two functions, reason becomes responsible for inference, demonstration, reasoning and the discovery of ideas it can use in reasoning. There are four 'degrees' of reason: (1) 'the discovery, and finding out of Proofs'; (2) the regular ordering of the proofs and of the steps in proofs; (3) perceiving the connection between proofs; and (4) drawing the correct conclusions (4.17.3). A large portion of this chapter of the *Essay* is directed towards the question, is the syllogism the proper instrument of reason? Locke's answer is 'no'. He believes we reason best when 'we only observe the connexion of the Proofs, without reducing our Thoughts to any Rule of Syllogism' (4.17.4).

Of the various faculties identified by Locke, the faculty of reason receives the strongest praise. A good case can be made for saying reason is the dominant faculty in Locke's philosophy. The *Conduct* calls it 'natural' reason, characterizing it as a touchstone which we all have 'to distinguish substantial gold from superficial glitterings, truth from appearances' (§3; in *Works*, iii. 211). The usefulness of this touchstone 'is spoiled and lost only by assumed prejudices, overweening presumption, and narrowing our minds' (*ibid.*). The description in the *Essay* of what reason can do is even more glowing: 'Though it penetrates into the Depths of the Sea and Earth, elevates our Thoughts as high as the Stars, and leads us through vast Spaces, and large Rooms of this mighty Fabrick, yet it comes far short of the real Extent of even corporeal Being' (4.17.9). He goes on to list conditions under which reason fails us. (1) The first is not directly the fault of reason, but a failure on our part to have the ideas necessary for reason to operate on. (2) If our ideas are obscure, confused or imperfect, reason will be hampered. An example is our lack of any 'perfect *Idea* of the least Extension of Matter, nor of Infinity, we are at a loss about the Divisibility of Matter' (4.17.10). Similarly, we do not have a good enough idea of the operations of our mind and of the beginning of motion or thought to enable us to discover 'how the Mind produces either of them in us'. (3) Reason also comes to a stand when it is unable to perceive the ideas that can show the *'certain or probable Agreement, or Disagreement of any two other* Ideas' (4.17.11). (4) Another failure of reason arises when it employs false principles: absurdities and contradictions result (4.17.12). Locke was suspicious of using any principles as the foundation for reasoning; he urged us to rely upon the natural ability of the mind to find and perceive the connection of ideas. (5) A fifth source of the failure of reason is the attempt to work with 'obscure and imperfect *Ideas*' or *'dubious Words*, and uncertain Signs' (4.17.13).

Reason is the touchstone for truth and knowledge; it is also the guide for action. In this latter role, Locke uses the phrase, 'light of Reason' (*Essays*, p. 115), or 'right reason' (*ibid.*, p. 111). Reason in this form is the source of 'certain definite principles of action from which spring all virtues and whatever is necessary for the proper moulding of morals' (*ibid.*). The reference is to the law of nature which reason can discover. This notion of moulding morals is a central theme of *Some Thoughts concerning Education*. Reason is to control desires in the child or, in some cases, it authorizes specific desires. The child's will should be submitted to reason (*ST*, §§33, 34, 36, 39). In their early years, children should follow adults' reason until they 'grow able to judge for themselves, and to find what is right, by their own Reason' (§61). Reason can advise and guide parents how best to raise their children (§94). The child should be taught how to be guided by reason, how to let reason control his passions, 'to get a Mastery over his Inclinations, and *submit his Appetite to Reason*' (§200; cf. §§77, 108). The goal of education should be to turn the child into a rational, moral person.

For Locke, reason is not the only, though it is the dominant, guide for how to live and what to believe. Faith in matters of religion is another guide. Reason discovers certainty or probability by deductions it makes from the ideas it acquires through the 'use of its natural Faculties, *viz.* by Sensation or Reflection' (*Essay*, 4.18.2). Faith 'is the Assent to any Proposition, not thus made out by the Deductions of Reason; but upon the

Credit of the Proposer, as coming from GOD, in some extraordinary way
of Communication. This way of discovering Truths to Men we call
Revelation' (*ibid.*). In the chapter on faith and reason in the *Essay* (4.18),
Locke is careful to show the domains of both; he also lays down some
stringent criteria for determining when some truth is above reason and
what events count as a REVELATION. Reason is also characterized as
'natural *Revelation*, whereby the eternal Father of Light, and Fountain of
all Knowledge communicates to Mankind that portion of Truth, which he
has laid within the reach of their natural Faculties' (4.19.4).

Reasonableness of Christianity   This work was published in 1695. It had
a second edition in 1696. Locke wrote two responses to the attacks on it by
John Edwards (*Some Thoughts concerning the Several Causes and Occasions of
Atheism*, 1695, and several other attacks). Locke's responses to Edwards
were two *Vindications of the Reasonableness* in 1696 and 1697. There were also
two editions of a French translation of his *Reasonableness* in 1696 and 1715.
In the preface to this book, Locke says that he has found unsatisfactory
the systems of divinity that claim to interpret the Scriptures. Those
systems are even often inconsistent among themselves, so Locke decided
to turn to the Scriptures himself and see what in fact they say. The
product of his 'attentive and unbiassed search' is contained in this book.
His opening topic is the doctrine of redemption. Since that doctrine is
'founded upon the supposition of Adam's fall' it was necessary for Locke
to understand 'what the Scriptures show we lost by Adam' (in *Works*, vii.
4). In the systems of divinity, he found two extremes of interpretation of
Adam's fall, neither of which seemed to fit what the Scripture says. The
one extreme 'shook the foundations of all religion', the other 'made
Christianity almost nothing'. The second alternative seems to be represented by those who found the first interpretation so severe that they
denied redemption was necessary and made Jesus 'nothing but the
restorer and preacher of pure natural religion; thereby doing violence to
the tenor of the New Testament' (pp. 4–5). The first extreme has 'all
Adam's posterity doomed to eternal, infinite punishment, for the transgression of Adam, who millions had never heard of, and no one had
authorised to transact for him, or be his representative' (p. 4). What
Adam fell from, Locke says, 'was the state of perfect obedience' (p. 5). The
state of paradise was a state of immortality, so what Adam lost by his
disobedience was 'life without end'. Death was the result.

The next question for Locke was, what is meant by death? Here too
there were different interpretations. Some will 'have it be a state of guilt,
wherein not only he, but all his posterity were so involved, that every one
descended of him deserved endless torment in hell-fire' (p. 6). Locke finds

this standard interpretation very strange since it says in effect that 'death' means 'eternal life in misery'. Death, for him, means death, non-existence. Without the redemption brought by Christ, there would be no life after death, whether in misery or happiness. Locke can find no place in the New Testament that tells us that corruption infects all because of Adam's sin. Each one of us is responsible for our sin (p. 7), 'though all die in Adam, yet none are truly punished, but for their own deeds' (p. 8).

Jesus Christ is the second Adam; he 'restored life again; that so by Adam's sin they may none of them lose anything, which by their own righteousness they might have a title to' (p. 9). The responsibility each one of us has for the actions we perform as a moral agent was an important notion for Locke, embodied in his concept of person in the *Essay*. No unrighteous person should be in paradise and hence will not be redeemed and rewarded by life eternal. But how is righteousness determined, what is it? It is, Locke says, 'an exact obedience to the law'. It is 'the eternal and established law of right and wrong' to which our actions must conform (p. 10). God's law, the law of nature, is that law. Violation of that law brings death; even a single violation, one transgression. In *Two Treatises*, the violator of the law of nature in the state of nature is not only a criminal, he is like a wild, savage beast who can be hunted and killed. That harsh view of punishment in his political work has his reading of the Scriptures on the law of God behind it: 'whoever is guilty of any sin should certainly die, and cease to be' (p. 11).

God's law comprises the law of works and the law of faith. The first is most important; it is also the law that can be known by reason (p. 13). Locke suggests a conceptual connection here: 'Where there is no law, there is no sin; all are righteous equally, with or without faith' (p. 11). Faith can save us if we fail in some aspect of the law of works. What is required by the law of faith? For Locke, we must accept Christ as the Messiah, his resurrection, his miracles, baptism and the morality set forth by Jesus's life and example.

The rest of *Reasonableness* is devoted to the details of Jesus's life and works. Towards the end, he raises doubts on a suggestion he made in the *Essay*, that we might be able to construct a demonstrative morality (p. 141).

John Edwards's various attacks on Locke's *Reasonableness* were also attacks on specific doctrines of the *Essay*, especially the latter's rejection of innate truths. Edwards's main complaint about the *Reasonableness* was that it omitted many of the doctrines he considered necessary for being a Christian. Edwards was not a good reader of texts. He missed what Locke says about another life for the righteous, being more concerned to charge him with being a Socinian. In his two *Vindications*, Locke strongly rejected this charge (in *Works*, vii).

recreation   The biographical information is lacking that would tell us what Locke did for recreation, but he held rather firm and explicit views about the value, even the therapeutic effects, of recreation. If we are to make good use of our life, we 'must allow a large Portion of it to Recreation' (*ST*, §197). This advice is especially relevant to young people: recreation in the correct spirit will help them stay young longer. 'The weakness of our Constitutions, both Mind and Body, requires, that we should be often unbent' (*ibid.*). We should not take recreation too seriously; it is important but it must be done with delight. He praises the ancients for their understanding the value of recreation: they 'understood very well how to reconcile manual Labour with Affairs of State, and thought it no lessening to their Dignity to make the one the Recreation to the other' (*ST*, §205). It was agriculture and gardening that men such as Gideon, Cincinnatus, Cato and Cyrus praised and practised. Manual arts, such as working in iron or brass or silver, even as a trade when one is not engaged in business, can serve a recreational role (*ST*, §209; cf. §201). Recreation is not just being idle (idleness for Locke was almost a sin; 'sauntering' in children is roundly condemned), 'but easing the wearied part by change of Business' (§206). The fact that our nature is such that we 'cannot be perfectly idle' is evidenced by the way 'Persons of Condition, especially Ladies, wast so much of their time' in forms of recreation, some of which produce little or no delight; e.g., 'Gaming leaves no Satisfaction behind it to those who reflect when it is over, and it no way profits the Body or Mind' (§207). Recreation is paired with business; it 'belongs not to People, who are Strangers to Business, and are wasted and wearied with the Employment of their Calling' (*ibid.*). Recreation relaxes and refreshes 'the part, that has been exercised, and is tired'.

Some types of recreation are not recommended; some are even dangerous. Cards, dice and drinking are examples of popular but dangerous (dangerous for the character) pastimes: a great many people 'throw away their spare Hours in them, through the prevalency of Custom, and want of some better Employment to fill up the Vacancy of Leisure, more than from any real delight is to be found in them' (*ibid.*). The best way to avoid wasting time at cards or dice is 'never to learn any Play upon them, and so to be incapacitated for those dangerous Temptations and incroaching Wasters of useful Time' (§208). Leisure time should be properly filled but only in the context, and as an antidote to or correlation, of business. The 'common, vicious, useless and dangerous Pastimes' must be made out of fashion: 'Men from their youth' should be 'weaned from that sauntring Humour, wherein some, out of Custom, let a good part of their Lives run uselesly away, without either Business or Recreation' (§208). Music is not listed as dangerous but it is not recommended: it, like dancing, wastes 'a

young Man's time, to gain but a moderate Skill in it, and engages often in
such odd Company, that many think it much better spared' (§197). Locke
gives music the last place on his list of accomplishments recommended for
a gentleman. Painting fares a bit better, but 'ill Painting is one of the worst
things in the World' (§203). Fencing and riding are also included as parts
of a gentleman's upbringing (§198). Painting is sedentary recreation
which involves more the mind than the body; Locke was concerned with
active recreations involving the body – bodily activity 'unbends the
Thought, and confirms the Health and Strength'.

Just as business, affairs of state and farming or manual labour can be
recreation to each other, so Locke urges parents and tutors to make
learning 'as much a Recreation to [children's] Play, as their Play is to
their Learning' (§74). Play can be turned into something a child hates,
were he ordered to 'spend so many Hours Morning and Afternoon' with
one of his playthings, e.g., whipping his top (§73; cf. §§124, 128, 129). The
lesson from this observation is that learning is made hateful in the same
way, by imposing it on the child as a task. We discourage children from
study by making it their business, forced on them or '*teazed* and *chid* about
it' (§76; cf. §148). Locke confesses that 'I have always had a Fancy, that
Learning might be made a Play and Recreation to Children; and that they
might be brought to desire to be taught, if it were propos'd to them as a
thing of Honour, Credit, Delight and Recreation, or as a Reward for doing
something else; and if they were never chid or corrected for the neglect of
it' (§148). He has some specific suggestions for using toys as a way of
making learning fun; learning the alphabet, for example, by employing a
die and other toys with letters on them can make 'this kind of *Learning a
Sport*' to children.

> Contrivances might be made *to teach Children to Read*, whilst they thought
> they were only Playing. For example, what if an *Ivory-Ball* were made like
> that of the Royal-Oak Lottery, with Thirty two sides, or one rather of
> Twenty four, or Twenty-five sides; and upon several of those sides pasted on
> an A, upon several others B, on others C, and on others D. I would have you
> begin with but these four Letters, or perhaps only two at first; and when he
> is perfect in them, then add another; and so on till each side having one
> Letter, there be on it the whole Alphabet. (§150)

Later, the letters can be changed into syllables, enabling the child to learn
to read 'without knowing how he did so'. Locke noticed that children will
take great pains to learn some game. He puts that energy to work in
learning to read by turning it into a game. He recounts a case where 'a
Person of Great Quality' would place vowels on six sides of a die

(including Y), eighteen consonants on the sides of three others, and found that his young son *'play'd* himself *into Spelling* with great eagerness, and without once having been chid for it, or forced to it' (§151; other suggestions are given in §§152–4). Locke's most ambitious plan for making learning play was to illustrate a book with pictures, such as *Aesop's Fables* or *Reynard the Fox* (§156).

Play can be instructive in another way. If the child can be observed while at play, without his being aware he is being observed, parents and tutor can learn about the child's natural traits and use those traits or change them later. Locke offers this suggestion particularly for spotting listlessness or 'sauntering'. If, when left entirely free to use his leisure time as he pleases, the child sits idly by or plays at nothing, that is evidence of sauntering, a trait that needs curbing. By the way the child uses his times of liberty, 'you will easily discern whether it be *listlesness* in his Temper, or aversion to his Book, that makes him *saunter* away his time of Study' (§125).

Locke recognized the importance of play for children, play unrelated to learning. While he recommends that children's desires and appetites should be carefully controlled and even silenced on occasion, the desire for recreation is an exception. Here, 'Fancy must be permitted to speak, and be hearken'd to also. *Recreation* is as necessary, as Labour, or Food. But because there can be no *Recreation* without Delight, which depends not alway on Reason, but oftener on Fancy, it must be permitted Children not only to divert themselves, but to do it after their own fashion; provided it be innocently and without prejudice to their Health' (§108). Playing and innocent folly in *'Childish Actions are to be* left perfectly free and *unrestrained*, as far as they consist with the Respect due to those that are present; and that with the greatest Allowance' (§63). Children should have playthings of different sorts but they should be kept by the tutor and given to the child 'but one at once, and should not be suffered to have another, but when he restor'd that' (§130). Too many toys can be harmful, nor should they be bought for the child. Encourage the child to make toys himself, or at least try to do so. Ordinary objects also can serve very well as toys: 'A Smooth Peble, a piece of Paper, the Mothers Bunch of Keys, or any thing they cannot hurt themselves with, serves as much to divert little Children, as those more chargeable and curious Toys from the Shops, which are presently put out of order, and broken' (§130).

reflection   The second of two sources of ideas (Locke uses the metaphor of 'fountains') is 'the *Perception of the Operations of our own Minds* within us, as it is employ'd about the *Ideas* it has got' (*Essay*, 2.1.4). Those operations of the mind are *'perceived and reflected on by our selves'* (2.1.2); the soul reflects

on and 'considers' those operations (2.1.4). Such reflecting and considering furnish the understanding with 'another set of *Ideas* which could not
be had from things without' (*ibid.*). Examples of the ideas acquired from
reflecting on the mind's operations are perceiving, thinking, doubting,
believing, reasoning, knowing, willing, 'and all the different actings of our
own Minds'. We are said to be 'conscious' of these ideas and we 'observe'
them in ourselves. Perceiving, being conscious of, are terms used to
indicate our awareness of those (or of any) ideas. 'Consciousness' is
defined as the 'perception of what passes in a Man's own mind' (2.1.19).
What passes in our minds are ideas of sense as well as ideas of reflection.
Being conscious of and having ideas go together for Locke. Just as we
cannot think without being conscious that we are thinking, so we cannot
have thoughts or ideas without being conscious of them. 'Being conscious
of' is not the same as reflection. Reflecting and considering identify the
operations or actions of the mind (he writes 'soul' or 'understanding' in
some passages) which yield ideas of the 'different actings of our own
Minds'. We can also reflect on or consider the acts of reflecting and
considering, as Locke is doing in these passages. 'Conscious of' is more
passive, reflecting is active and directive. But this distinction may be
difficult to maintain. Reflection is also characterized as 'that notice which
the Mind takes of its own Operations, and the manner of them, by reason
whereof, there come to be *Ideas* of these Operations in the Understanding'
(2.1.4). 'Noticing' may not be much different from 'being conscious of' or
even 'perceiving'. Reflection would seem to presuppose noticing, being
conscious of, or perceiving.

Locke also speaks of 'contemplating' the operations of the mind: in
contemplating we 'cannot but have plain and clear *Ideas*' of those operations, but unless we turn our 'Thoughts that way' and consider 'them
attentively', we will not have clear and distinct ideas of all the operations or
of 'all that may be observed therein' (2.1.7). In attacking the Cartesian
notion that the soul always thinks, Locke confesses that he has one of
those 'dull Souls, that doth not perceive it self always to contemplate
Ideas', as if one form of thinking is contemplating (2.1.10). He also refers to
ideas 'the Mind can receive, and contemplate without the help of the
Body' (2.1.15). Reflecting upon the past includes 'Reasonings, and
Contemplation' (*ibid.*). In his more extended discussion of memory, he
distinguishes between actual and potential recall, by saying 'we are said to
have all those *Ideas* in our Understandings, which though we do not
actually contemplate, yet we can bring in sight, and make appear again'
(2.10.2). Book Four opens by reaffirming that the mind contemplates its
own ideas; they are the only immediate objects that it can contemplate
(4.1.1). The last chapter of the *Essay* says we can contemplate our selves

since self is present to the understanding; otherwise, all that is present to the understanding are signs, the signs and representatives of other objects and that which we contemplate (4.21.4). But 2.19.1 says the mind turns 'inwards upon it self and contemplates its own Actions'. He goes on to say that if ideas are held 'under attentive Consideration', that mode of thinking is called 'Contemplation'.

Thus, contemplation is clearly related to reflection but is not quite the same. 'Being attentive' is a more systematic action than just contemplating. Just as a man will not have 'all the particular *Ideas* of any Landscape, or of the Parts and Motions of a Clock, who will not turn his Eyes to it, and with attention heed all the Parts of it', so we must pay heed and carefully observe the workings of the mind if we are to learn all we can about the mind's operations (2.1.7). 'Applying himself with attention' is required for both external and internal objects. Another phrase Locke uses for inward observation is 'turning inward upon it self'; 'turning inward' precedes reflection (2.1.8; 2.6.1). Locke is writing about children in this section: it is 'pretty late before most Children get *Ideas* of the Operations of their own Minds'. Distinct, lasting ideas of those mental operations will not occur 'till the Understanding turns inward upon it self, *reflects* on its own *Operations*, and makes them the Object of its own Contemplation' (2.1.8). Sense and reflection offer ideas to the mind 'for its Contemplation' (2.1.24); the simple ideas of reflection are 'as capable to be the Objects of its Contemplation, as any of those it received from foreign things' (2.6.1; cf. 2.19.3).

Ideas 'make their Approaches to our minds' via one sense, by several senses; some arise from reflection only and others are suggested to the mind '*by all the ways of Sensation and Reflection*' (2.3.1). The ideas of perception or thinking, and volition or willing (and presumably the various forms of these, cf. 2.19.2), arise from reflection alone (2.6.2). The list of ideas that 'approach' our minds from either source or from a combination of both is short. By examining his account of that short list, we may find some details on the working of reflection.

Pleasure or delight and its opposite are the first simple idea of sensation and reflection listed. Here, it is not the two sources working together that produce the idea, but the idea can arise from either source. His account in 2.7.2 deals with delight or uneasiness. He speaks of the 'affections of our Senses from without' or of 'any retired thought of our Mind within', saying that those affections and those thoughts 'produce in us *pleasure* or *pain*'. It is the affection or the thought, not some activity of the mind, that produces these ideas. Another phrase is: those ideas 'arise from' the thought or affection. When pleasure or pain are ideas of reflection, they arise not from thinking but from the thoughts we have. There seems to be no paying heed required. The 'infinite Wise Author of our being' has been 'pleased to join to several Thoughts, and several Sensations, a *perception* of *Delight*' (2.7.3). It is the delight that is attached to certain thoughts and sensations that causes us to attend to them. The attending (a form of reflection) seems to come after the pleasure or delight. Locke may mean to say that the *idea* of delight results from our attending to the pleasure we experience, thereby retaining the central notion of reflection as an activity of the mind which discovers or acquires ideas. The experience of pain or pleasure 'set[s] us on work', leading us to have direction and design in our actions, aiding us in the preservation of our life (2.7.4). Section 6 has the annexation by God of pleasure and pain to our *ideas*, not to the *experience* or feeling of pain and pleasure, so these ideas of reflection seem to be given to us; but of course, we must be aware of these ideas, and that awareness is of the contents of our minds.

Two other ideas Locke lists are existence and unity. God has not annexed these ideas to other ideas; they are 'suggested to the Understanding, by every Object without, and every *Idea* within' (2.7.7). But with these ideas, considering (a form of reflection) plays a role: 'we consider them as being actually there, as well as we consider things to be actually without us; which is, that they exist, or have *Existence*.' Power, another of the ideas on Locke's list of simple ideas of both sensation and reflection, involves the mind's observing: we observe 'in our selves, that we can, at pleasure, move several parts of our Bodies, which were at rest' (2.7.8), and thereby acquire the idea of power by that reflective observing. The acquisition of the idea of power is a bit more complex, involving mental operations of observing, noticing, reflecting and concluding (2.21.1). Another idea, not on his initial list in 2.7.1, is 'constantly offered us, by what passes in our own Minds', namely, the idea of succession. We acquire this idea by 'looking immediately' into ourselves and reflecting on 'what is observable there' (2.7.9). What we find is that 'our *Ideas* always, whilst we are awake, or have any thought, [are] passing in train, one going, and another coming, without intermission.' Reflecting on the 'appearances of several *Ideas* one after another in our Minds, is that which furnishes us with the *Idea* of *Succession*' (2.14.3).

The ideas on Locke's short list appear to us when observing, considering or attending to what goes on in our minds when we are conscious. Two questions arise: (1) do we not have to attend to the ideas of sense as well?; and (2) do these ideas on his list appear to the mind from perceiving or reflecting on the operations of the mind? There is a passive aspect to the ideas of pleasure and pain that God joins to almost every idea, just as we are largely passive in receiving many ideas of sensation. In both cases, the ideas catch our attention, they 'reach the mind', and we are conscious of them. If the impressions of sense 'are not taken notice of within' the mind, the idea will not be formed, but we cannot have an idea and not be conscious of it (2.9.3). The difference lies in the source or direction from which the idea reaches the mind: from external senses in the one case, from internal operations of the mind in the other. But the internal-external distinction applies only to the sources (to the physical stimuli in sensation, to internal awareness in reflection), not to the locus of ideas themselves. All ideas are internal, to use the spatial language Locke employs; they are all contents of awareness. So the answer to the first question is 'yes', but what we attend to in one instance is an idea of sense, in the other, a non-sensory idea of reflection. What Locke's brief analysis of the simple ideas of sensation and reflection reveals is that some ideas of reflection are the result of God's action, others result from our action of attending to our ability to move our body, and others to our awareness of the succession of ideas (all ideas, not just those of reflection). None of the ideas on the 2.7 list results from our reflecting on the *operations* of our mind. We can conclude, then, that the definition of reflection given in 2.1.2 and 2.1.4 which talked only of the operations of the mind must be emended to include these other ideas of pain, pleasure, power, existence, unity and succession. We do not become conscious of these ideas by reflecting on the operations of the mind.

Locke does devote a few chapters to specific mental operations, e.g., perception (2.9), retention (2.10), discerning, comparing, enlarging, abstracting (2.11), but there is very little information there about how reflection gives us ideas of these operations. That reflection is an important action of the mind is further indicated by its role in his account of personal identity: a PERSON is 'a thinking, intelligent Being, that has reason and reflection'. Reflecting on our lives, on our actions, is one way in which we become conscious of and responsible for moral actions.

relations   The idea of relations is one of three kinds of complex ideas, the other two being modes and substances. The idea of relation is formed by 'bringing two *Ideas*, whether simple or complex, together; and setting them by one another; so as to take a view of them at once, without uniting them into one' (*Essay*, 2.12.1). In the previous chapter on various operations of the mind, Locke speaks of 'that large tribe of *Ideas*' called 'relations' which are formed by comparing 'them one with another, in respect of Extent, Degrees, Time, Place, or any other Circumstance' (2.11.4; cf. 2.12.7). The chapter devoted to relation uses the terms 'relative' and 'respect' as well. Relations are expressed by terms *'that have others answering them, with a reciprocal intimation'*, such as father and son, bigger and less, cause and effect (2.25.2). On hearing one of these terms, 'the Thoughts are presently carried beyond the Thing so named.' Some relations are not so 'plainly intended' as relative, and some terms or names that are relative may not have in a particular language a correlative term (e.g., 'concubine'). All names signify ideas. When the idea is of something in the object named, it is a positive idea. If the idea 'arises from the respect the Mind finds in it [the object], to something distant from it, with which it considers it', then we have a relative term or idea (*ibid.*). Relative ideas and names are sometimes called 'external denominations', indicating some feature apart from the objects related. Some terms appear to be positive when they are implicitly relative, e.g., old, great, imperfect (2.25.3). We can agree on the idea of some relation while disagreeing about the nature of the relata (2.25.4).

Relations and ideas of relations, then, result from or consist in referring or comparing two things, 'from which comparison, one or both comes to be denominated' (2.25.5). Should the objects that are compared cease to be, or even just one cease to exist, the relation ceases as well. If a son dies, the relation of father-of between those two men no longer exists. One thing (idea, substance or mode) can have or stand in many different relations. Locke gives a list of thirty-two relations that a single man may have, from father, son, brother, grandfather to Englishman, servant, captain, contemporary.

There are as many relations as there are ways of comparing things (2.28.17). All relations terminate in simple ideas of sensation or reflection (2.28.18; cf. 2.25.9, 11). We may not often unpack a complex relational idea to exhibit all the simple ideas contained there, but analysis easily reveals some of the items in the collection. For example, the word 'father': '*First*, There is meant that particular Species, or collective *Idea*, signified by the Word Man; *Secondly*, These sensible simple *Ideas*, signified by the Word Generation; And, *Thirdly*, The Effects of it, and all the simple *Ideas*, signified by the Word Child' (2.28.18). Or the word 'friend': since it is 'taken for a Man, who loves, and is ready to do good to another, [it] has all those following *Ideas* to the making of it up. *First*, all the simple *Ideas*, comprehended in the Word Man, or intelligent Being. *Secondly*, The *Idea* of Love. *Thirdly*, The *Idea* of Readiness, or Disposition. *Fourthly*, The *Idea* of Action, which is any kind of Thought, or Motion. *Fifthly*, The *Idea* of Good, which signifies any thing that may advance his Happiness' (*ibid.*). Relations depend upon the simple ideas of which they are composed. Normally we have '*as clear a Notion of the Relation, as we have of those simple* Ideas, *wherein it is founded*' (2.28.19). The understanding of a relation between two individuals applies to all individuals exemplifying that relation. In this way, relations are universals. Locke gives an amusing example of this feature:

> If I know what it is for one Man to be born of a Woman, *viz. Sempronia*, I know what it is for another Man to be born of the same Woman, *Sempronia*; and so have as clear a Notion of Brothers, as of Births, and, perhaps clearer. For if I believed, that *Sempronia* digged *Titus* out of the Parsley-Bed, (as they use to tell Children,) and thereby became his Mother; and that afterwards in the same manner, she digged *Cajus* out of the Parsley-Bed, I had as clear a Notion of the Relation of Brothers between them, as if I had all the Skill of a Midwife; the Notion that the same Woman contributed, as Mother, equally to their Births, (though I were ignorant or mistaken in the manner of it,) being that on which I grounded the Relation (*ibid.*).

Since relations are universal, and since Locke defends an ontology of particulars, there is a problem about the status of relations. Earlier discussions of relations favoured a subjective interpretation. Locke sides with this view. Relations (not the idea of relations) are 'not contained in the real existence of Things but, something extraneous, and superinduced' (2.25.8). Relations are like mixed modes; they 'have no other *reality*, but what they have in the Minds of Men' (2.30.4). What is in the minds of men are ideas, so the distinction between relations and the ideas of relations is rather unclear. A similar difficulty surrounds his account of mixed MODES. An idea of a relation can be said to be real if there is a 'possibility of [something] existing conformable' to it. The ideas both of mixed modes and of relations are 'themselves Archetypes', they specify what features will fit or conform to the idea (*ibid.*). For the same reason, both kinds of ideas are adequate, that is, they have 'nothing to represent but themselves' (2.31.3). Later in this same chapter, he calls those ideas 'Originals, and Archetypes; [they] are not Copies, nor made after the Patterns of any real Existence, to which the Mind intends them to be conformable, and exactly to answer' (2.31.14). The ideas of mixed modes and relations are complex ideas, 'Collections of simple *Ideas*, that the Mind it self puts together' (*ibid.*). Just as a man's actions may fit the ideas we call justice or theft, so a man himself can 'stand in', 'exemplify', or 'fit' the ideas we call father, son or brother. The very same action we call theft may occur in another society lacking that idea and word. Certain features of persons that involve other persons may lack, in a particular society, the relational ideas and names that we employ to characterize those features. It makes sense to say that in those countries, actions of justice or theft do not exist, and that certain relations are not found in that country since it lacks the relevant names and ideas for those relations. In this way, relations are dependent upon specific ideas and names; when those ideas are missing, the relations they identify are also missing. *We* may observe people in that society and describe their actions even though that society is without those relational ideas and words. Locke makes this point about stabbing: in a country lacking the word 'stabbing' (and its signified idea), a person cannot stab another man, although, of course, he can perform the action *we* call 'stabbing' (3.5.11).

These examples may catch part of what Locke means when he says that relations have no reality save in the minds of men. He also wants to say, it seems, that 'brother of', for example, does not refer to a quality of the men whom we call 'brothers'. The word 'brother' does, however, refer to something other than itself or its ideas: it describes a specific characteristic two men have to each other, in this case as a result of biology. Such a relation 'exists' whether we mark it with a name or not. The same is true of social functions such as 'mayor' or 'senator': the functions can be filled whether a particular society has names for them or not. What, then, is the difference between the names and ideas of modes or relations and the names of substances? How do they differ in reality and adequacy? He likes to call the complex ideas of substances 'ectypes' or copies of what exists, although our ideas of substances are inadequate since we cannot be sure they 'exactly answer to' all the properties and powers of a substance (2.31.13). We can be sure that our complex ideas of modes and relations are adequate because *we* construct them; they specify what we want to conform to our ideas. Similarly for the reality of our ideas of substances: they are made 'in reference to Things existing without us, and intended to be Representations of Substances, as they really are' (2.30.5). The collection of simple ideas making up our complex idea of a substance must reflect the coexisting qualities of that substance.

In both cases, that of ideas of substances that and of ideas of modes or relations, the idea describes or characterizes features of objects, persons and actions. So the relation of 'conform to' between ideas and what they designate is the same. Our confidence that the ideas correctly describe or characterize what they designate is stronger with respect to ideas of modes or relations than it is with ideas of substances. That confidence results from the fact that *we decide* what goes into the ideas of modes and relations, whereas nature or the things themselves determine what goes into our ideas of substances. The difference is almost that between 'contingent' and 'necessary': for an action to be one of regicide or adultery, it *must* fit our ideas, while what is included in our idea of gold, e.g., is in part (but for Locke only in part) determined by what properties we will use to name or designate gold. The other part is what qualities exist together to form what we call 'gold'.

There are also some unobservable properties that Locke ascribes to substances, namely, POWERS to cause changes in bodies and in perceivers. The powers are part of the collection of coexisting qualities making our ideas of the nominal essence of gold, but such powers are a feature of gold, just as the power to melt lead is a feature of fire. Power is not an observable property or feature. Objects as well as persons clearly stand in specific relations. In fact, the division of the sciences on which the *Essay* ends identifies the first of the areas that fall within the compass of human understanding as 'The Nature of Things, as they are in themselves, their Relations, and their manner of Operation' (4.21.1). Do we have in this remark three aspects of things: as they are in themselves (unrelated to other objects), their relations, and their operations? If so, then we can say that relations are not part of the *nature* of things or the way things are in themselves; but he does not seem to deny here, as he does elsewhere, that things (objects and persons) do *have* relations, are related to other things. In this way, relations seem to have some kind of reality apart from our ideas and names; at least, some relations do. Instituted relations may be imposed or superinduced by men, but other relations, especially of objects, would seem to be more closely connected to the *natures* of objects. He does say that blood-relations, as in brother, father, son, are *natural* relations (2.28.2), so he may have meant what was much later called 'internal' relations for these sorts, relations that result from natural processes. His point in this last passage was simply that animals stand in similar natural relations to each other, but we do not always give names to those relations: "tis seldom said, This Bull is the Grandfather of such a Calf; or that two Pidgeons are Cousin-Germains' (2.28.2). So whether or not Locke's ontology permits him to say some relations are real properties in the world, there may be throughout his discussion an implicit distinction between natural and instituted relations. That distinction is explicit in 2.28.3. The forming of ideas of relations is not quite as free and under our control as he sometimes seems to say.

It should be noted too that what we include in our idea or name of justice or regicide is, in a very important sense, not up to us: 'Indeed, as any of them [relations] have the Names of a known Language assigned to them, by which, he that has them in his Mind, would signify them to others, so bare Possibility of existing is not enough; they must have a Conformity to the ordinary Signification of the Name, that is given them, that they may not be thought fantastical: as if a Man would give the Name of Justice to that *Idea*, which common use calls Liberality' (2.30.4).

Many different relations are mentioned in various places in the *Essay*; but three are important enough for specific doctrines in that work to merit some extended discussion. He ends 2.25.11 by saying of the first of these three, cause and effect, that it is 'the most comprehensive Relation, wherein all things that do, or can exist, are concerned'. The account of the construction by the mind of this idea is rather complex, resulting from our experience of changes (2.26.1; *see* CAUSE). In this same chapter, a few sections are given over to time and place, 'the Foundations of very large Relations ... [in which] all finite Beings at least are concerned' (2.26.3). The next chapter takes up the second of the three large relations, IDENTITY and diversity. These ideas arise because the mind often compares things with respect to their 'very Being', their 'existing at any determin'd time and place' (2.27.1). The third and perhaps most important kind of relation to receive extended discussion is moral relations. This sort of relation 'is the Conformity, or Disagreement, Men's voluntary Actions have to a Rule, to which they are referred, and by which they are judged of' (2.28.4).

There is one other relation of great importance for Locke, the knowledge-relation. Knowledge is defined in terms of perceiving the relations of ideas. There are four main types of knowledge-relations.

Hume also gave relations a prominent place in his account of knowledge and belief, listing seven relations, some of which deal with relations of ideas leading to certainty and knowledge, others which are the basis for our beliefs. For Hume, some ideas naturally introduce other ideas. Comparison is also for him the way we acquire ideas of relations (*Treatise*, Bk I).

The subject of relations enjoyed a lively period in the early twentieth century in the writings of G.E. Moore, Bertrand Russell and others. It has also been important for logical theory. (See *Encyclopedia of Philosophy*, ed. Paul Edwards, 1967, entry for 'relations'. For the history of relations prior to Locke, see J.R. Weinberg, *Abstraction, Relation, and Induction*, 1965.)

religion   Locke had an extensive and long-lasting interest in matters of religion. The largest group of books in his private library (870 titles, 23.8 per cent of his total collection) belongs to this category, what Harrison and Laslett list as 'theology' (*The Library of John Locke*, 1965; 2nd edn, 1972). In that collection were many books on various religious and theological subjects, books on different religious movements (e.g., Socinianism, Unitarianism), many copies of the Bible in different languages, and books of biblical interpretation. His own writings reflect the same interest. His *Paraphrases of St. Paul's Epistles* was the last book he wrote; it was preceded by *The Reasonableness of Christianity* (and by a number of replies to critics of that work), and by several *Letters* on toleration. There is also a *Discourse of Miracles* which was not published until after his death. Theologically related issues are found throughout *Two Treatises* and the *Essays on the Law of Nature*. Several chapters of the *Essay concerning Human Understanding* deal with topics of religious concern. His work on education, *Some Thoughts concerning Education*, urges parents, as a foundation for virtue, to 'imprint' on the mind of the child 'a true Notion of *God*, as of the independent Supreme Being, Author and Maker of all Things, from whom we receive all our Good, who loves us, and gives us all Things' (*ST*, §136). In that same passage, Locke's preference for the simple and practical in matters of religion is revealed: 'I am apt to think, the keeping Children constantly Morning and Evening to acts of Devotion to God, as to their Maker, Preserver and Benefactor, in some plain and short Form of Prayer, suitable to their Age and Capacity, will be of much more use to them in Religion, Knowledge and Vertue, than to distract their Thoughts with curious Enquiries into his inscrutable Essence and Being' (*ibid.*). Another firm conviction is indicated by his advice in a later section of that work where he says the 'Principles of Religion are to be drawn' from the Scriptures, but for children, reading the Bible must be fitted to their comprehensions (§158).

Frequently, religion and morality are coupled together, e.g., 'the true Principles of Morality and Religion' (*ST*, §200); '*the dignity of Principles* in Religion or Morality' (*Essay*, 1.3.22); 'Virtue and Religion are necessary' for happiness (2.21.60); the existence of God is a fundamental truth on which 'all Religion and genuine Morality depend' (4.10.7). Elsewhere in the *Essay* he praises plain and direct language in order to avoid making 'unintelligible both Morality and Religion' (3.10.13). In another passage which challenges a standard doctrine of orthodox Christianity, Locke asserts that 'All the great Ends of Morality and Religion, are well enough secured, without philosophical Proofs of the Soul's Immateriality' (4.3.6). The close tie between morality and religion comes with the law of nature which is the divine law, 'the Law which God has set to the actions of Men'; that law is 'the only true touchstone of *moral Rectitude*' (2.28.8). His *A Letter concerning Toleration* gives a simple definition of religion: 'the regulating of men's lives according to the rules of virtue and piety' (in *Works*, vi. 6).

For his religious beliefs, Locke looked to the Bible, and so recommended others to do. He eschewed systems of divinity, complaining that he found little satisfaction in them and little consistency (*Reasonableness*, in *Works*, vii. 3). Many doctrines that others claimed were in or supported by the Bible, Locke could not find there. What he found the New Testament required to be a Christian was acceptance of Christ as the Messiah. This was for him the fundamental article of faith (*ibid.*, p. 57). That article, however, entails a few others, such as Jesus's 'resurrection, rule, and coming again to judge the world' (*ibid.*, p. 151; for a clear, succinct account of Locke's religious beliefs, see Arthur Wainwright's introduction to his edition of the *Paraphrases*, pp. 28–59). He also accepted the miracles Jesus performed, and perhaps some performed by his disciples, but the *Essay* raises some tough questions about the criterion for something being a miracle (*see* REVELATION; *see also* MIRACLES). David Hume said that Locke 'seems to have been the first Christian, who ventur'd openly to assert, that *Faith* was nothing but a Species of *Reason*, that Religion was only a Branch of Philosophy, and that a Chain of Arguments, similar to that which establish'd any Truth in Morals, Politics, or Physics, was always employ'd in discovering all the Principles of Theology, natural and reveal'd' (*Dialogues concerning Natural Religion*, ed. John V. Price, Oxford, 1976, p. 156). Hume may have had in mind Locke's talk of a demonstrative morality, but there is no place where Locke suggested that the principles of theology might be derived through chains of arguments. Reason *is* given prominence in Locke's writings, but he also identified some truths that are above reason, e.g., the resurrection of the dead (*Reasonableness*, in *Works*, vii. 4, 18, 23).

The systems of divinity which Locke found objectionable and often unintelligible rested on some metaphysical doctrines which either went against reason (e.g., transubstantiation, which required a body to be in two places at once) or invoked concepts that Locke believed went beyond our knowledge. He believed that our knowledge is sufficient for our needs, but it falls short of an adequate knowledge of all reality. It was the limits to knowledge that worried many of Locke's orthodox readers. His claim that we do not know the real internal structure of matter (although he accepted as a useful hypothesis the corpuscular theory); his limiting what we can know to experience and observation; his rejection of innate truths; his claim that the immateriality of the soul is not necessary for immortality; his suggestion that God could give to certain systems of matter the property of thought; his questioning whether the same body would be resurrected: all of these were considered as undermining the metaphysical foundation of religion. His analysis of personal identity as sameness of consciousness also bothered his readers because it rejected the standard belief in an immaterial soul-substance as constituting the person. Neither in the text of his *Reasonableness*, nor in his replies to Stillingfleet's charges, did Locke affirm his acceptance of the doctrine of the Trinity. His evasion on this point led Stillingfleet and others to suspect he was sympathetic to the Anti-trinitarians (the Socinians and Unitarians). In all of these claims, denials and omissions, Locke was considered dangerous to religion. He bypassed most of the metaphysical categories usually blindly accepted.

He was writing at a time when several new, unorthodox movements in religion and theology were appearing in Europe, especially in Holland, where he spent the years 1683–8. He made friends among these new religious groups, Socinians, Unitarians and deists. Faustus Socinius (1539–1604) became popular in Poland, then his views spread to Holland

and England. The Socinians became the object of bitter attacks. The term 'Latitudinarian' was originally applied to the Cambridge Platonists but then broadened to include most of the unorthodox thinkers, men who stressed the rationality of religion and held other liberal views. (For a good discussion of these various groups, see G.R. Cragg, *From Puritanism to the Age of Reason*, 1950.) One of the attractions for Locke of these new approaches was their stress on rationality and a critical reading of Scriptures. The doctrine of the Trinity was openly rejected by some; an attitude of toleration for diverse views characterized the groups in Holland. The thinkers that came to be called 'deists' comprise different kinds of people, but Herbert of Cherbury (whom Locke discussed in the first book of the *Essay* as one who held a doctrine of innate truths) is usually classed among them, as is Charles Blount (1659–93), just to name a couple. Anthony Collins, a friend of Locke in the first years of the eighteenth century, is a more notorious and better-known figure classed as a deist. His *Essay concerning the Use of Reason* (1707) and his *Discourse of Free-Thinking* (1713) came under heavy attack, in both England and France. John Toland's *Christianity Not Mysterious* (1696) borrowed many doctrines from Locke's *Essay* and got Locke into trouble by the use he made of those doctrines. Deist or not, Toland typified for many the evils of Locke's philosophy for religion.

The label 'Cambridge Platonists' refers to a group of writers also important for understanding the metaphysical and theological environment within which Locke lived and wrote. These writers can be characterized as philosophical theologians. They wrote on several topics of interest to Locke; some defended a version of innateness, others wrote on space and time as related to God. This group was influenced by Descartes, as Locke was also. Locke had in his library most of the books of the members of this group: e.g., Ralph Cudworth, *The True Intellectual System of the Universe* (1678); Henry More, *An Antidote against Atheisme* (1653) and several other books, including some philosophical poems; John Smith, *Select Discourses* (1660). Nathanael Culverwel's *An Elegant and Learned Discourse of the Light of Nature* (1654) also belongs in this group.

As in most periods, there was a short set of labels which defenders of tradition hurled at those they perceived as attacking and undermining the doctrines they held as necessary for morality and religion: 'Socinian' and 'deist' in the hands of traditionalists in Locke's day were used to imply atheism. It is fairly certain that Locke fits none of these labels, certainly not 'atheist'. He did share some of the newer views of these different groups, but he is not properly classed as Socinian or deist. His was, as he was fond of saying, a Christianity of the Scriptures, but he insisted that many of the doctrines his attackers claimed to be based on the Bible were not there. Moreover, he stressed the importance of understanding the

Scriptures, of making sense of them as far as possible. The mysterious and unintelligible doctrines of systems of divinity were not needed to be a Christian, nor were they part of the Scriptures (*see* BIBLE; for a discussion of the relation of Locke's doctrines to the religious controversies of the seventeenth and early eighteenth centuries, see John W. Yolton, *Locke and the Way of Ideas*, 1956).

representation   This term and its cognate, 'represent', have a number of different uses in Locke's writings (mainly in his *Essay*). In one passage, he speaks of a woman grieving for her dead child who could think of nothing else, who was unable to cease lamenting her loss. The 'Consolations of Reason' were of no avail; 'all Representations, though never so reasonable, are in vain' (2.33.13). In another passage, after comparing the way ideas in memory gradually disappear to fading colours of a picture, he remarks that 'our Minds represent to us those Tombs, to which we are approaching; where the Brass and Marble remain, yet the inscriptions are effaced by time' (2.10.5). On a less sombre note, he mentions some people who 'have had lively representations set before their minds of the unspeakable joys of Heaven' (2.21.37). He also refers to the consciousness of some past action being 'but a present representation' of that action, going on to suggest (this is in the chapter on personal identity) that it is possible for some action to be represented to a person even though that action never existed. The question is open, 'why one intellectual Substance may not have represented to it, as done by it self, what it never did, and was perhaps done by some other Agent' (2.27.13). Locke thinks it possible that just as in dreams 'several representations' of actions or events can occur that never really happened, so representations made to a person awake may be without reality.

In his criticism of the syllogism as a tool for reasoning, he objects to 'Rhetorical Discourses' with their 'metaphorical Representations' that mislead and obscure the ideas on which the inference depends (4.17.4). Another abuse of language, this time of words, refers to those who have been 'bred up in the Peripatetick Philosophy' who are persuaded that terms such as 'substantial forms', 'vegetative souls', and 'intentional species' are real, that they 'are the Representations of some thing that really exists' (3.10.14).

The most frequent use of the words 'represent' and 'representation' relate to ideas (and to the words which stand for ideas). Sometimes ideas are said to *represent*, other times they are described as *representations*. There are five different referents for this relation of representation of ideas: God, substances, mixed modes, objects or things (sometimes actions), and classes.

While remarking on when children acquire the idea of God, Locke says that very often that idea resembles 'the Opinion, and Notion of the Teacher', rather than representing the true God (1.4.13). Even adults' idea of God falls short of God's nature which is simple and uncompounded: we join the idea of infinity to 'our *Ideas* of Existence, Power, Knowledge'. In that way, we make 'that complex *Idea*, whereby we represent to our selves the best we can, the supreme Being' (2.23.35). The idea of God, whether with children or adults, is what Locke elsewhere characterizes as an 'inadequate' idea, one which is 'but a partial, or incomplete representation of' the archetype to which it is referred (2.31.1). Adequate ideas 'perfectly represent those Archetypes, which the Mind supposes them taken from; which it intends them to stand for, and to which it refers them' (*ibid.*).

Another important class of inadequate ideas is that of substance. Whether we take these ideas to refer to 'a supposed real Essence of each Species of Things' (to which our knowledge does not extend), or whether our ideas of substances are 'only design'd to be Pictures and Representations in the Mind, of Things that do exist' (where the referent is to those qualities that are discovered to exist together), our ideas are imperfect and inadequate (2.31.6). Locke uses in this passage the term 'copy': we fail in our attempt to make our ideas of substances copies of the originals or archetypes. Our intention is to 'copy Things, as they really do exist; and to represent to our selves their Constitution, on which all their Properties depend' (2.31.3, 7). The names for substances suffer a similar deficiency since they are 'annexed to *Ideas*, that are neither the real Essences, nor exact Representations of the patterns they are referred to' (3.9.20). If we stay with the traditional idea of substance as a non-sensory support for properties, or even work with the scientific concept of the corpuscular structure of material objects, our ideas will be inadequate. If we take Locke's notion of the nominal essence as the collection of qualities we discover, we may still not form an adequate idea because some qualities will be left out of our idea: the nominal essence would include the actual and possible collection of qualities. What we can say about this Lockean idea of substance is that those ideas are real since they are 'intended to be Representations of Substances as they really are'; that is, our ideas are a combination of coexisting qualities (2.30.5). In this sense of substance, the ideas are 'such combinations of simple *Ideas*, as are taken to represent distinct particular things subsisting by themselves' (2.12.6). It is this concept of substance that Adam assumed when he named things (3.6.46).

Falsity of ideas results, for example, from an attempt to take an idea of substance 'as the Representation of the unknown Essences of Things' (2.32.18). An idea by itself, just as an idea that we have in our mind and that is not considered as representing something else, is neither true nor

false. Even if it is 'conformable . . . to the existence of Things', even if it is
an 'exact Representation' of things, it cannot be said to be false. Any ideas
that may differ from 'the reality of Things' cannot 'properly be said to be
false Representations', nor can such an idea be said to be an idea of
something that it fails to represent (2.32.20). Falsity lies in the judgement
we make on the basis of some complex idea; we also must intend our idea
to refer to some object or action (2.32.21–4). It is also inappropriate to say
that 'When I frame an *Idea* of the Legs, Arms, and Body of a Man, and
join to this a Horse's Head and Neck', I have made a false idea, since 'it
represents nothing without me' (2.32.25). Such an idea would be false if I
'call it a *Man*, or *Tartar*, and imagine it either to represent some real Being
without me, or to be the same *Idea*, that others call by the same name'
(*ibid.*).

There is another kind of idea that cannot be false: complex ideas, except
those of substances, and especially those of actions. These are described as
the '*Archetypes* of the Mind's own making, not intended to be the Copies of
any thing, nor referred to the existence of any thing, as to their Originals'
(4.4.5). Such an idea is not 'designed to represent any thing but it self';
hence it is not capable of a wrong representation (*ibid.*; cf. 2.32.2). The
notion of an idea that represents itself is a bit strange; what it means is
that such an idea sets the standards for actions. We might want to say
such ideas are always true because they are constructed by us, not taken
from things in the world. For example, 'He that at first put together the
Idea of Danger perceived, absence of disorder from Fear, sedate consideration of what was justly to be done, and executing of that without
disturbance, or being deterred by the danger of it' had a specific complex
idea in mind and intended it to be 'nothing else, but what it is' (2.31.3).
The name 'courage' was given to this idea, 'to signifie it to others, and
denominate from thence any Action he should observe to agree with it'.
When Locke imagines Adam forming complex ideas by observing and
giving names to actions, he says that Adam selected specific features that
he wished to identify by the name of 'disloyalty': 'His own choice having
made that Combination, it had all in it he intended it should, and so could
not but be perfect, could not but be adequate, it being referr'd to no other
Archetype, which it was supposed to represent' (3.6.44). Another example
of constructing a complex idea of an action is given in 2.32.17: 'Thus when
I have the *Idea* of such an Action of a Man, who forbears to afford himself
such Meat, Drink, and Cloathing, and other Conveniencies of Life, as his
Riches and Estate will be sufficient to supply, and his station requires, I
have no *false Idea*.' The truth-value is a function of the name given to that
description: 'when I give the name *Frugality*, or *Vertue*, to this Action, then
it may be called a *false Idea*, if thereby it be supposed to agree with that

Idea, to which, in propriety of Speech, the name *Frugality* doth belong; or to be conformable to that Law, which is the Standard of Vertue and Vice' (*ibid.*). It is easier and more usual for people to work with names rather than ideas, especially in the case of ideas of types of actions, since so many features are included in the idea: 'the *Name* occurs much easier, than the complex *Idea* it self, which requires time and attention to be recollected, and exactly represented to the Mind' (4.5.4).

Another way in which ideas represent is when a particular idea is made to stand for a class or kind. By the mental operation of abstraction '*Ideas* taken from particular Beings, become general Representations of all of the same kind' (2.11.9). By abstracting, particular ideas are made 'capable of representing more Individuals than one' (3.3.6). By combining several simple ideas 'we represent particular sorts of *Substances* to our selves' (2.23.6). Everything on Locke's ontology is particular, including ideas and words. Particular words become general when they are made the signs of general ideas. Particular ideas become general when they are 'set up, as the Representatives of many particular Things' (3.3.11). 'Signifying' or 'representing' many particulars are, in this last passage, closely linked; the 'or' seems to mark an equivalence. Representing is signifying; a representation is a signifier. In another passage, Locke speaks of specific particular ideas which 'more than one particular Thing can correspond with, and be represented by' (4.17.8). In still another section, 'representation' is coupled with 'picture': ideas of collective substances such as an army or the world are said to be *one* idea, 'it sufficing, to the unity of any *Idea*, that it be considered as one Representation, or Picture, though made up of never so many Particulars' (2.24.1).

The question of whether the relation of representation is one of picturing, corresponding, or signifying becomes important when considering the last of the ways in which ideas represent and are themselves representations: the idea-object relation. All three locutions for the relation of representation are found in the *Essay*. The term 'copy' is used with 'representation' and 'represent' in 2.31.3, 6, 7 and in 4.4.5. 'Picture' occurs in the passage just cited (2.24.1). The word 'image' is also used: simple ideas are real and 'agree to the reality of things. Not that they are all of them Images, or Representations of what does exist' (2.30.2). Locke reminds the reader of his earlier account about qualities, that the ideas of primary qualities are resemblances of the qualities of bodies. Does the phrase here, 'Images, or Representations', mean that the ideas of secondary qualities are neither the images nor the representations of qualities? Is he saying that to be a representation of a quality requires the idea to resemble the quality? The language of resemblance is also used in his first reply to Bishop Stillingfleet's attack on the *Essay*. The Bishop had argued that the ideas of colours, sounds, and tastes are, on Locke's account, only effects of bodies and hence we cannot acquire any knowledge of bodies from those ideas. Locke paraphrases Stillingfleet as follows:

> For I suppose your lordship argues, from my opinion concerning the simple ideas of secondary qualities, the little real knowledge we should receive from them, if it be true, that they are not representations or images of anything in bodies, but only effects of certain powers in bodies to produce them in us; and in that sense I take the liberty to read your lordship's words thus: so that we can really understand nothing certainly but these ideas by the effects those powers have upon us. (*A Letter to the Right Rev. Edward Lord Bishop of Worcester*, in *Works*, iv. 76)

Locke responds by pointing out that 'we as certainly know and distinguish things by ideas, supposing them nothing but effects produced in us by these powers, as if they were representations.' Apparently he is saying that our being able to distinguish objects by the colour or taste produced in us by objects is similar in function to working from representations: 'It is as if that colour and that taste were representations and resemblances of something in those bodies' (*ibid.*, p. 75). He also tells the Bishop that in his *Essay*, he affirms that 'the simple ideas of primary qualities are the images or representations of what does exist without us.'

When he writes about true and false ideas, however, simple ideas such as blue, yellow, sweet, bitter are said to 'answer to' the power in bodies that produces them *and* he says they represent that power (2.32.16). 'Answer to' may be another variant on 'represent'. No mention is made in this passage of images or resemblance. The 'answer to' locution is also used in 4.4.4 where he refers to 'the *Idea* of Whiteness or Bitterness, as it is in the Mind, exactly answering that Power which is in any Body to produce it there'. These ideas are said to 'represent to us Things under those appearances which they are fitted to produce in us', enabling us to distinguish and use the objects we need. In 2.32.19, Locke explains that strictly speaking, ideas are not true or false: it is 'some Judgment that the Mind makes, or is supposed to make' that has the truth-value. A judgement or proposition is the joining or separating of signs: 'The signs we chiefly use, are either *Ideas*, or Words, wherewith we make either mental, or verbal Propositions. *Truth* lies in so joining, or separating these Representatives, as the Things they stand for, do, in themselves, agree, or disagree: and *Falshood* is the contrary' (2.32.19).

The use of the word 'sign' indicates what may be the main feature of ideas as representations. The word-idea relation is elaborated in the third book of the *Essay*, particularly in the short chapter 2, 'Of the Signification of Words'. Words are sensible signs of the thoughts or ideas of speakers and listeners. Locke says ideas are 'collected from the Things, which they are supposed to represent' (3.2.2). Words signify ideas, conceptions or thoughts (he uses all of these terms). Ideas represent (signify) objects and qualities. When he discusses names, he says that those words are 'not put barely for our Ideas', but they are used 'ultimately to represent Things', making *that* representative relation clearly one of signification (3.11.24). The signification of these words, names for substances, 'must agree with the Truth of Things, as well as with Men's *Ideas*.' At the very end of the *Essay*, Locke speaks briefly of the doctrine of signs. He says that the most usual signs are words. The business of the doctrine of signs (he also calls it 'logic') is 'to consider the Nature of Signs, the Mind makes use of for the understanding of Things, or conveying Knowledge to others' (4.21.4). He then makes a very important but potentially misleading remark: 'For since the Things, the Mind contemplates, are none of them, besides it self, present to the Understanding, 'tis necessary that something else, as a Sign or Representation of the thing it considers, should be present to it: And these are *Ideas*.' 'Sign' and 'representation' seem to be the same in this passage. The relation of representation or of signification applies mainly to ideas but also, as the 3.11.24 passage said, to words. The potentially misleading part of this 4.21.4 remark is in the phrase, 'present to the understanding'. This is a phrase which received heavy use by Hume later. Malebranche and Arnauld had earlier debated the similar Cartesian notion of 'existence in the mind' (a notion which surfaced later in Berkeley's writing). Descartes's concept of the objective reality of ideas identified the representative role of ideas. Descartes explained the objective reality of ideas as the *being* of the object (the object that is known) in the mind. Arnauld laboured to convince Malebranche that what Descartes meant was that the being (reality) of objects in the mind was their 'being known'. 'Representation', 'being known' and 'being in the mind' refer, Arnauld insisted, to cognition and signification.

There are two pieces of evidence in the *Essay* that suggest that Locke had this Cartesian notion in mind. He was well acquainted with the Arnauld-Malebranche debate, especially with Arnauld's *Des vrayes et des fausses idées* (1683). In the fourth edition of his *Essay*, Locke says that the terms he had used in earlier editions, 'clear' and 'distinct' (Cartesian terms), might better be replaced by 'determinate' and 'determined' ('Epistle to the Reader', p. 13). These terms refer to, he says, '*some object in the Mind*'. Thus, a determinate or determined idea is one that is 'at any time objectively in the Mind'. The term 'representation' does not appear in this Epistle passage. The other textual evidence which suggests a Cartesian context for Locke's talk of 'present to the understanding' is a remark he makes while insisting that no truths or principles can be in the mind (as innatists were claiming) of which we are not conscious: 'For if these Words (*to be in the Understanding*) have any Propriety, they signify to be understood' (1.2.5). This remark is almost identical to one of the definitions used by Arnauld while trying to show Malebranche that he had confused cognitive with spatial presence. In that 4.21.4 passage on the doctrine of signs, Locke says the mind makes use of signs 'for the understanding of Things'. Arnauld insisted that 'to be in the understanding' just means 'to be known or understood'. He attacked Malebranche's notion that ideas are separately existing objects that stand proxy for objects in the world, but he agreed that ideas (Locke's signs) are our means for knowing objects. Ideas in the mind were the very things themselves, but things can only exist in the mind cognitively, as known.

representative   There is one passage in the *Essay* where this term is applied to ideas or, as Locke there says, appearances: a particular colour is made by the mind 'a representative of all of that kind' (2.11.9). But the term 'representative' and its plural are most applicable to Locke's concept of political society, to his version of representative government. Where men unite to form a political society, they give up the right and power each had in the state of nature to judge and punish violations of the law of nature. That power is given to the society, but since men join a society by choice and consent, the judgements against offences made by the society are really each member's own judgement made either directly by themselves or through their representatives (*T*2, §88). On the subject of taxation, the concept of a representative of the members is also invoked. Governments cost money to run, and it 'is fit every one who enjoys his share of the Protection, should pay out of his Estate his proportion for the maintenance of it' (§140). The payment must be 'with his own Consent'. Here, 'consent' means 'the consent of the Majority, giving it either by themselves, or their Representatives chosen by them'.

In certain political societies (or commonwealths, the term Locke uses frequently), the legislative is combined with the executive in one person, but Locke stresses the importance of that person being seen as 'the publick Person vested with the Power of the Law' which was jointly formed by that person and the members. That public person 'is to be consider'd as the Image, Phantom, or Representative of the Commonwealth, acted by the will of the Society' (§151). In other societies, the legislative may be in whole or part made up of representatives chosen by the people for set periods of time, and arrangements must be made for future elected representatives (§154). With changes in population, representatives chosen by the people may become 'very *unequal* and disproportionate to the reason it was at first establish'd upon' (§157). This disproportion may arise through the growth or decline of towns and cities, so that what was at one time a large inhabited area may now be just a few groups of persons. It would be wrong to retain the same numbers of representatives for that reduced population (*ibid.*). Locke had a concept of proportional representation. He does not give any figures for determining what he calls 'the true proportion' or a 'true reason' for deciding on the numbers of representatives from each region, but he does refer to a right that the people have 'to be distinctly represented' (§158). Another phrase is 'a fair and *equal Representative*', and he talks of the 'Power of Erecting new Corporations, and therewith new *Representatives*' (*ibid.*). This process of setting up a new group of representatives 'carries with it a supposition, that in time the *measures of representation* might vary, and those places have a just right to be represented which before had none; and by the same reason, those cease to have a right, and be too inconsiderable for such a Priviledge, which before had it' (*ibid.*). Free consent and selecting their representatives are the bases for legitimate government (§192).

In discussing the conditions under which a government can be dissolved, the conditions which make it illegitimate, Locke supposes the legislative body to be composed of three groups: a 'single hereditary Person', an 'Assembly of Hereditary Nobility', and 'an Assembly of Representatives chosen *pro tempore*, by the People' (§213). One way in which such a government could violate the trust of the people is if the hereditary person (the king) 'imploys the Force, Treasure, and Offices of the Society, to corrupt the *Representatives*, and gain them to his purposes' (§222). Solicitations, threats, promises might be used to buy the votes before debate on issues and against the wishes of those who elect the representatives. Tampering with the representatives of the people is a way to cut up 'the Government by the Roots, and poison the very Fountain of publick Security' (*ibid.*). The choice of representatives belongs to the people.

The concept of elected persons serving as the representatives of others goes along with Locke's stress upon community and his metaphor for the political structure of a living body with a will and soul directing the whole (*see* COMMONWEALTH). Hobbes developed the notion of representatives earlier in his *Leviathan* (1651). When the words and actions of a person are considered his own, Hobbes calls that person 'natural', but when those words and actions are 'considered as representing the words and actions of an other, then is he a *Feigned* or *Artificial person*' (Pt I, ch. XVI). Hobbes applied the distinction to actors on stage as well as to the political and social arenas. In one passage, he comes very close to anticipating Locke's notion of the body politic: 'A Multitude of men, are made *One* Person, when they are by one man, or one Person, represented; so that it be done with the consent of every one of the Multitude in particular. For it is the *Unity* of the Representer, not the *Unity* of the Represented, that maketh the Person *One*' (*ibid.*). Locke's stress on the majority acting for the whole also occurs in Hobbes: 'And if the Representative consist of many men, the voyce of the greater number, must be considered as the voyce of them all'.

resemblance   The importance of this term lies in its use in connection with Locke's discussion of the relation between ideas and qualities, concentrated mainly in *Essay* 2.8. There are a few other uses of this term, and the related 'image', that help us understand the resemblance-relation.

There are several places where Locke either cites the biblical notion, or employs it himself, of man being made in the image of God (e.g., *T*1, §30). When he deals with the topic of innate ideas of God, he refers to countries and people who have images of a deity (*Essay*, 1.3.6). One of these passages refers to 'their Images, and Representations of their Deities' (1.4.15). Images can have a representative role. In a manuscript entry on idolatry, he comments on the injunction against worshipping images, idols (printed in *Essays*, p. 261). It is doubtful that anyone ever meant such images to be likenesses of a God, but they may have played a representative role.

The passages where ideas are spoken of as images usually involve analogies. Much of Locke's description of ideas and perception makes use of visual and optical language. In *Essay* 2.1.15, it is a looking-glass which is used to attack the notion that our soul always thinks, even when we are not aware of doing so and have no recollection of thinking always: '*To think often, and never to retain it so much as one moment, is a very useless sort of thinking*; and the Soul in such a state of thinking, does very little, if at all, excel that of a Looking-glass, which constantly receives variety of images, or *Ideas*, but retains none; they disappear and vanish, and there remain no footsteps of them; the Looking-glass is never the better for such *Ideas*, nor the Soul for such Thoughts.' A later section in this chapter uses the analogy of the mirror again, this time to say that the understanding is passive in sensation: 'These *simple Ideas*, when offered to the mind, *the Understanding* can no more refuse to have, nor alter, when they are imprinted, nor blot them out, and make new ones in it self, than a mirror can refuse, alter, or obliterate the Images or *Ideas*, which, the Objects set before it, do therein produce' (2.1.25). A different analogy is used when he characterizes memory and the way ideas do not remain for ever in the mind. Just as the inscriptions on tombstones are effaced in time, and 'the Imagery moulders away', so '*The Pictures drawn in our Minds, are laid in fading Colours*; and if not sometimes refreshed, vanish and disappear' (2.10.5). Still another analogy is used to describe the succession of ideas in our awareness. He asks 'whether it be not probable that our *Ideas* do, whilst we are awake, succeed one another in our Minds at certain distances, not much unlike the Images in the inside of a Lanthorn, turned round by the Heat of a Candle' (2.14.9).

Analogies are never meant as literal likenesses. Locke was not of course saying that the mind *is* a mirror, or that ideas are in the mind just as the images are on a mirror. Nor did he want to say ideas are painted on the mind in the way in which images and pictures are painted on the lantern. There is *some* comparison, some similarity, between the rotation of the lantern casting its pictures for us to see and the mind or understanding being aware of the flow of ideas. 'Being aware of' thoughts and ideas is not the same as being visually aware of, seeing, the shapes and figures thrown out by the revolving, heated lantern. The problem arises when we try to say precisely how these analogies and comparisons apply to awareness and its contents. If ideas were not meant by Locke to be literally pictures, what does the term 'image' convey, what work does it perform? 'Representation' with which 'image' is coupled in some passages is a more neutral term, but it may be no less difficult to specify how ideas represent things or qualities.

The term 'resemble' poses similar problems. A more or less straightforward use of that term is found when Locke suggests that a way of explaining the taste of some unfamiliar fruit is to say it is like some other fruit which the person has tasted, even though the tastes are not the same (3.4.11). When we speak of plants as 'sensitive' because 'the different application of other Bodies to them, do very briskly alter their Figures and Motions', we do so because their motion 'has some resemblance to that, which in Animals follows upon Sensation' (2.9.11). But Locke suggests that this resemblance misleads, because the motion of plants 'is all bare Mechanism'. Another fairly clear example: if we form the idea of 'Legs, Arms, and Body of a Man, and join to this a Horse's Head and Neck' and then call it a man or a Tartar, we make a tacit false mental proposition, since there is no 'conformity and resemblance' between that complex idea and any living being in the world (2.32.25).

'Resemble' and 'image' come together in the discussion of primary and secondary qualities. Using the locution, 'Ideas, or Perceptions', he says we should not think they are 'exactly the Images and *Resemblances* of something inherent' in bodies (2.8.7). 'Perception' in this use (there are several such occurrences in the *Essay*) is not the act of perceiving, but a state of awareness, as we might say 'I perceive (see, touch) a chair in the corner', and then talk of the perception of the chair. This term does not lend itself so easily to an image or likeness interpretation as does the term 'idea'. Locke gives an example. Working with the corpuscular theory as the causal explanation of the production of sensory ideas, he says the colour and smell of a violet are caused by 'the impulse of such insensible particles of matter of peculiar figures, and bulks, and in different degrees and modifications of their Motions' (2.8.13). An alternative to the language of causation is the talk of God annexing 'such *Ideas* to such Motions, with which they have no similitude', pointing out that such an annexation is no more impossible to conceive than is the annexation of 'the *Idea* of Pain to the motion of a piece of Steel dividing our Flesh, with which that *Idea* hath no resemblance' (*ibid.*). The violet reappears in a much later passage where the question is raised: 'whether we think, that the *Idea* of Blue, be in the Violet it self, or in our Mind only' (2.32.14). His point there is not to answer the question but to say it makes no difference whether we take blue to be 'only a peculiar Texture of Parts, or else that very Colour, the *Idea* whereof (which is in us) is the exact resemblance' (*ibid.*). It makes no difference for our distinguishing violets or the colour blue from other flowers or colours because we do so on the basis of the appearance we call 'blue'. The word 'blue' 'notes properly nothing, but that Mark of Distinction, that is in a *Violet*, discernible only by our Eyes' (*ibid.*). It is beyond our capacities to know what features of the violet correspond with that mark. Nevertheless, Locke sets out a theory about that correspondence.

There are various words used to characterize the idea-quality relation. The ideas of primary qualities are said to be resemblances of those qualities, but in 2.8.15 Locke uses the word 'pattern': 'their Patterns do really exist in the Bodies themselves.' The ideas of secondary qualities '*have no resemblance*' to the qualities at all; there 'is nothing like our *Ideas*, existing in the Bodies themselves', presumably not even their 'patterns'. What corresponds to these ideas is 'only a Power to produce these Sensations in us' (*ibid.*). The next section says that the qualities 'are commonly thought to be the same in those Bodies, that those *Ideas* are in us, the one the perfect resemblance of the other, as they are in a Mirror' (2.8.16). Such is the common, ordinary opinion, an opinion that does not address the question of how a sensation or idea could be the mirror-image of a quality in an object. Berkeley was later to affirm that nothing could be like an idea save another idea, the ontological principle that there can be no causal interaction between mental and physical being extended to the resemblance-relation.

Besides the primary and secondary qualities, Locke distinguishes a third sort, 'The *Power* that is in any Body, *by* Reason of the particular Constitution of *its primary Qualities*, to make such a *change* in the *Bulk, Figure, Texture, and Motion of another Body*, as to make it operate on our Senses, differently from what it did before' (2.8.23). He went on to explain the difference in our thinking about the secondary and this third sort of quality (we might call the latter 'the indirectly secondary'). We do not believe the change in the colour or softness of wax caused by the sun resembles anything in the sun, yet we find it easy to think our ideas of heat or light *are* real qualities of the sun. But my being warmed by the sun is no different from the changes made in wax by the sun: 'They are all of them equally Powers in the Sun' (2.8.24). In the next section, he explains that since our ideas of colours, sounds, etc., contain 'nothing at all in them of Bulk, Figure, or Motion, we are not apt to think them the Effects' of the primary qualities. Because of this – 'Since Sensation discovers nothing of Bulk, Figure, or Motion of parts' in the production of these ideas, nor can reason show how that would work – 'we are so forward to imagine, that those *Ideas* are the resemblances of something really existing in the Objects themselves.'

This is a rather interesting analysis. The reason we think bodies are coloured is that the idea or sensation does not include the ideas of bulk, figure, etc., so we are not led to believe they are the effects of such qualities. Do we, then, suppose them to be the effects of colour in bodies? That seems to be what Locke is suggesting about the common view. With the third sort of qualities, 'in the Operations of Bodies, changing the Qualities one of another, we plainly discover, that the Quality produced, hath commonly no resemblance with any thing in the thing producing it; wherefore we look on it as a bare Effect of Power' (2.8.25). We 'plainly discover' because we can see that the sun does not manifest, does not appear to have, the qualities that the wax does when exposed to the heat of the sun: 'when we see Wax, or a fair Face, receive change of Colour from the Sun, we cannot imagine, that to be the Reception or Resemblance of any thing in the Sun, because we find not those different Colours in the Sun it self' (*ibid.*). We do discover a likeness or unlikeness between different sensible qualities, and we need only look at sun and wax or a fair face to discover the lack of resemblance. In our own case, 'not being able to discover any unlikeness between the *Idea* produced in us, and the Quality of the Object producing it, we are apt to imagine, that our *Ideas* are resemblances of something in the Objects.'

The fact that Locke is rather egregiously moving from theory to ordinary beliefs may be both confusing and disturbing. But if we recognize that, very much as Hume did in his *Treatise*, I, IV, II, Locke was attempting to explain how the ordinary belief about objects arises, the confusion and worry should disappear. As Hume said, philosophers 'suppose external objects to resemble internal perceptions' (*Treatise*, p. 216, Selby-Bigge edn.); the ordinary person rejects the notion of a double existence, of ideas and objects. The ordinary person, Hume said, believes the things he sees and touches are the objects in the world, not some internal resembling ideas. Locke's account of the common belief may straddle the single and double existence view when he says, 'we are apt to think, 'tis a Perception and Resemblance of such a Quality in the Sun' (*ibid.*). If it is a perception of the quality, this is close to Hume's account of the ordinary belief, but if 'perception' is taken as a resemblance, as the 'and' suggests, Locke's analysis places the common view on the side of Hume's philosophers. The issue that was to consume so much of the time and attention of philosophers throughout the eighteenth century, especially Berkeley, Hume, Leibniz, and most extensively of all, Kant, begins in *Essay* 2.8.

resurrection   In one of his replies to Stillingfleet, the Bishop of Worcester, Locke affirmed that 'The resurrection of the dead I acknowledge to be an article of the Christian faith' (*Mr. Locke's Second Reply*, in *Works*, iv. 303). Here and in other passages of this reply, Locke tells the Bishop that 'I read the revelation of the holy Scripture with a full assurance that all it delivers is true' (*ibid.*, p. 341). When Stillingfleet charged Locke's doctrines in the *Essay* with being inconsistent with another doctrine, that of the Trinity, Locke protested that his Bible says nothing about 'three persons in one nature, or . . . two natures and one person' (*ibid.*, p. 343). Locke never did say whether the Trinity was for him an article of faith, but since he based his Christianity on what the Bible says, we can probably conclude that that doctrine did not figure in his religion. For Locke what was necessary for being a Christian was basically to believe that Christ was the Messiah. To believe that, of course, entailed believing that he rose from the dead; his resurrection was a proof of his being the Messiah. These beliefs also involved the notion that Christ restored life to all men, the life which 'they receive again at the resurrection' (*Reasonableness*, in *Works*, vii. 9).

   The Bishop did not charge Locke with rejecting the doctrine of resurrection, only that Locke's account of knowledge in terms of ideas and his concept of person-identity are inconsistent with that doctrine. Stillingfleet understood, as other orthodox theologians did also, that the resurrection involved the *same* body. Locke told the Bishop that he could not find in the Bible any reference to same body; what he found was talk of the resurrection of the dead. In fact, in the first three editions of his *Essay*, Locke referred to the resurrection 'of our Bodies' (4.3.29), and he said 'the Bodies of Men shall rise again' (4.18.7). He changed these two passages after the third edition to read: 'The Resurrection of the Dead' and 'the dead shall rise and live again.' Apparently it was Stillingfleet's criticism that led Locke to make these changes, changes to an interpretation of the

resurrection that Stillingfleet attacked him for. 'When I writ that book, I
took it for granted, as I doubt not but many others have done, that the
Scripture had mentioned in express terms, "the resurrection of the body":
but upon the occasion your lordship has given me in your letter to look a
little more narrowly into what revelation has declared concerning the
resurrection, and finding no such express words in the Scripture, as that
"the body shall rise or be raised, or the resurrection of the body", I shall in
the next edition of it change those words of my book' (*Mr. Locke's Second
Reply*, in *Works*, iv. 333–4). Locke even went on to say that he did not
question 'that the dead shall be raised with bodies'; the question was, with
what bodies? Even in the addition to the second edition of the *Essay* of the
chapter on identity and diversity (where Locke develops his concept of
person), he said that a person at the resurrection would have a body 'not
exactly in make or parts the same which he had here' (2.27.15). So Locke
never said, even in those other passages in the first three editions, that the
same body will appear at the resurrection.

It was just that interpretation that Stillingfleet rejected: he took the
standard interpretation that the same body would be united with the same
soul as in mortal life. Stillingfleet did not fully understand Locke's
distinction between man and person, with the locus of person-identity
being in sameness of consciousness, and not, on the standard view, in an
immaterial substance. To Stillingfleet, this notion of the same person had
the consequence that what body a person has at any particular time is not
part of the personhood of a man. Locke had, too, rung the changes on one
consciousness in different substances, or even a day and night PERSON in
the same substance. These puzzles were his way of showing the irrele-
vance of substance to person-identity. He was not a defender of the
concept of substance, but he nowhere suggested that a person can be
disconnected from a body, not even at the resurrection. Just what happens
to the person in death is not discussed by Locke, but presumably persons
cease to exist until such time as God calls them to account. Nevertheless,
in the mortal life, and in the next life, we have bodies, earthly ones now,
heavenly bodies there. In a paper written in 1699, Locke says that the
Bible says many times that men shall be raised, 'But how they are raised
or with what bodys they shall come the Scripture as far as I have observed
is perfectly silent' (printed in *Paraphrases*, p. 684). Locke's commentary on
St Paul's letter to the Corinthians (1 Cor. 15) speaks of heavenly and
earthly bodies: 'those who are raised to an heavenly state shall have other
bodys' and those heavenly bodies will be beautiful and excellent, 'of a very
different constitution and qualitys from those they had before' (*ibid.*, p.
252). In another part of his commentary on 1 Corinthians, Locke glosses
St Paul as follows: 'This I say to you Brethren to satisfie those that aske

with what bodys the dead shall come, that we shall not at the resurrection have such bodys as we have now For flesh and blood cannot enter into the Kingdom which the saints shall inherit in heaven: Nor are such fleeting corruptible things as our present bodys are fitted to that state of immutable incorruptibility' (*ibid.*, p. 255).

Locke also has several long explanatory notes on the same Epistle, giving some details about the resurrection as outlined by St Paul. It will be done in stages: 'First of all Christ rose: Afterwards next in order to him the saints should all be raised, which resurrection of the just is that which he treats and gives an account of to the end of this discourse' (*ibid.*, p. 252). Locke even points out that 'we shall not all die but we shall all be changed in a moment in the twinkleing of an eye at the sounding of the last trumpet, for the trumpet shall sound and the dead shall rise, and as many of us believers as are then alive shall be changed' (*ibid.*, p. 255).

In arguing that it is the same body at the resurrection, Stillingfleet admitted that by 'same body' he did not mean the same particles of matter that a person, e.g., a sinner, had at a particular time (e.g. when he sinned), since we lose and change particles of the matter of our body throughout life. But committed as he was to the metaphysic of substances, Stillingfleet insisted that the same material substance that was united to the soul in this life had to be present and reunited with its soul at the resurrection. Locke runs through some of the arguments employed by the Bishop for this claim, reducing most to absurdity or to internal contradiction. There is some good conceptual analysis in the pages of Locke's *Second Reply*; there is also some fun and humour at the Bishop's expense. For example, if, as Stillingfleet quotes from John 5: 28–9, 'all that are in the graves shall hear his voice, and shall come forth', Stillingfleet must believe that the soul as a substance must also be in the grave: only what was in the grave can come out of the grave (in *Works*, iv. 306). If we ignore the problem of where the soul is when the body dies, another problem facing the Bishop is what particles does he believe come out of the grave? Again, those particles cannot be different from those that composed the body when it was placed in the grave, so all the particles that were united to the soul in life do not come out of the grave at the resurrection (*ibid.*, pp. 306–7).

Locke goes on to point out that we have different bodies at different times throughout our life, but whatever body we have at any specific time or period is *our* body: 'your lordship will easily see, that the body he had when an embryo in the womb, when a child playing in coats, when a man marrying a wife, and when bed-rid, dying of a consumption, and at last, which he shall after his resurrection; are each of them his body, though neither of them be the same body, the one with the other' (p. 308).

Whatever body we have at the resurrection will be *our* body. Another difficulty for the Bishop is that of the case of a man who has sinned over a long period of time (a 'long sinner', Locke calls him), the totality of the particles of such a 'long sinner' would be too vast to appear at the resurrection (pp. 308–9). The Bishop's response was, only *some* of the many particles a man's body had need to be united to the soul at the resurrection. Locke makes the obvious reply to this move: 'So that to take the numerical particles that made up his body at fifty, or any other season of his life; or to gather them promiscuously out of those which at different times have successively been vitally united to his soul; they will no more make the same body, which was his, wherein some of his actions were done, than that is the same body which has but half the same particles' (p. 310). Locke suggests that the particles of a 'decrepit, wasted, withered body' of an old sick man at death 'would be too few, or unfit to make such a plump, strong, vigorous, well-sized body, as it has pleased your lordship to proportion out in your thoughts to men at the resurrection' (*ibid.*). Even more telling against the Bishop's concept, 'what must an embryo do, who, dying within a few hours after his body was vitally united to his soul, has no particles of matter, which were formerly vitally united to it, to make up his body of that size and proportion which your lordship seems to require at the resurrection' (p. 311). The result is that an embryo that dies in the womb 'may be very little, not the thousandth part of an ordinary man', and that embryo would 'remain a man not an inch long to eternity: because there are not particles of matter, formerly united to his soul, to make him bigger; and no other can be made use of to that purpose.'

The chemist and friend of Locke, Robert Boyle, addressing the same topic, concluded that 'there is no determinate bulk or size that is necessary to make a human body pass for the *same*, and that a very small portion of matter will sometimes serve the turn: as an embryo, for instance in the womb, a new-born babe, a man at his full stature, and a decrepit man of perhaps a hundred years old, notwithstanding the vast difference of their sizes, are still reputed to be the same person' ('Some Physico-Theological Considerations about the Possibility of the Resurrection', 1675, reprinted in *Selected Philosophical Papers of Robert Boyle*, ed. M.A. Stewart, 1979, p. 199). Boyle was reflecting on the question of identity of a body from the point of view of a chemist. He took seriously what Locke made fun of in Bishop Stillingfleet, although Boyle was more concerned with what particles and how many that went into the grave God would need to enlarge them into a complete body at the resurrection. Boyle went to the same Epistle of St Paul, 1 Corinthians, that Locke paraphrased: in the question, 'How are the dead raised up?' Boyle mentions several possibilities: 'a plastic power in some of the matter of a deceased body, whereby, being divinely excited, it may be enabled to take to itself fresh matter, and so subdue and fashion it as thence sufficiently to repair or augment itself'; or an analogy with leaven in dough (*ibid.*, pp. 195–6). He does not commit himself to any explanatory hypothesis, but he does say that what St Paul says is consistent with the notion that 'a portion of the matter of a dead body, being united with a far greater portion of matter furnished from without by God himself, and completed into a human body, may be reputed the *same* that was dead before' (p. 197).

There were other writers who argued as Stillingfleet did, that the same body would be resurrected, although none of these offered the sort of detail that Boyle suggests for explaining how it might be accomplished: Matthew Hale, *The Primitive Origination of Mankind* (1677); Thomas Browne, *Religio Medici* (4th edn., 1656). Two writers came to Locke's defence on this topic: Samuel Bold, *A Discourse concerning the Resurrection of the Same Body* (1705); Catharine Cockburn, *A Letter to Dr. Holdsworth, Occasioned by His Sermon Preached before the University of Oxford, on Easter Monday* (1726) and 'A Vindication of Mr. Locke's Christian Principles', in her *Works* (1751). Holdsworth's sermon to which Cockburn replied was published in 1720; he replied to her defence in 1727. Holdsworth charged Locke with being a Socinian because of his rejection of the same body at the resurrection. Another divine, Daniel Whitby, also attacked Locke, siding with Stillingfleet (*Paraphrase and Commentary on the New Testament*, 1703). Whitby and Locke exchanged a few letters in 1699 and 1702, but Locke refused to be drawn into debate (*Corr.* 2533, vi. 545; 2536, vi. 548–9; 3188, vii. 676–7; 3203, vii. 697–8). In one letter to Whitby Locke simply said: 'For I being fully perswaded of the resurrection and that we shall have bodys fitted to that state, it is indifferent to me whether any one concludes that they shall be the same or not' (2536).

revelation Some truths can be discovered and some knowledge acquired by revelation. The early *Essays on the Law of Nature* list three kinds or sources of knowledge: inscription, tradition and sense-experience. A fourth kind, not one much discussed in these essays, is 'supernatural and divine revelation' (p. 123). There are in Locke's writings two sources of revelation: 'the light of Nature, and direct revelation' (*Essay*, 2.28.8). In that passage, he was talking about the divine law, 'that Law which God has set to the actions of Men'. The law of nature is often said to be knowledge obtained by our natural faculties (1.3.13), although in this same section he labels as 'extreme' the denial of a law of nature 'knowable by the light of Nature; i.e. without the help of positive Revelation'. The law he refers to here, however, is the claimed innate law, so he may only want to say we could not know an innate law (or know that it is innate) without the help of positive revelation. Certainly, the early *Essays* assert unequivocally that the law of nature 'can be known by the light of nature', that is, a law or truth 'which a man can attain by himself and without the help of another; if he make proper use of the faculties he is endowed with by nature' (p. 123). This essay is devoted to giving an affirmative answer to the question, 'Can the Law of Nature be Known by the light of Nature?' He also says we can know God's will by the light of nature or by 'God-inspired Men' (p. 187). In the *Essay*, reason is characterized as 'natural Revelation', the faculty 'whereby the eternal Father of Light, and Fountain of all Knowledge communicates to Mankind that portion of Truth, which he has laid within the reach of their natural Faculties' (4.19.4).

Talk of the light of reason or nature in the disclosure of truths about God's will and laws tends to disappear in later writings. It was a phrase invoked by innatists. The metaphor of light by which we 'see' special truths was also language Locke heavily criticized in the writings of those called 'enthusiasts' (4.19). The light of reason is replaced by reason itself in most of Locke's writings. For a long time, at least from the *Essay* to *Reasonableness* (from the 1680s to 1695), he held out hope that reason would be able by the means proper to that faculty (reasoning or even demonstration) to discover God's moral laws. In calling reason 'natural revelation' while writing against enthusiasm, he meant to preserve his conviction that our faculties, especially reason, are God-given, while avoiding falling into the enthusiast's trap of turning reason into a non-rational means of discovering important truths. Reason as natural revelation is also a way of bridging the gap between faith and reason, between reason and religion.

Another aspect of Locke's efforts to bring reason and revelation into harmony is indicated by his characterization of revelation (still in the chapter on enthusiasm) as 'natural *Reason* enlarged by a new set of Discoveries communicated by GOD immediately, which *Reason* vouches the Truth of, by the Testimony and Proofs it gives, that they come from GOD' (4.19.4). What is the role played by reason in discoveries communicated by God? How does reason vouch for the truth of those communications? Can we determine how reason vouches for these truths in specific cases where Locke assigns them to revelation?

The 'dictates of Nature and Reason, as well as his [God's] Reveal'd Command, requires us to preserve' our children (*T*1, §56). In this case, Locke only asserts that reason agrees with the natural instinct for the preservation of our children and what God commands. In another passage of this same work, Locke cites biblical texts to support his claim of parents' (not, as Filmer argued, the father's) power over the children or the honour due them by their children (*T*1, §61). Since Locke considers the Bible as the revealed word of God, these injunctions (e.g., that children should obey their parents) are revealed truths. The citations from the Bible come under the heading of 'testimony', as the way reason vouches for these truths. In the second of *Two Treatises*, the chapter on property says that revelation (i.e., the Bible) tells us of the 'Grants God made of the World to *Adam*, and to *Noah*, and his Sons' (*T*2, §25). God, we are told, quoting Psalm CXV, '*has given the Earth to the Children of Men*, given it to Mankind in Common'. Presumably, reason vouches for this truth because again reason accepts the Bible as God's revealed word. The *Essays* say 'we must believe that religion becomes known to men not so much by the light of nature as by divine revelation' (p. 167). Reason's role in this rather general revelation is unclear.

Another bit of information said by Locke to be disclosed to us by revelation is the existence of spirits, of SPIRITS other than ourselves and God. He is not always confident about whether this is knowledge or just belief. *Essay* 4.11.12 says that the existence of such spirits is *not* knowledge; just because we have ideas of such spirits (as Locke believed we do), it does not follow that we can claim to know that they exist. Nevertheless, he says that 'we have ground from revelation, and other Reasons, to believe with assurance, that there are such Creatures.' In this section, he is showing that the having of ideas is not by itself sufficient reason for saying the referents of those ideas exist; we cannot, at least, claim to know that they exist. He is a little more positive in 4.12.12 where he summarizes the limits of human knowledge, remarking that 'what we hope to know of separate Spirits in this World, we must, I think, expect only from Revelation.' An earlier passage in the *Essay* says that 'we have no certain information, so much as of the Existence of other Spirits, but by revelation', suggesting that revelation does give us *certain* information about spirits (4.3.27; cf. *ST*, §190). There are also two passages which say that if we were to know such and such, we could only do so by revelation. For example, it is 'impossible for us, by the contemplation of our own *Ideas*, without revelation, to discover' whether God has given to certain systems of matter the power to perceive and think (4.3.6). Or, it is impossible for us to know 'all the Effects of Matter' without revelation (4.6.14). Just how reason would accept such revelations is not clear.

It may be that Locke's claim that reason will vouch the truth of what God or God-inspired men reveal to us is a more general claim about criteria. In the *Essay*, he distinguishes *original* from *traditional* revelation. The *Paraphrases* talk of *immediate* revelation as distinguished from revelation *mediated* by the Scripture (4.18.3; cf. *Paraphrases*, p. 623n.). By original, he explains, 'I mean that first Impression, which is made immediately by GOD', while traditional revelation is 'those Impressions delivered over to others in Words, and the ordinary ways of conveying our Conceptions one to another' (4.18.3). Is original revelation non-verbal? Two examples suggest that it is. Locke speaks of 'things' discovered to St Paul 'when he was rapp'd up into the Third Heaven': he received new ideas in his mind in that state (*ibid.*). Another example: 'supposing GOD should discover to any one, supernaturally a Species of Creatures inhabiting, for Example, *Jupiter*, or *Saturn* . . . which had six Senses' (*ibid.*). That person would be unable by using words to produce in the minds of others 'those *Ideas*, imprinted by that sixth Sense'. In general, whatever impressions any one receives 'from the immediate hand of GOD, this Revelation, if it be of new simple *Ideas*, cannot be conveyed to another, either by Words, or any other Signs' (*ibid.*). The problem is not receiving new simple ideas of things never seen or experienced before; the problem lies in the inability to communicate those ideas to others. Original revelation can produce ideas in a mind without going through the channels of sensation and reflection.

Traditional revelation could discover to us truths which we are able to discover by our natural faculties, e.g., the truths in Euclid; but such revelations are unnecessary since we have God-given faculties for that purpose. Moreover, truths discovered 'from the Knowledge and Contemplation of our own *Ideas*, will always be certainer to us, than those which are conveyed to us by *Traditional Revelation*' (4.18.4). Even were God to reveal immediately to us (i.e. by original revelation) truths that we have or could reach by 'immediate intuition, or in self-evident Propositions, or by evident deductions of Reason', our assurance of these truths 'can be no greater, than our Knowledge is, that it is a *Revelation* from GOD' (4.18.5). Even where we have knowledge that some truth is revealed by God, if it contradicts 'the clear Evidence' of our understanding, that truth will not 'rationally prevail with any Man' (*ibid.*). The 'will not' is not replaced by 'should not', so it may be that Locke is merely describing how the mind works, what it can and cannot do, but the implicit tone suggests that he is really making a commendation when he says, 'we can never receive for a Truth any thing, that is directly contrary to our clear and distinct Knowledge.' He goes on to give, as an example, transubstantiation as something that contradicts our clear perception that one body cannot be in 'two distant Places at once'.

This example (and Locke rejects it in several places) is not revealed, is not found in the Bible. If anyone pretends to 'the Authority of a divine *Revelation*' for this doctrine (Locke is really taking a dig at church doctrine), it will never (and perhaps should never) gain the assent of rational men: 'Since the Evidence, *First*, That we deceive not our selves in ascribing it to GOD; *Secondly*, That we understand it right, can never be so great, as the Evidence of our own intuitive Knowledge, whereby we discern it impossible, for the same Body to be in two Places at once' (4.18.5). Were such propositions as this accepted as true, or even intelligible, 'this would be to subvert the Principles, and Foundations of all Knowledge, Evidence, and Assent whatsoever' (*ibid.*). The strength of any proposition said to be revealed 'depends upon our Knowledge, that GOD revealed it', but in the case of this claimed revealed truth, which contradicts our knowledge and reason, 'we cannot tell how to conceive that to come from GOD, the bountiful Author of our Being, which if received for true, must overturn all the Principles and Foundations of Knowledge he has given us' (*ibid.*). Even with immediate or original revelation, 'a Man has use of Reason, and ought to hearken to it' (3.18.6). However, he seems to allow for the possibility that some revealed propositions may have 'a greater Evidence' than the principles of reason (3.18.5). Revelation can also over-rule the *'probable Conjectures of Reason'*; the mind, he says, 'is bound to give up its Assent to such a Testimony, which it is satisfied, comes from one, who cannot err, and will not deceive' (4.18.8). Reason still must judge 'of the Truth of its being a Revelation, and of the signification of the Words, wherein it is delivered' (*ibid.*). With traditional revelation, second-hand revelation delivered in language, reason should judge the propositions as a 'matter of reason'. But by what means does reason decide that some set of words *is* a revelation?

When Locke writes about the distinction between faith and reason, he says there are some propositions that are above reason: these are proper objects of faith, but we must be sure that those propositions *are* 'beyond the Discovery of our natural Faculties' (4.18.7). He gives as examples 'that part of the Angels rebelled against GOD, and thereby lost their first happy state: And that the dead shall rise, and live again' (*ibid.*). These are propositions reported in the Bible, a source Locke accepted as mediated revelation. He was especially anxious to reject claims for direct, immediate revelation made by individuals who took themselves to be inspired by God but who in reality only pretend to have such revelation in order to secure their opinions and beliefs (4.19.5). To such claimants of immediate revelation from the hand of God, Locke demands a strong test: 'How do I know that GOD is the Revealer of this to me; that this Impression is made upon my Mind by his holy Spirit, and that therefore I ought to obey it?' (4.19.10). If I claim that God has revealed some truth to me, I must *know* 'that GOD is the revealer of it, and that what I take to be a Revelation is certainly put into my Mind by him, and is not an Illusion drop'd in by some other Spirit, or raised by my own phancy' (*ibid.*).

Locke's answer to the question he has raised is firm: if God 'would have us assent to' some proposition by 'his Authority, and convinces us that it is from him, by some Marks which Reason cannot be mistaken in', then we know we have a genuine revelation (4.19.14). He instances 'the holy Men of old, who had *Revelations* from GOD, [but] had something else besides that internal Light of assurance in their own Minds, to testify to them, that it was from GOD' (4.19.15). He also talks about 'marks' when he discusses how we can tell false MIRACLES from real ones; e.g., the burning bush, the fact that Moses's serpents ate the serpents of the magicians. Jesus's disciples had his miracles to testify that he was the Messiah. These marks pertain to first-hand, original revelations. *We* learn about them from the written word, from the Bible. What criteria does reason use to vouch that the Bible is God-inspired? Locke does not give a satisfactory answer; he simply says, 'we have Reason and the Scripture, unerring Rules to know whether it be from GOD or no' (4.19.16).

The role of reason in authenticating mediated revelation may be less important for Locke than its role in enabling us to assent to revealed propositions. We have to understand, find intelligible, any claimed revealed truth, even apparently those that are above reason, beyond our natural faculties. The *Paraphrases* interpret St Paul as enlarging the scope of truths that are beyond our natural faculties. The truths of the Gospel are made known to us 'by the spirit of god revealing' them; they may even 'seem foolish and absurd' to anyone who has only the natural faculties to work with (pp. 176–7). Locke has St Paul saying in 1 Corinthians: 'For who by the bare use of his natural parts can come to know the mind of the Lord in the designe of the gospel soe as to be able to instruct him [the spiritual man] in it? But I who renouncing all humane learning and knowledge in the case take all that I preach from divine revelation alone I am sure that therein I have the mind of Christ' (*ibid.*). But when he writes his commentary on St Paul's Epistle to the Ephesians, he explains in a note that '*Revelation*, is used by St *Paul*, not always for immediate Inspiration, but as it is meant here, and in most other Places, for such Truths which could not have been found out by humane Reason, but had their First Discovery from Revelation, though Men afterwards come to the Knowledge of those Truths by reading them in the Sacred Scripture, where they are set down for their Information' (p. 623n. h; for a discussion of revelation in the *Paraphrases*, see Wainwright, pp. 29–33).

rights   Locke does not have a definition or discussion of the concept of a right or rights, but references to a number of specific rights are found in his writings, along with a few references to natural rights and a sprinkling of general remarks about rights. There was a long tradition of the concept and a busy discussion of rights among some of his contemporaries and immediate predecessors. Commentators who have tried to reconstruct a theory of rights from Locke's writings do so by noting phrases and uses of rights-talk, mainly in *Two Treatises*, which can be identified with one or other prior theory in such authors as Suarez, Grotius, Pufendorf, Selden, Cumberland (see James Tully, *A Discourse on Property*, 1980, Pt II; Richard Tuck, *Natural Rights Theories*, 1979). Much of these discussions of rights are related to property, the law of nature, justice, duty and obligation.

In Lecture VIII of the *Essays on the Law of Nature*, Locke gives a negative answer to the question, is every man's own interest the basis of the law of nature? He refers to some ancient writers who argued that 'every right and equity be determined not by extraneous law but by each person's own self-interest' (*Essays*, p. 205). The 'more rational part of men [has] some sense of a common humanity, some concern for fellowship'. Locke does not want to say personal or private interests are opposed to 'the common rules of equity', but he believes that 'the strongest protection of each man's private property is the law of nature, without the observance of which it is impossible for anybody to be master of his property and to pursue his own advantage' (*ibid.*, p. 207). If we opt for self-interest rather than common equity as expressed in the law of nature, we would have to say that 'each person's own interest is the standard of what is just and right'; that alternative would lead to difficulties. Private interests must be constrained by common interests. What is morally best is not what most people desire; appetites and natural interests are not the basis for morality. When it is recognized that justice and equity should be based on law, on natural law in the first instance, we can appreciate that 'virtuous actions themselves do not clash nor do they engage men in conflict: they kindle and cherish one another. 'Justice in me does not take away equity in another, nor does the liberality of a prince thwart the generosity of his subjects' (p. 213). The right of ownership, of private property, is compatible with, is even sanctioned by the law of nature. Once we recognize that the basis of morality is the law of nature, God's law, we should be able to understand that 'The duties of life are not at variance with one another, nor do they arm men against one another.' Presumably Locke believed that the rights people have also do not clash, or that the tensions between competing interests and rights will be resolved.

The theme of a common human nature is also found in *Two Treatises* where Locke rejects Filmer's arguments for Adam's absolute and unlimited sovereignty over all others. He asserts that all men 'share in the same common Nature, Faculties and Powers . . . and ought to partake in the same common Rights and Priviledges' (*T*1, §67). The law of nature embodies and protects that common nature. Liberty and freedom for

Locke are always defined within laws, in the pre-civil society by the law of nature which 'willeth the Peace and *Preservation of all Mankind*' (*T*2, §7). The execution of the law of nature in the state of nature is placed in each person's hands; 'every one has a right to punish the transgressors of that Law', as a way of preventing the invasion of the rights of others (*ibid.*). Everyone is born 'with a Title to perfect Freedom [within the constraints of the law of nature], and an uncontrouled enjoyment of all the Rights and Priviledges of the Law of Nature' (*T*2, §87). When men decide to form a civil society, giving some of the power they had in the state of nature to a ruler or group, the rights of government should be explicit (*T*2, §111). The legislative body '*is bound to dispense Justice*, and decide the Rights of the Subject *by promulgated standing Laws, and known Authoris'd Judges*' (*T*2, §136). When a government violates its trust or fails to maintain order, 'the People become a confused Multitude, without Order or Connexion' (*T*2, §219). Justice cannot be administered under these conditions, men's rights can no longer be protected. Whether the dissolution of government be the fault of rulers or the people, 'whoever ... by force goes about to invade the Rights of either Prince or People, and lays the foundation for *overturning* the Constitution and Frame of *any Just Government*, is guilty of the greatest Crime' (*T*2, §230). Using force without right puts that person in a state of war with others (*T*2, §232).

Given his reliance on the law of nature as a basis for morality, we might expect Locke to talk about natural rights. The tradition of natural rights may be implicit in what he writes, but there are only a very few explicit references to that concept. While discussing the point that natural law is binding on all men, he explains that 'the binding force of civil law is dependent on natural law' and that we 'are not so much coerced into rendering obedience to the magistrate by the power of the civil law as bound to obedience by natural right' (*Essays*, p. 189). He also refers to 'natural right and the right of creation', explaining that 'all things are justly subject to that by which they have first been made' (*ibid.*, p. 185). The preface to *Two Treatises* makes a passing reference to '*the People of England, whose love of their Just and Natural Rights, with their Resolution to preserve them, saved the Nation when it was on the very brink of Slavery and Ruine.*' Most of the specific rights he cites in this and other books are so clearly linked with the law of nature that it is fair to say they were considered to be natural rights.

The right of self-preservation is one such right. God has given us a 'strong desire of Preserving [our] Life and Being' (*T*1, §86). Reason as the voice of God teaches us to preserve this natural inclination, telling us that we have a right to use the creatures of the earth that are 'necessar˙ and useful' to our existence (*ibid.*). The law of nature 'willeth the Pea˙

and *Preservation of all Mankind* (*T*2, §7); each man has a right to his preservation (*T*2, §25); all men have 'a right to preserve' what they have against a bad ruler (*T*2, §149); a despot makes force his rule of right, but those under his power have a right to preserve their lives (*T*2, §172); society has 'the Native and Original Right' to preserve itself (*T*2, §220).

Property is an important, central concept in Locke's social thought. He does not speak of the desire for possessions as a natural inclination, but he observes that children 'desire to have things to be theirs; they would have *Propriety* and Possession, pleasing themselves with the Power which that seems to give, and the Right they thereby have, to dispose of them, as they please' (*ST*, §105). His analysis of the origin of property occasionally uses the language of rights: I have a right to the acorns or apples that I gather, or to the grass 'my Horse has bit; the Turfs my Servant has cut' (*T*2, §28). He even speaks of a right to destroy 'any thing by using it', as the 'utmost Property Man is capable of' (*T*1, §39; cf. §§41, 42, 84, 85). We have a right to destroy 'that which threatens me with Destruction', as in war (*T*2, §16).

Another area where rights are mentioned is the parent-child relation. Inheritance and a father's right are briefly discussed in *T*1, §85; all of Adam's children have an 'equal Right to the use of the inferior Creatures' (*T*1, §87). Children have 'a Right to be nourish'd and maintained by their Parents' and they have 'a Title, and natural Right of Inheritance to their Fathers Goods' (*T*1, §§89, 90). The second of *Two Treatises* refers more generally to 'the distinct Rights and Powers' belonging to the '*Society betwixt Parents and Children*' (*T*2, §84).

There are rights that every person has in the state of nature, the right of punishing those who violate the law of nature and the right to seek reparation. The execution of the law of nature in that state is in everyone's hands; that means that 'every one has a right to punish the transgressors of the Law to such a Degree, as may hinder its Violation' (*T*2, §7). The person who has been damaged by the transgressor has 'a particular Right to seek *Reparation* from him that has done it' (*T*2, §§10, 11).

S

scepticism Locke did not have much patience with the sceptics, with those who 'disbelieve every thing, because we cannot certainly know all things' (*Essay*, 1.1.5). He characterizes such a disbeliever as being like a man 'who would not use his Legs, but sit still and perish, because he had no Wings to fly' (*ibid.*). We *are* limited in what we can know, but we can know some things, even attain certainty. Locke recommends an examination of our faculties and abilities, our cognitive powers, as a prelude to identifying the limits and bounds of human knowledge. If 'we let loose our Thoughts into the vast Ocean of *Being*, as if all that boundless Extent, were the natural, and undoubted Possession of our Understandings, wherein there was nothing exempt from its Decisions', we will be out of our depth and become confused and unsure (1.1.7). Questions will then arise, disputes will multiply, no clear resolutions will be achieved; we will then be confined to a 'perfect Scepticism'.

One certainty we can all have is 'that we have in us something that thinks, our very Doubts about what it is, confirm the certainty of its being' (4.3.6). To be sceptical about this truth, because we do not (unlike Descartes) know 'what kind of *Being* it is', is vain and unreasonable. The more important and, for Locke, more threatening scepticism concerns our claims for the existence of an external world. Scepticism here threatens because of Locke's definition of KNOWLEDGE in terms of the relation of ideas. As he recognized, on his definition, all our knowledge consists 'in the view the Mind has of its own *Ideas*' (4.2.1). The highest degree of certainty lies in what Locke calls 'intuitive knowledge'. Examples of intuitive, immediate, non-inferential knowledge are 'that *White* is not *Black*, That a *Circle* is not a *Triangle*, That *Three* are more than *Two*' (*ibid.*). In these examples, 'the Mind perceives at the first sight of the *Ideas* together, by bare *Intuition*, without the intervention of any other *Idea*.' He compares that kind of certain knowledge to the eye seeing light: intuitive knowledge is like bright sunshine. If anyone seeks a greater certainty than this, 'than to know that any *Idea* in his Mind is such, as he perceives it to be', such a person shows that he has 'a mind to be a Sceptick' (*ibid.*).

What about other ideas, those we commonly believe to be caused by and to refer to external, physical objects? This is the question raised by the sceptic. Locke formulates the problem as follows: 'There can be nothing more certain, than that the *Idea* we receive from an external Object is in our Minds; this is intuitive Knowledge. But whether there be any thing more than barely that *Idea* in our Minds, whether we can thence certainly inferr the existence of any thing without us, which corresponds to that *Idea*, is that, whereof some Men think there may be a question made, because Men may have such *Ideas* in their Minds, when no such Thing exists, no such Object affects their Senses' (4.2.14). Locke's initial answer to this problem is to appeal to the experiential differences between looking on the sun by day and thinking about it by night, or actually tasting wormwood or smelling a rose and thinking about that taste or that smell. The clear difference in such experiences should, Locke believed, answer the sceptic. When the sceptic appeals to dream experiences as a way of suggesting we may have all the ideas we do have without any external world, Locke tosses the sceptic this reply: 'he may please to dream that I make him this Answer, 1. That 'tis no great matter, whether I remove his Scruple, or no: Where all is but Dream, Reasoning and Arguments are of no use, Truth and Knowledge nothing. 2. That I believe he will allow a very manifest difference between dreaming of being in the Fire, and being actually in it' (*ibid.*). If the sceptic still persists in suggesting that all may be a dream, Locke refers him to the pain we feel when we are actually burned, as opposed to dreaming that we are burned. If such a person really doubts that he sees a fire, he can try putting his hand in it, and thereby become convinced of the real existence of the fire (4.11.7). After running over a number of examples of causing the appearance of the paper he writes on to change and thus affect the responses other people make to that writing, Locke returns to the sceptic's dream hypothesis. 'But yet, if after all this, any one will be so sceptical, as to distrust his Senses, and to affirm, that all we see and hear, feel and taste, think and do, during our whole Being, is but the series and deluding appearances of a long Dream, whereof there is no reality; and therefore will question the Existence of all Things, or our Knowledge of any thing: I must desire him to consider, that if all be a Dream, then he doth but dream, that he makes the Question; and so it is not much matter, that a waking Man should answer him' (4.11.8).

Locke was convinced that 'no body can, in earnest, be so sceptical, as to be uncertain of the Existence of those Things which he sees and feels' (4.11.3). He was not moved by the theoretical problems raised by sceptics; he found no practical difficulties in discovering that we are affected by the physical world. As others at that time also did, he does distinguish certain of our sense experiences as giving us specific information about the nature of objects (the primary qualities), and he accepted the corpuscular theory about the structure of matter. He did not think we are able to discover the full nature of matter, but his friends in the Royal Society were pushing the frontiers back here and there. Moreover, he was of the opinion that God gave us our faculties in order to live in this world, to make those discoveries relevant to our well-being. There is no discussion in Locke's writings where he tries to reconstruct how we come to have a belief in an external world, as Descartes did in the sixth Meditation. Nor does Locke examine the various attempts made by Malebranche and Arnauld (as later Hume did in the *Treatise*), to defend a realism within the way of ideas. He did understand why some might find a problem with his definition of knowledge in terms of ideas, but he believed that the actual receiving of sensory ideas was sufficient grounds for accepting realism. Scepticism with regard to the senses was simply not a problem for him.

science This is a word that has a meaning and a referent for us somewhat different from those it had in the seventeenth and eighteenth centuries. We use it to designate disciplines such as physics, astronomy, biology, as well as the social sciences of anthropology, sociology, or psychology. For Locke and his contemporaries, science had a more general meaning. Locke lists as sciences divinity, ethics, law and politics (*Essay*, 2.22.12), arithmetic, geography, chronology, history, geometry (*ST*, §178), and even accounting (*ST*, §210). The final chapter of the *Essay* offers a threefold classification or division of the sciences. The first is natural philosophy which is described as 'The Knowledge of Things, as they are in their own proper Beings, their Constitutions, Properties, and Operations' (4.21.2). Matter and spirits were included in the 'things' studied by natural philosophy. The end of this science 'is bare speculative Truth, and whatsoever can afford the Mind of Man any such', again including in what may yield such truths God, man, angels, spirits and bodies or 'any of their Affections, as Number, and Figure'. The other two sciences in this division of all sciences are ethics and logic (or, as Locke prefers, the doctrine of signs).

Francis Bacon was among modern writers the first to devote attention to a classification and analysis of different sciences, different bodies of knowledge. In the second decade of the eighteenth century, Ephraim Chambers offered in the preface to his *Cyclopaedia; or An Universal Dictionary of Arts and Sciences* (1728) an extensive analysis of the many different disciplines and activities leading to knowledge. The chart used in that preface echoes Bacon but is also more specific and systematic. Chambers defines science in his preface as a system of propositions 'relating to some one Syllogism, orderly and artfully laid down in Words' (p. viii). The entry on 'science' is slightly different: 'a clear and certain Knowledge of any Thing, founded on self-evident Principles, or Demonstrations', or a 'form'd System of any Branch of Knowledge'. Locke's division of the sciences is reproduced in that entry. The title page of Chambers's *Cyclopaedia* speaks of human and divine science. Under 'natural and scientific' knowledge, the chart distinguishes sensible from rational knowledge, sensible including meteorology, hydrology, mineralogy, physiology, and zoology. These are said to consist in 'the Perception of Phenomena, or External Objects'. The category of rational knowledge includes physics, natural philosophy and metaphysics. These rational sciences are said to deal with the 'Perception of the intrinsick Characters or Habitudes of sensible Objects'. Many other sciences or bodies of knowledge are listed under the heading 'Artificial and Technical' on Chambers's chart. They are described in notes.

The term 'natural philosophy' used by Locke and Chambers comes closest to what we normally think of as science, except for Locke's remark about its dealing with speculative truths. Chambers's definition under that term leaves out the word 'speculative': 'that Science which considers the Power of *Nature*, the Properties of *Natural* Bodies, and their mutual action on one another'. Chambers says that this description fits what was also called 'physics', but he distinguishes physics as natural philosophy from experimental physics. The former is 'the Doctrine of Natural Bodies, their Phenomena, Causes, and Effects, their various Affections, Motions, Operations' (entry under 'physicks'). Experimental physics for Chambers enquires into the reasons and natures of things by experiment. Locke's use of the phrase 'natural philosophy' reflects this double reference of rational and experimental activities. Most of Locke's remarks concern the difficulties in speculative or rational natural philosophy, difficulties that stand in the way of reaching certainty. He comments in *Some Thoughts* that the world is filled with rational systems of natural philosophy, none of which contains truth and certainty suitable to teach a young man. Still, a gentleman should be acquainted with some systems, should learn their hypotheses and understand their language. The student should not hope to obtain 'scientifical' knowledge from these systems, although Locke believes the modern corpuscularians talk more intelligibly than others do. Boyle is also cited (*ST*, §93). In that same work, Locke refers to 'the abstruse Speculations of Natural Philosophy, and Metaphysicks'; children's heads are filled with unclear ideas from those systems (*ST*, §94). Even systems of physics come in for criticism, except Newton's, which is praised for its combination of mathematics and matters of fact (*ST*, §194). He urges his readers in the *Essay* not to take doubtful systems for complete sciences, not to mistake 'unintelligible Notions, for scientifical Demonstrations' (4.12.12). Ill use of words, obscure terms and their misuse have characterized most systems of natural philosophy (3.11.5; 3.10.2).

The reference to 'scientifical demonstrations' is not, as we might think, to empirical or experimental work. It has the meaning of a demonstration about what leads to certainty, not to the probable conclusions we associate with science today. Similarly, when he says of natural philosophy as a speculative science that it will never be made into a science, the term 'science' means 'demonstrative science', as with geometry (*ST*, §190). Elsewhere, he suggests that some men may be able to make better guesses about the nature of bodies and their unknown properties, but such conjectures will only be judgements and opinions, not certain knowledge (4.12.10). He goes on in this passage to repeat that 'natural Philosophy is not capable of being made a Science.' The term 'science' again has the sense of reaching certainty about the nature of bodies by discovering their inner structure: such a discovery would give us an understanding and knowledge of the power of bodies and their effects even prior to experience. In 4.3.26, he says of experimental philosophy that it will not yield a '*scientifical Knowledge*'; such knowledge is out of our reach with respect to the physical world. The reason given for this inability is that 'we want perfect and adequate *Ideas* of those very Bodies, which are nearest to us.' Our classifications of kinds of objects by means of observable properties are 'very imperfect, and incompleat'; they will not produce scientifical knowledge, again meaning demonstrative certainty. What would be necessary for such a knowledge of nature would be to have an accurate description of the corpuscular structure of matter in particular objects (*ibid.*). Had we such an insight into the inner structure, we would be able to derive the effects of objects from that knowledge; we would have a deductive knowledge of necessary connections in nature (*see* CONNEXION (NECESSARY)).

Given the limitations of human knowledge when dealing with the physical world, we must acquire what knowledge we can from experience and experiments (4.12.12). Our science of nature must be based upon experience and observation, upon discovering coexisting qualities (4.3.9). In these injunctions about the method to science, Locke was reflecting the tenets of the Royal Society, the method practised by those great men mentioned in the 'Epistle to the Reader' of his *Essay*: Boyle, Sydenham, Huygenius, and Newton. These men did employ some hypotheses, but those hypotheses had to explain observed phenomena and they were taken as probable. Locke was cautious about HYPOTHESES, but he did accept as the most intelligible the corpuscular hypothesis about the structure of matter. He even uses that hypothesis in an explanation of why the same water can feel hot to one hand and cold to the other (2.8.21). Nevertheless, Locke and the Royal Society scientists were busy trying to replace the rational natural philosophy found in systems of science with an empirical science based upon careful observation and experimentation. The epistemology of the *Essay* is supportive of this new approach to science.

There is one curious small piece of writing by Locke which may look as if it does not quite fit this model of proceeding by experience and observation. His *Elements of Natural Philosophy* is a brief summary of the knowledge then available from various sciences: chapters on matter and motion, on the solar system, on air and the atmosphere, on meteors, on springs and rivers, vegetables and plants, animals, our senses, etc. (in *Works*, iii. 303–28). The final chapter in this short summary is on the understanding: it gives a very brief account of his theory of ideas and knowledge. So this piece is not really an example of a rational system. It differs from the *Essay*'s remarks about science just in the fact that it records the information then known about the physical world.

signs   In the classification of the sciences at the end of the *Essay*, Locke identifies the third class as the doctrine of signs. This science is also called 'logic'; its task is 'to consider the Nature of Signs, the Mind makes use of for the understanding of Things, or conveying its Knowledge to others' (4.21.4). This definition of logic was a departure from the traditional view; it indicates Locke's interest in a logic of use rather than a discipline concerned with form and validity. The doctrine of signs would aid us in understanding 'things', a vague term meant to cover the referents of our ideas, such as physical objects or events and human actions. The doctrine of signs will also help convey our knowledge to others. The fact that 'the Scene of *Ideas* that makes one Man's Thoughts, cannot be laid open to the immediate view of another' makes it important that the signs of ideas be clear and unambiguous. Understanding and communicating are the key features of such a doctrine.

Locke suggests in this same section that a proper doctrine of signs might give us 'another sort of Logick and Critick' than has so far been produced. Does the *Essay* go some distance in elaborating such a new LOGIC? Locke certainly devotes much attention to signs throughout that work: he goes to great lengths in Book Three to show what is needed for understanding and communicating, and to describe the nature and function of linguistic signs. He likes to characterize ideas as 'invisible, and hidden from others'; they cannot be made to appear by themselves (3.2.1). By means of visible, public signs, ideas and thoughts can be made to appear, made known to others. He links this need for public signs of ideas with the 'Comfort, and Advantage of Society' which depends upon the 'Communication of

Thoughts' (*ibid.*). For communication, 'some external sensible Signs, whereby those invisible *Ideas*, which his thoughts are made up of' are required. This signification of ideas by words is conventional, not natural. Were there a natural connection between words and ideas, there would be just one universal language.

Words as sounds or as written marks are without meaning until they are linked by convention and custom to specific ideas (1.2.23). Children assent to propositions only after they have learned the connections between sounds and ideas. From repeated sensations, children acquire ideas; then by degrees they 'learn the use of Signs' by framing articulate sounds and thus acquire the use of words (2.11.8). More generally, 'Before a Man makes any Proposition, he is supposed to understand the terms he uses in it, or else he talks like a Parrot, only making a noise by imitation, and framing certain Sounds, which he has learnt of others; but not, as a rational Creature, using them for Signs of *Ideas*, which he has in his Mind' (4.8.7). The distinction between sounds and words is illustrated by Locke's listing of the components of mixed modes. With a word such as 'lie', those components are: '1. Articulate Sounds. 2. Certain *Ideas* in the Mind of the Speaker. 3. Those words the signs of those *Ideas*. 4. Those signs put together by affirmation or negation' (2.22.9). It is the connection between the sound and the idea that transforms the sound (or written characters) into a word. The sound 'man' stands for 'an Animal of such a certain Form' (2.27.8); words such as 'justice', 'gratitude', or 'glory' stand for ideas in the minds of those who use them or hear and understand them (2.32.11).

Words are not the only kinds of signs. Ideas are also signs, but in their case, the signification does not arise from convention or custom. Truth is defined as the joining or separating of ideas or words 'as the Things they stand for, do, in themselves, agree, or disagree' (2.32.19). Words stand for ideas (although they are, Locke observes, often taken to refer to things); ideas stand for things. These two kinds of signs function in two different sorts of propositions, verbal and mental, resulting in two kinds of truth (4.5.2).

Individual words signify particular ideas, verbal propositions express or signify mental propositions. The components of both verbal and mental propositions are signs. Signs signify and have meaning. What do ideas signify or mean? The term 'signify' or 'signification' is mainly restricted in Locke's text to words (e.g., 2.13.18; 2.3.3, 6; 3.1.6; 3.2.2; 3.3.10). There is one passage that may use 'signification' to refer to ideas, but that passage is ambiguous (2.32.1). What signifies in that passage may be the terms 'true' and 'false'. Otherwise, ideas are not characterized as signifying. There is at least one passage that links 'represent' with words

(3.3.10), but usually 'represent' is a feature of ideas, not words. Is the sign-function of ideas, then, better characterized as representing rather than as signifying? There are other terms Locke uses to indicate the relation between ideas and things: correspond, resemble, copy. But the general feature of all signs is their significatory function. So both word-signs and idea-signs must signify, stand for, or carry meaning. Ideas do this by representing what they stand for or signify. The signification relation for words is *conventional*. The significatory or representative relation for ideas cannot be conventional; ideas do not signify by convention. Can we say the signification of ideas is *natural*? Sensory ideas are the natural result of causal sequences from object to perceiver. There is also a sense in which they are universal: we all do tend to receive the same ideas from objects – certainly, the same kinds of simple ideas of colours, sounds, extension, solidity, motion. Variations in specific tastes or sounds, or of shapes and sizes, are still experiences of the same kind of ideas. The signification-relation between ideas and things is very important for Locke's perception theory. It is also relevant in understanding the nature of his ideas. The causal theory of perception is overlaid by a significatory relation: ideas may be caused by objects (although Locke admitted that he did not know how that causal process worked); but more importantly for cognition, ideas signify, represent, their causes.

Locke's attention to language and words as signifiers was a substantial addition to the interest in language among his contemporaries, but his interpreting ideas as signifiers, as signs, was perhaps of greater import-ance (*see* IDEA; *see also* REPRESENTATION). Berkeley in the next century elaborated the notion of idea-signs into the language of God, making ideas no longer modes of mind. Idea-signs even become for him the objects themselves. Kant uses the term 'representations' for what Locke, Berkeley and Hume called 'ideas'. Thomas Reid also developed a notion of natural signs.

sin   The Latin word *peccata* (sins) usually signifies 'in general ill Actions, that will draw on punishment upon the Doers' (*Essay*, 1.3.19). Locke was commenting upon the claimed innateness of the proposition, '*Men must repent of their Sins.*' He remarks that until we know what particular sins there are, such a supposed innate rule would be of little use. However, he does accept this rule: 'Indeed, this is a very true Proposition, and fit to be inculcated on, and received by those, who are supposed, to have been taught, what Actions in all kinds are *sins*' (*ibid.*). He gives a list of actions which the worship of God proscribes: 'Not to kill another Man; Not to know more Women than one; Not to procure Abortion; Not to expose their Children; Not to take from another what is his'. He refers to these actions as sins, not just as vices. The *Letter concerning Toleration* writes of idolatry as a sin. His interest in these actions is with making the point that the civil magistrate has no jurisdiction over that sin; he ought not to punish those who practise idolatry (in *Works*, vi. 36–7). He also lists three other sins there: covetousness, uncharitableness and idleness. Not even the sins of lying and perjury are punishable by civil law. The first of *Two Treatises* says "twould always be a Sin in any Man of Estate, to let his Brother perish for want of affording him Relief out of his Plenty' (*T*1, §42).

Some Thoughts lists covetousness along with pride as coming from 'those wrong Inclinations, which they [children] should restrain and suppress' (§52). There are also discussions of craving in children, although he does not characterize this as a sin (§§38–9; 106–7). In general, desires in children are to be suppressed; the educator and parents are to help the child learn self-control. Lying is said to debase 'a Man to the lowest degree of a shameful meanness, and ranks him with the most contemptible part of Mankind, and the abhorred Rascality' (*ST*, §131). The first time lying is discovered in a child, it should be described as 'a monstrous Thing in him' (*ibid.*; cf. §37). There are many other negative traits to be avoided in children, many vices, but whether Locke viewed these all as sins is unclear.

The more interesting question is, 'did Locke have an opinion about original sin, about Adam's Fall?' His *Reasonableness of Christianity* identified two extreme interpretations of the Fall, both of which Locke rejects. One extreme 'would have all Adam's posterity doomed to eternal, infinite punishment, for the transgression of Adam, who millions had never heard of, and no one had authorised to transact for him, or be his representative', the view of Calvin (in *Works*, vii. 4). The other extreme view is that the claim for eternal punishment for all Adam's posterity was inconsistent with the 'justice and goodness of the great and infinite God', and that 'there was no redemption necessary, and consequently, that there was none', the deists' view. Locke's interpretation of Adam's sin is that what Adam lost was eternal life. The state of paradise was one of immortality. When Genesis 2: 17 says, 'In the day, that thou eatest thereof, thou shalt surely die', Locke points out that Adam did not actually die that day. From that time to his actual death, Adam's life began 'to shorten, and waste, and to have an end' (*ibid.*, p. 5). Death then entered: mortality replaced immortality. Locke agrees with those who said that death in Adam's sentence did not mean an eternal life in misery. Such a punishment is, Locke agrees, inconsistent with a just God. He also rejected the notion that Adam's sin corrupted 'human nature in his posterity' (p. 7). Nowhere does the New Testament 'tell us that corruption seized on all, because of Adam's transgression'. Most importantly of all for Locke, he reads the Bible as saying 'every one's sin is charged upon himself only.'

In his *Paraphrase and Notes upon the Epistles of St. Paul*, this reading of Adam's Fall is elaborated. For example, St Paul speaks of sin entering the world by one man's action, 'and death by sin; and so death passed upon all men, for that all have sinned' (*Paraphrases*, p. 523). St Paul also says that death reigned 'even over them that had not sinned after the similitude of Adam's transgression' (*ibid*.). Locke understands St Paul as saying Adam's posterity became mortal, adding a long note in an earlier passage claiming that this interpretation of 'have sinned' as 'became mortal' is consistent with what Paul says in 1 Cor. 15: 22, where he says 'as in Adam all die', meaning 'become mortal' (p. 247). In his commentary on this proposition, Locke writes: 'For as the death that all men suffer is oweing to Adam' (p. 250). In another passage, Locke affirms that 'Mankind without the positive law of god knew by the light of nature That they transgressed the rule of their nature, Reason, which detailed to them what they ought to doe', reflecting his general trust in reason to guide our actions (p. 524). In a note on p. 533, Locke gives a list of phrases about sin, all of which mean 'giveing our selves up to the conduct of our sinful carnal appetites, to allow any of them the command over us'. The note on 'carnal lusts' speaks of 'Sinful lusts, at least those to which the Gentiles were most eminently enslaved' (p. 534, n. 13). On carnal desires again, Locke speaks of 'the law or right reason' and of man's 'natural inclination pushing him to the satisfaction of his irregular sinful desires' (p. 545, n.18). When Paul says, 'deliver me from this body of death', Locke interprets him as meaning: 'The State he had been describeing was that of humane weakness, wherein notwithstanding the law even those who were under it and sincerely endeavoured to obey it were frequently carried by their carnal appetites into a breach of it' (p. 546, n. 24).

There is much additional discussion of sin in these *Paraphrases*, but Locke's commentary always takes the same form. Some recent accounts of this aspect of his thought have focused attention on his position on the doctrine of original sin. See W.M. Spellman, *John Locke and the Problem of Depravity* (1988), esp. ch. 1, and Wainwright's introduction to his edition of the *Paraphrases*, pp. 35–7.

slaves, slavery   There are a number of references to slaves in Locke's *Two Treatises*. One such reference is in the chapter on the state of war. Anyone who 'attempts to get another Man into his Absolute Power, does thereby *put himself into a State of War* with him' (*T2*, §17). Such absolute power or dominion over another person violates that person's right to freedom and makes that person a slave. The fear in such attempts to enslave me is that that person may have designs on my life. The example Locke uses in the next section is of a thief who steals my money: 'I have no reason to suppose, that he, who would *take away my Liberty*, would not when he had me in his Power, take away every thing else' (*T*2, §18). Freedom from absolute, arbitrary power is a prerequisite for our preservation. 'For no Man, or Society of Men, having a Power to deliver up their *Preservation*, or consequently the means of it, to the Absolute Will and arbitrary Dominion of another whenever any one shall go about to bring them into such a Slavish Condition, they will always have a right to preserve what they have not a Power to part with' (*T*2, §149). Thus the seriousness of any attempt to exert that kind of power over another person. No one can, even by compact or agreement, '*enslave himself* to any one' (*T*2, §23).

There is one apparently legitimate situation in which absolute power over another can arise: when that person, 'by his fault, forfeited his own Life, by some Act that deserves Death' (*ibid.*). Then, 'he, to whom he has forfeited it, may (when he has him in his Power) delay to take it, and make use of him to his own Service.' How does a man forfeit his life? What acts deserve death? It may be an act of theft, since Locke says that we may kill a thief because he may have designs on our life (*T*2, §18), but the more likely reference is to the person who, in the state of nature, violates or transgresses a law of nature (*T*2, §8). In the state of nature, every man is the executioner of the law of nature. Anyone who transgresses such a law can be punished by any other member of the state of nature. Violators of the law of nature cease to be human. In this earlier passage, Locke rules out anyone's having an absolute, arbitrary power over such a transgressor; at least, the criminal could only be used 'so far as calm reason and conscience dictates' (*ibid.*). Whether calm reason and conscience would permit using the transgressor in your service (e.g., as a servant) is not clear. The apparent justification of so doing in the section on slavery is that whenever the transgressor 'finds the hardship of his Slavery out-weigh the value of his Life, 'tis in his Power, by resisting the Will of his Master, to draw on himself the Death he desires' (*T*2, §23). What we can say is that such a person was indeed enslaved, albeit perhaps justifiably so. An arbitrary, unjustified enslavement is different, as a passage in the first of *Two Treatises* makes clear: 'a Man can no more justly make use of another's necessity, to force him to become his Vassal, by with-holding that Relief, God requires him to afford to the wants of his Brother, than he that has more strength can seize upon a weaker, master him to his Obedience, and with a Dagger at his Throat offer him Death or Slavery' (*T*1, §42).

There are other passages where Locke refers to slaves being part of the larger family. Early in the second of *Two Treatises*, he distinguishes political power from other sorts of powers: from the power of 'a *Father* over his Children, a *Master* over his Servant, a *Husband* over his Wife, and a *Lord* over his Slave' (*T*2, §2). That section also contains a passing reference to 'a Captain of a Galley' (cf. §154). A later section identifies the 'subordinate Relations of *Wife, Children, Servants*, and *Slaves* united under the Domestick Rule of a Family' (*T*2, §86). The section just preceding this one speaks of two sorts of servants, one whose services are paid for, another called by 'a peculiar Name', i.e., 'slaves'. Why Locke should characterize this name as 'peculiar' is not clear. His reference is to captives taken in a just war: they are 'by the Right of Nature subjected to the Absolute Dominion and Arbitrary Power of their Masters' (*T*2, §85). Justification by a natural right is a strong claim. It rests on the war's being just, on the captives' being the aggressors and hence participants in an unjust war of aggression. Being an aggressor entails seeking absolute dominion over those that are attacked. Such aggressors when captured have 'forfeited their Lives, and with it their Liberties, and lost their Estates; and being in the *State of Slavery*, not capable of any Property, cannot in that state be considered as any part of *Civil Society*' (*T*2, §85). Absolute, arbitrary power 'one man has over another, to take away his Life, whenever he pleases' is characterized as 'despotical power' (*T*2, §172). Locke then seems to contradict the natural right he referred to earlier. No man comes by such despotical power by nature or by compact, 'for Man not having such an Arbitrary Power over his own Life, cannot give another Man such a Power over it' (*ibid.*). The exception is forfeiture by the aggressor, forfeiture 'which the aggressor makes of his own Life, when he puts himself into the state of War with another'. The same harsh attitude Locke expresses towards a thief, emerges here: those who use war to achieve their unjust ends have left humankind and descended down the scale of being to the level of beasts. If the aggressor is successful and conquers and subdues another society, that absolute, arbitrary power is unjustified. The descendants of those who were conquered have the right to shake off that dominion 'and free themselves from the Usurpation, or Tyranny', brought about by the sword (*T*2, §192). Those living under a government without their consent, especially when ruled by an aggressor, 'are direct Slaves under the Force of War' (*ibid.*).

There is another way in which men would be enslaved, namely, if Robert Filmer's hereditary monarchy descending from Adam were realized. A large part of the attack against Filmer in the first of *Two Treatises* centres on this notion that Filmer's account of government would make slaves of all the subjects; all mankind would be in chains (*T*1, §1). Along with other writers, Filmer in effect says we are all born slaves (*T*1, §2; cf. §4). Locke also finds Filmer's account of parental power objectionable: that power is 'like that of Absolute Monarchs over their Slaves' (*T*1, §51). Whether it be Filmer's monarch descended from Adam or any arbitrary ruler, living in such a society is to be a slave in chains (*T*2, §§220, 239).

In his extended attack on Filmer, the term 'slave' is used often to describe or characterize the lack of freedom and consent which the subjects in a Filmerian society would suffer. Captives taken in just wars become slaves in a somewhat different sense: they are truly enslaved and have no rights. There was in Locke's time another kind of slave, those that were bought and sold and held in bondage. While working for Shaftesbury Locke held several positions which brought him into direct knowledge of slaves and the slave trade in America. Along with Shaftesbury, he invested money in several companies that were involved in the slave trade. In 1673–4 he was secretary to the Council of Trade and Plantations, of which Shaftesbury was the president. From 1668 to 1675, Locke was secretary to the Lords Proprietors of Carolina. In connection with this latter position, he helped draft, under Shaftesbury's supervision, the Fundamental Constitutions of Carolina. A surviving copy in Locke's hand among the Shaftesbury papers in the Public Record Office has sometimes been taken as evidence that Locke was the author. He may have had some influence on the drafting of this document, but caution should be used in placing it among Locke's writings. Several clauses in that draft have led some commentators on Locke to conclude that he may have accepted or even favoured this kind of slaves. One clause reads: 'Every freeman of Carolina shall have absolute power and authority over his negro slaves, of what opinion or religion soever' (in *Works*, x. 196). Another, longer, clause gives slaves the option of which church they wish to belong to, but that option does not exempt them from 'that civil dominion his master hath over him, but be in all other things in the same state and condition he was in before'.

Locke opens the first section of the first of *Two Treatises* by this remark: 'Slavery is so vile and miserable an Estate of Man, and so directly opposite to the generous Temper and Courage of our Nation; that 'tis hardly to be conceived, that an *Englishman*, much less a *Gentleman*, should plead for't.' Did he mean this condemnation of slavery to apply only to the result Locke thought would be the case on Filmer's account, to the subject-slaves of an absolute monarch? For a recent treatment of the question of Locke and slavery, see Wayne Glausser, 'Three Approaches to Locke and the Slave Trade', *Journal of the History of Ideas*, (1990), pp. 199–216.

social contract   *see* COMPACT OR CONTRACT

society   In several places, Locke refers to 'a certain propensity of nature' which leads men into 'a life in society' (*Essays*, p. 157). The *Essay* tells us that God 'designed Man for a sociable Creature', made him 'with an inclination, and under a necessity to have fellowship with those of his own kind' (3.1.1). *Two Treatises* strikes the same theme: 'God having made Man such a Creature, that on his own Judgment, it was not good for him to be alone, put him under strong Obligations of Necessity, Convenience, and Inclination to drive him into *Society*' (*T2*, §77). In each of these texts, the sociality of man is linked with language. In this last passage, man is said to be equipped with understanding and language. The *Essay* passage has man furnished with 'Language, which was to be the great Instrument, and common Tye of Society' (3.1.1). The early *Essays* say that man is prepared 'for the maintenance of society by the gift of speech and through the intercourse of language' (p. 157). The *Essay* also says that 'Language . . . was given us for the improvement of Knowledge, and bond of Society' (3.10.13). Speech is said to be 'the great Bond that holds Society together' (3.11.1). For that reason, those who employ 'logical Niceties, or curious empty Speculations' affect negatively the 'great Concernments of Humane Life and Society' (3.10.12). Unclear language, the abuse of words, can 'destroy the Instruments and Means of Discourse, Conversation, Instruction, and Society' (3.10.10). The stress Locke gave to language in Book Three of the *Essay* was not just to ensure clear thinking: language had social importance as well. It was viewed as a fundamental aspect of society; it was for him one of several key features of his concept of society.

The inclination we have to be sociable is reinforced by certain conditions in the state of nature. That state is not quite asocial, but people do, on Locke's description of that state, tend to stay with small units, such as the family, or even to operate on their own. The conditions in the state of nature are not entirely conducive to happiness and security, two other features in his concept of society. God has made an 'inseparable connexion' between '*Virtue* and publick Happiness'. Thus, the practice of virtue is 'necessary for the preservation of Society' (1.3.6). Human society rests on two factors, 'a definite constitution of the state and form of government, and secondly, the fulfilment of pacts' (*Essays*, p. 119). Equity and justice themselves, not their utility, make the fulfilment of promises one of the safeguards of society (*ibid.*, p. 219). Writing against the innatist's claim for innate moral principles, Locke remarks that history shows that 'there is scarce that Principle of Morality' that has not been slighted somewhere, with the exception of those that 'are absolutely necessary to hold Society together'; even those are often ignored in relations between societies (*Essay*, 1.3.10). He recognized that virtue and praise are united, in most men's minds, so much so that laws of fashion rather than real virtue tend to dominate (2.28.11). Praise and respect from one's companions are powerful forces in society: no one 'can live in Society, under the constant Dislike, and ill Opinion of his Familiars, and those he converses with' (2.28.12).

The laws and rules of society should function for the good of the whole (*T*1, §93; cf. *T*2, §§136, 137). The purpose of human society should be peace and tranquility (*T*1, §106). The concept of government includes 'the establishment of Society upon certain Rules or Laws, which require Conformity to them' (4.3.18). Laws should be made 'conformable to the Laws of Nature' (*T*1, §97), but in any case, a society requires the agreement of the members on the positive laws. The '*Liberty of Man, in Society*, is to be under no other Legislative Power, but that established, by consent' (*T*2, §22). In this passage, Locke is writing about political or civil society, the purpose of which is the preservation of property and possessions (*T*2, §138). In his discussion of civil society, terms such as 'community', 'commonwealth', 'the body of the people' and 'government' keep appearing. The final section of *Two Treatises* illustrates this interplay of these terms and phrases: 'The *Power that every individual gave the Society*, when he entered into it, can never revert to the Individuals again, as long as the Society lasts, but will always remain in the Community; because without this, there can be no Community, no Common-wealth, which is contrary to the original Agreement. So also when the Society hath placed the Legislative in any Assembly of Men, to continue in them and their Successors, *the Legislative can never revert to the People* whilst that Government lasts' (*T*2, §243).

Political or civil society is not the only society identified by Locke. A family has some resemblance 'in its Order, Offices, and Number . . . with a little Common-wealth, yet is very far from it, both in its Constitution, Power and End' (*T*2, §86). Should it be suggested that a family might resemble a monarchy, 'and the *Paterfamilias* [resemble] the absolute Monarch in it, absolute Monarchy will have but a very shattered and short Power, when 'tis plain, by what has been said before, That the *Master of the Family* has a very distinct and differently limited *Power*, both as to time and extent, over those several Persons that are in it' (*ibid.*). Political society is characterized by the power it has to preserve the property of its members, a power which each person had in the state of nature but agrees by consent and contract to give up and place in 'the hands of the Community' (*T*2, §87). The community becomes the arbiter by settled standard rules applied equally to all parties to disputes. It is the uniting into one body, and the having 'a common establish'd Law and Judicature to appeal to, with Authority to decide Controversies between them, and punish Offenders' that define and constitute a civil society (*ibid.*). It is important to understand that the natural power each man has in the state of nature is not given to those who govern, but to the 'public', the 'Body Politick', which in turn authorizes individuals as their representatives to make laws for 'the public good of the Society' (*T*2,

§89). The act of forming one commonwealth comes first, then a body politic with form and structure. The power that is delegated to legislators in civil society reverts to the people when the trust placed in them has been violated (*T*2, §§240–42).

Locke does not say that a family must have laws, but any other type of society will dissolve 'and break to pieces, unless it be regulated by some laws, and the members all consent to observe some order' (*A Letter concerning Toleration*, in *Works*, vi. 13). He there lists as societies 'philosophers for learning, . . . merchants for commerce, or . . . men of leisure for mutual conversation and discourse', a rather loose-knit set (*ibid.*). A church is a well-defined society, 'a voluntary society of men, joining themselves together of their own accord, in order to the public worshipping of God, in such a manner as they judge acceptable to him, and effectual to the salvation of their souls' (*ibid.*). He insists that, especially in a church-society, 'the right of making its laws can belong to none but the society itself, or at least, which is the same thing, to those whom the society by common consent has authorised thereunto' (*ibid.*, p. 14; *see also* COMMONWEALTH; GOVERNMENT).

solidity   Solidity is one of the primary qualities. It is often listed together with extension, figure and motion (e.g., *Essay*, 2.8.9; 2.23.2, 3, 15; 2.31.2; 3.6.5). Alone among the primary qualities, it receives a chapter devoted to it, *Essay* 2.4. The language used in 2.8 to characterize all primary qualities, those which the mind and the senses find inseparable from matter, is used in Locke's discussion of solidity. The idea of solidity is the idea that seems 'most intimately connected with, and essential to Body' (2.4.1). Its essentiality is perhaps stronger than that of other primary qualities. 'Essential' does not refer to 'essence', as Descartes said extension is in relation to matter. Locke did not believe we could discover the essence of mind or body, but there is more to his use of the term 'essential' in relation to solidity than just 'essential for our idea of solidity'. Bodies for him are hard, solid and impenetrable. The corpuscular theory of matter, which Locke accepted as the most probable theory, extended solidity to the corpuscles as well. Thus, the essentiality of solidity for body is more than epistemic, more than essential for our idea of body. We receive this idea from touch or from experiences of trying to squeeze a football. It is an idea that is reinforced by the feeling of being supported whenever we move or rest (2.4.1). It is a property that is illustrated by the resistance which one body shows in keeping other bodies out of its space. Even a drop of water manifests solidity: 'All the Bodies in the World, pressing a drop of Water on all sides, will never be able to overcome the Resistance, which it will make, as soft as it is, to their approaching one another' (2.4.3). Hardness is not the same as solidity, as this example shows. '*Solidity* is hereby also *differenced from hardness*, in that Solidity consists in repletion, and so an utter Exclusion of other Bodies out of the space it possesses; but Hardness, in a firm Cohesion of the parts of Matter, making up masses of a sensible bulk, so that the whole does not easily change its Figure' (2.4.4).

Rearranging the parts of matter, the corpuscles, will not make a body more or less solid. Two slabs of marble 'will more easily approach each other, between which there is nothing but Water or Air, than if there be a Diamond between them', but this is not because 'the parts of the Diamond are more solid than those of Water, or resist more' (2.4.4). The reason for this difference in the approach of two pieces of marble to a diamond and a drop of water is that 'the parts of Water, being more easily separable from each other, they will by a side-motion be more easily removed, and give way to the approach of the two pieces of Marble.' Were it possible to prevent this side-motion, the water 'would eternally hinder the approach of these two pieces of Marble, as much as the Diamond'. Hard and soft are irrelevant to solidity. Locke mentions several ordinary examples that illustrate this fact, e.g., filling 'a yielding soft Body well with Air or Water', or a football with air, but the most interesting example is the experiment Locke reports that was performed in Florence 'with a hollow Globe of Gold fill'd with Water, and exactly closed'. When this filled globe was placed in a press 'which was driven by the extreme force of skrews, the water made it self way through the pores of that very close metal, and finding no room for a nearer approach of its Particles within, got to the outside, where it rose like a dew, and so fell in drops, before the sides of the Globe could be made to yield to the violent compression of the Engine, that squeezed it' (*ibid.*). The idea of solidity also includes the notion of filling SPACE.

Some Considerations of the Consequences of the Lowering of Interest

This title continues, '*and Raising the Value of Money*'. It was published in 1692, followed by several other pamphlets on the same topic in 1695–6. A collection of these writings was published in 1696 under the title *Several Papers Relating to Money, Interest and Trade, &c.* There were second and third editions of some of these papers, papers written to influence members of government at a time when the questions of lowering interest rates and devaluing the money were urgent topics. The importance of this aspect of Locke's thinking was recognized in his own day, but has only recently been given the serious attention of scholars. Patrick Hyde Kelly's two-volume edition (*Locke on Money*, 1991) gives the full text of the pamphlets and has an extended introduction and commentary on the background and composition of them.

Some Thoughts Concerning Education   This work originated in long letters Locke wrote while he was living in Holland to his friends in England, Mr and Mrs Edward Clarke. They had sought Locke's advice on raising their young son. It was to be advice on rearing and educating the son to become a gentleman. There were four official editions in Locke's lifetime, but five in effect since there were two different look-alike editions printed in 1693 (with minor variants between them). The fifth was actually published in 1705, one year after Locke's death. A third edition appeared in 1695, a fourth in 1699. The original letters grew in number, some additions were made before publishing them as a book, and changes were made in the editions subsequent to the two in 1693.

This work attracted the attention of many of Locke's friends, especially those with young children. There are a few references to girls here and there, but primarily the book was written as advice for parents on raising a son. This work has assumed a major place in the history of educational thought, despite its rather limited focus on producing a young gentleman. There is, in fact, much sound advice on raising children and some sage observations on children's nature, motives, desires and activities. In its larger scope, this is a work that reflects Locke's longstanding concern to develop moral character. He has a number of sections on the health of the body, but the well-being of the moral person was perhaps his dominant concern in this work. He does address the nature of a curriculum, he talks about the value of travel for a young man, he has several novel suggestions for learning foreign languages, and he recommends observing children at play as a way of studying their character. He believed that children are born with certain character traits, some of which can be altered, others of which must be worked with or around.

It is safe to say that the notion of education was a central one in his thinking about people and society: the transmission of the values of society rested with the rearing and education of children. The process of culturation took place within the family. The guidance the tutor and parents are urged to give the growing child in order to help him acquire knowledge runs parallel with the hints at a genetic psychology in the *Essay*. Parental guidance also plays an important role in his *Two Treatises*. *Some Thoughts* emerged from a body of educational literature in the seventeenth century, but Locke systematized and made more readable what some of the earlier tracts attempted.

For the standard edition, with details on the composition of this work and extensive textual notes, see the Clarendon edition with introduction, notes and a critical apparatus by John W. and Jean S. Yolton, Oxford, 1989.

sorts, sortals   The only use of the word 'sortal' cited by the *Oxford English Dictionary* is Locke's in the *Essay*. Locke explains that he derived it from the more common 'sort', meaning 'kind' (3.3.15). This is the only time he uses 'sortal' in that work. Both 'sort' and 'sortal' designate a name which in turn signifies a complex idea which represents a set of coexisting qualities. Usually, he writes of sorts or of the act of sorting or ranking into kinds of things. While he does hold the notion that mixed modes have or are nominal essences (in their case, there is no real essence), most of his discussion of classification relates to physical things, e.g., gold, silver, lead. These discussions involve other concepts, such as abstract general ideas, essences, and the ontology of particulars. Abstraction separates the particularity of some idea from its representative role as a standard for ranking 'real Existences into sorts' (2.11.9). Those ideas, with their names, also designate kinds of qualities, e.g., whiteness. With substances, our ideas of sorts are 'nothing but several Combinations of simple *Ideas*, co-existing in such, though unknown, Cause of their Union, as makes the whole subsist of itself' (2.23.6). Locke was sceptical about our ability to know the internal nature of substances such as gold, although he accepted the corpuscular theory as the most likely hypothesis about matter. His point was that our ideas and names for kinds of things, such as man, horse, sun, water, iron, signify not the internal corpuscular structure but the observable qualities of such objects (*ibid.*). Included in those qualities designated by our sortal names are some unobservables, the active and passive powers credited to the corpuscular structure on his version of that theory. He gives the example of 'the power of drawing Iron' as part of the complex idea of what we call a loadstone (a magnet), 'and a Power to be so drawn is a part of the Complex one we call *Iron*' (2.23.7). Strictly, these powers are not part of observed coexistences; the fact that iron is drawn to a loadstone, the fact that wax melts when exposed to heat, are reasons for saying the loadstone has a power to attract iron, or that iron has the passive power to be attracted, or that the power to melt wax or turn wood into charcoal or ash is a property of the sun or fire. The account of qualities presented in *Essay* 2.8 traces the ideas we receive of primary and secondary qualities to the powers of the insensible corpuscles (at least, to the primary qualities of those corpuscles). So our sortal ideas and names include the non-observable powers of objects. Some of the observable qualities to which our idea of gold refers are not strictly properties of gold itself: 'Yellowness, great Weight, Ductility, Fusibility, and Solubility, in *Aqua Regia*' are 'nothing else, but so many relations to other

Substances; and are not really in the Gold, considered barely in it self, though they depend on the real, primary Qualities of its internal constitution, whereby it has a fitness, differently to operate, and be operated on by several other Substances' (2.23.37; cf. 2.31.6).

To be ranked under a general name *is* to be of a particular sort: 'the *Essences of* the *sorts, or* (if the Latin word please better) *Species* of Things, are nothing but these abstract *Ideas*' that general names signify (3.3.12). Locke repeats this remark: 'the having the Essences, and the having the Conformity' to the complex idea are the same. Sortals share a characteristic with mixed modes: both serve as standards for what falls under the idea, a kind in the one case, an action in the other. The name and essence of the species or kinds are the same. Both mixed modes and kinds are, as he says of the latter, *'the Workmanship of the Understanding'* (3.3.14). The difference between mixed-mode ideas of actions and abstract general ideas for kinds of things is that the latter are based upon the fact that there are similarities between natural substances which are reflected in the sortals. Nature, Locke affirms in an effort not to be misunderstood, 'in the Production of Things, makes several of them alike: there is nothing more obvious, especially in the Races of Animals, and all Things propagated by Seed' (3.3.13). The 'especially' clause would not seem to rule out natural productions of gold or wood also being alike in different instances. The naming and sorting is done by the understanding, not nature, but the sorting works from the similitudes discovered in experience.

It is the fact that 'several particular Substances do, or might agree' that makes them 'capable to be comprehended in one common Conception, and be signified by one Name' (3.6.1). Noticing the similarities, selecting the features to be collected in a complex idea with a name attached, are obviously activities that we undertake. In this sense, the sorting can be said, in Locke's language, to be the workmanship of the understanding. What we capture in our names for such substances does not include all the ways in which instances of man, horse, water, wood or gold have similarities with other men, horses, water, etc. In some cases, what the sortal names designate are a set of coexisting qualities that we find important or useful. Different persons for different reasons may disagree on what to include in the idea of a kind (3.6.30). In these ways, the abstract idea with its name is called by Locke a *nominal essence*, the 'named' essence, the term under which the sorting will be conducted (3.6.2). The contrast is not with some real essence that, as it were, sorts things into kinds itself; rather, it is with Locke's real essence which is 'the constitution of the insensible parts of' some body on which the observed qualities 'and all the other Properties' depend (*ibid.*; cf. 3.6.6).

Locke was anxious to avoid any implication that his real essence naturally sorted things into kinds, mainly because he wanted to distinguish his concept of real essence from the older notion of a fixed number of natural kinds – 'moulds', as he characterized that notion – into which properties and qualities were poured (3.3.17; cf. 4.4.13). But he recognized that his real essences are related to sorts since they are the bases for the qualities and properties which we use to classify things. It was a consequence of his denial of natural kinds that 'there is no individual parcel of Matter, to which any of these Qualities are so annexed, as to be *essential* to it, or inseparable from it' (3.6.6). The term 'essential' 'belongs to it [any object] as a Condition, whereby it is of this or that Sort'. This distinction between individuals or particulars and classes or kinds of particulars receives a forceful illustration with the example of Locke himself: 'Tis necessary for me to be as I am; GOD and Nature has made me so: But there is nothing I have, is essential to me. An Accident, or Disease, may very much alter my Colour, or Shape; a Fever, or Fall, may take away my Reason, or Memory, or both; and an Apoplexy leave neither Sense, nor Understanding, no nor Life' (3.6.4). To make any of these qualities I have essential for being a man requires me to form an abstract idea of 'man'. Thus, if Locke is asked 'whether it be *essential* to me, or any other particular corporeal Being to have Reason? I say no; no more than it is *essential* to this white thing I write on, to have words on it' (*ibid.*). To call the first a man, or the second a treatise, each must fit certain criteria which we select and to the ideas of which we give names. In general, 'It would be absurd to ask, whether a thing really existing, wanted any thing *essential* to it' (3.6.5).

It is difficult not to think in terms of distinct species and kinds of plants, animals, metals, minerals in nature. Locke's talk of classes being the workmanship of the understanding makes it sound as if we do in fact group qualities or properties into different kinds of things. He did not of course mean that man makes plants and animals, or gold or diamonds, but he did subscribe to the ontology of particulars: all that exist are particulars. Was he just making an epistemic claim: *our* concept of kinds *is* a product of which qualities we put together? One of Locke's friends, William Molyneux, put the problem which disturbs us about Locke's account. In a letter to Locke of 22 December 1692, Molyneux said that what Locke said 'concerning Genera and Species is Unquestionably true', but he then went on to explain his hesitation: 'it seems hard to assert, that there is no such sort of Creatures in Nature as Birds; for tho we may be Ignorant of the Particular Essence that makes a Bird, or that Determines and Distinguishes a Bird from a Beast, or the just Limits and boundarys between each; Yet we can no More doubt of a Sparrows being a Bird, and an Horses being a Beast, than we can of this Colour being

Black and tother White, tho by Shades they may be made so Gradually to Vanish into each other, that we cannot tell where either Determines' (*Corr.* 1579; iv. 601). Locke's response to Molyneux's comment is instructive. 'In the objection you raise about species I fear you are fallen into the same difficulty I often found my self under when I was writing of that subject, where I was very apt to suppose distinct species I could talk of without names' (*ibid.*, 1592; iv. 626). He asks Molyneux what he means when he says we cannot doubt a sparrow's being a bird? Locke suggests the answer: 'the combination of simple ideas which the word bird stands for, is to be found in that particular thing we call a sparrow.' The next remark is even more significant: 'And therefore I hope I have no where said, *there is no such sort of creatures in nature as birds*; if I have, it is both contrary to truth and to my opinion.' So there are in nature sorts of creatures. He reaffirms that the simple ideas we receive come from the real constitution of creatures, and also 'that there are real distinctions and differences in those real constitutions one from another, whereby they are distinguished one from another, whether we think of them or name them or no.' What he denies is that we 'rank particular substances into sorts or genera and species' by means of 'those real essences or internal constitutions'. We rank and sort by means of the qualities (he writes 'ideas' here) we observe in the objects around us.

Locke's clarification for Molyneux is a fairly unequivocal affirmation that there are kinds of animals in nature with differing internal constitutions. The fact that we cannot discover those internal structures means that we cannot classify animals (and other objects) by means of those structures. As in knowledge generally, we are limited to experience and observation. So when we list the characteristics that make a sparrow or gold, we are relying only on observed coexisting qualities. We can make an inference to differences in internal structure from observed differences in qualities, but this inference is part of theory, not observational knowledge (3.6.22). Locke would seem to allow, then, that there are natural kinds, but those kinds are a product of different corpuscular structures or other (biological) internal parts, not a product of the discredited doctrine of species fixed by a finite number of forms.

Whether Locke's clarification to Molyneux is consistent with Locke's talk of the chain of being not having any chasms or gaps, and his claimed examples of animals mating across species, is not clear. Nor can we say just how he thought his commitment to the ontology of particulars is consistent with his assertion of sorts of creatures in nature, unless he just means that 'sorts' or 'kinds' are not part of nature, which does seem to be correct: we do not find classes over and above members of classes. So we might suggest that Locke accepts the following propositions:

(1) There are sorts of birds, horses, minerals in nature.
(2) Those sorts have different internal constitutions which are the source of our simple ideas composing our complex ideas of substances.
(3) The internal differences between animals do not preclude mixing of species.
(4) Our talk about birds, horses, gold, water is done in the language of observed qualities, of coexisting qualities.
(5) We classify objects in terms of those observed coexisting qualities; hence, the classifications we have and work with are those we make by identifying groups of qualities and giving them a name.

Interest in Locke's account of sortal terms surfaced in very recent times in writers such as Putnam and Kripke. For a discussion of their interest and analysis, see J.L. Mackie, *Problems from Locke* (1976) and Michael Ayers, *Locke* (1991) vol. II (*see also* ESSENCE; PROPERTIES).

soul   There can be no question about Locke's belief in immortality. He accepted the biblical teaching that the dead shall rise, but he took issue with those who said the *same* body shall be resurrected. He seems to have accepted St Paul's talk of heavenly, spiritual bodies (*see* RESURRECTION). Were these spiritual bodies to be joined with souls? Locke never speaks directly to this question. It is the PERSON whom God shall judge on Judgement Day, the moral person characterized by Locke in terms of sameness of consciousness and the acceptance of responsibility for the actions done in this life. There are scattered phrases here and there where Locke does speak of the soul as if he did accept its existence and its immortality. Remarking that men have different views about what is right and good (some men even doubt God's existence and the immortality of the soul), Locke asserts: 'Even if God and the soul's immortality are not moral propositions and laws of nature, nevertheless they must be necessarily presupposed if natural law is to exist' (*Essays*, p. 173). In the *Letter concerning Toleration*, he insists that the civil magistrate should have no concern with the salvation of souls, even when men neglect their care (in *Works*, vi. 23, 28). Near the end of the *Essay*, he speaks of 'everlasting Happiness, or Misery', suggesting the need for every man 'to think of his Soul, and inform himself in Matters of Religion' (4.20.3). The same theme is found in 2.21.60 where he refers to the 'endless Happiness, or exquisite Misery of an immortal Soul hereafter'.

When we turn to the concepts and doctrines of the *Essay*, we find references to the mind far outnumber those to the soul. The 'Epistle to the Reader' says the understanding is '*the most elevated Faculty of the Soul*'

(p. 6), and 1.2.24 refers to the reasoning faculties of the soul. He also uses some Cartesian and Christian language in saying man is a creature consisting of soul and body (1.4.4). Another passage has the soul reflecting on its ideas, but that same passage speaks of the actions of the mind (2.1.4). A passage in 2.10.7 speaks of 'the Eye of the Soul', but it is the mind that he deals with there. Both terms appear in 2.21.6 where he speaks of the mind while discussing faculties, warning against mistaking them for 'some real Beings in the Soul'. The soul itself is described in one passage as 'a real Being' (2.23.19), and another section gives the soul the power of 'exciting of Motion by Thought' (2.23.28). A few places find Locke using 'spirit' instead of 'soul'. For example: 'But how inconsiderable a rank the Spirits that inhabit our Bodies hold amongst those various, and possibly innumerable, kinds of nobler Beings' is beyond our grasp (4.3.17). Most of the other references to soul in this work occur when he discusses specific doctrines or claims that he opposes: the claim for innate principles; the Cartesian claim that thought is the essence of the soul and hence the soul always thinks; the claim that personal identity requires sameness of soul; Locke's suggestion that God could add thought to some organized bit of matter; and the question about natural kinds raised by changelings and monsters.

The rejection of innate ideas and principles in his opening statement of the claim employs the language used by the innatists of the soul receiving principles in its 'very first Being; and [it] brings [them] into the World with it' (1.2.1). But even here, Locke paraphrases this view by saying those supposed principles were said to be 'as it were stamped upon the Mind of Man'. Throughout the rest of his polemic, 'mind' is the term used, except for one or two brief references to 'soul' (e.g., 1.2.14, 15). Otherwise, the question is directed towards men or children assenting to propositions, rather than talking about the location of those supposed innate principles.

The long sequence of sections attacking the Cartesian notion that the soul always thinks (the implication of saying thought is the essence of the soul) contains frequent references to the soul, including several remarks that sound as if Locke does accept the existence of a soul. He says in 2.1.10 that he has 'one of those dull Souls, that doth not perceive it self always to contemplate Ideas'. Towards the end of that section, he says: 'I do not say there is no Soul in a Man, because he is not sensible of it [that he is thinking] in his sleep.' The next section grants 'that the Soul in a waking Man is never without thought, because it is the condition of being awake' (2.1.11). But for the most part, these sections (2.1.9–19) use the term 'soul' to state the claim and Locke's counter-claims that the soul always thinks. Whether we can conclude from these uses of the word 'soul', that Locke accepted that we do have a soul, is a bit dubious. There is one passing remark that suggests that either he did not, or (the more likely reading) that he did not think he needed to talk of the soul: 'I would be glad also to learn from these Men, who so confidently pronounce, that the humane Soul, or which is all one, that a Man always thinks, how they come to know it' (2.1.18).

One of his objections to the claim that the soul always thinks is that, since we are not aware that it is always thinking, thinking could be dissociated from the man: 'But whether sleeping without dreaming be not an Affection of the whole Man, Mind as well as Body, may be worth a waking Man's Consideration' (2.1.11). The disconnection of thinking from being aware that we are thinking leads to some of those puzzle cases Locke presents in his account of personal identity. For example, 'if it be possible, that the Soul can, whilst the Body is sleeping, have its Thinking, Enjoyments, and Concerns, its Pleasure or Pain apart, which the Man is not conscious of, nor partakes in: It is certain, that *Socrates* asleep, and *Socrates* awake, is not the same Person; but his Soul when he sleeps, and *Socrates* the Man consisting of Body and Soul when he is waking, are two Persons' (*ibid.*). He elaborates the sequences in the next section. 'Let us suppose that the Soul of *Castor*, whilst he is sleeping, retired from his Body, which is no impossible Supposition for the Men I have here to do with, who so liberally allow Life, without a thinking Soul, to all other Animals' (2.1.12). In the chapter on personal identity, these puzzle cases are repeated and extended. At the end of that discussion, Locke reports that we ordinarily take 'the Soul of a Man, for an immaterial Substance, independent from Matter', but given our ignorance about the operations of thinking and memory, or their connection with the physiology of the body, there is 'no Absurdity at all, to suppose, that the same Soul may, at different times be united to different Bodies, and with them make up, for that time, one Man' (2.27.27).

The reference to the relation between thinking (or, that 'thinking thing that is in us, and what we look on as our selves') and the body mechanism ('a certain System of Fleeting Animal Spirits') is picked up later when Locke makes his suggestion about God being able to add the power of thought to certain systems of matter. In that long section (4.3.6), he says he does not mean, by this suggestion, to 'lessen the belief of the Soul's Immateriality', but he assures us nevertheless that 'All the great Ends of Morality and Religion, are well enough secured, without philosophical Proofs of the Soul's Immateriality.' He makes the same point when replying to the Bishop of Worcester (*Mr. Locke's Second Reply*, in *Works*, iv. 476). It was this claim, along with his suggestion about thinking matter, that led many of his readers to conclude that either he did lean towards materialism or he doubted the existence of the soul. Neither seems to be the case. The concept of soul was just not one that he needed in his analysis of the topics in his *Essay*. Nor did it play any significant role in his writings about religion.

The one final place in the *Essay* where Locke uses the word 'soul' is in those passages where he raises questions about natural kinds. There, he introduced examples of misshapen men about whom doubt was expressed as to their humanity. He also used examples of changelings and reported monstrous births as evidence against natural kinds fixed by nature. The question about the Abbot of St Martin who *'had so little of the Figure of a Man, that it bespake him rather a Monster'* was 'did he have a rational soul?' (3.6.26). The issue is raised again in 4.4.15 where Locke appears to criticize those who place the decision upon 'a certain Superficial Figure' rather than on a soul: 'This is to attribute more to the outside, than inside of Things; to place the Excellency of a Man, more in the external Shape of his Body, than internal Perfections of his Soul.' Others take the criterion of humanity for odd-shaped creatures to be 'the issue of rational Parents', concluding that such beings must 'therefore have a rational Soul' (4.4.16). In these passages, Locke is mainly raising criteria questions and arguing his case that sorts and kinds (species) are our own making (*see* SORTS, SORTALS).

space   The idea of space is a simple idea acquired by sight or touch. We perceive by sight 'a distance between Bodies of different Colours, or between the parts of the same Body' (*Essay*, 2.13.2). We can do the same by feeling and touch, even in the dark. Distance is space 'considered barely in length between any two Beings, without considering any thing else between them' (2.13.3). If we take into account the length, breadth, and thickness, we have the idea of capacity. 'Each different distance is a different Modification of Space' (2.13.4). We have standard measures for the different modifications: inch, feet, miles, etc. These ideas can be repeated as often as we like 'without mixing or joining to them the *Idea* of Body, or any thing else' and in that way form the ideas of shapes such as cube or square. The ideas of such figures can be formed by seeing or touching the boundaries or extremities of bodies, but the idea of figure can also be had from space itself by varying the idea of space in terms of angles and lines (2.13.5). We can, it seems, think of parts of space and form in our mind space-shapes. The ideas of figures are, in fact, just 'so many different *simple Modes of Space*' (2.13.6). He does not seem to mean filled space, space marked out by occupying bodies.

The idea of space is distinct from the idea of SOLIDITY, the essential feature of body for Locke. Moreover, we can form the idea of extension without reference to bodies, another break with the Cartesians. Extended space lies 'between any two Bodies, or positive Beings, . . . whether there be any Matter or no between' (2.13.26). Space is extended, as body is also, but Locke suggests using the term 'expansion' for the extension of space (2.13.24, 25). Space also has parts, but unlike body, the parts of space are inseparable, even in thought (2.13.13). The parts of space are also immovable and they are not resistant to the motion of body (2.13.14). Space is, he says in 2.15.1, 'often applied to Distance of fleeting successive parts, which never exist together, as well as to those which are permanent'. But this is to confuse filled space with pure (empty) space. Expansion (extension of space) is more properly the 'Idea *of lasting distance, all whose parts exist together*' (2.15.12). The mind 'is not able to frame an *Idea* of any Space, without Parts' (2.15.9). He even identifies the 'least Particle of Matter or Space we can discern, which is ordinarily about a Minute, and to the sharpest eyes seldom less than thirty Seconds of a Circle, whereof the Eye is the centre' (*ibid.*)

The idea of place is another mode of space formed by 'considering the relation of Distance between any two Bodies, or Points' (2.13.7). It is not clear whether the points referred to are on bodies (e.g., their edges) or in space. He frequently speaks of space not only having parts, but also points. In this passage, points are contrasted with 'larger Portions of sensible Objects', which is the more ordinary way of thinking about place. 'Thus a Company of Chess-men, standing on the same squares of the Chess-board, where we left them, we say they are all in the *same Place* or unmoved, though, perhaps, the Chess-board hath been in the mean time carried out of one Room into another, because we compared them only to the Parts of the Chess-board, which keep the same distance one with another' (2.13.8). Identifying place by reference-points is more precise and accurate (2.13.9). Locke gives a variety of examples illustrating these notions of place: the place of a ship in relation to land; the place of individual chessmen; the location of verses in Virgil; the place of Virgil's book in Bodley's Library. He also remarks that 'we can have no *Idea* of the Place of the Universe, though we can of all the parts of it' (2.13.10). The reason we cannot locate the universe is that 'we have not the *Idea* of any fixed, distinct, particular Beings, in reference to which, we can imagine it to have any relation of distance' (*ibid.*).

Place refers to objects in space in relation to other objects. Beyond the universe 'is one uniform Space or Expansion, wherein the Mind finds no variety, no marks' (2.13.10). The space beyond the universe is described in various ways: as 'the undistinguishable *Inane* of infinite Space' (2.13.10); 'those boundless Oceans of Eternity and Immensity' (2.15.5); 'the infinite Abysses of Space and Duration' (2.15.6). The mind is able to 'come to the end of solid Extension; the extremity and bounds of all Body', but nothing hinders the mind from thinking of the 'endless Expansion' of space beyond those bounds (2.15.2). Locke makes one qualification about those endless spaces beyond the world: they are empty of bodies but not of all Beings: God inhabits immensity, just as he does eternity, although just how we are to understand God's presence in space is left obscure. It was a notion that played a role in the dispute between Samuel Clarke (Newton's disciple) and Leibniz in the early years of the eighteenth century.

Other eighteenth-century writers discussed the nature of space, including its relation to God, for example, Samuel Colliber, John Clarke, Edmund Law. (See the bibliography in this *Dictionary* for titles and dates. For a discussion of these writers, as well as Newton, Berkeley and Hume on space, see J.W. Yolton, *Thinking Matter*, 1984.) One of the issues between some of these writers was whether space is absolute or relative, a substance or an accident. Newton suggested that space is the sensorium of God, a phrase that puzzled Leibniz, but Newton's space was not just a relation. Locke took space to be a component of the world; some space is filled, some is empty. The precise characterization of space was something about which Locke was uncertain (2.13.15). Those who denied empty space or who said 'that *Space* and *Body* are *the same*' leave us with a dilemma: 'Either this *Space* is something or nothing; if nothing be between two Bodies, they must necessarily touch; if it be allowed to be something, they ask, whether it be Body or Spirit' (2.13.16). Locke's response to this dilemma is startling in its hint of breaking away from the traditional categories: 'To which I answer by another Question, Who told them, that there was, or could be nothing, but solid Beings, which could not think; and thinking Beings that were not extended?' He went on to offer a number of examples illustrating the reality of empty space. Supposing, one example suggests, 'God placed a Man at the extremity of corporeal Beings' (2.13.21). Can that man stretch his hand beyond his body? 'If he could, then he would put his Arm, where there was before *Space* without *Body*; and if there he spread his Fingers, there would still be *Space* between them without *Body*' (*ibid.*) Another example: 'No one, I suppose, will deny, that God can put an end to all motion that is in Matter, and fix all Bodies of the Universe in a perfect quiet and rest, and continue them so as long as he pleases' (2.13.21 *bis*). The example goes on to have God destroy one body, take it out of existence. 'Whoever then will allow, that God can, during such a general rest, annihilate either this Book, or the Body of him that reads it, must necessarily admit the possibility of a *Vacuum*.' If pressed by the standard ontological question, 'whether this *Space* void of *Body*, be *Substance* or *Accident*' (2.13.17), Locke confesses he cannot answer that question until he has been given a clear, informative definition of substance, which he does not find in those writers who use that term. Moreover, he finds the idea of SUBSTANCE very obscure.

spirits   If we read the entry for 'spirit' in Chambers's *Cyclopaedia* (1728), he tells us that one use of this term was to designate any incorporeal being or intelligence, e.g., God, Angels, or the Devil. It was also, Chambers reports, used to refer to the human soul. We find both these uses in Locke. Our idea of spirit is as inadequate as our idea of body (*Essay*, 2.23.30). Because our 'Notion of immaterial Spirit may have, perhaps, some difficulties in it, not easie to be explained', this is not a reason to doubt spirits' existence (2.23.31; cf. 2.23.32). When late in Book Four of the *Essay* Locke refers to 'the *Operations of Spirits*, both their thinking and moving Bodies', he is using 'spirit' in the second sense discerned by Chambers: as soul or immaterial substance (4.6.14). In some sections, 'spirit' and 'soul' are used interchangeably (e.g., 2.23.20, 21). Most uses of the plural form refer to finite spirits or spiritual beings other than humans. About these he is sometimes tentative, saying, 'We have ground from revelation, and several other Reasons, to believe with assurance, that there are such Creatures' (4.11.12).

   How do we go about forming ideas of such creatures? How do we interpret the scriptural references? 'For the Mind getting, only by reflecting on its own Operations, those simple *Ideas* which it attributes to *Spirits*, it hath, or can have no other Notion of *Spirit*, but by attributing all those Operations, it finds in it self, to a sort of Beings, without Consideration of Matter' (3.6.11). These are ideas of spirits separate from matter. Even the idea of God is formed by enlarging various ideas of existence, knowledge, power and joining them to infinity. He recognizes that it is not easy to form ideas of 'different *Species of Angels*' because we are unsure which of our properties, or what degrees of those properties, should be extended to other species of spirits (*ibid.*). They are conceivable: at least 'It is not impossible to conceive, nor repugnant to reason, that there may be many *Species of Spirits*, as much separated and diversified one from another by distinct Properties', even though we lack specific ideas for such species (3.6.12). Conceiving of 'more *Species* of intelligent Creatures above us' is possible because 'in all the visible corporeal World, we see no Chasms, or Gaps'; we extend the chain of being above us in the same way (*ibid.*). We can even 'guess at some part of the Happiness of superior Ranks of Spirits, who have a quicker and more penetrating Sight, as well as a larger Field of Knowledge' (4.3.6; cf. 2.23.36).

   Various properties and abilities are ascribed to such spirits by Locke. Our faculty of memory is much inferior to that faculty possessed by 'some superiour created intellectual Beings' (2.10.9). Locke speculates that God may even 'communicate to those glorious Spirits' some of his perfections (*ibid.*). Locke is unsure what the relation is to space of such spirits, 'or how they communicate in it' (2.15.11), but he is convinced that 'Spirits, as well as Bodies, cannot operate, but where they are' (2.23.19). It was a generally accepted dictum that, to use a formulation employed by Samuel Clarke, 'Nothing can any more act, or be acted upon, where it is not present, than it can be, where it is not' (*A Collection of Papers . . . between . . . Mr. Leibniz and Dr. Clarke*, 1717, Clarke's second reply, §4). Locke says that finite 'Spirits do operate at several times in several places', so they must be able to change, as well as be located at, specific places (2.23.19). He includes humans in this remark: 'For my Soul being a real Being, as well as my Body, is certainly as capable of changing distance with any other Body, or Being, as Body it self; and so is capable of Motion' (*ibid.*). 'Motivity' is the term he uses to characterize the motion of finite spirits (2.23.28). In one passage he makes a fascinating conjecture about spirits other than us: 'Spirits can assume to themselves Bodies of different Bulk, Figure, and Conformation of Parts. Whether one great advantage some of them have over us, may not lie in this, that they can so frame, and shape to themselves Organs of Sensation or Perception, as to suit them to their present Design, and the Circumstances of the Object they would consider' (2.23.13). He describes this as 'so wild a Fancy', a way of conceiving 'the ways of Perception in Beings above us'.

He also suggests that spirits 'may excite . . . *Ideas* in me, and lay them in such order before my Mind, that I may perceive their Connexion' (4.19.10). We do not understand how they communicate their thoughts to each other, 'Though we must necessarily conclude, that separate Spirits [separate from matter], which are Beings that have perfecter Knowledge, and greater Happiness than we, must needs have also a perfecter way of communicating their Thoughts, than we have' (2.23.36; cf. *Letter to Bishop of Worcester*, in *Works*, iv. 18). He suggests that they have an immediate communication without the need to use signs (words or sounds), but he admits it is difficult to form any notion of that kind of communication. We find it difficult to understand 'how spirits that have no Bodies, can be Masters of their own Thoughts, and communicate or conceal them at Pleasure, though we cannot but necessarily suppose they have such a Power' (*ibid.*). He also thinks that angels use a form of direct, non-discursive knowledge (4.17.14). He even believes that 'the Spirits of just Men made perfect, shall have in a future State' a knowledge and understanding of 'Thousands of Things' which escape us now.

Just what kinds of spirits there may be above us is not specified, except for a few examples cited by Locke. He seems confident that there are (at least, probably) 'infinite numbers of *Spirits*' (4.3.27), 'innumerable kinds of nobler Beings' (4.3.17). He speaks of them inhabiting an 'intellectual World', a world that is greater 'and more beautiful' than the material one we live in (*ibid.*). He mentions angels, whose existence we know by revelation, from the Bible. *Some Thoughts concerning Education* also says the Bible tells us about the operations of spirits (*ST*, §192). *Essay* 4.16.12 mentions angels and devils.

His work on education confirms that he does speak of evil as well as good spirits, although it is not entirely clear whether evil spirits were considered by Locke to be real (*ST*, §138). The only evil spirits mentioned in that work are '*Goblins, Spectres*, and *Apparitions*' (*ST*, §191), or '*Sprites* and *Goblins*' (*ST*, §138). It seems unlikely that Locke believed there really were such spirits outside of story-books or tales told to children. His concern was to prevent such stories and notions being given to children. Even with good spirits, children should be exposed to the idea of them only after they have learned about the infinite spirit, God. All the child should know about God is that he is 'the independent Supreme Being, Author and Maker of all Things, from whom we receive all our Good, who loves us, and gives us all Things' (*ST*, §136). To say more about God's nature would require explaining about spirits, but 'by talking too early to him [the child] of Spirits, and being unseasonably forward to make him understand the incomprehensible Nature of that infinite Being, his Head [may] be either fill'd with false, or perplexed with unintelligible Notions of him' (*ibid.*). Locke's advice to parents is to wait until the child brings up the topic of spirits; then you can give him some information about them from the Scriptures. Some notion of spirits is a good prerequisite for the child's study of natural philosophy. Too much exposure to the study of matter may make it difficult for the child to accept the notion of '*immaterial Beings in rerum natura*' (*ST*, §192). *Some Thoughts* confirms what the *Essay* says, that natural philosophy should include the study of spirits, their nature and qualities, not just bodies (*ST*, §190; *Essay*, 4.21.2).

state of nature   Locke defines political power as '*a Right* of making Laws with Penalties of Death, and consequently all less Penalties, for the Regulating and Preserving of Property, and of employing the force of the Community, in the Execution of such Laws, and in defence of the Common-wealth from Foreign Injury, and all this only for the Publick Good' (*T*2, §3). He then tells us in the next chapter that if we are to have a good understanding of political power, we should discover how it arises. For that, we need to 'consider what State all Men are naturally in' prior to political society. Understanding the origins of political society will explain how those features of political power he lists arose, perhaps even find their justification: the right of making laws, the use of penalties including death for those who violate the laws, the regulating and preserving of property, and the employment of the force of the community in the execution of laws. The other two features of political power, defending against foreign aggression and always acting for the public good, fit less tightly into the account of the origin of that power. Locke of course is concerned with legitimate political power, not power seized by aggression. In the first of *Two Treatises* he had firmly rejected Filmer's account of political power descending from God to Adam and then to Adam's posterity.

It was not so much the monarchial form of government defended by Filmer that Locke objected to (he does not rule out all forms of political societies that have a king and legislative body). What he rejected was the hereditary nature of Filmer's account with all power placed in the king, the subjects having no role in the structure or running of the government. Legitimate political power for Locke is derived from specific features of people living in the state of nature. Each of the main characteristics of Lockean civil society finds its prototype in Locke's state of nature. We need to speak of *Locke's* state of nature, because his account of that condition differs from that of others, most markedly from Hobbes's concept. Those differences reflect a divergence in their views of human nature, as well as of God's relation to man. Highlighting these differences between Locke and Hobbes will help us understand Locke's state of nature and see the ways in which his civil society reflects that state.

1. The condition men are in naturally is described by Locke as 'a *State of perfect Freedom* to order their Actions, and dispose of their Possessions, and Persons as they think fit' (*T*2, §4). Hobbes defines liberty as 'the absence of external impediments', a liberty 'each man hath, to use his own power, as he will himself for the preservation of his own Nature; that is to say, of his own Life; and consequently, of doing any thing, which in his own Judgment, and Reason, he shall conceive to be the aptest means thereunto' (*Leviathan*, Pt I, ch. XIV, p. 189, Penguin edn.). So far, the two definitions are fairly similar, except for the term 'power' in Hobbes's definition. The concept of power for Hobbes does encompass strength, prudence, nobility, reputation and even knowledge, so it is not just physical force, and so the presence of that term in Hobbes's definition may not mark a major difference (*ibid.*, ch. X). Where a significant difference arises is in Locke's qualification that perfect freedom in the state of nature occurs 'within the bounds of the Law of Nature' (*T*2, §4). This law obliges everyone in that state: it 'teaches all Mankind ... that being all equal and independent, no one ought to harm another in his

Life, Health, Liberty, or Possessions' (T2, §6). In Hobbes's state of nature, 'every man has a Right to every thing; even to one another's body' (*Leviathan*, Pt I, ch. XIV, p. 190). It is questionable what kind of 'right' this can be, or how it arises, since he says (and this is a large difference from Locke) that 'Right and Wrong, Justice and Injustice have there no place'; that is, in the state of nature, they 'relate to man in Society, not in Solitude' (*ibid.*, ch. XIII, p. 188)). There seem to be two concepts of 'right' for Hobbes: one derives from laws within political society; the other simply means, as he says, 'the liberty to do, or to forebeare' (ch. XIV, p. 189). Locke agrees that rights are related to laws, although there are for him some natural rights as well, but these are closely linked to the law of nature. Hobbes talks of a law of nature (a 'Precept, or generall Rule, found out by Reason') which forbids a man 'to do, that, which is destructive of his life, or taketh away the means of preserving the same', but this is a prudential rule, not a law which, as with Locke, God gives to man.

2. Locke's law of nature is also discovered by the faculty of reason, but reason for him is natural revelation, the voice of God. What reason discloses are God's laws, moral injunctions. Locke quotes Richard Hooker who talked of an obligation of 'mutual Love amongst Men' (T2, §5) and he stresses the importance of men being the workmanship of God and hence God's property (T2, §6). In the state of nature for Locke, we all share in the community of mankind. The liberty men have in that community is constrained by the law of nature, even though he characterizes man's liberty in the state of nature as 'uncontroleable'. One constraint is against suicide; another precludes destroying 'any Creature in his Possession, but where some nobler use, than its bare Preservation calls for it' (*ibid.*). The law of nature also precludes anyone harming another in his life, liberty, health or goods; that law 'willeth the Peace and *Preservation of all Mankind*' (T2, §7).

3. Hobbes finds all mankind have 'a general inclination' which he characterizes as 'a perpetual and restlesse desire of Power after power, that ceaseth onely in Death' (*Leviathan*, Pt I, ch. XI, p. 161). Even recognizing the breadth of his concept of power, the result of this general trait of human nature is that the state of nature is a war of 'every man against every man', not necessarily in actual fighting, but 'the known disposition thereto' (ch. XIII, pp. 185–6). Hobbes would probably agree with Locke's definition of a state of war: 'a State of Enmity and Destruction; And therefore declaring by Word or Action, not a passionate and hasty, but a sedate setled Design, upon another Mans Life' (T2, §16). Hobbes identifies the state of nature with the state of war, Locke carefully distinguishes them. For Locke, the state of nature is a condition of peace,

goodwill, mutual assistance and preservation. The state of war is one of enmity, malice, violence, mutual destruction: a good characterization of Hobbes's state of nature.

One other feature of Locke's state of nature is that 'the *Execution* of the Law of Nature is in that State, put into every Mans hands' (*T2*, §7). Locke says that this notion is a 'strange doctrine', meaning a new notion (*T2*, §13). That doctrine gives to every one in the state of nature the right 'to punish the transgressors of that Law to such a Degree, as may hinder its Violation' (*T2*, §7). Hobbes had insisted that, in the state of nature, there is no common power which could keep the people quiet or in awe. A common power, a strong ruler, could enforce laws and turn the state of nature (war) into a political society. For Locke, some authority for enforcement and overseeing the law of nature is required, but he disperses that authority to every person in the state of nature. Under that strange doctrine, that every man in the state of nature has the executive power of the law of nature, every man has two distinct rights: 'the one of *Punishing* the Crime *for restraint*, and preventing the like Offence . . .; the other of taking *reparation*, which belongs only to the injured party' (*T2*, §11). It is from these two rights in the state of nature that the magistrate in political society acquires those rights on behalf of all the members of the civil society.

Locke raises a possible objection against his doctrine of everyone's having the executive power of the law of nature. Can men be objective in judging others and in assessing appropriate punishments? Will not self-love 'make Men partial to themselves and their Friends'? Or will not 'Ill Nature, Passion and Revenge' lead them to impose harsh punishments that are not appropriate to their crimes? (*T2*, §13). If these objections are valid, would not 'Confusion and Disorder' result? His answer to these objections is to admit that the 'Inconveniences of the State of Nature . . . must certainly be Great, where Men may be Judges in their own Cases, since 'tis easily to be imagined, that he who was so unjust as to do his Brother an Injury, will scarce be so just as to condemn himself for it' (*T2*, §13). But he reminds us that absolute monarchs are men too, so the same dangers of bias and unfairness may apply to their judgements. Not every government is better in this respect than the state of nature. Moreover, every man in the state of nature 'is answerable for it [his judgement] to the rest of Mankind' (*ibid.*). What Locke does not say here, but what is most important for understanding his concept of political power, is that wherever the locus of executive power is in civil society, it takes its origin and legitimacy from the fact that every man in the state of nature has that power in relation to the law of nature.

The state of nature was used by Locke and many earlier writers as a concept to explain the origin of political power and specific features that characterize civil society (positive laws, enforcement of those laws, rights and duties, public good). The question has been raised, did these writers believe that the concept referred to some actual pre-political condition? Locke gives several answers to this question. First, he suggests some historical examples, while admitting that our records are rather thin (*T*2, §101). He suggests that Rome and Venice began 'by the uniting together of several Men free and independent one of another', so they were in a state of nature prior to the uniting (*T*2, §102). He also cites a book by Josephus Acosta in which it is said that 'in many parts of *America* there was no Government at all' (*ibid.*). Acosta's examples were of Peru, Brazil and Florida. Locke believes these people began their political societies from 'a voluntary Union, and the mutual agreement of Men freely acting in the choice of their Governours, and forms of Governments' (*ibid.*; cf. §92 where he refers to the woods of America). He also cites another account by Justin (Marcus Julianus Justinus) where Sparta and the establishment of a government by free and independent men is described (*T*2, §103).

Locke clearly took these examples and instances 'out of History, of *People free and in the State of Nature*' who met together and incorporated themselves into a commonwealth (*ibid.*). His second answer to the question about the existence of a state of nature is more conceptual, although it captures a fundamental condition for a legitimate civil society. Any absolute ruler 'is as much *in the state of Nature*, with all under his Dominion, as he is with the rest of Mankind' (*T*2, §91). The criterion for a state of nature is, he says in this passage, 'where-ever any two Men are, who have no standing Rule, and common Judge to Appeal to on Earth for the determination of Controversies of Right betwixt them'. He extends the scope of men living in a state of nature to 'all *Princes* and Rulers of *Independent* Governments all through the World', because, even if the subjects have made some sort of agreement with the rulers, they may not have met the proper criterion for the social contract (*T*2, §14). The consent or compact that moves men from the state of nature to political society must take the specific form of 'agreeing together mutually to enter into one Community, and make one Body Politick' (*ibid.*).

A more detailed description of what is agreed to when men incorporate themselves into a civil society is given later in *Two Treatises*: 'The only way whereby any one devests himself of his Natural Liberty, and *puts on the bonds of Civil Society* is by agreeing with other Men to joyn in and unite into a Community, for their comfortable, safe, and peaceable living one amongst another, in a secure Enjoyment of their Properties, and a greater

Security against any that are not of it' (*T*2, §95). There are very specific reasons for leaving the state of nature: want of 'an *establish'd*, settled, known *Law*' agreed to as the standard of right and wrong; the lack of '*a known and indifferent Judge*' with proper authority; and the lack of power to 'back and support the Sentence when right, and to *give* it due *Execution*' (*T*2, §124–6; *see* SOCIETY).

Locke followed in a long tradition of writers using the concept of a state of nature. There are many similarities between his account and those of writers in earlier centuries. For a discussion and analysis of those writers, see Quentin Skinner, *The Foundations of Modern Political Thought* (1978), vol. II.

substance   When we think and talk about the objects we touch, see, or use in our ordinary experience, we think of those objects (e.g., a football, a table, a piece of gold) as the possessors or subjects of qualities, powers, and abilities that we discover in our use or exploration of them. It would never occur to us to think the football or the desk was just the qualities we discover, or might discover. The notion of these objects being nothing more than a collection of qualities is a notion we ordinarily find obscure, if not meaningless. When pressed to say what the object is if not just a group of qualities, we find it difficult to respond. We use words such as 'it', 'they', 'thing'. The word 'apple' is taken to refer to something that has specific properties: a colour, a taste, a shape and texture. We think the word refers to *that which* has those qualities or properties. But the 'it' or the 'that which' seems elusive, seems never to come within our experience.

Philosophers, ancient and modern, formulated this ordinary way of thinking about objects in the technical language of substance, mode, attribute, property. Referring to properties such as thinking, willing, believing, Descartes used the dictum, 'nothingness possesses no attributes or qualities', meaning that qualities or attributes belong to something, to some *thing* or (the technical term) *substance* (*Principles of Philosophy*, Pt I, §11). The general definition of substance with which Descartes worked is the standard one: 'a thing which exists in such a way as to depend on no other things for its existence' (*Principles*, Pt I, §51). Spinoza's definition is a bit more precise and complex: 'By substance, I understand that which is in itself and is conceived through itself; in other words, that, the conception of which does not need the conception of another thing from which it must be formed' (*Ethics*, Pt I, Def. III). Spinoza's substance turns out to be God, the only substance there is, but it has all the attributes – an infinite number, in fact – two of which (extension and thought) 'the intellect perceives of substance, as if constituting its essence' (*ibid.*, Def.

IV). For Descartes God is also the only proper substance, but the concept of substance is applied in a derivative sense to mind and body, immaterial and material substances. These qualify as substances because they are the supporters of qualities or attributes, that to which specific qualities belong. Just as for Spinoza, the two attributes we can understand, thought and extension, enable us to gain some knowledge of substance, so for Descartes, we become aware of these derivative substances through specific qualities or attributes. These substances themselves have no effect on us. It is only through the attributes we experience that we can 'infer that there must also be present an existing thing or substance' (*Principles*, Pt I, §52). Each of these two kinds of substances has an essential or principal attribute or property 'which constitutes its nature and essence, and to which all its other properties are referred, extension for body, thinking for mind' (*ibid.*, §53).

With the doctrine of substance outlined thus far, two questions arise: (1) 'can we say anything about the nature of substance apart from its attributes?', and (2) 'does our concept of substance rest only on the inference we make from the dictum that qualities cannot exist alone, that they must have a substance to which they belong?' Descartes had trouble with these questions. At one point, he seems to answer the first question in the negative; he comes close to identifying substance with its essential attribute. Principle 63 tells us that the essential attributes of mind and body really are, or are thought to be, the substances themselves: thought 'must then be considered as nothing else but thinking substance itself'. The same remark is made about extension and extended substance. Whether he meant these remarks to be taken in an ontological way (substances are the same as essential properties) or only as pertaining to our knowledge is not clear. He says it is 'much easier for us to have an understanding of extended substance or thinking substance than it is for us to understand substance on its own, leaving out the fact that it thinks or is extended' (*ibid.*). But the question remains unanswered: 'can there *be* a substance without some essential attribute?'

The doctrine of substance in Descartes and Spinoza is complex and subtle, but this quick sketch is sufficient to provide us with the background against which Locke wrote. He reflects Descartes's admission that the word 'substance' does not apply univocally to God, finite minds and bodies, but this fact leads Locke to be critical of the term and concept. He interrupts his account of the simple modes of space to indicate his doubts about the meaningfulness of 'substance'. If it is applied to God, minds, and bodies in the same sense, it may devalue the important differences (*Essay*, 2.13.18). If it is claimed that it applies to each of these in a different sense, then these philosophers should use three different words 'to prevent in so important a Notion, the Confusion and Errors, that will naturally follow from the promiscuous use of so doubtful a term' (*ibid.*). The next section suggests that it was the taking of accidents (i.e., non-essential properties) 'as a sort of real Beings, that needed something to inhere in' that forced earlier philosophers 'to find out the word *Substance*, to support them' (2.13.19). Locke's critical tone becomes more strident at this point. Referring to the story of the Indian philosopher who thought the earth needed support, and suggested an elephant supported it and a tortoise supported the elephant (thereby opening an infinite regress), Locke says that this way of talking is no less meaningful or meaningless than the European philosophers' talk of substance as a support for qualities (cf. 2.32.2, where he says both are talking like children). The notion of substance supporting qualities or of qualities inherent in substance is equally unclear (2.13.20).

When Locke turns his attention to describing the idea of substance, he exemplifies the way we ordinarily think and talk about objects. It is the *ideas* of substances that he describes as 'such combinations of simple *Ideas*, as are taken to represent distinct particular things subsisting by themselves; in which the supposed, or confused *Idea* of Substance, such as it is, is always the first and chief' (2.12.6). The long chapter on our complex ideas of substances reaffirms this description: we notice that certain ideas (i.e., qualities) always go together in what we call 'external objects'. But we cannot imagine 'how these simple *Ideas* [qualities] can subsist by themselves, [so] we accustom our selves, to suppose some *Substratum*, wherein they do subsist, and from which they do result, which therefore we call *Substance*' (2.23.1). If we try to form an idea of the substance itself apart from the qualities (what he calls 'pure substance in general'), we can only find a supposition of we know not what support of those qualities (2.23.2). The ideas of particular kinds of things, substances, are formed by combining those simple ideas that 'are by Experience and Observation of Men's Senses taken notice of to exist together' (2.23.3). He gives examples of a man, horse, gold, water, iron, diamond. All of these ideas are of coexisting qualities, with the added 'confused *Idea* of *something* to which they belong, and in which they subsist' (*ibid.*).

The same account is offered of our idea of mind, the supposed immaterial substance, Descartes's *res cogitans*: it too is the complex idea of various mental actions and powers such as thinking, reasoning, fearing, which we suppose belong to some thing called 'spirit' or 'mind' (2.23.5). So the twin notions of material and immaterial substances are equally unclear, once we go beyond the collection of properties associated with some particular sort of these physical or mental 'things'. The next section makes it clear that Locke is talking about our *ideas* of these things, not the supposed substance itself. 'Whatever therefore be the secret and abstract Nature of *Substance* in general, all *the* Ideas *we have of particular distinct sorts of Substances*, are nothing but several Combinations of simple *Ideas*' (2.23.6). He does not say, substances are only collections of qualities, but he does repeatedly insist that our ideas of particular substances are nothing but such collections. The 'nothing but' locution is used a number of times, but always for our ideas of particular kinds of substances (cf. 2.23.14). Not even the idea of substance in general is given that formulation: that idea is always referred to as the confused idea of a supposed support for qualities. The nature of such support is beyond our knowledge.

For a traditional philosopher schooled in the language of substance, property and accidents, especially for such a person with theological interests, Locke could be seen as undercutting the traditional ontology. He *was* so viewed by Edward Stillingfleet, the Bishop of Worcester. In his *Letter to the Bishop of Worcester*, Locke speaks to Stillingfleet's concluding from the limitation of ideas to sensation and reflection that substance does not come within the compass of human reason. Stillingfleet had charged that those who employed this new language of ideas (the new way of ideas, is how he characterized it) 'have almost discarded substance out of the reasonable part of the world' (cited by Locke in his *Letter*, in *Works*, iv. 5; see Stillingfleet's *A Discourse in Vindication of the Doctrine of the Trinity*, 1697, pp. 233–5). Stillingfleet seized on the elephant example used by Locke, especially Locke's remark in 2.23.2 that those who use the language of substance talk like children. Locke's response is to say he does not know what it is to discard substance out of the world. He then quotes from *Essay* 2.23.4–6 in support of his distinction between talking about substance and talking about the idea of substance. He claims that these passages all 'intimate that the [physical] substance is supposed always something, besides the extension, figure, solidity' (*ibid.*, p. 7). He also says that as long as there is any sensible quality or simple idea, substance cannot be discarded, since ideas and qualities carry the supposition of a substratum. He confesses to Stillingfleet that he did say the idea of substance is unclear, but he has not found any clear definitions of it, not even in the standard logic books (*ibid.*, p. 8). He also points out that saying an idea is inadequate or confused does not entail a denial of what the idea is supposed to refer to (*ibid.*, pp. 18–21). He even claims that the mind perceives a necessary connection between qualities and inherence in a substance, but this may be a claim designed to calm the Bishop, rather than reflecting Locke's own belief.

The strongest passage in the *Essay* suggesting that Locke did accept the real existence of substances in the world is found in 2.23.29, a summary conclusion of previous sections in that chapter. He there says that

'Sensation convinces us, that there are solid extended Substances; and Reflection, that there are thinking ones: Experience assures us of the Existence of such Beings; and that the one hath a power to move Body by impulse, the other by thought; this we cannot doubt of.' The phrase, 'the Existence of such Beings', is not a claim about our ideas, but about reality. The next sentence even says that experience 'every moment furnishes us with these clear *Ideas*' of both kinds of 'Beings', mind and body. The 'clear ideas', though, cannot refer to the substance component, since he has so firmly and repeatedly said that idea is confused at best. So what are the 'Beings' that experience assures us exist? The ideas are identified as those 'received from their proper Sources', beyond which 'our Faculties will not reach' (*ibid.*). The 'proper sources' may just be sensation and reflection, but there is evidence in this chapter (and elsewhere in the *Essay*) that Locke has in mind for the ideas of bodies, the causes of those ideas, causes which for him are expressed by the corpuscular theory of matter (*see* CORPUSCULAR HYPOTHESIS).

As early in this chapter as section 3, he speaks of coexisting ideas (he probably means 'qualities'; see 2.8.8) as 'supposed to flow from the particular internal Constitution, or unknown Essence of that Substance'. The presence of the words 'supposed' and 'unknown essence' suggests a close, perhaps intended, parallel with the language he uses to talk about the supposed substratum of qualities which is beyond our faculties. We may suspect that the corpuscular theory is replacing the vague notions of substratum and support which characterized the traditional doctrine of substance. 'Flow from' (a causal notion) replaces the vague idea of a 'support' and the 'unknown essence' replaces the supposed substratum. He tells us in 2.23.8 that our senses fail us 'in the discovery of the Bulk, Texture, and Figure of the minute parts of Bodies, on which their real Constitutions and Differences depend'. Section 10 is clear: observed secondary qualities are said to be powers in an object (as 2.6 explains) 'operating, by the Motion and Figure of its insensible Parts' and cause us to have specific ideas of heat, sound, etc. The unknown essence of this scientific theory of matter is the specific structure and organization of the insensible corpuscles.

This quiet move, from the traditional concept of substance to the concept of body as a combination of qualities caused by insensible corpuscles, yields an account of bodies which still gives them two components, an observable set of qualities and an unknowable internal, insensible corpuscular structure as the cause of the observable qualities (as well as the cause of our ideas of those qualities). So we can say the Bishop was correct if he meant to charge Locke's analysis with discarding the *concept* of substance which he and many philosophers had accepted, but the

bodies of everyday life, the substances on which chemists such as Boyle
worked in their laboratories, are all preserved with the new scientific
concept which Locke joined to the phenomenal objects of ordinary experience. So the 'Beings' to which Locke attests are the particular sorts of
objects in our world. For us those objects are just a collection of qualities,
but Locke agrees that we cannot conceive of objects as just qualities, so
he employs the scientific hypothesis used by most members of the scientific community to fill out our concept of physical objects. When he uses
the term 'substance', as he continues to do, most of its meaning and all
of its reference are exhausted by the observed coexisting qualities. Our
knowledge of bodies is limited to what we can discover by experience and
observation. What he called the 'nominal essence' of bodies is the set of
qualities that we discover to occur together. For example, the word 'gold'
or our idea of gold refers to the set of qualities we have discovered always
goes with objects of that sort. More precisely, 'gold' means the collection
of qualities such as malleable, soluble in certain solutions, yellow, etc. No
reference to substance or to something over and above those qualities.
The same holds for other things: lead, wood, mercury. In forming our
ideas of nominal essences, we must be careful to fit our ideas to the
qualities we find going together in our experience. Scientific descriptions
are more detailed and precise in listing the qualities and powers comprising gold, lead, wood, but any idea of these 'substances' must conform to
those groups of qualities. Names for Locke are signs of ideas, and ideas
are signs of things, but his 'things' tend to dissolve into collections of
qualities, into the nominal ESSENCE.

What happens to the second of Descartes's two substances, the immaterial, thinking soul? There was not available any alternative to the description of the soul as that which thinks in us. It was considered to be
immaterial, immortal, and indivisible; it also excluded bodily extension,
although for some the soul had an extension of its own kind (as space did
also). Locke startled orthodox philosophers and theologians by affirming
that immateriality was not necessary for immortality. He also angered
many of his readers with his suggestion that God could give to certain
organized matter the power of thought. These two features in Locke's talk
of soul disturbed the traditionalists, but it was his novel account of the
person which puzzled them most. Sameness of person is independent of
sameness of soul. 'Mind' is a term Locke uses more frequently than 'soul',
but whichever term we choose, Locke insists that our knowledge is limited
to what we can discover by reflecting on ourselves when we think, will,
or perceive. If there is a counterpart with soul or mind to the corpuscular
theory for bodies, it may be the physiology of nerves and brain. Whether
he accepted the usual account of animal spirits activating nerves and

muscles, or whether he extended the corpuscular theory to the biological matter of the living body, both were largely theory and hypothesis, so they would not enlarge our knowledge of mind or soul beyond experience. As well, special problems arise when trying to explain physiological causation of mental events. We cannot quite say that Locke's 'person' replaces the more traditional 'soul', but to the extent that it assumes some of the older functions of SOUL, the PERSON turns out to be a collection of actions and mental operations, a sort of counterpart to bodies as collections of qualities.

The concept of body in Locke's account lends itself easily to his extension of 'substance' to collective bodies such as an army, a city, the world. Just as particular substances are a collection of qualities, so these groups are a collection of particular substances: 'the *Idea* of such a collection of Men as make an Army, though consisting of a great number of distinct Substances, is as much one *Idea*, as the *Idea* of a Man' (2.24.1). These collective ideas of substances have the same feature of uniting in one concept a number of particulars as do the ideas of any one of the substances comprising an army, a troop, the universe.

The elimination or bypassing of the traditional concept of substance accelerated after Locke. Berkeley even rejected the scientific notion of insensible structure, favouring the notion of physical objects as combinations of qualities. Hume pronounced the concept of substance meaningless (there is no impression of sense or reflection for that idea), and challenged the notion of an immaterial soul. Hume's 'self' is not, as it has for so long been presented, just a string of perceptions: he firmly identified 'the true idea of the human mind ... as a system of different perceptions or different existences, which are link'd together by the relation of cause and effect, and mutually produce, destroy, influence, and modify each other' (*Treatise*, I, IV, VI, p. 261). Nevertheless, even recognizing the stress on a system of causally related existences, we are probably correct in hearing in Hume an echo or extension of Locke's concept of person.

T

tabula rasa This phrase, which in the Latin form does not appear in the *Essay*, is popularly used to characterize what is usually referred to as Locke's 'empiricism'. The notion of the soul as a blank or empty tablet at birth was used by Locke for two purposes: (1) as a counter to the claim for innate characters inscribed on the soul or mind, and (2) as a way of starting his account of the acquisition of ideas. It was a metaphor with a distinguished history, going as far back as Aristotle's *De Anima*. Making the point that 'mind is in a sense potentially whatever is thinkable, though actually it is nothing until it has thought', Aristotle goes on to say: 'What it thinks must be in it just as characters may be said to be on a writing-tablet on which as yet nothing actually stands written: this is exactly what happens with mind' (*De Anima*, 429b, 30–430a3). The mind, on this use of the tablet comparison, has the potentiality to receive thoughts; that is a way in which we can say it has thoughts, but not actual ones until they appear. St Thomas Aquinas referred to this passage in Aristotle, glossing it as saying the mind (the 'intellect', he says) is 'at first *like a clean tablet on which nothing is written*' (*Summa Theologica* I, Q. 79). The same metaphor is used by Gassendi (along with other anticipators of Locke), and the Cambridge Platonist, Nathanael Culverwel, uses it in opposition to his own version of innateness: he tells us that Aristotle says his '*Understanding* came *naked* into the World. He shews you an . . . *abrasa tabula*, a *Virgin soul*' (*An Elegant and Learned Discourse of the Light of Nature*, 1654, pp. 73–4). Leibniz characterized one of the differences he had with Locke on the nature of the soul: is it 'vuide entierement comme des tablettes, ou n'a encore rien écrit (*tabula rasa*) suivant Aristote et l'Auteur de Essai'? Or is the soul, as Leibniz claimed, already in possession of certain principles or notions for which external objects provide the occasion for it to become aware of them (*Nouveaux Essais*, Raspe edn., p. 4)?

The phrase *tabula rasa* appears in Locke's early *Essays on the Law of Nature* where he says that 'the newly-born are just empty tablets' ('rasae tabulae', p. 137). He also used the phrase in Draft B of the *Essay*: 'It being then probable to me that there is noe notion, idea or knowledge of any thing orig(in)aly in the soule, but that at first it is perfectly rasa tabula, quite void but altogether capable of those characters notions or ideas which are the proper objects of our understandings' (*Drafts*, ed. Nidditch and Rogers, §12, p. 128). In the *Essay* itself, he gets his programme of idea-acquisition started by saying: 'Let us then suppose the Mind to be, as we say, white Paper, void of all Characters, without any *Ideas*' (2.1.2). Another passage talks of the mind as a dark room: sensation and reflection are said to be 'the Windows by which light is let into this *dark Room*. For, methinks, the *Understanding* is not much unlike a Closet wholly shut from light, with only some little openings left, to let in external visible Resemblances, or *Ideas* of things without' (2.11.17). Another version of this metaphor is found earlier: 'The Senses at first let in particular *Ideas*, and furnish the yet empty Cabinet' (1.2.15). The newly-born, empty tablet of Draft B is slightly modified in the *Essay*: 'If we will attentively consider new born *Children*, we shall have little Reason, to think, that they bring many *Ideas* into the World with them' (1.4.2). Not many, but perhaps a few: 'some faint *Ideas*, of Hunger, and Thirst, and Warmth, and some Pains, which they may *have* felt in the Womb' (*ibid.*). These ideas (sensations) still result from experience, from stimuli in the womb, and of course, they are nothing like the specific moral or logical ideas claimed by innatists. We may need to modify the blank tablet comparison a bit, or just carry it back to the foetus. One other related comparison is made with the infant's learning. Its early days in this world are spent sleeping much of the time (2.1.22). As it gradually spends more time awake, it acquires more and more ideas. The movement from sleeping to waking is compared to learning. Locke also concluded *Some Thoughts* by saying that he considers a gentleman's son when very little as white paper or wax, to be moulded and formed (*ST*, §217).

Despite the various uses of the white tablet and associated metaphors, it is important not to let those metaphors mislead us. What Locke's use of it shows is that the mind lacks ideas and truths; no moral or logical principles are inscribed on the soul or mind prior to birth. But the tablet (the mind) is of course there; it has the potentiality to acquire ideas and knowledge. The mind also has various faculties waiting to be used and developed. There is even an innate principle of seeking pleasure and avoiding pain, and children are born with certain character traits. Moreover, while the mind is passive (as the blank tablet metaphor suggests) in its early days, it soon becomes active in many ways. These metaphors of the blank tablet, empty cabinet, dark room are not offered, nor do they reflect, the full account of the mind present in Locke's *Essay*; they have a limited role to play in the total account of the human understanding in the *Essay*.

tempers This is a term used by Locke in his *Some Thoughts concerning Education* for dispositions of the mind, what we can call 'character traits'. It was a word in use in this sense earlier in the century in treatises on education (e.g. Jean Gailhard's *The Compleat Gentleman*, 1678). It had a more general use as well. Occasionally, Locke speaks of 'the Temper both of Body and Mind' (*ST*, §63), or of the temper of the brain (*ST*, §67), but it is tempers of the mind, its constitution and inclinations, that he singles out for the attention of the tutor. He refers to the age, temper and inclination of the child (§81); he says children have all sorts of tempers (§87), 'various Tempers, different inclinations, and particular Defaults' (§217).

Some tempers are natural, others acquired. Both are important for education, the natural ones for telling the tutor how best to work with each individual; the acquired tempers are important for the developed character of the person. He speaks of 'the Child's natural Genius and Constitution' as important to be 'consider'd in a right Education', but, he warns, 'we must not hope wholly to change their Original Tempers' (§66). For example, we cannot make the 'Gay Pensive and Grave, nor the Melancholy Sportive, without spoiling them'. He even says 'God has stampt certain Characters upon Mens Minds, which, like their Shapes, may perhaps be a little mended; but can hardly be totally alter'd, and transform'd into the contrary' (§66). In a later section, he speaks of 'the natural make of his [the child's] *Mind*' inclining him to certain dispositions or tempers (§101). Writing there also of men, he says 'Some Men by the unalterable Frame of their Constitutions are *Stout*, others *Timorous*, some *Confident*, others *Modest*, *Tractable*, or *Obstinate*, or *Careless*, *Quick* or *Slow*' (*ibid.*). This list gives us some examples of tempers or traits, apparently due to natural inclinations. He remarks that what he calls here 'the peculiar *Physiognomy of the Mind* is most discernable in Children, before Art and Cunning hath taught them to hide their Deformities, and conceal their ill Inclinations under a dissembled out-side' (*ibid.*). Perhaps not all on that list are entirely due to nature, but the passage seems to suggest they are.

Other examples are given in section 102: 'Fierce or Mild, Bold or Bashful, Compassionate or Cruel, Open or Reserv'd'. Listlessness and 'sauntering' are also listed as tempers (§§123, 125). Locke urges the tutor or the parents to observe the child at play, when 'he is under least restraint', when his natural tempers can be discerned (cf. §108). He refers to tempers as '*native Propensities*, these prevalencies of Constitution'; they may be 'mended, and turned to good purposes' but 'the Byass will always hang on that side, that Nature first placed it' (§102). A later section comments that 'few of *Adam's* Children are so happy, as not to be born with some Byass in their natural Temper, which it is the Business of Education either to take off, or counter-balance' (§139). Having observed 'the Characters of his Mind' in the 'first Scenes of his Life, you will ever after be able to judge which way his Thoughts lean, and what he aims at, even hereafter, when, as he grows up, the Plot thickens, and he puts on several Shapes to act it' (§102). Other references to natural tempers can be found in sections 115, 116, 131, and 167.

The value of knowing what the child's natural tempers are is in enabling the tutor or parents to adapt their methods of raising and educating the child to that particular individual. There are times when the child is more receptive to learning, 'seasons of aptitude', which the tutor can discover by coming to know the child's natural tempers (§§74, 88). To decide how best to expose the young gentleman to the vices of the world without unduly influencing him, the tutor needs to 'judge of the Temper, Inclination and weak side of his Pupil' (§94). Pride, obstinacy and 'softness of Mind' can be corrected by a knowledge of 'the particular Temper of the Child' (§114). Even such a specific task as teaching the child a foreign language can be aided if the tutor understands the child's temper and inclination for such learning (§115). More importantly for moral education, 'As he grows up, the Tendency of his natural Inclination must be observed; which, as it inclines him, more than is convenient, on one or t'other side, from the right Path of Vertue, ought to have proper Remedies applied' (§139).

The concept of natural tempers, then, indicates that Locke recognized that children are not entirely 'blank tablets' to be formed and moulded by environment and education. Besides the various faculties of the mind, a child also has some natural character traits, tempers of mind, which will influence his subsequent development.

thinking matter   While discussing the extent and limits of human knowledge, how far our knowledge extends to 'the reality of Things' or 'the extent of Allbeing', Locke expresses confidence that 'Humane Knowledge, under the present Circumstances of our Beings and Constitutions may be carried much farther, than it hitherto has been' (*Essay*, 4.3.6). On his definition of knowledge, we are limited to the ideas we have and to our ability to perceive their relations. But even with the ideas we do have, there is much that we do not know or understand: e.g., we do not understand how physical processes can cause ideas; we do not understand the cohesion of particles; and, while we have the ideas of a square and a circle, we do not know whether there can be a square circle. Our ideas of body and mind also fall short of their real essences. He then offers another example of the limitations of knowledge. 'We have the *Ideas* of *Matter*, and

Thinking, but possibly shall never be able to know, whether any mere material Being thinks, or no; it being impossible for us, by the contemplation of our own *Ideas*, without revelation, to discover, whether Omnipotency has not given to some Systems of Matter fitly disposed, a power to perceive and think, or else joined and fixed to Matter so disposed, a thinking immaterial Substance' (4.3.6).

The suggested option is that God could add to matter either a power to perceive and think or another substance, a thinking, immaterial substance. The operation of 'adding' or, as he usually says, 'superadding' apparently would not change the nature of the matter to which thought or a thinking immaterial substance was added. Most writers at that time would have said such addition *would* alter the nature of matter, causing it to cease to be matter. These writers were wedded to the ontology of two substances whose essential properties could not cross over one to the other. Thus, thought could not be added or superadded to matter, since thought and extension (the essences of mind and matter) are incompatible. Apparently, not even God could, for these writers, add thought to matter without changing the nature of matter. Locke considers this claim unwarranted and a detraction from God's power. We simply do not know 'wherein Thinking consists, nor to what sort of Substances the Almighty has been pleased to give that Power' (*ibid.*).

Edward Stillingfleet, the Bishop of Worcester, was one of those writers who found Locke's suggestion of God being able to superadd thought to matter objectionable and threatening. It sounded to him like materialism. At the very least, Stillingfleet insisted, this suggested possibility would confuse or confound the ideas of matter and spirit. Locke patiently explained that these two ideas are no more confused by that possibility than they are in the idea of a horse. To say that 'matter in general is a solid extended substance; and that a horse is a material animal, or an extended solid substance with sense and spontaneous motion' is not to make the matter of the horse any the less material (*Mr. Locke's Second Reply*, in *Works*, iv. 460). Locke draws a distinction between matter and body: the latter has more properties than the former. A plant or animal is a combination of matter and biological or life processes. With animals, the matter of the body has other properties added to it, such as sense, perception, and the ability to move. The power of propagation in plants and animals is another added property. Gravity is the result of forces and powers added to the material universe. Locke had said in the *Essay* that wherever thought is located, in whatever substance it is found, it is there by 'the good pleasure and Bounty of the Creator' (4.3.6). In his reply to Stillingfleet, he points out the consequences if God had not added sense and spontaneous motion to animals: they would become animal machines, as Descartes had argued (in *Works*, iv. 463).

It could be said that these remarks by Locke beg the question of interaction between mind and body, since he assumes that sense and perception are added to the material body. Thus, to suggest that thought might also be added to some bit of matter (the brain) is no different. The relation of 'added to' may be unclear. At the very best, it means 'is a property of the animal', if an animal or a man is viewed (as some writers did) as a combination of two substances, each with its own essential property; then we run into the problem faced by Descartes, Malebranche and Leibniz of accounting for the total behaviour of those organisms. The creation-scenario for these traditionalists has God creating two different substances. Malebranche and Leibniz kept these two substances with their different properties in parallel relations; what happens in extension corresponds with what happens in thought, but without interaction. Descartes recognized that with humans, these two substances formed a new unit, constituting one whole, working together and interacting. He did not have metaphysical categories for this unified, integrated whole of mind and body, but it was a reality he freely admitted exists.

What we find in Locke is a further erosion of the standard two-SUBSTANCE ontology (*see* SUBSTANCE). Substance itself becomes less important; the different properties of extension, solidity, motion, sensing, perceiving, thinking, willing and the various powers of body and mind become prominent. Without a strong commitment to the two-substance ontology, Locke is free to examine with an open mind what we in fact know in our own case, and what we suppose is true of some animals, namely, that they are organized biological matter with specific mental properties. The question raised by Locke's suggestion about God adding thought to some matter is 'is the two-substance ontology adequate for understanding ourselves, even our world?' Locke still preserves the difference of properties; there is no suggestion that thought might be only brain processes. Even were God to dispense with immaterial substance and make thought a property of the brain, that would not turn thought into a physical property of the brain. Locke differed sharply with those who said that making thought a property of the brain would change the brain into a non-material substance. For Locke there is a fundamental difference between 'being part of the nature of' and 'being a property of'. The latter need not affect the former.

The previous remarks catch what seems to be implicit in Locke's suggestion about God adding thought to matter. His response to Stillingfleet was more direct. He tried to work with the two substances accepted by Stillingfleet, showing him how God might have proceeded in the act of creation. First, God creates 'a solid extended substance' (*Mr. Locke's Second Reply*, in *Works*, iv. 464). Locke asks: 'is God bound to give it, besides being, a power of action?' He thinks God has a choice: 'He

therefore may leave it in a state of inactivity, and it will be nevertheless
a substance; for action is not necessary to the being of any substance, that
God does create.' Locke then tries to have God create another kind of
substance, an immaterial substance. What are the characteristics of this
second substance? We can infer that it is not solid or extended, but does
it have any positive properties besides existence? Locke describes it as
having 'bare being'. His point is that this second substance, on the
creation-scenario he is developing, has not been given any kind of active
powers either; both substances are inactive. The next stage in his scenario
is to ask 'is there some property which God can give to one of these two
substances but not to the other?' God can 'put an end to any action of
any created substance, without annihilating' that substance. Similarly, he
can give 'existence to such a substance, without giving that substance any
action at all'. Locke sees no reason preventing God from giving the same
power to either of these two substances. 'Let it be, for example, that of
spontaneous or self-motion, which is a power that it is supposed God can
give to an unsolid substance, but denied that he can give to a solid
substance' (*ibid.*, p. 464). Locke's suggestion is that there is 'no reason to
deny Omnipotency to be able to give a power of self-motion to a material
substance, if he pleases, as well as to an immaterial; since neither of them
can have it from themselves' (*ibid.*, p. 465).

Appeals to what we can or cannot conceive, which Stillingfleet and
others called for, are irrelevant to the issue. There are features of matter,
such as gravitation, which are just as difficult for us to understand or
conceive as how any substance thinks. Our understandings can hardly be
a measure of what God can do. So Locke then moves from self-motion,
which he thinks God could attach either to the solid, extended and
inactive substance or to the unsolid, unextended and inactive substance.
God could add thought to either, but 'it is equally beyond our capacity
to conceive how either of these substances thinks.' Locke agrees that God
cannot make 'a substance to be solid and not solid at the same time', but
'that a solid substance may not have qualities, perfections, and powers,
which have no natural or visibly necessary connexion with solidity and
extension, is too much for us (who are but of yesterday, and know
nothing) to be positive in.'

These remarks and the *Essay*'s suggestion about thought and matter
resulted in a long debate in Britain through the eighteenth century. That
controversy also migrated to Europe, where Locke's suggestion and his
replies to Stillingfleet were frequently cited. For the details, see Yolton,
Thinking Matter (1984) and *Locke and French Materialism* (1991).

thoughts   This is a term that may seem innocent and in no need of definition or explication, but when its use in the *Essay* is examined, it turns out to be another term in the developing language of mind. It goes along with other mental terms such as 'notion', 'conception', 'idea' and 'impression'. In many passages, 'thoughts' is an alternative to 'ideas'; in others it is employed with words and discussion of communication; in still other passages, the mind is said to act on or with its thoughts.

The 'Epistle to the Reader' speaks of setting one's '*Thoughts on work, to find and follow Truth*', or of letting '*loose their own Thoughts, and follow them in writing*' (*Essay*, p. 6), of using '*thy own Thoughts in reading*' (p. 7). Locke reports that while discussing with his friends, '*it came into my Thoughts, that we took a wrong course.*' He confesses that he has not written his *Essay* for '*the Information of Men of large Thoughts and quick Apprehensions*', and he explains modestly that what the reader will find in this work is what has been '*spun out of my own course Thoughts*' (p. 8). In explaining a change in terminology introduced into the fourth edition, changing 'clear and distinct' to 'determined and determinate' ideas, he says that the latter are '*more likely to direct Men's thoughts to my meaning*' (p. 13).

Passages in Book One speak of directing our thoughts, setting them to work (1.1.6), and he warns of the difficulties in letting our thoughts loose 'into the vast Ocean of *Being*' (1.1.7; cf. 2.15.9). He also speaks of following and applying our thoughts, of the labour of our thoughts, and of principles on which our thoughts rest (1.2.1, 8, 10; 1.3.24). He refers to the employment of thoughts 'to enquire into the Constitution and Causes of things' (1.4.11), to thoughts enlarging themselves as we become acquainted with more sensible things (1.4.13). Many Book Two passages speak of turning thoughts to the operations of the mind, of examining one's thoughts as one searches the understanding, of the memory of thoughts, and simply of having thoughts (2.1.5, 7, 15, 17; cf. 2.21.30). He also rejects unconscious thoughts (1.2.10). Other locutions have us extending our thoughts beyond matter (2.7.10), abstracting thoughts (2.13.27; cf. 2.15.8), fixing our thoughts on some object and reflecting on the number and succession of thoughts (2.14.4, 5). Sometimes he writes of the progression of thoughts, remarking that our thoughts 'can never arrive at the utmost *Divisibility*' of matter (2.17.12).

Such expressions are found throughout the other books of the *Essay*. There are also places where thoughts and ideas (occasionally, notions) are linked. For example, Book Four ends by asserting that 'the Scene of *Ideas* that makes one Man's Thoughts, cannot be laid open to the immediate view of another' (4.21.4). When discussing the reality of knowledge, he urges us not to confine '*our Thoughts* and abstract *Ideas* to Names' (4.4.13). Ideas of substances 'must not consist of *Ideas* put together at the pleasure of our Thoughts, without any real pattern they were taken from' (4.4.12). That same book opened by affirming that 'our Knowledge is only conversant about' ideas, 'since *the Mind* in all its Thoughts and Reasonings, hath no other immediate Object' (4.1.1). If we are to 'think well, it is not enough, that a Man has *Ideas* clear and distinct in his Thoughts ... he must think in train, and observe the dependence of his Thoughts and Reasonings, one upon another' (3.7.2). Confusion in ideas can result in disorders in 'Men's Thoughts and Discourses' (2.29.12). Discussing relations, Locke gives an example: 'when a man says, Honey is sweeter than Wax, it is plain, that his Thoughts in this Relation, terminate in this simple *Idea*, Sweetness' (2.28.18). Contrasting ideas of mixed modes with those of substances, he suggests using the term 'notion' in order to indicate that these ideas 'had their Original, and constant Existence, more in the Thoughts of Men, than in the reality of things' (2.22.2). In the chapter on duration, he writes of reflecting on the train of ideas which come 'constantly of themselves into our waking Thoughts' (2.14.27).

Words, names especially, are also associated in his text with thoughts. Some complex tastes and smells lack names and hence 'are less taken notice of, and cannot be set down in writing; and therefore must be left without enumeration, to the Thoughts and Experiences of my Reader' (2.18.5). Giving names to complex ideas is 'a very short and expedite way of conveying their Thoughts one to another' (2.18.7). Elsewhere, he refers to the 'Communication of Thoughts' by means of 'external sensible Signs, whereby those invisible *Ideas*, which his thoughts are made up of' are signified (3.2.1). That same section has words being the signs of ideas (his usual way of speaking), but the very next section says words are used to record thoughts. Section 4 returns to words as signifying ideas, but men are said 'in their Thoughts [to] give them a secret reference to' ideas in other men's minds and to things (3.2.4). Words are also said to 'express to one another those Thoughts and Imaginations' men have (3.2.6). The names of mixed modes '*lead our Thoughts to the Mind*' (3.5.12).

The more frequent locution involving ideas is to locate them *in* the mind, but several passages place thoughts in the mind. For example: 'any retired thought of our Mind' (2.7.2), 'the Mind has great power in varying and multiplying the Objects of its Thoughts' (2.12.2), although the next section uses the more general, 'thoughts of man' (cf.2.21.12: 'Thoughts of our Minds' or the power the mind has over its thoughts). A number of passages cite specific thoughts: of infinity (2.17.1), of space (2.15.4), of extension (2.15.2), of duration (2.14.24–8), of mad men (2.11.13), of children (1.4.3).

These samples from Locke's use of the term 'thoughts' indicate the need he felt for another word for describing and talking about the mind, its contents and operations. The terminology of ideas which struck his contemporaries as new and radical was only part of the language of mind employed in the *Essay* (*see also* CONCEPTION; NOTION).

time 'To understand *Time* and *Eternity* aright, we ought with attention to consider what *Idea* it is we have of *Duration*, and how we came by it' (*Essay*, 2.14.3). Time is, as this chapter title indicates, one of the modes of duration. Locke presents duration as 'another sort of Distance, or Length, the *Idea* whereof we get not from the permanent parts of Space, but from the fleeting and perpetually perishing parts of Succession' (2.14.1). He refers to St Augustine's puzzlement about time, but he thinks he can show how we acquire a clear and distinct idea of it from his two sources, sensation and reflection (2.14.2). The source of the idea of duration begins with our being aware of 'a train of *Ideas*' passing in our mind. By reflecting on the successive appearances of ideas in our mind, we acquire the idea of succession (2.14.3). He then applies the notion of distance to the succession of ideas, 'the distance between any parts [ideas] of that Succession'. The result is the idea of duration defined in terms of succession and the interval between the parts of the members of that successive train of ideas or (as he sometimes writes) thoughts.

Once we have acquired the idea of duration in this way, we can apply it to things which exist while we are not aware of any flow of ideas. We can think of the world existing while we slept last night (2.14.5). Since we have experienced the revolutions of days and nights, we can think of the world existing during the interval when we were not aware of it. That prior experience is necessary for such an extension of duration; otherwise we would have no basis for predicating duration of the world while we are unaware of it. Locke suggests that had Adam and Eve slept the first twenty-four hours after their creation, 'the Duration of that 24 hours had been irrevocably lost to them, and been for ever left out of their Account of time' (*ibid.*). We can also multiply lengths of duration to form ideas of hours, days, months. We can even extend it 'beyond the existence of all corporeal Beings, and all the measures of Time, taken from the great Bodies of the World, and their Motions' (2.15.3). We cannot, however, extend duration beyond all being because God fills all eternity. Eternity, it seems, is duration without end, perhaps without parts or intervals.

Locke raises the possibility, urged by some writers, that the idea of duration might be acquired from 'our Observation of Motion by our Senses', but he points out that the motion of objects produces a train of ideas in our mind (2.14.6). Without the train of ideas, we could not acquire the idea of duration. We can obtain the idea of succession even when no observable motion is available, as when becalmed at sea; our thoughts still succeed each other though nothing may appear to move around us. He also remarks that there are motions that are outside our range of awareness, motions too slow or too fast to be perceived. Thus, the train of ideas is the more fundamental source for the idea of succession and duration. There is also a suggestion that the train of ideas is more regular than some observable motions. He compares the succession of ideas in the mind to the regular appearances of images on a lantern lighted and turned by the heat of a candle (2.14.9).

Because of the '*constant and regular Succession of Ideas* in a waking Man', that succession is 'as it were, *the Measure* and Standard *of all other Successions*' (2.14.12). It is the measure in terms of the regular succession of ideas, 'the Consideration of Duration, as set out by certain Periods', that is what is called 'time' (2.14.17). But there is a difficulty: unlike measuring extension where we can apply the standard measure to the object we want to measure, 'in the measuring of Duration, this cannot be done, because no two different parts of Succession can be put together to measure one another' (2.14.18). We do not have a standard measure of duration apart from the experience of a constant fleeting succession of ideas (*ibid.*). This fact has led people to take the motion of the sun as a standard for duration, a standard outside the succession of ideas. The result has been a tendency to confuse time with motion (2.14.19). Motion is only relevant to measuring duration to the extent that it 'brings about the return of certain sensible *Ideas*' (2.14.22). We can also apply duration in our thoughts to events prior to the regular motions of the sun, e.g., 'beyond the Duration of Bodies or Motion', as we can apply the measure of a mile 'to Space beyond the utmost Bodies' (2.14.25). Duration without motion, space without body: that is the parallel Locke draws.

The independence of duration (at least, our concept of it) from motion is given another illustration: 'I can imagine that Light existed three days before the Sun was, or had any motion, barely by thinking' (2.14.30). Similarly, 'I can have an Idea of the *Chaos*, or Angels, being created before there was either Light, or any continued motion, a Minute, an Hour, a Day, a Year, or 1000 Years' (*ibid.*). Locke distinguishes between 'Duration it self, and the measures we make use of to judge of its length' (2.14.21). Duration 'goes on in one constant, equal, uniform Course'. He has various descriptive phrases for it and space: 'those Boundless Oceans of Eternity and Immensity', the 'infinite Oceans of Duration and Space'; both are described as 'uniform and boundless' (2.15.5). Time and place are portions of duration and space, they are 'determinate distinguishable Portions of those infinite Abysses of Space and Duration' (2.15.6). In a strict sense, time is only applied to events that begin and end within our sensible world, but in a broader sense it 'is applied to Parts of that infinite Duration' (2.15.7). Both space and duration have parts: 'Every part of Duration is Duration too; and every part of Extension [i.e., the extension of space, expansion] is Extension, both of them capable of addition or division *in infinitum*' (2.15.9). He goes on to talk of the smallest part of either space or time which we can discern and from which we form a clear and distinct idea.

Duration is also described as '*the length of one straight Line*', whereas space forms three-dimensional figures (2.15.11). That straight time-line is 'one common measure of all Existence'. Time is part of duration; our idea of time is of '*perishing distance, of which no two parts exist together*' (2.15.12). In contrast, expansion (space) is '*lasting distance, all whose parts exist together*'. The relation between space and duration is not just that both are characterized in terms of length and distance: 'Expansion and Duration do mutually imbrace, and comprehend each other; every part of Space, being in every part of Duration; and every part of Duration in every part of Expansion' (*ibid.*). Is this a concept of space-time? There is one other passage that links them together. While giving examples of modes of motion, such as slide, roll, tumble, walk, creep, run, dance, leap, skip, he says that these modes 'answer those of Extension' (2.18.2). The term 'extension' here is clearly referring to space; he has told us earlier that space is extended, suggesting the word 'expansion' for it as a way of distinguishing it from the extension of body. He continues in this passage: '*Swift* and *Slow* are two different *Ideas* of Motion, the measures whereof are made of the distance of Time and Space put together, so they are complex *Ideas* comprehending Time and Space with Motion.'

The subsequent discussion of space and time, by writers such as Berkeley, Hume, Leibniz in debate with the Newtonian Samuel Clarke, tended to concentrate on the question of absolute versus relative concepts of both. Locke's view belongs with the absolute side of this debate, but not in the sense of time or space being a substance. What he queried about space – why it must fit the traditional category of substance and mode – can be raised for time. Nevertheless, we can say he is with the Newtonians in holding space and duration to exist whether they are filled or not. No one seems to have picked up on his suggestion that space and time 'imbrace' each other. Curiously, in his extended commentary on Locke, Leibniz (*Nouveaux Essais*) has little to say about Locke's account of time or duration, but in his exchange with Clarke, he gave much attention to the topic. Chambers, in his *Cyclopaedia* (1728), gives some attention to Locke and also traces some of the previous history of the notion of time. Later in the eighteenth century, Kant gave much attention to space and time as concepts which we bring to the experience of phenomena. Kant's discussion clearly eclipsed that of Locke on these two concepts.

toleration   *see* LETTERS ON TOLERATION

truth   Locke defines truth as *'the joining or separating of Signs, as the Things signified by them, do agree or disagree one with another'* (*Essay*, 4.5.2). He explains that the signs referred to are components of propositions. Thus, strictly, truth belongs to propositions. There are two kinds of proposition, mental and verbal. The former consists of ideas related in certain ways, the latter is composed of words. The best way to analyse the concept of truth would be to separate truths of thought from truths of words, but this is very difficult to do, since we can hardly deal with mental propositions without using words. Were we able to make the separation, a mental proposition would be 'nothing but a bare consideration of the *Ideas*, as they are in our Minds stripp'd of Names' (4.5.3). Most of us, perhaps all of us, 'make use of Words instead of *Ideas*', especially when dealing with complex ideas (4.5.4). It may be the case that in thinking or reasoning about simple ideas and their propositions (e.g., propositions about white, sweet, bitter) 'we can and often do frame in our Minds the *Ideas* themselves, without reflecting on the Names' (*ibid.*). But with propositions involving complex ideas (e.g., a man, vitriol, fortitude), we usually put the name for the idea. Still, Locke preserves the distinction between mental and verbal propositions, characterizing the mental as putting together or separating ideas without the use of words: 'When *Ideas* are so put together, or separated in the Mind, as they, or the Things they stand for do agree, or not' (4.5.6). Verbal truth, the truth of words, is characterized as 'the affirming or denying of Words one of another, as the *Ideas* they stand for agree or disagree' (*ibid.*).

Locke recognized that a question about the reality of truth can be raised, a question similar to the one he briefly discussed about his definition of knowledge in terms of the relation of ideas: is it real or merely verbal, just a matter of expressing 'the *Chimæras* of Men's Brains', a visionary world in our imagination? His answer is that a merely verbal or 'barely nominal' truth would be a proposition where the ideas the words stand for lack 'an agreement with the reality of Things' (4.5.8). He thinks he has answered the sceptic earlier about knowledge (*see* SCEPTICISM; *see also* PROPOSITIONS).

There are different sorts of truths, particular and general (4.6.2). General truths are of kinds or classes, so they require a knowledge of species. In substances, knowledge and truth refer only to the nominal essence, to the classes we make for our purposes by identifying coexisting qualities (4.6.4, 5; *see* SORTS, SORTALS). Even limiting our truth-claims to observable coexisting qualities for things, we cannot be certain of anything other than that our propositions do correctly report the coexisting qualities. If certainty requires necessity, we do not have that kind of certainty in science or everyday experience (4.6.6; cf. 4.6.7–11).

Locke also mentions moral truths, meaning not truths about morality but opinions, 'speaking Things according to the perswasion of our own Minds, though the Proposition we speak agree not to the reality of Things' (4.5.11). Another type of truth is 'metaphysical', 'which is nothing but the real Existence of Things, conformable to the *Ideas* to which we have annexed their names' (*ibid.*). Metaphysical truth is not propositional, it is simply a way of referring to what exists. He suggests that this kind of truth involves a tacit proposition 'whereby the Mind joins that particular Thing, to the *Idea* it had before settled with a name to it' (*ibid.*). Chambers, in his *Cyclopaedia* (1728), reports that this kind of truth was sometimes called 'transcendental truth'; he gives an example of a clock: it may be said to be true 'when it answers the Idea or intention of the Person who made it' (see his entry for 'Truth').

Truth was important for Locke. He praised the pursuit of it; he contrasted that pursuit with living '*on scraps of begg'd Opinions*' of others: '*every moment of his Pursuit, will reward his Pains with some Delight*' (*Essay*, 'Epistle to the Reader', p. 6). He tells the reader that '*there is nothing in this Treatise of the Truth whereof I am not fully persuaded*' (p. 7). He also says 'Justice and Truth are the common ties of Society' (1.3.2). His work on education stressed the importance for children to tell the truth (*ST*, §§37, 139, 150; cf. *Essays*, p. 129). Parents and tutor are urged to be truthful in talking with children (*ST*, §120).

The topic of truth is not given special attention by subsequent writers, although some do talk of truth in the course of discussing other concepts. Hume echoes several of Locke's descriptions of truth, Chambers cites several passages from the *Essay*, Berkeley has very little mention of the concept. Theories of truth, e.g., coherence, correspondence, pragmatic, came into vogue much later.

Two Tracts on Government   The publication with this title consists of two early writings by Locke on toleration, the authority of the civil magistrate in relation to religious practices, the nature of society and its laws. Philip Abrams edited these tracts in 1967, publishing them with a long introduction and notes. One of these tracts was in Latin. Abrams prints the Latin text along with an English translation. The other tract was written in English and seems to have been intended for publication. Locke later changed his mind and did not publish it. That English tract

was written in 1660; it carried the title: 'Question: whether the civil
Magistrate may lawfully impose and determine the use of indifferent
things in reference to Religious Worship'. It was written as a reply to
Edward Bagshaw's *The Great Question Concerning Things Indifferent in Religious Worship* (1660). The Latin tract carries the title: 'An Magistratus
civilis possit res adiaphoras in divini cultus ritus asciscere, eosque populo
imponere?' That tract was written in 1660–1; Abrams reminds us that
those were close to the years in which Locke's essays on the law of nature
were being written and delivered as lectures at Oxford. Both of Locke's
tracts deal with issues raised by Bagshaw. Abrams provides us with the
sequence of writings by Bagshaw and Locke on this topic: 'Bagshaw's
Great Question, published 15 September 1660; Locke's English *Tract*,
finished by 11 December 1660; Bagshaw's *Second Part of the Great Question*,
published in September 1661; Locke's Latin *Tract*; and Bagshaw's *Third
Part*, published January 1662' (*Two Tracts on Government*, Cambridge
University Press, 1967, p. 17)

The mood of Locke while writing the first tract reflects the social unrest
prior to the restoration of Charles II to the English throne; it also
indicates his belief that the return of the legitimate king will bring peace
and social order. Early in that tract, Locke remarks: 'As for myself, there
is no one can have a greater respect and veneration for authority than I.
I no sooner perceived myself in the *world* but I found myself in a storm,
which hath lasted almost hitherto, and therefore cannot but entertain the
approaches of a calm with the greatest joy and satisfaction' (p. 119). The
tensions between oppression and disorder, between tyranny and anarchy,
were very real in Locke's mind; the 'smartest scourges can fall upon
mankind' is his description of them. Authority goes with the first of these,
liberty with the second. He was not defending oppression or tyranny, but
equally he was frightened of disorder and anarchy. The relief he believed
the restoration of Charles II would bring led him to give strong support
to that kind of ordered authority. The tone of this tract clashes rather
sharply with his later defence of toleration in his 1689 *Epistola de Tolerantia*,
or even with a manuscript draft of a 1667 essay on toleration to which
Abrams refers. Locke speaks of the 'submission I have for *authority*', along
with the 'love of *liberty* without which a *man* shall find himself less happy
than a *beast*' (p. 120). But he warns that 'a *general freedom* is but *a general
bondage*', commenting that those who claim they are defenders of public
liberty 'are the greatest engrossers of it', hogging it for themselves (*ibid.*).
He worries that the specific liberty Bagshaw defended 'would prove only
a *liberty* for *contention, censure* and *persecution* and turn us loose to the *tyranny*
of a *religious rage*' (*ibid.*).

The reference to Bagshaw's 'liberty of indifferent things' identifies the particular object of Locke's attack. It was a question about the authority of the civil magistrate over matters of dress and ceremonies in church. A more precise explanation of what indifferent things are is given in the second tract: 'Now things are said to be indifferent in respect of moral good and evil, so that all things which are morally neither good nor evil are called indifferent' (p. 221). Since good and evil, or moral actions, 'imply a law as a standard', Locke finds it necessary to give an account of different sorts of laws, chiefly divine and human, the latter of various kinds and falling into an order of importance. Divine law does not cover all the details of life and action, details that are 'indifferent' from God's point of view. But these matters have been handed by God to 'his deputy the magistrate' (p. 223). So indifferent matters are controlled by the magistrate for 'the wise regulation of . . . the welfare of the commonwealth' (*ibid.*). In this tract, 'indifferent things' cover whatever is not included in the higher law (God's law), but then it belongs to a lower law. 'For where the divine law sets bounds to its action, there the authority of the magistrate begins, and whatever is classed as indeterminate and indifferent under that law is subordinate to the civil power' (p. 227).

The issue was, are there areas where no law, no authority, supervenes between individuals and society, especially areas that fall outside civil laws? Bagshaw and others argued that matters of worship escape the bounds of the civil magistrate, especially matters of style, place and time of worship, and dress. Locke argues in both tracts against this view, insisting that matters 'regarding divine worship, must be subjected to governmental power' (p. 229). His defence of this position in the second, Latin tract is more formal and systematic than in the first, English tract, but in both Locke is a strong (ardent, even) defender of law and order, opposed to freedom and toleration in even such matters as what to wear in church. There had been much debate and turmoil within his college, Christ Church, itself on religious practices; Locke and Bagshaw were both members of that college. Locke opposes those who use appeals to liberty 'to pull down well-framed constitutions, that out of its *ruins* they may build themselves fortunes' (p. 121). Similarly, he rejects the notion of those who would be 'Christians so as not to be Subjects', or those who 'like to engage us in perpetual dissension and disorder'. He announces in firm tones that 'All the *freedom* I can wish my country or myself is to enjoy the *protection* of those *laws* which the prudence and providence of our ancestors established and the happy return of his Majesty hath restored' (*ibid.*).

Whether it is said that 'the magistrate's crown drops down on his head immediately from *heaven* or be placed there by the *hands of his subjects*', Locke proclaims that 'the supreme magistrate of every nation what way soever created, must necessarily have an *absolute* and *arbitrary power* over all the indifferent actions of his people' (pp. 122–3). A few paragraphs later, he reaffirms this point: 'it is impossible there should be any supreme legislative power which hath not the full and unlimited disposure of all indifferent things' (p. 129). He even goes further: 'subjects may be obliged to obey those laws which it may be sinful for the magistrate to enact' (p. 152). The magistrate is to govern 'for the common good and the general welfare' of all (p. 219), but should he fail to do so, there is no appeal against his sinful legislation (p. 220). Perhaps the most striking contrast with the 'liberal' Locke of *Two Treatises* and the various letters on toleration is his claim that magistrates are invested with power and are 'by their power, superior to the laws themselves and to the subjects they govern' (p. 222).

It is not too difficult to hear the voice of Hobbes in some of these statements. Filmer's defence of monarchy descending from God is also not far off in many passages. That Locke did not publish either of these tracts may indicate a change of values and attitudes, but these views are nevertheless ones he held and placed in writing. Some of these early views were softened in later writings, others were abandoned altogether. The difference of situation and context between the 1660s in England and the 1680s in Holland (where he wrote his *Epistola*) is also a factor in under-standing the strong defence of authority (even where it goes against the well-being of the subjects) in 1660 and the ringing support for religious toleration in the late 1680s.

Two Treatises of Government   This work by Locke, especially the second of the two treatises, has undoubtedly been the most popular, most widely known and used of his many books. Only the *Essay concerning Human Understanding* could vie with it for prominence, but *Two Treatises* has outstripped the *Essay* in the intensity with which it has been studied and probably in its influence on liberal political theory. This work was probably written in the early 1680s; Peter Laslett argues for a date between 1679 and 1683, thus disposing of the long-held view that Locke wrote the book to justify the 1688 'glorious revolution' when William and Mary came to the English throne. (See Laslett's introduction to his edition of *Two Treatises*, pp. 49–53.) There has been much discussion of Laslett's dating of this work. Gradually, scholars have come around to his view, or at least to the view that much, if not all, of *Two Treatises* was written close to the date Laslett suggested.

This work had many printings in Britain during Locke's lifetime and in the following century. By the beginning of the nineteenth century, there had been about two dozen editions and reprintings, sometimes only of the second treatise on civil government. There were French translations of the second treatise from 1690, Italian translations from the end of the eighteenth century, and later translations into Spanish, German, Swedish, Norwegian and Russian. Translations of the whole work have only appeared recently: in Czech (in 1965), in German (in 1906, 1966 and 1967), in Italian (1948 and 1960), and Spanish (1966). It is a work constantly read and studied today in many countries.

Most of the focus has been on the second treatise. The first is a long polemic against Robert Filmer's *Patriarcha, or The Natural Power of Kings* (1680). In that work, Filmer argued for a monarchial form of government based on the descent from Adam via God. The father of the family was in effect the ruler of that group. The king of a country played a similar role. Filmer used various arguments from the Bible to support his argument. Locke countered with detailed readings of the Scriptures, showing that Filmer read into them rather than finding justification for his views in that book. There are many features of the first treatise which are picked up and elaborated in the second; for example, Locke's insistence on parental, not fatherly, power in the family; some references to the concepts of person and property, and also to the doctrine of laws of nature.

Locke opens the second treatise with a quick summary of what he has argued in the first: '1°. That *Adam* had not either by natural Right of Fatherhood, or by positive Donation from God, any such Authority over his Children, or Dominion over the World as is pretended. 2°. That if he had, his Heirs, yet, had no Right to it. 3°. That if his Heirs had, there being no Law of Nature nor positive Law of God that determines, which is the Right Heir in all Cases that may arise, the Right of Succession, and consequently of bearing Rule, could not have been certainly determined. 4°. That if even that had been determined, yet the knowledge of which is the Eldest Line of *Adam's* Posterity, being so long since utterly lost, that in the Races of Mankind and Families of the World, there remains not to one above another, the least pretence to be the Eldest House, and to have the Right of Inheritance' (*T2*, §1)

There was another view of government cited by Locke in this section, that it is the 'product only of Force and Violence, and that Men live together by no other Rules but that of Beasts, where the strongest carries it, and so lay a Foundation for perpetual Disorder and Mischief, Tumult, Sedition and Rebellion' (the view of Hobbes).

A third view is the one put forward in the second treatise. What he presents there is an account that starts with all men having certain powers and obligations in a pre-civil society, a society within which the laws of nature (God's laws) function, from which people move by consent and contract to a civil society, placing some of the power and rights all had in the state of nature in the hands of an appointed official or a group whose task it is to govern for the good of all the members, protecting their life, property, possessions and persons. There is a strong element of individualism in this account, but Locke also stressed the power of the community and the importance of majority rule.

It is the second treatise which is best-known and read. Its title was *An Essay concerning the True Original, Extent, and End of Civil Government*. Many of its chapters have become classics in the literature of liberal views. His account of the state of nature, of property, of political or civil society (its ends, structure, operation), of representation, of dissent have for long defined much of the discussion of political theory and its history.

U

understanding The subject of Locke's *Essay* was the understanding, human understanding, which he characterized as '*the most elevated Faculty of the Soul*', a faculty that '*searches after Truth*' ('Epistle to the Reader', p. 6; cf. 2.21.6). The objective of that work was '*to examine our own Abilities, and see, what Objects our Understandings were, or were not fitted to deal with*' (p. 7). If the understanding is in fact one of the faculties in Locke's account, it is not of the same order as the faculties of sensation, reasoning, or memory. As a faculty, it is pre-eminent; it 'sets Man above the rest of sensible Beings, and gives him all the Advantage and Dominion, which he has over them' (1.1.1; cf. *Elements of Natural Philosophy*, in *Works*, iii. 329). The *Conduct of the Understanding* refers to the different faculties (there, they are said to be faculties of the mind) and says that the 'supreme command belongs to the will' with respect to man as an agent, but he affirms in that passage what he modified in the second edition of the *Essay*, that man determines himself to voluntary action 'upon some precedent knowledge or appearance of knowledge, in the understanding' (*Conduct*, §1; in *Works*, iii. 205; cf. *Essay*, 2.21.6).

He thinks a survey of the understanding, with the aim of setting the boundaries of knowledge by discovering its powers, will be a useful enterprise (1.1.7). At one point, he identifies the 'chief end of all our Thoughts, and the proper business of all Understandings' to be the 'knowledge and veneration' of God (2.7.6), but there are lesser goals too, goals such as truth, belief, judgement, perception: all the topics of the *Essay*. The limits of the understanding in these matters are frequently drawn (e.g., 2.15.2). The understanding is said to judge objects and to search after truth; it considers things and is able to 'carry any *Idea*, as it were, beyond it self, or, at least, look beyond it, to see how it stands in conformity to any other' (2.25.1); 'Custom settles habits of Thinking in the Understanding' which account in part for the association of ideas (2.33.6).

Some of the operations of the understanding, such as considering and enlarging ideas, are more often credited to the mind. The mind is also usually the locus of ideas, but a number of passages speak of ideas in the understanding. One of the sections in the chapter on memory gives the mind the power to revive ideas, and ideas are said to be in the mind, but in that same section, ideas are also spoken of as in the understanding (2.10.2). A similar switch occurs with the analysis of the succession of ideas: sometimes they 'pass in the mind', other times the 'train of *Ideas* ... take their turns in our Understandings' (2.14.4; cf. 2.19.3). In his discussion of mixed modes, he speaks of the mind putting the parts of these ideas together, but those ideas are said to be 'consistent in the Understanding' (2.22.2). Very early in Book Two, the understanding is said 'not to have the least glimmering of any *Ideas*, which it doth not receive from' external sensation or internal reflection. It is the mind which furnishes the understanding with the idea of the mind's operations (2.1.5). The previous section had experience furnishing the understanding with this second kind of ideas. The apology for his frequent use of the term 'idea' explains that it is a term which he uses to 'stand for whatsoever is the Object of the Understanding when a Man thinks' (1.1.8). It was not one of the aims of this work to discover whether ideas are caused by physical and physiological processes, but he again locates ideas in the understanding (1.1.2). Another passage has simple ideas appear to the *mind* which the *understanding* cannot refuse (2.1.25). Still another section seems to have some ideas being offered to the understanding directly, without the action of the mind: 'some *Ideas* forwardly offer themselves to all Men's Understandings', although this section says this happens 'as soon as the mind puts them [the ideas] into Propositions' (1.4.22).

The precise relation between the understanding and the mind in Locke's analysis is not clear. His *Essay* is on the understanding, not the mind – at least, if we take the title of that book as our guide. But references to and uses of the mind far outnumber those of the understanding. Often, the two seem to be interchangeable. The understanding does play a faculty role when it considers and enlarges, but often it is the mind that performs these and other operations. The *Conduct* was another extended bit of writing about the understanding: it is not directed to the conduct of the mind. On the other hand, his work on education, *Some Thoughts*, makes extensive use of the mind, not the understanding. The best we can conclude is that the understanding in Locke's account is more than just one of the faculties of the mind; even as a faculty, it plays a special role in the search for truth and knowledge. Locke also sometimes viewed it as pre-eminent in action, in determining the will, but on this point he was troubled and, in the end, drew back from such a strong cognitivism (*see also* UNEASINESS; MIND).

uneasiness The motive to change our state or condition is 'some *uneasiness*' we feel. Uneasiness is 'the great motive that works on the Mind to put it upon Action' (*Essay*, 2.21.29). It is this feeling that Locke identifies as 'the *determinating of the Will*'. Uneasiness is closely linked with desire: 'The uneasiness a Man finds in himself upon the absence of any thing, whose present enjoyment carries the *Idea* of Delight with it, is that we call *Desire*, which is greater or less, as that uneasiness is more or less vehement' (2.20.6). He goes on to say that the 'chief if not only spur to humane Industry and Action is uneasiness'. If we are easy and content without having some particular object or state, 'there is no desire for it, nor endeavour after it; there is no more but a bare *Velleity*, the term used to signifie the lowest degree of Desire' (*ibid.*; cf. 2.21.39: 'where-ever there is *uneasiness* there is *desire*'). A number of passions and emotions are defined in terms of uneasiness. Sorrow, for example, is 'uneasiness in the Mind, upon the thought of a Good lost, which might have been enjoy'd longer; or the sense of a present Evil' (2.20.8). Fear is 'an uneasiness of the Mind, upon the thought of future Evil likely to befal us' (2.20.10). Envy 'is an uneasiness of Mind, caused by the consideration of a Good we desire, obtained by one, we think should not have had it before us' (2.20.13). Shame is another uneasiness of the mind 'upon the thought of having done something, which is indecent, or will lessen the valued Esteem, which others have for us' (2.20.17). Blushing does not always accompany this uneasiness. Even hatred and love are forms of uneasiness (2.20.5). In general, pleasure and pain, delight and uneasiness, refer to bodily pains and pleasures as well as to 'whatsoever *Delight* or *Uneasiness* is felt by us, whether arising from any grateful, or unacceptable Sensation or Reflection' (2.20.15).

We are not capable of more than one determination of the will to one action at a time. It is present uneasiness that determines the will (2.21.36). If we judge some end or action is unattainable, even the strongest degree of uneasiness will not spur us to act (2.21.40). If we judge that various ends *are* attainable, then the 'most important and urgent *uneasiness*, we at that time feel, is that, which ordinarily determines the *will* successively, in that train of voluntary actions, which make up our lives' (*ibid.*; cf. 2.21.47). There are also *natural* and *fantastical* uneasinesses. The former are 'the *uneasiness* of *Hunger*, *Thirst*, *Heat*, *Cold*, *Weariness*', the latter include the 'itch after *Honour*, *Power*, or *Riches*' (2.21.45). The fantastical ones are 'acquir'd habits by Fashion, Example, and Education'. The same sources produce 'a thousand other irregular desires, which custom has made natural to us'. These two, natural and fantastical (or acquired), desires produce 'a constant succession of uneasinesses' (*ibid.*). The natural desires or uneasinesses are implanted in us by God, they are part of human nature, guiding our preservation (2.21.34).

This chapter on power, where much of the discussion of uneasiness and the determination of the will occurs, went through a number of revisions.

It was the chapter in the *Essay* that gave Locke most trouble. In the first edition, he accepted the view that 'good, the greater good, determines the will' (2.21.35). He explains in this section that he has now, in the second edition, 'ventur'd to recede from so received an Opinion'. From the second to the fifth editions of the *Essay*, he asserts that '*good*, the *greater good*, though apprehended and acknowledged to be so, does not determine the *will*, until our desire, raised proportionably to it, makes us *uneasy* in the want of it' (*ibid.*). A man might be convinced that 'plenty has its advantages over poverty', that conveniences of life are better than 'nasty penury', but, if he is content with his present condition, he will not act to change his situation. What he recognizes intellectually will not move him to seek a change. Even with virtue, we can be fully persuaded of its importance in this and the next world, but until we 'hunger and thirst after righteousness', until we feel uneasy in its absence, we will not be determined to seek virtue. Locke even cites the case of the drunkard who, recognizing that his health is endangered by excess drinking and that he is spending too much money at the tavern, will nevertheless allow the uneasiness he feels for his drinking companions and 'the habitual thirst after his Cups, at the usual time' to drive him back there (*ibid.*).

Good and evil, both present and absent, work upon the mind, but what immediately determines the will is 'the *uneasiness* of *desire*' (2.21.33). He does not mean that desire forces our will to act (although the example of the drunkard may sound that way). He is speaking of *voluntary* actions. Knowledge of good and evil, of virtue and vice, is not sufficient for us to will to act. For voluntary action, we must not only want and desire to attain some end, we must feel that want. Strictly, to desire *is* to feel, but it is important to see that Locke is stressing the feeling, the felt need or felt importance of acting morally. Desire is the uneasiness that motivates us to act voluntarily to attain some goal. Locke's talk of 'determining the will' may sound as if he believes desire *drives* us to act, even against our will. The struggle he had in this long chapter was over how to understand voluntary action. His analysis is in terms of volition, not compulsion, but the will does not by itself set us on a course of action: it must be moved, determined. We might prefer to speak of the motives of actions rather than the determination of the will, but whichever language we use, we need to recognize that we are the agents that act. As agents, we do not act without motives. Some would say it is *reasons* that motivate us (or ought to do so), others say it is a knowledge of what is good or virtuous. After the first edition of his *Essay*, Locke came to a different conclusion. It is desire, restlessness, uneasiness for some absent good or condition that motivates us to act, to change our present state. It is correct to say we are, on this account, driven by our desires, so long as we do not interpret the 'driven' in a compulsive way. It would be better to say we are *motivated* by our desires, not by knowledge or reason, a conclusion reached in the eighteenth century by Hume also (cf. 2.21.31)

Even so, this is a rather surprising conclusion to reach for someone such as Locke, who elsewhere extols the value of reason and rationality. Doubtless, he would have preferred reason to be the motivator of human agents, but he made a realistic assessment of the actual psychology of motivation as he struggled with revising this chapter. He linked his revised understanding of human psychology with the ontological principle that nothing can operate where it is not: "'tis against the nature of things, that what is absent should operate, where it is not' (2.21.37). He admits that the *idea* of some absent good, by contemplation, can be 'brought home to the mind, and made present', but the idea will not move us to act unless or until that idea 'raises our desire, and the *uneasiness* of that has the prevalency in determining the *will*' (*ibid.*). Without uneasiness, that idea is in the mind 'only like other *Ideas*, the object of bare unactive speculation'. Even the idea or representation of 'the unspeakable Joys of Heaven' will not motivate us as long as we are content with our condition in this life (cf. 2.21.38: 'The infinitely greatest confessed good being often neglected, to satisfy the successive *uneasiness* of our desires pursuing trifles').

Locke does recognize that desires can get out of hand, can *drive* us in a compulsive way by dominating the will. The will is still the source of action, but in these cases, desires lead us to less than responsible actions. The drunkard example may be read in this way. More generally, he refers to such dominating desires as 'any very great, and prevailing *uneasiness*, having once laid hold on the *will*, lets it not go' (2.21.38). Examples are 'any vehement pain of the Body; the ungovernable passion of a Man violently in love; or the impatient desire of revenge' (*ibid.*). What happens in such situations is that 'the *will* thus determined never lets the Understanding lay by the object, but all the thoughts of the Mind, and powers of the Body are uninterruptedly employ'd that way . . . as long as it lasts' (*ibid.*; cf. 2.21.32).

Aware of the power of desires, and the role they play in human action, it was important for Locke to find ways of controlling desires, turning some into motivations for good, uprooting or silencing others. The way to do this is through education and training children. Education becomes the vehicle for rational behaviour. The tensions between reason and desire are addressed directly in *Some Thoughts concerning Education*. His extended remarks on this topic often seem as if they were written, as in fact they were, in their initial form as letters to Locke's friends, Mr and Mrs Edward Clarke, prior to the revisions Locke made in the second edition of the *Essay*. There are no changes on this topic in the four subsequent editions of *Some Thoughts*. Section 54 is clearly of the same vintage as the first edition passages in *Essay 2.21*: '*Good and Evil, Reward* and *Punishment*, are the only Motives to a rational Creature; these are the Spur and Reins, whereby all Mankind are set on work, and guided, and therefore they are to be made use of to Children too' (*ST*, §54). The phrase, 'rational creature', may indicate that this is what a rational person will do. Reaching the standard of rationality is the goal of *Some Thoughts*. Locke is fully aware of the motivating force of desire: 'For where there is no Desire, there will be no Industry' (*ST*, §126); but he recommends a strict programme for curbing the most violent and disruptive desires in favour of the modest ones, those that are consistent with 'Application, Industry, Thought, Contrivance, and Good Husbandry' (*ST*, §130).

Rewards and punishments are useful in getting children to have 'a Liking and Inclination to what you propose to them to be learn'd' (*ST*, §72). They are also useful in leading children to desire virtue and commendation and to avoid disgrace. 'In this way, the Objects of their Desires are made assisting to Vertue' (*ST*, §58). As he did in the *Essay*, so here he identifies specific natural desires and wants, e.g., 'Pains of Sickness and Hurts, Hunger, Thirst and Cold; want of Sleep, or Rest and Relaxation of the Part wearied with Labour' (*ST*, §107). He suggests in this passage that with some help, reason may be able to minimize the effects and demands of these desires, even to 'seek their removal'. At the same time, the pains 'that come from the Necessities of Nature, are Monitors to us, to beware of greater Mischiefs, which they are the Forerunners of' (*ST*, §107). But helping children learn to endure some of these pains can 'make them Stronger in Body and Mind'. In fact, he identifies 'the great Principle and Foundation of all Vertue and Worth . . . That a Man is able to *deny himself* his own Desires, cross his own Inclinations, and purely follow what Reason directs as best, tho' the appetite lean the other way' (*ST*, §33). Children should accordingly be urged 'to consult, and make use of their Reason, before they give allowance to their Inclinations' (*ST*, §107). He wants children 'to learn the Art of stifling their Desires as soon as they rise up in them, when they are easiest to be subdued' (*ibid.*). Preparation for learning this art should begin early, very early; even '*from their very Cradles*' they should 'be used to submit their Desires, and go without their Longings' (*ST*, §38; cf. §104). Desires should be curbed early and children should be encouraged to 'submit to Reason' (*ST*, §52).

Some Thoughts, then, offers a programme for controlling and using desires in order to motivate children to act; but reason seems to be the controlling factor in that programme – at least, it is the ideal and the standard used by the tutor and parents. The *Conduct of the Understanding* also expresses confidence in reason and knowledge as the determiners of the will. The opening section of that work strikes a confident rational tone: 'The last resort a man has recourse to, in the conduct of himself, is his understanding' (§1; in *Works*, iii. 205). Reason, not desire or uneasiness, activates man. The understanding, with reason, leads: all the 'operative powers' of a man are directed by reason and understanding. Even the will itself, 'how absolute and uncontrollable soever it may be thought, never fails in its obedience to the dictates of the understanding'.

Locke does not seem to have resolved the uneasy tension between reason and desire as motivators of men. It may be that his appeals to reason and understanding were what he hoped for, while the detailed account of uneasiness as that which moves us to act was his realistic recognition of what in fact is the case. His training programme for children in *Some Thoughts* can be seen as his attempt to resolve this tension between ideal and reality, to recommend ways in which parents and tutors can turn certain desires and inclinations to the direction of reason.

V

Vindication of the Reasonableness of Christianity   This was a forty-page pamphlet published by Locke in 1696, replying to a vicious attack against his *Reasonableness* by John Edwards (*Some Thoughts concerning the Several Causes and Occasions of Atheism,* 1695). The *Vindication* is usually included in the second edition of Locke's *Reasonableness.* A *Second Vindication* appeared in 1697, a 480-page extension of the main points in the original small pamphlet. A French abridgement of the *Vindications* was published in 1703 (as vol. 2 of the French translation of the *Reasonableness*) and reprinted later. A German version of this condensed translation can be found in a two-volume work published in 1733. As the *Reasonableness* was, so the two *Vindications* were published anonymously. Locke was rather incensed at the charges of atheism and Socinianism levelled by Edwards, but the burden of his reply was to point out that Edwards, like most other religious writers then, accepted doctrines and articles of faith which Locke could not find supported by what Jesus said. Locke liked to say that he based his religious views on what the Bible reported Jesus as saying. When critics such as Edwards or Stillingfleet tried to show that Locke did not accept some church doctrine, Locke usually replied that that doctrine (e.g., the Trinity, resurrection of the same body) was not in his Bible. Some men, Locke remarked (with Edwards clearly in mind, but others as well), 'will not bear it, that any one should speak of religion, but according to the model that they themselves have made of it. Nay, though he proposes it upon the very terms, and in the very words which our Saviour and his apostles preached it in, yet he shall not escape censures and the severest insinuations. To deviate in the least, or to omit any thing contained in their articles, is heresy, under the most invidious names in fashion, and it is well if he escapes being a downright atheist.' (*Vindication,* in *Works,* vii. 165)

The first *Vindication* is one of the best brief statements of Locke's own religion. Had Edwards not continued his attack in *Socinianism Unmask'd* (1696), Locke probably would have stayed silent. The fact that the *Second Vindication* is so massively long (and rather uninteresting) is an indication

of how much Locke resented the charge of being a Socinian or an atheist
(*see* ATHEISM).

virtue Having distinguished three laws that are used to justify the
'Rectitude, or Obliquity' of actions (divine, civil, and the law of opinion
or reputation), Locke points out that under the third of these, the words
'virtue' and 'vice' 'are Names pretended, and supposed every where to
stand for actions in their own nature right and wrong' (*Essay*, 2.28.10).
These words are applied 'to such actions, as in each Country and Society
are in reputation or discredit'. The measure of 'what is every where called
and esteemed *Vertue* and *Vice* is the approbation or dislike, praise or blame,
which by a secret and tacit consent establishes it self in the several
Societies, Tribes, and Clubs of Men in the World' (*ibid.*). He characterizes
this as the 'common *measure of Vertue and Vice*' (2.28.11). This common and
prevalent measure is contrasted with 'the only true touchstone of *moral
Rectitude*', which is the divine law, the law of nature (2.28.8). Locke was
puzzled and somewhat angry that he was misread as identifying the true
measure of virtue with the common measure. He did believe that often
the two agreed, or did not differ greatly, in what was judged virtue or
vice; but he is very clear and firm in identifying the divine law as the true
measure. James Lowde, in *A Discourse Concerning the Nature of Man* (1694),
misread Locke in this way. Locke added a long comment in the preface
to the fourth edition of the *Essay* responding to Lowde, pointing out the
several places where he identified the 'eternal and unalterable nature of
right and wrong, and what I call *Vertue* and *Vice*' with God's law, the law
of nature (see note † in Nidditch's edition for 2.28.11; cf. 1.3.6).

Elsewhere, Locke characterized the Golden Rule as 'that most un-
shaken Rule of Morality, and Foundation of all social Virtue' (1.3.4). The
social dimension of virtue is stressed in other passages. Keeping compacts
(contracts, promises) is an 'undeniable Rule of Morality', the justification
of that rule for Christianity: 'Because God, who has the Power of eternal
Life and Death requires it of us' (1.3.5). This same passage says that 'the
old *Heathen* Philosophers' invoked that rule because violating it is dishonest and below the dignity of man; it is also 'opposite to Vertue' which is
'the highest Perfection of humane Nature'. More generally, God has, 'by
an inseparable connexion, joined *Virtue* and publick Happiness', making
the practice of virtue 'necessary to the preservation of Society, and visibly
beneficial to all, with whom the Virtuous Man has to do' (1.3.6). *Some
Thoughts* also remarks that virtue makes a man valued and beloved by
others (*ST*, §135; cf. §200).

But the early essays on the law of nature guard against making utility
or social benefit the sole value of virtue: 'In fact a great number of virtues,

and the best of them, consist only in this: that we do good to others at our own loss' (*Essays*, p. 207). He cites the heroic actions of men such as Hercules, Marcus Curtius (362 BC), or the Roman leader, G. Fabricius Luscinus (*ibid.*, p. 209). Self-preservation is also ruled out as the foundation of the law of nature: were it the foundation, 'virtue would seem to be not so much man's duty as his convenience' (p. 181). Locke recognized that men frequently praise vice and shameful actions instead of virtue (p. 167), and he considers the causes that lead us away from virtue, piety and religion (*Essay*, 2.21.57). Nevertheless, he remained confident that virtue and religion are necessary for happiness. Virtue frequently accompanies, or even includes, wisdom, good breeding, and learning (*ST*, §134).

Virtue is perhaps the most important topic in his work on education. His concern is with building moral character, 'forming the Mind to Virtue', raising children in such a way that virtue and a virtuous life will become their goal (*ST*, §142). He realized that, as he said, 'Vertue is harder to be got, than a Knowledge of the World' (*ST*, §70), but he came to the recognition that knowledge of virtue is not sufficient to motivate children or adults to seek virtue (*Essay*, 2.21.35). He was critical of the usual way parents raised their children: 'if we look into the common Management of Children, we shall have reason to wonder, in the great Dissoluteness of Manners which the World complains of, that there are any Foot-steps at all left of Virtue' (*ST*, §37). His recommended programme involved much denial of desires and making desires subservient to reason: 'the Principle of all Vertue and Excellency lies in a power of denying our selves the satisfaction of our own Desires, where Reason does not authorize them' (*ST*, §38). He who has 'not a Mastery over his Inclinations, he that knows not how to *resist* the importunity of *present Pleasure or Pain*, for the sake of what Reason tells him is fit to be done, wants the true Principle of Vertue and Industry; and is in danger never to be good for any thing' (*ST*, §45; cf. §§52, 107; *see also* MORALITY; GOOD AND EVIL).

W

women   References to, some discussion of, and a few debates about
women are found in several of Locke's books. Women as wives and
mothers, as members of the conjugal society, take up a fair amount of the
first of *Two Treatises* and a smaller space in the second. Women as
mothers, a few remarks about girls and daughters, appear in *Some
Thoughts*. The *Paraphrases* contains an interesting interpretation of St
Paul's injunction against women preaching or being in church uncovered
or unveiled. References to women are also made in the *Essay*, mainly to
illustrate some principle or claim.

The *Essay* references are not especially significant; they do not reveal
any of Locke's views about or attitudes towards women. In the discussion
of innate ideas and principles, he cites as an example of moral principles
which one would think would be innate, if any principles were innate:
'Not to kill another Man; Not to know more Women than one; Not to
procure Abortion; Not to expose their Children' (1.3.19). One of the
puzzle cases about personal identity involves the conjecture that 'a Man
born of different Women, and in distant times, may be the same Man'
(2.27.21). He also reports, apparently with belief, that history tells us that
women 'have conceived by Drills' (i.e., mandrills); this is in connection
with his argument against fixed kinds in nature (3.6.23). An example of
children's acquisition of ideas is the way they soon learn to tell their
mother from a stranger (1.4.3; cf. 4.7.9). The ideas of mother and nurse
are given as examples of general ideas (3.3.7); and the point he makes
about mixed modes being man-made is illustrated by commenting that
killing a man's father or mother is, in most societies, recognized as a
distinct kind of action, and given a name, while other sorts of killing are
not named (3.5.6, 7). Another mixed-mode example involves Adam
naming actions that he witnesses, e.g., the actions of Lamech's wife which
Adam mistook for adultery, thereby introducing into the language a new
word, even though that word had not yet any exemplification (3.6.44).

The early sections of his work on education give advice to parents on
the health of the body. Locke's prescriptions are rather harsh: exposing
children to cold and wet, getting then inured to rough, plain living

conditions. At the beginning of a series of sections containing this advice, he suggests 'one short Rule, *viz*. That Gentlemen should use their Children, as the honest Farmers and substantial Yeomen do theirs. But because the Mothers possibly may think this a little too hard and the Fathers too short, I shall explain my self more particularly; only laying down this as a general and certain Observation for the Women to consider, *viz*. That most Children's Constitutions are either spoiled, or at least harmed, by *Cockering* and *Tenderness*' (*ST*, §4). His recommendations are mainly for a boy, since it was the son of his friends the Clarkes for whom Locke wrote *Some Thoughts*. He recognizes that his harsh regimen will not, in all respects, 'so perfectly suit the Education of *Daughters*' (*ST*, §6), but he thinks the anticipated reaction of mothers is not entirely justified: 'How fond Mothers are like to receive this Doctrine, is not hard to foresee. What can it be less than to Murder their tender Babes to use them thus? What! put their Feet in cold Water in Frost and Snow, when all one can do is little enough to keep them warm?' (*ST*, §7) He gives an example from Seneca to support his recommendations. Exposure to wind and sun also helps to toughen the body and ward off illness. This was a recommendation Locke believed important for boys and girls. 'And if my young Master be to be kept always in the Shade, and never exposed to the Sun and Wind, for fear of his Complexion, it may be a good Way to make him a *Beau*, but not a Man of Business. And although greater Regard be to be had to Beauty in the Daughters, yet I will take the Liberty to say, that the more they are in the *Air*, without prejudice to their Faces, the stronger and healthier they will be; and the nearer they come to the Hardships of their Brothers in their Education, the greater Advantage will they receive from it all the remaining Part of their Lives' (*ST*, §9). In a long letter to Mrs Clarke, Locke responds to her request for further advice about her daughters. He there advises that 'the meat drink and lodging and clothing should be ordered after the same manner for the girls as for the boys' (*Corr*. 809; ii. 686). A healthy constitution in girls requires 'a stomach able to digest ordinary food, and a body that could endure upon occasion both wind and sun'. He does in this letter make one concession:

> You know my opinion is that the boys should be much abroad in the air at all times and in all weathers, and if they play in the sun and in the wind without hats and gloves so much the better. But since in your girls care is to be taken too of their beauty as much as health will permit, this in them must have some restriction, the more they exercise and the more they are in the air the better health they will have, that I am sure: but yet 'tis fit their tender skins should be fenced against the busy sunbeams, especially

when they are very hot and piercing: to avoid this and yet to give them
exercise in the air, some little shady grove near the house would be
convenient for them to play in. (*ibid.*)

Most of the other recommendations about wet shoes, spare clothing, in
this letter, are urged for girls (*ibid.*, pp. 687–9).

There are in *Some Thoughts* a few other interesting comments about
daughters that may reveal something about the way girls were treated in
families. No one believes, Locke says, that the 'Retirement and Bashful-
ness, which their Daughters are brought up in, make them less knowing
or less able Women. Conversation, when they come into the World, soon
gives them a becoming assurance' (*ST*, §70). Two other comments involve
mothers and daughters. 'A prudent and kind Mother, of my Acquaintance, was, on such an occasion [when the daughter was very stubborn],
forced to whip her little Daughter, at her first coming home from Nurse,
eight times successively the same Morning, before she could master her
Stubbornness, and obtain compliance in a very easy and indifferent matter'
(*ST*, §78). Locke was opposed to whipping except in very recalcitrant
cases. A positive example is given later: 'I cannot but commend both the
Kindness and Prudence of a Mother I knew, who was wont always to
indulge her Daughters, when any of them desired Dogs, Squirils, Birds,
or any such things, as young Girls use to be delighted with' (*ST*, §116).
But Locke goes on to point out that those girls often failed to take good
care of their pets. It was important for him that 'People should be
accustomed, from their Cradles, to be tender to all sensible Creatures,
and to spoil or *waste* nothing at all' (*ibid.*).

Locke had many quarrels with Robert Filmer, one of which was about
Filmer's slighting of women in his interpretation of several passages in
the Bible. Filmer tried to extract from Genesis 1: 28 a basis for Adam's
sole dominion over the earth and all men, as well as of Eve. Locke objects
that the biblical passage does not speak of a private dominion; it says,
'God blessed them', both Adam and Eve. The dominion he gave was
given to both male and female and in effect to all mankind. This passage
was also the basis for Locke's analysis of property in the second of *Two
Treatises*. 'If it be said that *Eve* was subjected to *Adam*, it seems she was
not so subjected to him, as to hinder her *Dominion* over the Creatures, or
Property in them: for shall we say that God ever made a joint Grant to two,
and one only was to have the benefit of it?' (*T*1, §29; cf. §30). Even more
questionable is Filmer's reading of Genesis 3: 16, where God addresses
Eve after the Fall, telling her he will 'greatly multiply your pain in
childbearing; in pain you shall bring forth children, yet your desire shall
be for your husband, and he shall rule over you.' Filmer turned this

passage into a sanction for a grant of government to Adam, apparently taking the words about the husband ruling over her as a political statement. Locke had little trouble pointing out that this passage is about Eve's punishment. Even when we take Eve as a representative of all women, the subjection of women to men referred to is certainly not part of civil society. It entails, Locke says, 'no more but that Subjection they should ordinarily be in to their Husbands' (*T*1, §47). Locke's interpretation of this Genesis passage strikes a rather unorthodox note: 'But there is here no more Law to oblige a Woman to such a Subjection, if the Circumstances either of her Condition or Contract with her Husband should exempt her from it, then there is, that she should bring forth her Children in Sorrow and Pain, if there could be found a Remedy for it' (*ibid.*). Neither the subjection nor the pain of childbirth, on Locke's gloss, is fixed and unavoidable. He even goes further before this section closes: 'God, in this Text, gives not, that I see, any Authority to *Adam* over *Eve*, or to Men over their Wives, but only foretels what should be the Womans Lot' (*ibid.*; cf. §67). He does end the section by commenting that the laws of mankind and the customs of societies have generally sanctioned what Genesis foretold. Locke even grants that there is 'a Foundation in Nature' for such an arrangement. And in the next section, he modifies his interpretation: if 'these words here spoke to *Eve* must needs be understood as a Law to bind her and all other Women to Subjection, it can be no other Subjection than what every Wife owes her Husband' (cf. *T*1, §49).

However that subjection is interpreted, Locke's passing reference in *T*1, §47 to a marriage contract suggests an agreement between two persons. He characterizes this 'conjugal contract' as 'personal' (*T*1, §98). There, the contrast is with the father-son relation: 'the Power of the Husband being founded on Contract, and the Power of the Father on *Begetting*'. The '*Society of Man and Wife should be more lasting*, than of Male and Female amongst other Creatures', just because a woman 'is capable of conceiving, and *de facto* is commonly with Child again, and Brings forth too a new Birth long before the former is out of a dependancy' on the parents (*T*2, §80). But Locke raises the question, 'why this *Compact*, where Procreation and Education are secured, and Inheritance taken care for, may not be made determinable, either by consent, or a certain time, or upon certain Conditions, as well as any other Voluntary Compacts, there being no necessity in the nature of the thing, nor to the ends of it, that it should always be for life' (*T*2, §81). The next section makes the point that husband and wife may have differences of understanding and wills. There is some ambiguity in his concept of a marriage contract in this passage. Given that there will be differences, Locke says, it is necessary 'that the last Determination, *i.e.* the Rule, should be placed somewhere', its locus being the man's share, since he is 'the abler and the stronger'. Does the phrase, 'the rule', refer to the terms of the contract? Does it give the husband the right or power to decide issues between them? Is it only with the issues that they agree on that the wife has some rights and free choice? The next sentence may clarify these questions somewhat: 'But this reaching to the things of their common Interest and Property, leaves the Wife in the full and free possession of what by Contract is her peculiar Right, and gives the Husband no more power over her Life, than she has over his' (*T*2, §82). The power of the husband is unlike the power of an absolute monarch (Filmer had argued they were the same): 'the *Wife* has, in many cases, a Liberty to *separate* from him; where natural Right, or their Contract allows it, whether that Contract be made by themselves in the state of Nature, or by the Customs or Laws of the Countrey they live in' (*ibid.*; cf. *T*1, §62). Procreation and mutual support are the ends of conjugal society, but the contract covers other aspects of marrage: 'Community of Goods, and the Power over them, mutual Assistance, and Maintenance, and other things' (*T*2, §83). These can all be 'varied and regulated by that Contract, which unites Man and Wife in that Society'.

Filmer defended the father's right and power within the family (and, as ruler, within the nation). Locke always countered with a stress on paternal power, the power and rights of both parents (see *T*1, §§6, 11, 60, 61). In the second of *Two Treatises*, the chapter on paternal power insists that the mother shares in the power over their children, a power which includes nourishing and educating. At the beginning of that section, he says that 'if we consult Reason or Revelation, we shall find she hath an equal Title' (*T*2, §52; cf. *T*1, §55). There is no right of nature peculiar to the father in relation to his children. When the father 'quits his Care of them, he loses his power over them' (*T*2, §65). Locke raises some questions in this passage about situations where one woman has more than one husband at a time; where, as was reported from America, husband and wife part; where the father dies (*T*1, §123; *T*2, §§182, 183).

There is one other area where Locke offers a more liberal, unorthodox view about women than that held by most of his contemporaries. In his letter to the Corinthians, St Paul addressed the question of whether women could pray or prophesy in church with their heads uncovered. This passage is, as Locke acknowledged, 'as difficult a passage as most in St. Paul's Epistles' (*Paraphrases*, p. 200). Locke's long note interpreting St Paul on this matter begins with several preliminary remarks. (1) It was 'the custome, for women, who appeared in public, to be veiled. ... Therefore it could be noe question at all, whether they ought to be veyled when they assisted at the prayers ... in the publick assemblys' (*ibid.*). (2) 'It is plain that this covering the head in women is restrained to some particular actions which they performed in the assembly.' (3) If 'women were to be veiled in the assemblys, let those actions be what they will, the women joyning in them were still to be veyled.' Locke's note suggests that prophesying meant speaking when one received 'a spiritual gift [from] the immediate and extraordinary motion of the holy ghost'. He sees no reason to exclude the possibility that women could receive such a gift and then speak in church. In a later passage on the same Epistle, St Paul enjoins silence on women. Locke interprets this injunction as excluding a liberty for women to speak 'where they had an immediate impulse and revelation from the spirit of god' (p. 245n.).

Wainwright tells us that this interpretation was unusual in Locke's day: 'Locke's interpretation, restrained and cautious as it appears to be, posed a threat to the accepted practice of restricting leadership in public worship to the male sex' (p. 443; cf. introduction to his edition of the *Paraphrases*, pp. 68–9).

Z

zealots Locke was greatly concerned for the pursuit of truth. He was equally insistent that claims for truth be based on adequate evidence, proofs or demonstrations. He worried about those who 'applaud themselves as zealous Champions for Truth, when indeed they are contending for Error' (*Essay*, 2.33.18). Such mistaking error for truth can be sincere, can result from 'wrong and unnatural Combinations of *Ideas*', especially among the 'different Sects of Philosophy and Religion' (*ibid.*). Not everyone knowingly maintains falsehoods, but the strength of custom, education 'and the constant din of their Party' force ideas together that lead to errors and false beliefs. It is difficult to throw off those beliefs we have accepted uncritically, difficult to depart from accepted doctrines: 'all the world are born to orthodoxy; they imbibe at first the allowed opinions of their country and party, and so never questioning their truths, not one of an hundred ever examines. They are applauded for presuming they are in the right' (*Conduct*, in *Works*, iii. 267–8). The 'zealous bigots' of all parties never stop to examine their beliefs and doctrines. In a passage which reflects some of the opposition Locke himself ran into by questioning or rejecting established doctrines, he suggests it is difficult to 'bear the name of Whimsical, Sceptical, or Atheist, which he is sure to meet with, who does in the least scruple any of the common Opinions' (1.3.25). Especially when the received doctrines are believed to be 'Standards set up by God ... to be the Rule and Touchstone of all other Opinions', people never think to question the claims that those doctrines *are* God's standards. Thus, 'It is easy to imagine, *how* by these means it comes to pass, that *Men* worship the Idols that have been set up in their Minds; grow fond of the Notions they have been long acquainted with there; and *stamp the Characters of Divinity, upon Absurdities and Errors*, become zealous Votaries to Bulls and Monkeys; and contend too, fight, and die in defence of their Opinions' (1.3.26).

Attacking intolerance and those who 'persecute, torment, destroy, and kill other men upon pretence of religion', Locke urges 'those firey zealots' to apply the same methods to their friends that they used for forcing others to believe and practise as they do (*Letter concerning Toleration*, in *Works*, vi.

67). He complains that those zealots 'hardly have patience to refrain from violence and rapine' in order to make others conform to the customs, ceremonies, and mysteries of their particular church or religion (*ibid.*, p. 22). These zealots 'condemn all things that are not of their mode' (*ibid.*, p. 25).

The chapter on 'Enthusiasm', added to the fourth edition of the *Essay*, is an elaboration of these examples of intolerance, error and conviction based upon feelings of being inspired or being the vehicles for the word of God, in contrast with basing their beliefs on evidence or clear signs of genuine revelation. The enthusiasts are characterized by Locke as 'Men, in whom Melancholy has mixed with Devotion, or whose conceit of themselves has raised them into an Opinion of a greater familarity with GOD, and a nearer admittance to his Favour than is afforded to others' (4.19.5). They often flatter themselves 'with a perswasion of an immediate intercourse with the Deïty, and frequent communications from the divine Spirit' (*ibid.*). These 'untractable Zealots' rely not on rational proofs of divine REVELATION or on evidence, but only on their own persuasions (4.19.11).

BIBLIOGRAPHY

A   WORKS BY LOCKE

Complete edition: *The Works of John Locke*, A New Edition Corrected, 10 vols (London: Printed for Thomas Tegg, 1823; fac. repr. Aalen, Germany: Scientia Verlag, 1963).

The Clarendon Edition of the Works of John Locke (Oxford: Clarendon Press, 1975 to date) has definitive editions of individual works. The following works appear in chronological order.

1   *Epistola de tolerantia, ad clarissimum virum T.A.R.P.T.O.L.A. scripta à P.A.P.O.I.L.A.* (Goudae: Apud Justum ab Hoeve, 1689)
    Anonymously published work addressed to Philipp Limborch. Reprinted in Amsterdam in 1705. All the 'toleration letters' (this Latin edition, its English translation described below, the second, third and part of a 'fourth') were reprinted together by Thomas Hollis in 1765.

2   *A Letter concerning Toleration* (London: Printed for Awnsham Churchill, 1689)
    Published anonymously. Translation of the *Epistola de tolerantia* by William Popple. There was a second edition in 1690, and frequent reprints in Britain, Scotland and North America from 1740 to 1800. There were four editions of a Dutch translation, and four of a German translation, with only one separately appearing French edition (in 1764). For a modern edition, see *Epistola de Tolerantia/ A Letter on Toleration*, ed. R. Klibanski, trans. J. W. Gough (Oxford: Clarendon Press, 1968). Latin and English on facing pages.

3   *Two Treatises of Government; in the Former, The False Principles and Foundation of Sir Robert Filmer and His Followers are Detected and Overthrown. The Latter is an Essay concerning the True Original, Extent, and End of Civil Government* (London: Printed for Awnsham Churchill, 1690)
    Published anonymously. There were two more editions published in Locke's lifetime, in 1694 and 1698. Some twenty-eight further editions and translations (into Dutch, French, German, Italian and Swedish), chiefly of the second treatise only, had appeared by 1800. The definitive edition is that by Peter Laslett (Cambridge: Cambridge University Press, 1960; 2nd edn., 1971).

4   *An Essay concerning Humane Understanding: in Four Books* (London: Printed by
    Eliz. Holt for Thomas Basset, 1690)
    A second issue has the imprint: Printed for Thomas Basset, and Sold by Edw.
Mory. Locke readied for the press the first five editions (1690, 1694, 1695, 1700
and 1706). For the sixth edition (1710), the title's spelling was changed to
'Human'. There were further editions and translations (into Latin, French and
German) to the number of forty-eight by 1800. Pierre Coste translated it into
French and had revised his edition at least three times by 1742. An abridgement
(chiefly of Books 2–4) was made by John Wynne in 1696, had been revised and
reprinted some seventeen times by 1800, and served as the basis for several
French, German, Italian and Greek translations. The definitive edition has been
edited by Peter Nidditch for the Clarendon Edition of the Works of John Locke
(Oxford: Clarendon Press, 1975). Two supplementary volumes entitled *Drafts for
the* Essay *and Other Philosophical Writings* have been edited by Peter Nidditch and
G.A.J. Rogers (vol. 1, 1990; vol. 2 in press).

5   *A Second Letter concerning Toleration* (London: Printed for Awnsham and John
    Churchill, 1690)
    Written in answer to Jonas Proast's *The Argument of the 'Letter concerning Toleration'
Consider'd and Answer'd* (Oxford: Printed by H. West and A. Clements, 1690).
Published anonymously. Reprinted in editions of the *Works* and in the Hollis
edition of the 'toleration letters' (see no. 1 above). A Dutch translation appeared
with that of the first *Letter* in 1774.

6   *Some Considerations of the Consequences of the Lowering of Interest, and Raising the
    Value of Money: in a Letter to a Member of Parliament* (London: Printed for
    Awnsham and John Churchill, 1692)
    Locke's anonymous response to the 'Great Recoinage' controversy of the 1690s.
A second edition was published in 1696, and is usually found in the collection,
Several Papers Relating to Money, Interest and Trade, &c. An Italian translation was
published in Florence in 1751. The definitive edition of this work, of *Short
Observations* (no. 9 below), and of *Further Considerations* (no. 11 below) prepared by
Patrick Kelly for the Clarendon Edition of the Works of John Locke, was
published in 1991 under the title, *Locke on Money*.

7   *A Third Letter for Toleration, to the Author of the 'Third Letter concerning Toleration'*,
    (London: Printed for Awnsham and John Churchill, 1692)
    A second anonymous reply to Proast. Reprinted in Hollis's edition of the
'toleration letters' (see no. 1).

8   *Some Thoughts concerning Education* (London: Printed for A. and J. Churchill,
    1693)
    Written to help his friends Mary and Edward Clarke rear their children, the
first two editions were anonymous. The second edition is a line-for-line reprint of
the first and almost indistinguishable from it, also published in 1693. Following
editions in Locke's lifetime appeared in 1695 (called the 'third'), in 1699 (the
'fourth'), and in 1705 (the 'fifth'. One of his more popular works, it had been
reprinted in England, Ireland and Scotland nineteen more times by 1800. A Dutch
translation was published in 1698 and in 1753. A French translation (by Pierre

Coste) first appeared in 1695, with revisions and reprints eighteen times. There were several different German translations from 1708 to 1787, six in all; as well as some seven editions of different Italian translations, 1735–92; two Russian translations (1760 and 1788), and one Swedish edition in 1709. The definitive edition in the Clarendon Edition of the Works of John Locke was edited by John W. and Jean S. Yolton, and published in 1989.

9 *Short Observations on a Printed Paper, Intituled, For Encouraging the Coining Silver Money in England, and after for Keeping It Here* (London: Printed for A. and J. Churchill, 1695)

Published anonymously. The second edition (1696) is usually found in *Several Papers Relating to Money, Interest and Trade, &c.* (London: Printed for A. and J. Churchill, 1696). Included in the Italian edition of *Some Considerations* (see no. 6).

10 *The Reasonableness of Christianity, As Delivered in the Scriptures* (London: Printed for Awnsham and John Churchill, 1695)

Published anonymously, this work is the result of Locke's efforts to reconcile the divisive controversies amid Christians and to consider 'wherein the Christian faith consists'. A second edition was published in 1696: *ibid.*, '*To Which Is Added a Vindication of the Same, from Mr. Edwards's Exceptions*'. Another edition was published in 1731 and reprinted in 1736, both with the *Vindication*. The *Reasonableness* alone was further reprinted four more times in the eighteenth century. Pierre Coste translated the *Reasonableness* into French in 1696, and contrived an abridgement of the *Vindication* and the *Second Vindication* (see no. 13) which was published in 1703. The French *Reasonableness* and its *Vindications* were again published in 1715, 1730 (an unauthorized edition), 1731 and 1740. There was a Dutch translation of the *Reasonableness* in 1729; two German translations of Coste's translation of the *Reasonableness* and his abridgement of its *Vindications* were published in 1733 and 1758–9. John Higgins-Biddle has edited the definitive edition of the *Reasonableness* for the Clarendon Edition of the Works of John Locke (in press).

11 *Further Considerations concerning Raising the Value of Money; Wherein Mr. Lowndes's Arguments for It in His Late Report concerning 'An Essay for the Amendment of the Silver Coins' Are Particularly Examined* (London: A. and J. Churchill, 1695)

One of the 'papers on money' published anonymously. Lowndes, Secretary of the Treasury, had proposed raising the nominal value of coins. Locke had to make several revisions in the text of this work, chiefly mathematical computations, so that there was a '*Second Edition*' in 1695, and a '*Second Edition*' (actually the third) in 1696. Either of these 'second' editions is to be found in the collection, *Several Papers Relating to Money, Interest and Trade, &c.: Writ upon several Occasions and Published at Different Times*, by John Locke, Esq; (London: Printed for A. and J. Churchill, 1696). Cf. nos. 6, 9.

12 *A Letter to Edward Ld Bishop of Worcester, concerning Some Passages Relating to Mr. Locke's Essay of Humane Understanding: in a Late Discourse of His Lordship's, in Vindication of the Trinity* (London: Printed for A. and J. Churchill, 1697)

The second issue is entitled, more properly, *A Letter to the Right Reverend Edward Ld Bishop of Worcester....* Edward Stillingfleet, the Bishop of Worcester, had charged Locke with unorthodox religious beliefs, in his *A Vindication of the Doctrine of the Trinity* (1696). This *Letter* is the first of Locke's three defences of his *Essay*.

13   *A Second Vindication of the Reasonableness of Christianity, &c.* (London: Printed for A. and J. Churchill, 1697)

Anonymous publication of a further defence of his religious views. For French and German editions, see no. 10.

14   *Mr. Locke's Reply to the Right Reverend the Bishop of Worcester's Answer to His Letter, concerning Some Passages Relating to Mr. Locke's Essay of Humane Understanding: in a Late Discourse of His Lordships, in Vindication of the Trinity* (London: Printed by H. Clark for A. and J. Churchill, and E. Castle, 1697)

A further defence, written in response to Stillingfleet's *The Bishop of Worcester's Answer to Mr. Locke's Letter* (1697). This *Reply* includes an answer to Thomas Burnet's *Remarks upon 'An Essay concerning Human Understanding'*, also published in 1697 (7 pp. at end).

15   *Mr. Locke's Reply to the Right Reverend the Lord Bishop of Worcester's Answer to His Second Letter: Wherein, besides Other Incident Matters, What His Lordship Has Said ... Is Examined* (London: Printed by H.C. for A. and J. Churchill, and E. Castle, 1699)

Known as *Mr. Locke's Second Reply*.

A reply to Stillingfleet's *The Bishop of Worcester's Answer to Mr. Locke's Second Letter* (1698).

16   *Posthumous Works of Mr. John Locke* (London: Printed by W. B. for A. and J. Churchill, 1706)

Published from among the many manuscript papers Locke left behind, this collection includes (1) 'Of the Conduct of the Understanding', (2) 'An Examination of P. Malebranche's Opinion of Seeing All Things in God', (3) 'A Discourse of Miracles', (4) 'Part of a Fourth Letter for Toleration', (5) 'Memoirs relating to the Life of Anthony First Earl of Shaftesbury', and (6) 'His New Method of a Common-Place-Book'. The 'Conduct' was frequently reprinted separately, as well as translated into Dutch, German and Italian. The fourth 'toleration letter' appears in the Hollis edition of *Toleration Letters* (see no. 1).

17   *A Paraphrase and Notes upon the Epistles of St. Paul to the Galatians, I & II Corinthians, Romans [and] Ephesians; to Which Is Prefix'd, An Essay for the Understanding of St. Paul's Epistles, by Consulting St. Paul Himself* (London: Printed by J. H. for Awnsham and John Churchill, 1707)

The first posthumous publication, these *paraphrases* were first published separately: *Galatians* in 1705, *1 Corinthians* and *2 Corinthians* in 1706, *Romans, Ephesians*, and the introductory 'Essay' in 1707. There were eight further editions or reprintings of the collected edition by 1800. A German translation of the collection was published in 1768, and a Dutch translation of his paraphrase of the Epistle to the Romans was reported published in 1768. The definitive edition of the *Paraphrases* was edited by Arthur W. Wainwright for the Clarendon Edition of the Works of John Locke (2 vols., Oxford: Clarendon Press, 1987).

18 *Some Familiar Letters between Mr. Locke and Several of His Friends* (London: Printed for A. and J. Churchill, 1708)
Chiefly correspondence with William and Thomas Molyneux, and Philipp Limborch, the first of many exchanges to be published up to 1959. The definitive edition of the complete correspondence is the collection edited by E. S. de Beer for the Clarendon Edition of the Works of John Locke (*The Correspondence of John Locke*, 8 vols, Oxford: Clarendon Press, 1976–89).

19 *A Collection of Several Pieces of Mr. John Locke, Never before Printed, or Not Extant in His Works. Published by* [Pierre Desmaizeaux] (London: Printed by J. Bettenham for R. Francklin, 1720)
The collection includes (1) a translation of Pierre Coste's 'Eloge de M. Locke' (from *Nouvelles de la république des lettres*, Feb. 1705), (2) 'The Fundamental Constitutions of Carolina', (3) 'A Letter from a Person of Quality, to His Friend in the Country' (now, like the 'Constitutions of Carolina', thought to be written by the first Earl of Shaftesbury), (4) 'Remarks upon Some of Mr. Norris's Books', (5) 'Elements of Natural Philosophy', (6) 'Some Thoughts concerning Reading and Study for a Gentleman', (7) correspondence with Anthony Collins, Henry Oldenburg and others, and (8) 'Rules of a Society' for the support of religion. Only the 'Remarks' on John Norris, the 'Elements', 'Reading and Study' and some of the letters were written by Locke. The 'Elements' had been separately reprinted six times by 1800, sometimes with 'Reading and Study', and both were translated into French in 1757.

20 *Observations upon the Growth and Culture of Vines and Olives, the Production of Silk, the Preservation of Fruits; Written at the Request of the Earl of Shaftesbury ...* (London: Printed for W. Sandby, 1766)
Written while Locke was in France, November 1675 to May 1679.

21 *John Locke: Essays on the Law of Nature: the Latin Text, with a Translation, Introduction and Notes, Together with Transcripts of Locke's Shorthand in His Journal for 1676*, ed. W. von Leyden (Oxford: Clarendon Press, 1954)
Several manuscripts found in the Lovelace Collection of Locke materials in the Bodleian Library, Oxford.

22 *John Locke: Two Tracts on Government*, ed. with an introduction, notes and translation by Philip Abrams (Cambridge: Cambridge University Press, 1967)
Tracts, written in 1660–1: (1) 'Question: whether the civil Magistrate ...'; (2) 'An Magistratus Civilis ...'

23 *The Library of John Locke*, ed. John Harrison and Peter Laslett, 2nd edn. (Oxford: Clarendon Press, 1971)
Based on Locke's interleaved copy of *Catalogus impressorum librorum Bibliothecae Bodlejanae in Academia Oxoniensi*, compiled by Thomas Hyde (1674), the first edition of this printed record was published in Oxford Bibliographical Society Publications, new ser. 13 (1965). It is Locke's own record of books he has owned. The compilers identify fully each work, and list its present location if known.

B   PRE-NINETEENTH-CENTURY WORKS

The place of publication, unless otherwise specified, is London.

Aquinas, Thomas, *Basic Writings*, ed. A. C. Pegis (New York: Random House, 1945)

Aristotle, *De Anima*, in *Basic Works*, ed. R. McKeon (New York: Random House, 1941)

Arnauld, Antoine, *Des vrayes et des fausses idées, contre ce qu'enseigne l'auteur de la Recherche de la verité* (Cologne: N. Schouten, 1683); translated as *On True and Fake Ideas*, trans. Stephen Gaukroger (Manchester: Manchester University Press, 1990)

Arnauld, Antoine and Pierre Nicole, *La Logique, ou L'Art de penser* (Paris: Chez Charles Savreux, 1662); translated as *Logic, or The Art of Thinking* (T.B. for H. Sawbridge, 1685)

Bayle, Pierre, *Dictionnaire historique et critique*, 2nd edn, 3 vols (Amsterdam: R. Leers, 1702)

Berkeley, George, *An Essay towards a New Theory of Vision* (Dublin: Printed by A. Rhames for J. Pepyat, 1709)

Berkeley, George, *A Treatise concerning the Principles of Human Knowledge* (Dublin: Printed by A. Rhames for J. Pepyat, 1710)

Bold, Samuel, *A Discourse concerning the Resurrection of the Same Body; with Two Letters concerning the Necessary Immateriality of Created Thinking Substance* (S. Holt for A. and J. Churchill, 1705)

Bold, Samuel, *Some Considerations on the Principal Objections and Arguments Which Have Been Publish'd against Mr. Lock's Essay* (For A. and J. Churchill, 1699)

Bonnet, Charles, *Essai analytique sur les facultés de l'âme* (Copenhague: Cl. & Ant. Philibert, 1760)

Boulainvilliers, Henri de, *Histoire de l'ancien gouvernement de la France*, 3 vols (A la Haye et à Amsterdam: Aux dépends de la Compagnie, 1727)

Boyle, Robert, *Selected Philosophical Papers*, ed. M. A. Stewart (Manchester: Manchester University Press, 1979)

Browne, Peter, *The Procedure, Extent, and Limits of Human Understanding* (W. Innys, 1728)

Browne, Peter, *Things Divine and Supernatural Conceived by Analogy with Things Natural and Human* (Printed for William Innys and Richard Manby, 1733)

Buffon, Georges-Louis Leclerc, comte de, *L'Histoire naturelle, générale et particulière*, 15 vols (Paris: A l'Imprimerie du Roy, 1749–67)

Campbell, George, *A Dissertation on Miracles: Containing an Examination of the Principles Advanced by David Hume, Esq; in 'An Essay on Miracles'* (Edinburgh: Printed for A. Kincaid & J. Bell . . . 1762)

Carpenter, Richard, *The Conscionable Christian: Or, The Indevour of Saint Paul, to Have and Discharge a Good Conscience Always towards God and Men, Laid Open and Applyed in Three Sermons* (F.K. for John Bartlett, 1623)

Carroll, William, *A Dissertation upon the Tenth Chapter of the Fourth Book of Mr. Locke's*

Essay . . . Wherein the Author's Endeavours to Establish Spinoza's Atheistical Hypothesis . . . Are Discover'd and Confuted (J. Matthews, 1706)

Chambers, Ephraim, *Cyclopaedia, or An Universal Dictionary of Arts and Sciences*, 2 vols (J. and J. Knapton, 1728)

Chillingworth, William, *The Religion of Protestants, a Safe Way to Salvation* (Oxford: Printed by Leonard Lichfield, 1638)

Cicero, M. T. (also called Tully), *De Officiis* ('Offices', or 'On Moral Duties'), with English translation by Walter Miller, Loeb Classical Library (London: Heinemann, 1921)

Clarke, John, *A Defence of Dr. [Samuel] Clarke's Demonstration of the Being and Attributes of God; Wherein Is Particularly Consider'd the Nature of Space, Duration, and Necessary Existence . . .* (J. and J. Knapton, 1732)

Clarke, Samuel, *A Collection of Papers Which Passed between the Late Learned Mr. Leibniz and Dr. Clarke, in the Years 1715 and 1716, Relating to the Principles of Natural Philosophy and Religion* (Printed for J. Knapton, 1717)

Cockburn, Mrs Catharine Trotter, *A Defence of the Essay of Human Understanding . . . Wherein Its Principles with Reference to Morality, Reveal'd Religion, and the Immortality of the Soul, Are Considered and Justify'd* (Will. Turner, 1702)

Colliber, Samual, *An Impartial Enquiry into the Existence and Nature of God . . . With an Appendix concerning the Nature of Space and Duration* (Printed and Sold by the Booksellers, 1718)

Collins, Anthony, *A Discourse of Free-Thinking, Occasion'd by the Rise and Growth of a Sect Call'd Free-Thinkers* (J.J. & P. Knapton, 1713)

Collins, Anthony, *An Essay concerning the Use of Reason in Propositions, the Evidence Whereof Depends upon Human Testimony* ([s.n.], 1707)

Comenius, Johann Amos, *Naturall Philosophie Reformed by Divine Light, or A Synopsis of Physicks . . .* (Printed by Robert and William Leybourn, for Thomas Pierrepont . . . 1651); translation of *Physicae ad lumen divinum reformatae synopsis*

Condillac, Étienne Bonnot de, *Essai sur l'origine des connoissances humaines; ouvrage où l'on réduit à un seul principe tout ce qui concerne l'entendement humain* (Amsterdam: P. Mortier, 1746)

Crousaz, Jean-Pierre de, *Système de réflexions qui peuvent contribuer à la netteté et à l'étendue de nos connoissances, ou Nouvel essai de logique*, 2 vols (Amsterdam: F.L. Honoré, 1712); English translation: *A New Treatise of the Art of Thinking, or, A compleat System of Reflections, concerning the Conduct and Improvement of the Mind* (Tho. Woodward, 1724)

Cudworth, Ralph, *The True Intellectual System of the Universe. The First Part: Wherein All the Reason and Philosophy of Atheism is Confuted, and Its Impossibility Demonstrated* (R. Royston, 1678)

Culverwel, Nathanael, *An Elegant and Learned Discourse of the Light of Nature, with Several Other Treatises* (T.R. and E. M., 1654)

Descartes, R., *Comments on a Certain Broadsheet*, in his *The Philosophical Writings*, trans. J. Cottingham *et al.* (3 vols, Cambridge: Cambridge University Press, 1985–90), vol. 1, pp. 293–311

Descartes, R., *Rules for the Direction of the Mind*, in his *The Philosophical Writings*, vol. 1, pp. 7–78

Duncan, William, *The Elements of Logick* (R. Dodsley, 1748)

Edwards, John, *Socinianism Unmask'd: a Discourse Shewing the Unreasonableness of a Late Writer's Opinion concerning the Necessity of Only One Article of Christian Faith, and of His Other Assertions in His Late Book . . . The Reasonableness of Christianity* (J. Robinson, 1696)

Filmer, Robert, *Patriarcha, or The Natural Power of Kings* (Ric. Chiswell, 1680)

Fleetwood, William, *An Essay on Miracles* (Charles Harper, 1701)

Grotius, Hugo, *De jure belli ac pacis libri tres: in quibus jus natura & gentium item juris publici praecipua explicantur*, ed. secunda (Amsterdam: Guilielmum Blaeuw, 1631); first published in 1625

Hale, Sir Matthew, *The Primitive Origination of Mankind Considered and Examined According to the Light of Nature* (Wm. Godbid, 1677)

Hartley, David, *Observations on Man: His Frame, His Duty, and His Expectations*, 2 vols (S. Richardson, 1749)

Herbert, Edward, Baron Herbert of Cherbury, *De veritate, prout distingvitur a revelatione, a verisimili, a possibili et a falso*, [rev. edn.] (Per A. Matthaevm, 1633); first published in Paris, 1624

Hoadly, Benjamin, *A Letter to Mr. Fleetwood* (J. Nutt, 1702)

Hobbes, Thomas, *Leviathan*, ed. C. B. Macpherson (Harmondsworth: Penguin Books, 1968)

Hobbes, Thomas, *The English Works*, ed. Sir William Molesworth, 11 vols (Longman, 1845)

Hooke, Robert, *Micrographia, or Some Physiological Descriptions of Minute Bodies Made by Magnifying Glasses, with Observations and Illustrations Thereupon* (Printed by Jo. Martyn and Jo. Allestry, 1665)

Hume, David, *A Treatise of Human Nature: Being an Attempt to Introduce the Experimental Method of Reasoning into Moral Subjects*, 3 vols (J. Noon, 1739–40); modern edn ed. L. A. Selby-Bigge, 2nd (rev.) edn P. H. Nidditch (Oxford: Clarendon Press, 1978)

Hume, David, *Dialogues concerning Natural Religion*, ed. John V. Price (Oxford: Clarendon Press, 1976)

Hutcheson, Francis, *An Essay on the Nature and Conduct of the Passions and Affections; with Illustrations on the Moral Sense* (J. Osborn and T. Longman, 1728)

King, William, *De Origine Mali* (Benj. Tooke, 1702); English translation by Edmund Law, as *An Essay concerning the Origin of Evil* (For W. Thurlbourn Bookseller in Cambridge; and Sold by R. Knaplock [et al.] 1731)

Law, Edmund, *An Enquiry into the Ideas of Space, Time, Immensity and Eternity* (Cambridge: W. Fenner and W. Thurlbourn, 1732)

Leibniz, G. W., *Oeuvres philosophiques, latines & françoises . . .* publiés par Rud. Eric Raspe (Amsterdam & Leipzig: J. Schreuder, 1765); chiefly contains his *Nouveaux Essais sur l'entendement humain* (pp. 1–496)

Leibniz, G. W. 'The Monadology, 1714', in his *Philosophical Papers and Letters*, ed. L. E. Loemker (New York: Humanities Press, 1970), pp. 643–53

Malebranche, Nicolas, *De la recherche de la verité, où l'on traite de la nature de l'esprit de l'homme & de l'usage qu'il en doit faire pour éviter l'erreur dans les sciences* (Paris, André Pralard, 1674); translated as *The Search after Truth*, trans. T. M. Lennon and P. J. Olscamp (Columbus: Ohio State University Press, 1980)

Maupertuis, Pierre-Louis Moreau de, *Oeuvres*, 2 vols (Berlin: Etienne de Bourdeaux [et al.], 1753)

Mayne, Charles, *An Essay concerning Rational Notions* (W. Innys, 1733)

Mayne, Zachary, *Two Dissertations concerning Sense and the Imagination; with an Essay on Consciousness* (J. Tonson, 1728)

Maynwaring, Everard, *Praxis medicorum antiqua et nova: the Ancient and Modern Practice of Physick Examined, Stated and Compared* (J.M. and are to be sold by T. Archer, 1671)

Molyneux, William, *Dioptrica Nova: a Treatise of Dioptricks, in Two Parts* (Benj. Tooke, 1692)

More, Henry, *An Antidote against Atheisme, or An Appeal to the Natural Faculties of the Minde of Man, Whether There Be Not a God* (Roger Daniel, 1653)

Paley, William, *A View of the Evidences of Christianity* (Dublin: J. Pasley for J. Milliken, 1794)

Parker, Samuel, *A Demonstration of the Divine Authority of the Law of Nature, and of the Christian Religion* (M. Flesher, 1681)

Perronet, Vincent, *A Second Vindication of Mr. Locke, Wherein His Sentiments relating to Personal Identity Are Clear'd from Some Mistakes of the Rev. Dr. Butler* (Fletcher Gyles, 1738; facsim. rept. by Thoemmes, Bristol, 1991)

Perronet, Vincent, *A Vindication of Mr. Locke, from the Charge of Giving Encouragement to Scepticism and Infidelity* (J.J. and P. Knapton, 1736)

Power, Henry, *Experimental Philosophy: in Three Books, Containing New Experiments, Microscopical, Mercurial, Magnetical* (T. Roycroft, for J. Martin and J. Allestry ... 1664)

Priestley, Joseph, *Disquisitions Relating to Matter and Spirit; to Which Is Added, The History of the Philosophical Doctrine concerning the Origin of the Soul, and the Nature of Matter* (Printed for J. Johnson, 1777)

Priestley, Joseph, *Hartley's Theory of the Human Mind* (J. Johnson, 1775)

Proast, Jonas, *The Argument of the 'Letter concerning Toleration' Briefly Consider'd and Answer'd* (Oxford: G. West, 1690)

Pufendorf, Samuel, *De jure naturae et gentium libri octo* (Lund: Sumtibus Adami Junghans, imprimebat Vitus Haberegger, 1672)

Pufendorf, Samuel, *De officio hominis et civis, juxta legem naturalem libri duo* (Lund: Sumtibus Adami Junghans, 1673)

Reid, Thomas, *Essays on the Intellectual Powers of Man* (Edinburgh: J. Bell, 1785)

Rousseau, Jean-Jacques, *Du contrat social* (Paris: Chez Marc-Michel Rey, 1762)

Sclater, William, *A Key to the Key of Scripture, or An Exposition with Notes, upon the Epistle to the Romans* (Printed by T.S. for George Norton, 1611)

Selden, John, *Mare clausum, seu De dominio maris libri duo* (W. Stanesbeius, pro R. Meighen, 1635)

Sergeant, John, *Solid Philosophy Asserted, Against the Fancies of the Ideists; or The Method to Science Farther Illustrated* (Roger Clavil, 1697); facism. reprint by Garland Publishers, New York, 1984

Sergeant, John, *The Method to Science* (W. Redmayne, 1696)

Sherlock, William, 'A Digression concerning Connate Ideas, or Inbred Knowledge', in his *A Discourse concerning the Happiness of Good Men* (W. Rogers, 1704)

Sherlock, William, *A Vindication of the Doctrine of the Holy and Ever Blessed Trinity* (W. Rogers, 1690)

Simpson, William, *Hydrologia Chymica, or The Chymical Anatomy of the Scarbrough, and Other Spaws in York-Shire* (W.G. for Richard Chiswell, 1669)

Smith, John, *Select Discourses Treating of the True Way or Method of Attaining to Divine Knowledge* (W. Morden, 1660)

South, Robert, *Animadversions upon Dr. Sherlock's Book, Entituled A Vindication of the Holy and Ever-Blessed Trinity* (Randal Taylor, 1693)

South, Robert, *Tritheism Charged upon Dr. Sherlock's New Notion of the Trinity* (John Whitlock, 1695)

Spinoza, B. *Ethics*, in his *Selections*, ed. John Wild (New York: C. Scribner's Sons, 1930), pp. 94–400

Sprat, Thomas, *The History of the Royal Society for the Improvement of Natural Knowledge* (T.R. for F. Martyn, 1667)

Stillingfleet, Edward, *A Discourse in Vindication of the Doctrine of the Trinity; with an Answer to the Late Socinian Objections Against It from Scripture* (J.H. for Henry Mortlock, 1697)

Stillingfleet, Edward, *Origines Sacræ* (R. W. for H. Mortlock, 1662)

Stillingfleet, Edward, *The Bishop of Worcester's Answer to Mr. Locke's Letter concerning Some Passages Relating to his Essay* (J.H. for Henry Mortlock, 1697)

Suarez, Francisco, *Selections from Three Works: De legibus, ac Deo legislator, 1612; Defensio fidei catholicae et apostolicae adversus anglicanae sectae errores, 1613; De triplici virtute theologica, fide, spe et charitate, 1613*, 2 vols (Oxford: Clarendon Press, 1944)

Toland, John, *Christianity Not Mysterious, or A Treatise Shewing That There Is Nothing in the Gospel Contrary to Reason, Nor Above it, and That No Christian Doctrine Can Be Properly Call'd a Mystery* ([s.n.] 1696)

Tully, *De Officiis* ('Offices') *see* Cicero

Voltaire, F.-M. Arouet de, *Elémens de la philosophie de Neuton, mis à la portée de tout le monde* (Amsterdam: Chez E. Ledet & cie, 1738)

Voltaire, F.-M. Arouet de, *Letters concerning the English Nation* (C. Davis and A. Lyon, 1733); French edn, *Lettres écrites de Londres sur les Anglois, et autres sujets* (Basle: [s.n.] 1734)

Watts, Isaac, *Logick, or, The Right Use of Reason in the Enquiry after Truth* (J. Clark and R. Hett, 1725)

Watts, Isaac, *Philosophical Essays on Various Subjects, viz. Space, Substance, Body, Spirit, the Operations of the Soul in Union with the Body, Innate Ideas, Perpetual Consciousness, Place and Motion of Spirits, the Departing Soul, the Resurrection of the Body, etc.* (Richard Ford, 1733)

Whitby, Daniel, *A Paraphrase and Commentary upon All the Epistles* (A. & J. Churchill, 1700)

Wilkins, John, *An Essay towards a Real Character, and a Philosophical Language* (S. Gellibrand and J. Martyn, 1668)

Wilkins, John, *Of the Principles and Duties of Natural Religion* (A. Maxwell for T. Basset, 1675)

Wollaston, William, *The Religion of Nature Delineated* (S. Palmer, 1722)

C SECONDARY SOURCES

Aarsleff, Hans, 'Leibniz on Locke on Language', *American Philosophical Quarterly*, 1 (1964), 165–88

Aarsleff, Hans, *The Study of Language in England, 1780–1860* (Princeton: Princeton University Press, 1967)

Ashcraft, Richard, *Revolutionary Politics and Locke's 'Two Treatises of Government'* (Princeton: Princeton University Press, 1986)

Ayers, Michael, *Locke: The Arguments of the Philosophers*, 2 vols (London: Routledge & Kegan Paul, 1991)

Biddle, John C., 'John Locke's Essay on Infallibility: Introduction, Text, and Translation', *Journal of Church and State*, 19 (1977), 317

Bourne, H.R. Fox, *The Life of John Locke*, 2 vols (London: H.S. Knight; New York: Harper, 1876)

Burns, J. H. (ed.), *The Cambridge History of Political Thought, 1450–1700* (Cambridge: Cambridge University Press, 1991)

Cohen, Murray, *Sensible Words: Linguistic Practice in England, 1640–1785* (Baltimore and London: Johns Hopkins University Press, 1977)

Colman, John, *John Locke's Moral Philosophy* (Edinburgh: Edinburgh University Press, 1983)

Cragg, G.R., *From Puritanism to the Age of Reason: A Study of Changes in Religious Thought within the Church of England, 1660–1700* (Cambridge: Cambridge University Press, 1950)

Cranston, Maurice, *John Locke: A Biography* (London: Macmillan Co., 1957)

Davies, Catherine Glyn, *'Conscience' as Consciousness: The Idea of Self-Awareness in French Philosophical Writing from Descartes to Diderot*, Studies on Voltaire and the Eighteenth Century, 272 (Oxford: Voltaire Foundation, 1990)

Dewhurst, Kenneth, *John Locke (1632–1704), Physician and Philosopher: a Medical Biography; with an Edition of the Medical Notes in His Journals* (London: Wellcome Historical Medical Library, 1963)

Duchesneau, François, *L'Empirisme de Locke* (La Haye: Martinus Nijhoff, 1973)

Dunn, John, *The Political Thought of John Locke: An Historical Account of the Argument of the 'Two Treatises of Government'* (Cambridge: Cambridge University Press, 1969)

Edwards, Paul (ed.), *The Encyclopedia of Philosophy* (London and New York: The Macmillan Co. and the Free Press, 1967)

Franklin, Julian H., *John Locke and the Theory of Sovereignty: Mixed Monarchy and the Right of Resistance in the Political Thought of the English Revolution* (Cambridge: Cambridge University Press, 1978)

Gobetti, Daniela, *Public and Private: Individuals, Households and Body Politic in Locke and Hutcheson* (London: Routledge, 1992)

Goyard-Fabre, S., *John Locke et la raison raisonnable* (Paris: Librairie Philosophique J. Vrin, 1986)

Grant, Ruth W., *John Locke's Liberalism* (Chicago and London: University of Chicago Press, 1987)

Hacking, Ian, *The Emergence of Probability: A Philosophical Study of Early Ideas about Probability, Induction and Statistical Inference* (Cambridge: Cambridge University Press, 1975)

Hoppen, K. Theodore, *The Common Scientist in the Seventeenth Century: A Study of the Dublin Philosophical Society 1683–1708* (London: Routledge & Kegan Paul, 1970)

King, Peter, *The Life of John Locke; with Extracts from His Correspondence, Journals, and Common-Place Books* (London: H. Colburn, 1829; 2nd edn, 2 vols, London: Colburn & Bentley, 1830)

Knowlson, James, *Universal Language Schemes in England and France, 1600–1800* (Toronto: University of Toronto Press, 1975)

Machamer, Peter K. and R.G. Turnbull (eds.), *Motion and Time, Space and Matter: Interpretations in the History of Philosophy and Science* (Columbus: Ohio State University Press, 1976)

Mackie, J. L., *Problems From Locke* (Oxford: Clarendon Press, 1976)

Nuchelmans, Gabriel, *Judgment and Proposition from Descartes to Kant* (Amsterdam, Oxford, New York: North Holland Publishing Co., 1983)

Obertello, Luca, *John Locke e Port-Royal: il problema della probabilità* (Trieste: Istituto di Filosofia, 1964)

Passmore, John, 'Locke and the Ethics of Belief', the Dawes Hicks Lecture for 1978, *Proceedings of the British Academy*, 64 (1978), 185–208

Pastore, Nicholas, *Selective History of Theories of Visual Perception, 1650–1950* (New York: Oxford University Press, 1971)

Price, H. H., *Belief*, the Gifford Lectures delivered at the University of Aberdeen in 1960 (London: George Allen & Unwin, 1969)

Russell, Bertrand, *Problems of Philosophy* (London: Oxford University Press, 1912)

Seliger, M., *The Liberal Politics of John Locke* (London: George Allen & Unwin, 1968)

Skinner, Quentin, *The Foundations of Modern Political Thought*, 2 vols (Cambridge: Cambridge University Press, 1978)

Spellman, W. M., *John Locke and the Problem of Depravity* (Oxford: Clarendon Press, 1988)

Tuck, Richard, *Natural Rights Theories: Their Origin and Development* (Cambridge: Cambridge University Press, 1979)

Tully, James, *A Discourse on Property: John Locke and His Adversaries* (Cambridge: Cambridge University Press, 1980)

Vaughn, Karen Iversen, *John Locke, Economist and Social Scientist* (Chicago and London: University of Chicago Press, 1980)

Vienne, Jean-Michel, *Expérience et raison: les fondements de la morale selon Locke* (Paris: Librairie Philosophique J. Vrin, 1991)

Weinberg, Julius R., *Abstraction, Relation and Induction: Three Essays in the History of Thought* (Madison: University of Wisconsin Press, 1965)

Wiener, Philip P. (ed.), *Dictionary of the History of Ideas: Studies of Selected Pivotal Ideas*, 4 vols (New York: Charles Scribner's Sons, 1968)

Yolton, Jean S. and John W. Yolton, *John Locke: A Reference Guide* (Boston: G.K. Hall & Co., 1985)

Yolton, John W., *John Locke and the Way of Ideas*, Oxford Classical and Philosophical Monographs (London: Oxford University Press, 1956; repr. Oxford: Clarendon Press, 1968)

Yolton, John W. (ed.), *John Locke: Problems and Perspectives; A Collection of New Essays* (Cambridge: Cambridge University Press, 1969)

Yolton, John W., *Locke and French Materialism* (Oxford: Clarendon Press, 1991)

Yolton, John W., *Locke, an Introduction* (Oxford: B.H. Blackwell, 1985)

Yolton, John W., *Locke and the Compass of Human Understanding: A Selective Commentary on the 'Essay'* (Cambridge: Cambridge University Press, 1970)

Yolton, John W., *Perceptual Acquaintance from Descartes to Reid* (Minneapolis: University of Minnesota Press; Oxford: Basil Blackwell, 1984)

Yolton, John W., *Thinking Matter: Materialism in Eighteenth-Century Britain* (Minneapolis: University of Minnesota Press; Oxford: Basil Blackwell, 1984)

Index

Note: Page numbers in bold refer to the main entries or to especially significant discussions of given terms.